Dr. Effie Maclellan
Department of Educational Studies
University of Strathclyde
Southbrae Drive
GLASGOW   G13 1PP
Tel:- 0141 950 3355
e-mail:- e.maclellan@strath.ac.uk

SOCIAL CONSTRUCTIVIST TEACHING

AFFORDANCES AND CONSTRAINTS

ADVANCES IN RESEARCH ON TEACHING

Series Editor: Jere Brophy

ADVANCES IN RESEARCH ON TEACHING   VOLUME 9

SOCIAL CONSTRUCTIVIST TEACHING:

AFFORDANCES AND CONSTRAINTS

EDITED BY

JERE BROPHY

College of Education, Michigan State University, USA

2002

JAI
An Imprint of Elsevier Science

Amsterdam – Boston – London – New York – Oxford – Paris
San Diego – San Francisco – Singapore – Sydney – Tokyo

ELSEVIER SCIENCE Ltd
The Boulevard, Langford Lane
Kidlington, Oxford OX5 1GB, UK

First edition 2002

Library of Congress Cataloging in Publication Data
A catalog record from the Library of Congress has been applied for.

British Library Cataloguing in Publication Data
A catalogue record from the British Library has been applied for.

ISBN: 0-7623-0873-7

∞ The paper used in this publication meets the requirements of ANSI/NISO Z39.48-1992 (Permanence of Paper).
Printed in The Netherlands.

CONTENTS

vi

LIST OF CONTRIBUTORS

Jere Brophy	College of Education, Michigan State University, USA
Daniel Chazan	College of Education, Michigan State University, USA
Kailonnie Dunsmore	College of Education, State University of New York at Albany, USA
Carol Sue Englert	College of Education, Michigan State University, USA
Ralph P. Ferretti	College of Education, University of Delaware, USA
Jennifer Hauver James	College of Education, University of Maryland, College Park, USA
Charles D. MacArthur	College of Education, University of Delaware, USA
Graham Nuthall	Education Department, University of Canterbury, New Zealand
Cynthia Okolo	College of Education, Michigan State University, USA
Kathleen J. Roth	LessonLab, Inc., USA
Marty Schnepp	Holt High School, Holt, Michigan, USA

Alan H. Schoenfeld   Graduate School of Education,
                                University of California, Berkeley, USA

Bruce A. VanSledright   College of Education,
                                University of Maryland, College Park, USA

Gordon Wells   Department of Education,
                                University of California, Santa Cruz, USA

INTRODUCTION

This volume was conceived as an attempt to address issues associated with social constructivist approaches to teaching, which recently have attained widespread popularity. Their popularity can be seen in the previous volume in this series (Brophy, 2001), in which authors representing 14 school subjects (beginning reading, later content area reading and literature studies, writing, number, geometry, biology, physics, chemistry, earth science, history, physical geography, cultural studies, citizenship education, and economics) synthesized what is currently known (or at least believed to be true) about best practices in teaching their respective subjects. Most of these authors cited notions of learning community, social construction of knowledge, or sociocultural learning to argue that learning is most likely to be meaningful and accessible for use when it is socially negotiated through classroom discourse.

Social constructivism is primarily a theory of learning rather than a theory of teaching, so educators who identify themselves as social constructivists can and do advocate a range of teaching approaches. However, these approaches tend to share the key assumption that, ideally, learning involves negotiating understandings through dialogue or discourse shared by two or more members of a community of people who are pursuing shared goals. In school settings, the social construction of understandings typically occurs in whole-class or small-group discussions or in dialogues between pairs of students. The teacher plays an important role in structuring or guiding this discourse, but this is a quite different role from that of the traditional frontal teacher who focuses on transmission of information through lecture, demonstration, and recitation methods. The traditional transmission approach and the more recently articulated social constructivist approach are often contrasted along several dimensions. The following contrasts, taken from Good and Brophy (2000), are representative; see Table 1.

Such comparisons are useful, but they must be interpreted carefully to avoid three common oversimplifications: (1) reducing discussions of teaching to this single dimension, when teaching has other important components that do not fit easily into a transmission vs. social constructivist comparison; (2) implying that one must choose between these two approaches, when logic and some data indicate the need for a judicious blend; and (3) implying that a particular choice or blend will have universal applicability, when there is good reason to believe

Table 1.   Teaching and Learning as Transmission of Information Versus as
Social Construction of Knowlegde.

Transmission View	Social Construction View
Knowledge as fixed body of information transmitted from teacher or text to students	Knowledge as developing interpretations coconstructed through discussion
Texts, teacher as authoritative sources of expert knowledge to which students defer	Authority for constructed knowledge resides in the arguments and evidence cited in its support by students as well as by texts or teacher; everyone has expertise to contribute
Teacher is responsible for managing students' learning by providing information and leading students through activities and assignments	Teacher and students share responsibility for initiating and guiding learning efforts
Teacher explains, checks for understanding, and judges correctness of students' responses	Teacher acts as discussion leader who poses questions, seeks clarifications, promotes dialogue, helps group recognize areas of consensus and of continuing disagreement
Students memorize or replicate what has been explained or modeled	Students strive to make sense of new input by relating it to their prior knowledge and by collaborating in dialogue with others to coconstruct shared understandings
Discourse emphasizes drill and recitation in response to convergent questions; focus is on eliciting correct answers	Discourse emphasizes reflective discussion of networks of connected knowledge; questions are more divergent but designed to develop understanding of the powerful ideas that anchor these networks; focus is on eliciting students' thinking
Activities emphasize replication of models or applications that require following step-by-step algorithms	Activities emphasize applications to authentic issues and problems that require higher-order thinking
Students work mostly alone, practicing what has been transmitted to them in order to prepare themselves to compete for rewards by reproducing it on demand	Students collaborate by acting as a learning community that constructs shared understandings through sustained dialogue

that what constitutes optimal teaching varies with grade level, instructional
goals, and other context factors. Given that teaching approaches are means
rather than ends in themselves, it is logical to assume that optimal teaching
involves an eclectic mixture of components that is suited to the students and

the instructional goals, and that the prominence of particular components will wax and wane as lessons or units progress and students develop expertise in the domain.

Applefield, Huber, and Moallem (2001) synthesized commonly expressed constructivist views on learning and teaching. First, they noted that constructivists tend to agree on four characteristics as central to all learning: (1) learners construct their own learning; (2) new learning depends on students' existing understandings; (3) social interaction/dialogue plays a critical role; and (4) authentic learning tasks are needed to ensure meaningful learning. Other commonly emphasized concepts include situated cognition, scaffolding, cognitive apprenticeship, cooperative learning, learning communities, generative learning, and teaching in the zone of proximal development. They also discussed five myths about constructivist-based teaching and concluded with principles for optimizing such teaching.

Five myths about constructivist-based teaching are:

(1) It has no focus for learning or clear goal (although it does not prescribe particular sequences of learning activities, it involves designing learning environments to support goal-oriented knowledge construction and should not be confused with idle discussion or exploratory activities that lack clear focus).

(2) It is not carefully planned (working from clear goals, constructivist teachers identify a challenge, case, or problem – ideally, an authentic activity – that is suited to the learning goals; scaffold students' learning; and assess their goal attainment).

(3) There is no structure for learning (engagement in the activity, with the learning goals in mind, provides direction to activities such as exploring the causes of the problem to be solved, noting similarities and differences with already familiar tasks, and classifying it with reference to larger systems).

(4) Learning will take place automatically as long as learners are involved in discussion or other forms of social interaction (in fact, teachers need to monitor discussions and group activities and be prepared to intervene to redirect the discussion or address misconceptions).

(5) Since teachers are not primarily delivering instruction (lecturing and explaining), their role in the classroom is less important (the teacher's role shifts from primarily telling to primarily guiding, but the latter is a crucial role that calls for sophisticated decision making about when and how to intervene and what is required to mentor, coach, and facilitate students' learning effectively).

Challenges in implementing constructivist teaching include deciding how much to structure learning tasks, dealing with the breadth/depth dilemma, and finding ways to enable students to struggle productively with the confusions and conflicts involved in collaboratively addressing ill-structured, real-world problems.

Applefield, Huber, and Moallem (2001) concluded by suggesting that the following pedagogical recommendations flow from fundamental constructivist principles of learning:

(1) The overall goal is to stimulate thinking in learners that results in meaningful learning, deep understanding, and transfer to real-world contexts.
(2) The teacher encourages knowledge construction through primarily social learning processes by selecting authentic tasks and emphasizing ill-defined problems and higher order questions.
(3) Lessons feature clear content goals and multiple ways of representing key ideas.
(4) Learners are encouraged to raise questions, generate hypotheses, and test their validity.
(5) Learners are challenged by ideas and experiences that generate inner cognitive conflict or disequilibrium. Errors are viewed positively as opportunities to explore conceptual understanding.
(6) Students are given time to engage in reflection through journal writing, drawing, modeling, and discussion, to facilitate learning through reflective abstraction.
(7) The learning environment provides ample opportunities for dialogue within a community of discourse that engages in activity, reflection, and conversation.
(8) Within this community of learners, it is the students themselves who must communicate their ideas to others, defend them, and justify them.
(9) Students work with big ideas – central organizing principles that have the power to generalize across experiences and disciplines.

Like most contemporary educators, I find much that is attractive in social constructivist approaches to learning and teaching. This is especially the case when they are contrasted with transmission approaches, because certain difficulties with transmission methods are well known. When transmission methods of teaching are implemented poorly or simply used too exclusively, they tend to lead to student boredom, reliance on rote learning methods, and the acquisition of disconnected items of knowledge that are mostly soon forgotten or retained only in inert forms.

However, certain predictable difficulties with social constructivist techniques can also be expected. Airasian and Walsh (1997), Weinert and Helmke (1995), Windschitl (1999), and others have observed that these techniques are difficult to implement effectively: They require teachers to possess a great deal of subject-matter knowledge (including knowledge about how to teach the subject to students at the grade level) and an ability to respond quickly to only partially predictable developments in the discourse, and they require students to participate more actively and take more personal risks in their learning. Furthermore, heavy reliance on social constructivist discourse models increases the possibility that the discourse will stray from the lesson's intended goals and content, and that even when it remains goal-relevant, progress toward construction of the intended understandings may be erratic and include frequent verbalization of misconceptions. In terms originally introduced by Jacob Kounin (1970) in the context of studying classroom management, it might be said that such lessons have a rough rather than a smooth *flow*, frequently interrupted or sidetracked *momentum*, and a poor *signal* (valid content)-*to-noise* (irrelevant or invalid content) *ratio*.

Research on the learning of strategies, including strategies for teaching effectively, indicates that three kinds of knowledge must be acquired and integrated to enable people to implement the strategies optimally: (1) propositional knowledge of facts, concepts, and generalizations needed to understand the rationale for and nature of the strategy; (2) procedural knowledge of how to implement the strategy skillfully; and (3) conditional knowledge about when to use the strategy and how to adapt it to situational contexts. As scholarly literature on social constructivist approaches to teaching has developed, there has been considerable progress in building a base of propositional and procedural knowledge, but little progress in generating conditional knowledge. In fact, instead of offering balanced assessments of the trade-offs embedded in social constructivist approaches or discussions of when a teacher should or should not use them, writers presenting social constructivist models too often imply that teachers should use them all the time. Furthermore, although there are exceptions, most writing on social constructivist teaching has been confined to statements of rationales coupled with classroom examples of the principles being implemented in practice, without including systematic assessment of outcomes.

This problem was exemplified in a special issue of the *Review of Research in Education* that focused on social constructivist teaching. Noting that a large corpus of work had accumulated in which social constructivist views had been

used to design instruction, the editors asked O'Connor (1998) to assess the
effect of social constructivist teaching on measurable outcomes of learning.
O'Connor concluded that this question could not be addressed yet, partly
because social constructivism is interpreted in many different ways, making it
difficult to generalize, and partly because of the limited availability of research
speaking to the question. Therefore, O'Connor instead wrote a lengthy chapter
illustrating and contrasting some of these different approaches. His descriptions
are useful, as are his analyses of the complexities embedded within the editors'
challenge. Nevertheless, it remains true that O'Connor was given an open
invitation to build a case for the efficacy of social constructivist approaches to
teaching and confessed an inability to do so.

   This is troubling, because romantic or otherwise misguided interpretations of
social constructivism have led to questionable practices in teaching and teacher
education. Some teachers are being led to believe that frontal teaching, skills
practice, and independent work on assignments are simply inappropriate and
should not occur in their classrooms (which should focus instead on
whole-class discussions and small-group cooperative learning activities). Other
teachers are getting the impression that anything that involves discussion or
hands-on activity serves worthwhile curricular purposes and will induce students
to construct significant understandings.

   Concerns about such problems have caused leading social constructivist
spokespersons to criticize much of what has been advocated in the name of
social constructivism and to clarify that a complete instructional program will
include transmission as well as constructivist aspects (Sfard, 1998; Staver, 1998;
Trent, Artiles & Englert, 1998; Wells, 1998) and that its constructivist aspects
embody principles that are much more complex and sophisticated than a simple
admonition not to equate teaching with telling (Chazan & Ball, 1999).
Furthermore, social constructivist leaders in mathematics and science education
have emphasized the need for teachers to provide modeling and explanations,
to support students' construction of knowledge through well-chosen questions
and activities, and to scaffold the students' work. They have rejected the notion
that teachers need only to facilitate students' intrinsically motivated
explorations, characterizing this romantic view as a fundamental misunder-
standing and misapplication of constructivist theory (Cobb, 1994; Driver, Asoko
et al., 1994).

   The field clearly needs more research on social constructivist teaching that
includes attention to a variety of student outcomes. However, it also needs more
theoretical development concerning "conditional knowledge" questions about
when and why social constructivist approaches are optimally used and when
and why other approaches would be more appropriate.

For example, although he did not address social constructivism specifically, Larson (2000) asked six high school social studies teachers to talk about their conceptions of classroom discussion and about factors influencing the degree to which they would emphasize discussion as opposed to transmission forms of instruction in their classrooms. He found that teachers' reported uses of discussion were influenced by five factors: student diversity, lesson objectives, the age and maturity of students, the sense of community in the classroom, and the interest level of students. *Diversity* in student ability, ethnicity, culture, and other factors increases the potential for awareness of different perspectives, but it also increases the likelihood of conflict. The teachers reported talking more and beginning to dominate classroom interactions when their students became embroiled in conflict. They also reported being more likely to dominate interactions when *lesson objectives* emphasized content coverage but being more open to discussion when they did not feel pressured to cover particular content, especially if students already possessed information believed to be important or had spent time gathering background information to support discussion. Individual differences complicate this rule of thumb: Students who know more tend to discuss more, some students are reticent about participating, and students cannot make up for absences because discussions cannot be recreated and teachers' notes are insufficient for accomplishing the goals that led to use of discussion in the first place. The *age and maturity of students* was emphasized in teacher comments about using discussion more with older, more mature, more knowledgeable, less defensive, and more socially adept students. Even though these were high school teachers, some complained that discussions were difficult with younger students, whom they viewed as requiring more teacher effort to keep them on topic and appropriate in their responses to one another. Discussion was more likely where *the sense of community in the classroom* had developed, featuring trust and respect for one another, feelings of personal safety, and common goals for exploring issues. Class size affected this factor: The teachers reported that whole-class discussions were difficult in larger classes. Finally, the *interest level* of students was considered a factor: The teachers felt that students needed to be interested in a topic if they were to participate in a discussion on it, and to believe that discussion was a worthwhile way to learn.

I believe that the development of conditional knowledge about when and why social constructivist approaches are optimally used has been slowed by two pervasive characteristics of the social constructivist literature. First, social constructivists tend to have a lot more to say about learning than about teaching. In particular, they tend to focus on epistemological issues (What is the nature of knowledge and how is it constructed and validated?) rather than pedagog-ical issues (What combination of approaches to teaching will optimize the students' construction of knowledge that reflects the course's intended outcomes?). Second, to the extent that they do talk about teaching, social constructivists tend to put forth their particular model as if it applied univer-sally, without saying much if anything about when it would or would not be used or how it might need to be adjusted to different types of students, different subject matter, different learning activities, and so on.

CONCERNS AND INSIGHTS DEVELOPED FROM MY OWN RESEARCH

My interest in these issues has been fueled in part by my own scholarly activities. In recent years, I have been collaborating with Janet Alleman in developing instructional units on cultural universals (food, clothing, shelter, transportation, etc.) for use in primary-grade social studies, and in studying the teaching of Barbara Knighton, who implements the units with first and second graders. Our unit plans include a blend of transmission and social constructivist elements, as does Barbara's teaching (in all subjects, not just social studies).

In planning our units, in monitoring their implementation in Barbara's classes, and in noting other aspects of Barbara's teaching not directly related to our unit plans, we frequently encounter evidence of a need for qualifications on the feasibility of social constructivist approaches to classroom discourse, especially when students' cognitive development and domain expertise are limited. We have been trying to move beyond vague notions of "balancing" transmission and social constructivist approaches by developing principles specifying how and why these approaches might be combined, and their mixture adjusted, as lessons and units progress. Our tentative conclusions are as follows (Alleman & Brophy, 2001).

First, it appears that transmission techniques are best used for efficiently communicating canonical knowledge (initial instruction establishing a knowledge base) and social constructivist techniques are best used for constructing knowledge networks and developing processes and skills (synthesis and application). In the early elementary grades where our research has focused, this contrast is somewhat muted: Most transmission occurs during teacher-student interaction segments that include a lot of teacher questioning and little or no extended lecturing, and most opportunities for students to engage in the social construction of knowledge are closely monitored and highly scaffolded by teachers. Later grades more often feature lesson or activity segments that are more exclusively either transmission or social construction of knowledge.

I noted earlier that overreliance on social constructivist discourse models can lead to lessons that have a rough rather than a smooth flow, frequently interrupted or sidetracked momentum, and a poor signal-to-noise ratio. These dangers become acute when teachers face either of two conditions that we observe regularly: (1) young learners with as-yet poorly developed skills for learning through speaking and listening and undeveloped skills for learning through reading and writing; and (2) learners whose prior knowledge (domain expertise) is very low and poorly articulated, so that questions about the topic frequently fail to produce responses or elicit irrelevant or invalid statements. This commonly occurs in social studies lessons in the early grades, even when the questions deal with food, clothing, shelter, or other cultural universals with which the students have had frequent life experiences.

The problems that we have observed when teachers overuse social constructivist discourse models (or use them ineffectively) have sensitized us to the need for adaptation of these models when teaching in the early grades, especially when addressing topics about which students have minimal prior knowledge. One adjustment that we suggest is to rely more heavily on transmission techniques early in a lesson or unit, to establish a common base of information that includes clear articulation of big ideas. Another is to adapt the discourse model that has been developed with middle- and secondary-school classrooms in mind to make it more attuned to the discourse forms and rhythms that are predominate in the primary grades (e.g. more frequent but shorter exchanges, with more teacher scaffolding to help students express themselves). Our goal is to incorporate as much of the social constructivist ideal as is possible under the circumstances, but in ways that result in more smoothly flowing lessons that have more acceptable signal-to-noise ratios. In this regard, it is important to plan to either avoid predictable misconceptions or focus attention on them, especially if they involve big ideas and are particularly memorable or difficult to eradicate once verbalized.

Attempts to use social constructivist discourse with young children often are complicated by the problem of egocentrism. Primary-grade students often use questions posed by the teacher as occasions for launching stories that they want to tell. These stories may have little or nothing to do with the topic, in which case they distract from the focus of the lesson. In the case of lengthy anecdotes, they derail lesson momentum completely. Our observations of Barbara Knighton indicate that she is skilled at using helpful and constructive comments to prevent this from happening in the learning community that she has established. She also follows up by making time for one-to-one sharing during later interactions, such as while eating lunch with her students.

A core idea of constructivism is that each student builds his or her own unique representation of what is communicated. However, a student may or may not create a complete and accurate reconstruction of what the teacher intended to convey, so that learning is often incomplete or distorted. Barbara blends and balances transmission and constructivist teaching in ways that address these limitations of young learners, yet encourage them to personalize their learning and apply it to their lives outside of school. She provides basic information during whole-class instruction early in a lesson or unit, then follows up with small-group or partner activities that allow every student to draw on what he or she knows or has experienced. If necessary, she uses direct instruction with checking for understanding at the beginning of the segment, then gradually moves to reflective/interactive discussions.

Barbara models the knowledge construction process by using examples from her own life to articulate and illustrate major understandings in ways that legitimate students' feelings and encourage them to share their insights. She also frequently laces metacognitive self-talk into the conversation, to help students learn to reflect on how they know things or what implications their new learning might have.

Because topic-focused whole-class discussions are difficult to sustain for long with young learners, Barbara frequently scaffolds her students' participation in these lessons or shifts to alternative formats. Her scaffolding may include cueing the students to "listen for," "think about," "listen to the story and be ready to share," "listen and decide how you would choose," and so on. If students struggle to respond to her questions, she may help them to express themselves, thus minimizing interruptions and sidetracks. As she scaffolds students' thinking, she often revoices their contributions in ways that focus on big ideas.

Following (or even in between segments of) whole-class lessons, Barbara frequently will arrange for the students to communicate in small groups ("Talk with your table group to decide what you think was the most important idea") or pairs ("Turn to your partner and share your ideas"). Even these small-group and paired activities, however, may need to be kept short and to be carefully scaffolded if they are to function as worthwhile learning experiences for young learners.

One way that our unit plans compensate for young learners' limited capacities for sustained knowledge construction in classrooms is to arrange for them to engage in such knowledge construction at home with their parents or other family members. Our lessons include daily home assignments calling for students to collaborate with their parents in carrying out some activity that applies what the students learned that day in class. These home assignments are not conventional worksheets or other traditional "homework." Instead, they call for students to engage in sustained conversations with their parents as they talk about how the family came to live where it currently lives, inspect clothing labels to identify where their clothes were made, talk about how the furnace works, or discuss other lesson-based content.

Both the parents and the children tend to find these interactions enjoyable. In the process, the children learn a lot about the goals and decision making that lie behind much of their parents' behavior, and the parents learn that their children are more curious and knowledgeable than they realized. Discussions that begin in our home assignments often lead to personal or family projects, trips to the library, expansion of discussion to other topics, or other elaborations that provide opportunities for both social construction of knowledge and reinforcement of family ties. We believe that the home has great potential for exploitation as a site for extension of knowledge construction begun in the classroom (Alleman & Brophy, 1994).

RATIONALE AND PLAN FOR THIS VOLUME

I envisioned this volume as a sympathetic but analytic and critical view of social constructivist teaching principles, developed with the recognition that instructional approaches are not ends in themselves but means – tools to accomplish certain jobs (In this regard, I recognize that many educators might argue that reflective discussion and other desired classroom processes are ends in themselves. I would argue, however, that upon finer analysis, these processes can be seen as aspects of designed learning experiences that have been included because they are believed to support students' progress toward ultimate outcomes – not just narrow content and skills objectives but broader dispositions toward reflective and critical thinking, use of disciplinary discourse genres, etc.). Like other tools, particular instructional approaches are ideal for accomplishing some jobs, useable but not ideal for accomplishing others, and irrelevant or even counterproductive for accomplishing still others.

The volume explores the applications of this truism to social constructivist teaching. It was planned as an attempt to generate conditional knowledge about such teaching by inviting researchers who value social constructivist approaches to draw on their own work and any other work that they viewed as appropriate to address this issue. Its contributors include people who have done research on relatively generic aspects of teaching as well as people who have studied instruction in particular subject areas. They were invited to participate because I viewed them as scholars who emphasize teaching for understanding and are sympathetic to social constructivist perspectives, but not so committed to social constructivist teaching models that they could not be analytic and objective. I asked them to focus on theory and research relating to social constructivist teaching, not social constructivist ideas about learning (except to the extent of clarifying the rationales for the teaching strategies). I also asked them to address the following six questions:

(1) What does social constructivist teaching mean in the area(s) of teaching on which your scholarly work concentrates?
(2) What is the rationale for using these approaches, and what forms do they take?
(3) What are the strengths/areas of applicability of these teaching approaches, and what are their weaknesses/areas of irrelevance or limited applicability?
(4) When, why, and how are social constructivist approaches used optimally?
(5) When, why, and how do these approaches need to be adjusted from their usual form in order to match the affordances and limitations of certain students, instructional situations, etc.?
(6) When and why are these approaches irrelevant or counterproductive (and what methods need to be used instead in these situations)?

Unfortunately, educational innovations commonly get oversimplified, taken to extremes, or otherwise distorted. This volume attempts to counteract that tendency with respect to social constructivist teaching approaches by combining sympathy (exploring their affordances) with realism (acknowledging their limitations).

In my original conception, the volume would have focused on classroom discussion, particularly whole-class discussion, which I viewed as the prototypical social constructivist teaching method. However, review of the literature and discussions with some of the authors made it clear that many educators who identify themselves as social constructivists emphasize the interactions that occur in pairs or small groups as much or more than the interactions that occur in whole-class discussions in their models of teaching, and that they emphasize the nature of the task or activity as much as the discussion that occurs within it. Consequently, the title of the book uses the term "social constructivist" rather than the term "discussion," because the former term better describes the contents of most of the chapters.

It also is worth noting that my original ideas about the title of the volume and my early correspondence with chapter authors referred to social constructivist teaching "methods." Most of the authors objected to this term because it carries connotations that conflict with social constructivist philosophy. Some authors even expressed discomfort with the term "social constructivist teaching." They were more comfortable talking about learning and ways to support students' construction of knowledge, and they viewed such support as highly contextual and dependent on instructional goals, emergent student discourse or task responses, and other factors. Several were leery of any attempt to talk about social constructivist "teaching" in terms that might lead to its representation as a set of "methods." Some of the authors comment on these issues in their chapters.

I understand these concerns, and sympathize with them to an extent (for example, in my own contributions to the volume, I have avoided the term "method" and instead referred to social constructivist "teaching," "approaches," or "principles"). However, I believe that social constructivist (or any other) views on learning that are used as a basis for planning teaching need to lead ultimately to relatively systematized models of teaching, for two main reasons. First, I believe that it is unrealistic to expect to be able to educate teachers to implement social constructivist principles without systematizing them into operational models of teaching (especially given the widespread agreement that these principles are much harder to implement successfully than transmission principles). Second, systematic models of social constructivist teaching, or at least operational descriptions of social constructivist principles in action, are needed to provide a basis for conducting research on such teaching. Much more research on the feasibility and effectiveness of social constructivist teaching is needed, and this assumes the existence of reasonably clear teaching models and the possibility of reliably assessing the degree to which these models are being implemented in classrooms.

The contributors to this volume have studied social constructivist teaching as implemented at various grade levels and in several subject areas. In the process, they have developed or identified both general models and situational adaptation strategies for applying social constructivist principles in ways that match the students, the subject matter, and other affordances and constraints embedded in the schools in which they work. They summarize what they have learned in the first eight chapters. Then, in the last chapter, I conclude the volume with a discussion of what their collective efforts suggest as state-of-the-art responses to the six questions listed previously.

REFERENCES

Airasian, P., & Walsh, M. (1997). Constructivist cautions. *Phi Delta Kappan, 78,* 444–449.
Alleman, J., & Brophy, J. (1994). Taking advantage of out-of-school learning opportunities for meaningful social studies learning. *Social Studies, 85,* 262–267.

Alleman, J., & Brophy, J. (2001, April). *Adjusting the knowledge transmission/construction mix to student expertise levels in elementary social studies*. Paper presented at the annual meeting of the American Educational Research Association, Seattle.

Applefield, J., Huber, R., & Moallem, M. (2001). Constructivism in theory and practice: Toward a better understanding. *High School Journal, 84*, 35–53.

Brophy, J. (Ed.). (2001). *Subject-specific instructional methods and activities*. New York: JAI (an imprint of Elsevier Science).

Chazan, D., & Ball, D. (1999). Beyond being told not to tell. *For the Learning of Mathematics, 19*(2), 2–10.

Cobb, P. (1994). Where is the mind? Constructivist and sociocultural perspectives on mathematical development. *Educational Researcher, 23*(7), 13–20.

Driver, B., Asoko, H., Leach, J., Mortimer, E., & Scott, P. (1994). Constructing scientific knowledge in the classroom. *Educational Researcher, 23*(7), 5–12.

Good, T., & Brophy, J. (2000). *Looking in classrooms* (8th ed.). New York: Addison Wesley Longman.

Kounin, J. (1970). *Discipline and group management in classrooms*. New York: Holt, Rinehart & Winston.

Larson, B. (2000). Influences on social studies teachers' use of classroom discussion. *Clearinghouse, 73*, 174–181.

O'Connor, M. (1998). Can we trace the "efficacy of social constructivism?" In: P. D. Pearson & A. Iran-Nejad (Eds), *Review of Research in Education* (Vol. 23, pp. 25–71). Washington, D.C.: American Educational Research Association.

Sfard, A. (1998). On two metaphors for learning and the dangers of choosing just one. *Educational Researcher, 27*(2), 4–13.

Staver, J. (1998). Constructivism: Sound theory for explicating the practice of science and science teaching. *Journal of Research in Science Teaching, 35*, 501–520.

Trent, S., Artiles, A., & Englert, C. (1998). From deficit thinking to social constructivism: A review of theory, research, and practice in special education. In: P. D. Pearson & A. Iran-Nejad (Eds), *Review of Research in Education* (Vol. 23, pp. 277–307). Washington, D.C.: American Educational Research Association.

Weinert, F., & Helmke, A. (1995). Learning from wise Mother Nature or Big Brother Instructor: The wrong choice as seen from an educational perspective. *Educational Psychologist, 30*, 135–142.

Wells, G. (1998). Some questions about direct instruction: Why? To whom? How? and When? *Language Arts, 76*, 27–35.

Windschitl, M. (1999). The challenges of sustaining a constructivist classroom culture. *Phi Delta Kappan, 80*, 751–755.

Jere Brophy
Series Editor

LEARNING AND TEACHING FOR UNDERSTANDING: THE KEY ROLE OF COLLABORATIVE KNOWLEDGE BUILDING

Gordon Wells

INTRODUCTION

In this chapter, I wish to explore the role of language – and of meaning-making practices more generally – in promoting students' learning in all areas of the curriculum.[1] As might be expected, I shall give some attention to reading, broadly conceived, since acquiring information from books, maps, diagrams, and texts of all kinds, plays an increasingly important role in education as students increase in age (Kress, 1997; Lemke, in press). I shall also devote some attention to writing – in non-narrative as well as narrative genres – as, with Langer and Applebee (1987), I believe that it is in the writer's dialogue with his or her emerging text that an individual's understanding of an issue or topic is most effectively developed and refined.

However, meaning making is not restricted to interaction with texts. It can certainly also occur in design work, both aesthetic and practical (Smagorinsky, 1995), and in planning and carrying out experiments, surveys and other forms of empirical investigation. But, most importantly, it is taking place almost continuously in almost all classrooms, in the various kinds of talk that constitute or accompany the vast majority of activities. Some twenty years ago,

Social Constructivist Teaching, Volume 9, pages 1–41.
ISBN: 0-7623-0873-7

it was calculated that, in a typical classroom, somebody is talking for at least two thirds of each lesson, and that two thirds of that talk is contributed by teachers (Flanders, 1970). Clearly that estimate needs to be qualified according to subject and grade level and will probably need to be radically revised for those classrooms in which group work for different purposes constitutes a significant form of activity. Nevertheless, until recently, the talk through which learning and teaching is enacted was treated – like water by fish – as transparent and taken for granted. It was therefore rarely considered as a matter for serious investigation or as a domain deserving efforts at improvement.

My argument will be, therefore, that, first, we need to give adequate recognition to all the modes of making and representing meaning through which the activities of learning and teaching are enacted and that, second, of these, talk in particular deserves sustained attention. This is because, as I have suggested, it is the medium in which meaning is most readily and ubiquitously negotiated. It is also, I believe, the foundation of a social constructivist approach to education. Before continuing, therefore, I need to justify this latter claim.

THE SOCIAL CONSTRUCTION OF MIND:
A VYGOTSKYAN PERSPECTIVE

The term "social constructivist", used in the title of this book and in several of the chapter titles, certainly identifies some key assumptions that all the authors share. For example, there would be general agreement that knowledge is constructed by individuals through an active relating of new information to their personal experience and their current frameworks for making sense of that experience. There would also be agreement about the ineluctably social nature of knowing and coming to know, if only because, in John John Donne's memorable words, "No man is an island . . ." Therefore, although we each construct our own knowledge, we do so in the context of activities carried out in conjunction with others – in the family, the community, and in public institutions such as school, church and workplace. More disputable is the status of any particular item or body of knowledge. Some would make a distinction between 'public' knowledge and 'personal' knowledge – between 'what is known' and 'what *I* know' – treating the former as independent of individual knowers. For others, by contrast, the relativity of all knowledge seems to be an inescapable implication of acceptance of the fact that knowledge in any domain is constructed and reconstructed by countless unique individuals who occupy different locations in time and space and belong to different cultures that have diverse worldviews and systems of values (Chinn, 1998).[2]

A somewhat similar divergence also occurs with respect to learning and teaching. While there is a considerable degree of consensus about social constructivism as a theory of *learning*, when it comes to a social constructivist theory of teaching, on the other hand, there is probably much less agreement. Or at least there is disagreement about what such a theory might look like in practice and, indeed, whether it is appropriate to talk about social constructivist *teaching* at all. This latter position is the one that I believe follows from the conception of learning-and-teaching that is at the heart of the cultural historical activity theoretical (CHAT) approach to education, which has been derived from the work of Vygotsky (1978, 1981, 1987), Leont'ev (1978, 1981), Bakhtin (1986) and those who have developed their seminal ideas.

There are a number of key tenets of the CHAT approach:

- Purposeful collaborative activity is both the setting and the motivator for the interactions through which learning and development occur, both on the time-scale of cultural history and that of individual life trajectories.
- Such activities are always uniquely situated in space and time and are mediated by the particular cultural resources available, both the material and semiotic artifacts that are to hand and the practices in which they are deployed. They are also mediated by the knowledgeable skills of the human participants.
- Meaning making is an essential aspect of all activity, both mediating participants' actions and giving rise to semiotic artifacts in which the knowledge and skills developed in and through the activity are embodied for use as resources in future activity.
- From this perspective, learning can fruitfully be conceptualized as appropriating and personally transforming the knowledge and skills enacted in such activities, and developing the dispositions to use these resources responsibly and effectively to contribute to further projects of personal and social significance.
- Learning requires the assistance of other participants who both model the knowledgeable skills involved in activity and guide the learner toward independent mastery.
- Because new learning always builds on personal prior experience, individuals construct different meanings from the same event. Starting from different cultural niches, individual learning trajectories are therefore both diverse and unique, as are the identities that are formed over time. This diversity constitutes a rich resource within society, both for creatively meeting new demands and for challenging and transforming the status quo.

I have spelled out these tenets and their implications in considerable detail elsewhere (Wells, 1999, 2000, 2001), so here I shall focus only on those that help to clarify the role of teaching in a CHAT approach to education.

Fundamental to this approach is that teaching is construed as providing developmentally oriented assistance that enables learners to achieve the goals that they themselves have set or have taken over and made their own. Ideally, it is this 'ownership' that provides the major motivation for the "learning that leads development" (Holzman, 1995). Vygotsky (1978, 1987) proposed the metaphor of the "zone of proximal development" (ZPD) to characterize this conception of teaching. Teaching occurs when a more expert member of a culture assists a learner by managing the overall organization of a task to the extent necessary to enable the learner to participate within his or her current ability, and by providing guidance and assistance with those aspects that he or she cannot yet manage unaided. In recent years, the term "scaffolding" has been used to refer to such assistance when offered with a tutorial intention (Wood, Bruner & Ross, 1976; Cazden, 1988). However, the corollary of scaffolding is that its purpose is to enable the learner to manage without assistance in the future and to take over responsibility for all aspects of the task (Maybin et al., 1992). At the same time, it should also be emphasized that it is not only adults designated as 'teachers' who provide assistance in the zpd. Participants in a joint activity of any scope and complexity nearly always differ in their knowledgeable skills and so can both assist others and learn from them with respect to the different tasks involved. On many occasions, too, it is recognized that no-one has the answer sought or a solution to the problem involved but that, by working together, an outcome can be achieved that is superior to what any individual participant could have achieved alone.

However, the responsive support of individuals or groups of students is not the teacher's only responsibility – important though this is. There is also the responsibility for planning and organizing the sequence of activities through which students are brought into contact with the 'content' of the prescribed curriculum, and presented with tasks that challenge them to "go beyond themselves" (Vygotsky, 1987) in developing new interests, skills and understanding and in making connections between the new information and what they already know. For this reason, I have suggested that it is helpful to think of teaching as taking place on two levels. On the first level, that of 'curriculum manager', the teacher's responsibility is to manage and evaluate the learning trajectory of the class as a whole and, on the second, it is to work with individual students or similarly performing groups and to provide them with assistance that is responsive to their individual needs and appropriately pitched in their zones of proximal development (Wells, 1999). The challenge, of course, is to carry out the first responsibility in such a way that it allows the opportunities necessary to fulfill the second.

A second consequence of adopting the CHAT approach is that due recognition is given to the situated nature of all activities, both in relation to the cultural and historical settings in which they occur and to the life trajectories and current identities of the individual students who make up the class community. From this it follows that it is inappropriate to think that the prescribed curriculum can or should be realized in the same way in all classes at the same grade level. If one takes seriously the need to build on what students bring to their encounters with curricular material as a consequence of their diverse cultural backgrounds, individual previous experiences, and current strengths and interests, it is clear that the activities through which the curriculum is enacted will differ, both in organization and in outcomes, according to the unique characteristics of each classroom community.

It was because of these considerations that I earlier doubted the appropriateness of talking about social constructivist teaching for, if the goal of teaching is to assist and guide learning, the form that teaching might ideally take on any particular occasion cannot be determined independently of the particular group of learners that it is intended to assist. Better, it seems to me, is to think of teaching within the theoretical framework provided by social constructivism – and particularly by the CHAT version of social constructivism – as being, not a set of methods, but rather an overall stance with respect to the two levels of responsibility that I proposed above.

DIALOGIC INQUIRY

Seen in this light, I suggest, learning-and-teaching needs to be seen as essentially an enterprise of inquiry that is dialogically coconstructed by teacher and students together. This was the conclusion that was reached by the group of teacher researchers with whom I collaborated for nearly a decade at OISE/University of Toronto. While recognizing that our common 'vision' would be enacted in different practices by individual members, we agreed on the principles that would guide the learning and teaching for which we were responsible. The key components, we suggested, included:

- creating communities characterized by: inclusiveness, equity and caring, as well as by intellectual achievement;
- giving a high priority to knowledge building and understanding through inquiry, while not neglecting the routine processes and skills needed to engage in them;

- encouraging collaboration – between teacher and students, as well as among students; valuing and building, whenever possible, on students' contributions to the activity in progress, so that knowledge is co-constructed, rather than unilaterally delivered;
- broadening participants' interests and recognizing and valuing the contributions of 'experts' beyond the classroom; bringing the classroom community into a two-way relationship with communities beyond the classroom (local/world-wide, practical/intellectual) by participating in their practices;
- acknowledging and taking into account that, whatever the activity, the whole person is always involved (body as well as mind, feelings and values as well as rational thinking);
- providing for the growth and self-determination of each individual as well as for the development of the classroom community as a whole.

As will be seen, we placed a strong theoretical emphasis on inquiry. The motivating force for learning that is generated by inquiry is developed at some length in the writings of Dewey (1974) and, while not made explicit in Vygotsky's theoretical work, it has become a key feature of many of the pedagogical developments of his work in recent years (Stetsenko & Arievich, in press).[3] An orientation toward inquiry also has advantages from an organizational point of view since, when students share the responsibility for selecting the topics to be investigated and the methods they will use to do so, the resulting sense of 'ownership' of their activities enables them to sustain their engagement and to develop strategies of responsible collaboration that lead to successful completion. Another important advantage of this approach is that it maximizes the opportunity for the teacher to provide individualized assistance, since less of her or his time and energy need to be given to matters of discipline and control.

In such an approach to the curriculum, language clearly plays a central role. Whether in group or whole class activities, provision is made for multiple occasions of goal-oriented dialogue, or what Bereiter (1994) has called "progressive discourse", in which participants propose, explore and evaluate alternative ideas, explanations and problem solutions and, together, construct the most satisfactory outcome of which they are capable. As he argues when likening classroom discussion to "the larger discourse of knowledge building communities" in the world beyond school:

> . . . classroom discussions may be thought of as part of the larger ongoing discourse, not as preparation for it or as after-the-fact examination of the results of the larger discourse. The fact that classroom discourse is unlikely to come up with ideas that advance the larger

discourse in no way disqualifies it. . . . The important thing is that the local discourses be progressive in the sense that understandings are being generated that are new to the local participants and that the participants recognize as superior to their previous understandings (1994, p. 9).

Approached in this way, teaching is no longer seen as transmitting the results of knowledge building activities already completed by distant experts, but as preparing for, encouraging, facilitating, and extending dialogue about curricular-related issues that are of personal interest and concern to the particular community for which the teacher is responsible.

However, it is not being suggested that such episodes of discussion are the only worthwhile learning activities. As will be exemplified below, there are occasions when teacher exposition or direct instruction is the most effective way of bringing relevant information into the arena (Bruner, 1990), and guided learning and practice of particular constituent procedures and skills may on occasion be a prerequisite for launching into some new domain of activity.[4] Furthermore, there needs to be opportunity for solo as well as group work. Not only are group or class discussions much more productive when individual participants have thought about, and prepared themselves to contribute to, the issues to be addressed, but it is in such 'dialogue with self' – often in the form of journal entries, written notes, or other permanent representations of their thinking – that they recognize the gaps in their own understanding and, at the same time, more fully appropriate the dialogic genres and strategies that they have encountered in interaction with others.

A third point also needs to be emphasized. While it is in dialogue with others that the significance of activities is made explicit, questioned and clarified, this does not in any way diminish the importance of action itself, as a site for putting understanding to use and for testing conjectures, hypotheses and problem solutions. Indeed, as I have argued elsewhere (Wells, 1999, 2001), the purpose of learning is not to amass knowledge, as in a bank account (Freire, 1970), but to be able to act effectively and responsibly in situations of personal and social import.

UNDERSTANDING AND KNOWLEDGE BUILDING

I argued earlier that, because of the diversity of participants' cultural origins and individual life trajectories, there can be no universally appropriate method of teaching. It can nevertheless be plausibly argued that, at a rather abstract level, there is a universal sequence to the kind of learning that leads to increased under-standing.[5] This I have attempted to represent in the 'spiral of knowing' (Fig. 1).

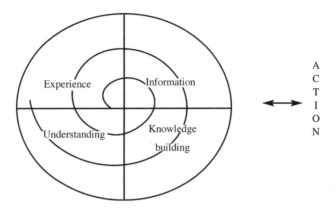

Fig. 1. The Spiral of Knowing (Adapted from Wells, 1999).

Learning is an inherent aspect of participation in almost all activities except the most routine (Lave & Wenger, 1991) and is continually extended and refined over the whole life-span through particular, situated occasions of knowledge building. Figure 1 is thus intended to represent a spiral progression through many cycles of 'coming to understand.' On each occasion, one starts with a personal resource of interpreted past experience that one uses to make sense of what is new. The new is encountered as 'information', either through feedback from action into the world (Freeman, 1995) or from reading, viewing and listening to representations of the experiences, explanations and reflections of others. However, for this information to lead to an enhancement of understanding – which is the goal of all useful learning – it must be actively transformed and articulated with personal experience through "knowledge building" (Bereiter & Scardamalia, 1996).

Knowledge building can take a variety of forms but all are essentially social and interactional in nature. The aim is to create a common, or shared, understanding to which all contribute, whether overtly or through responding internally to the contributions of others (Bakhtin, 1986). Most typically, this goal is attempted through face-to-face oral discourse (which may, of course, include reference to artifacts present in the situation, such as material tools, diagrams, graphs and quotations from written texts of present or absent authors). In Bereiter and Scardamalia's research, the discourse takes the form of messages written at a computer and posted to a central classroom computerized database, to which other students are encouraged to respond with questions, objections or confirming evidence (Scardamalia et al., 1994). By contrast, in the Grades 6 and 7 class taught by Karen Hume, a DICEP teacher, the written dialogue is carried on in the medium of messages posted on the 'Knowledge Wall', a notice board that extends along one wall of the classroom (Hume, 2001). Another possibility that is being increasingly exploited is to carry on the dialogue via the internet.

A second desirable feature of knowledge building is that it occurs in relation to an object that the community, or some members of it, are trying to improve. Such an object can take many forms, ranging from a functioning model to a work of art (e.g. a drawing, a story or poem, a musical performance) and from a scientific explanation to a geometric proof, a map or diagram. Such an 'improvable object' provides a clear focus for discussion, particularly if it is a representation of its creators' current understanding and a rationale has to be given for proposing a change. It is also likely to motivate revision, since the effect of making a change can readily be judged for the improvement it brings or fails to bring about.

One question that is frequently asked about such student-led knowledge building is: What should the teacher do if the knowledge that is collaboratively constructed about a particular topic is at variance with the culturally sanctioned knowledge? This is certainly a serious issue, particularly if the students are to be assessed in terms of performance on tests that consider only whether answers are 'correct' or not and that ignore the processes involved in reaching them. One possible solution to this potential predicament is for the teacher to give a group of students the responsibility for ascertaining the points of view of particular experts who have contributed to the larger dialogue within the discipline and for introducing "what Newton (or some other authority) said" into the discussion as one perspective to be considered among others. Another possibility is for the teacher to suggest additional evidence (and where it could be found) that needs to be taken into account for the class to construct as complete an account or explanation of the topic or phenomenon as possible. To be avoided at all costs, on the other hand, is for the authorized version to be presented at the conclusion of the discussion as the 'correct' view, which should replace the collaboratively constructed one, simply because it is authorized.

Rather than teaching students to accept 'what is known' simply on the basis of authority, then, the aim of knowledge building is to help them to recognize that all knowledge of the world in which we live is tentative and open to improvement – that is to say, knowledge is simply the account that currently best fits the available evidence and has not been shown to be false in terms either of internal inconsistency or of the consequences of actions that put it to the test. Furthermore, since advances in knowledge come from just the sorts of progressive discourse in which students are engaging, they should be encouraged to see that, by being apprenticed into this form of discourse, they can gradually take on the role of expert in their chosen field and contribute to the larger enterprise of creating knowledge that will have consequences for action and, hopefully, for improving the human condition. It is also important that they understand that, in some areas – for example, in relation to ethical and aesthetic judgements or in constructing explanations of complex events with multiple causal influences – there is no single 'right answer' since there are alternative points of view that are equally acceptable.

Finally, it is worth reemphasizing a point made earlier about the extent to which the whole person is involved in learning of the kind we have been discussing here. Learning through participation in collaborative knowledge building is not simply a matter of acquiring more knowledge. It also involves changes in attitudes and dispositions toward the topics investigated and in the knowledgeable skills that such investigations require. In other words, learning, seen as increasingly full and effective participation in activities of interest and concern to the learner, is also a major influence on the formation of his or her identity and self-image and, by the same token, of the ways in which he or she is regarded by others. For this reason, it is important that participation in dialogue be a positive experience for every student. With this in view, students should be encouraged to ensure that all contributions to the dialogue are both formulated as clearly and coherently as possible, and accepted and treated with respect – even if this takes the form of disagreement.

So far, drawing on cultural historical activity theory, I have argued for an approach to teaching that construes the teacher's role as essentially that of assisting learners in appropriating the knowledgeable skills necessary to develop and pursue interests and concerns that are both personally and socially valued. I have also suggested that this role involves two levels of responsibility: that of selecting, organizing and evaluating the activities in which students engage, and that of providing responsive guidance and assistance to enable them to complete tasks that they cannot yet manage on their own. In outlining this approach, I have also tried to explain why special emphasis should be given to dialogic inquiry as the means by which the goals of education can best be met. In the remainder of this chapter, I shall attempt to make these suggestions more concrete by describing particular activities in more detail and by presenting examples drawn from different areas of the curriculum, as these occurred in classrooms with which I am familiar.

A TAXONOMY OF ACTIVITIES AND PARTICIPANT STRUCTURES

There are many types of classroom activities in which students can be occupied, some more obviously 'constructivist' than others. Rather than comment on each of them in turn, however, I want to sketch a framework that may be helpful to teachers when thinking about which activities to select on particular occasions and for particular purposes. The activities are arranged with respect to two dimensions: their relationship to the spiral of knowing introduced above, and to the participant structures in which they may be appropriately used (see Table 1). Not included, but also very important, are related activities in which students develop and refine the skills, such as observing, reading, writing, measuring, and so on, that are necessary for engaging in these activities. These are not included as separate activities because, in principle, they are best learned and practiced as they are used as means for achieving the goals of the activities in which they occur.

The participant structures in Table 1 will certainly be familiar; they range from a student working alone to the whole class functioning as a single group. The labels given to the types of activity are perhaps less self-explanatory; however, the activities themselves would be recognizable to almost every teacher, even though they themselves may rarely choose them. As mentioned above, they are arranged sequentially (from top to bottom) in relation to the four components in the spiral of knowing: experience, information, knowledge building and understanding. It must be emphasized, though, that it is not envisaged that they would necessarily all occur in any particular curricular unit, nor that those that were selected would occur in the order in which they are presented above. Furthermore, while each of the activities can, in principle, involve any of the participant structures, some of them seem likely to be more effectively carried out in some participant structures than others. With these provisos, I will start with descriptive definitions of the types of activity. Suggestions as to how they might be used with different participant structures will be considered in the section that follows.

EXPERIENCE

It is a common practice to elicit students' prior knowledge of a curricular topic before introducing new information. Typically this happens in oral mode, with the teacher asking leading questions to the whole class. However, if we take

Table 1. A Taxonomy of Curriculuar Activities.

Type of Activity	Participant Structure				
	Individual Student (solo)	Student + Teacher	Group (2 or more students)	Group + Teacher	Whole Class
Experience					
Recap Relevant Knowledge					
Brainstorm Possible Questions, Approaches, Procedures, etc.					
Plan: Goals, Procedures, Materials, etc.					
Information					
Gather Information					
Obtain Evidence					
Observe, Experiment, etc.					
Knowledge Building					
Identify Patterns and Make Connections					
Evaluate Evidence					
Formulate Solution, Explanation, Conclusion, etc.					
Present Interim/Final Results + Receive Feedback					
Understanding					
Reflect on: Current Understanding, Strategies Used, What Next?					

seriously the constructivist principle that knowledge is built on the basis of what learners bring to the encounter with new material, it is important to give them the opportunity to reflect individually on what they already know and to communicate this to others. In the framework developed by the DICEP group, we typically start with a two part activity, which we refer to as 'launching' the unit (Wells, 2001). The aim is to capture the students' interest and to encourage them to make connections to their previous experience.

Recap Relevant Knowledge or Experience

In the first part, the teacher presents some form of aesthetic event to the whole class by, for example, reading or telling a story (Egan, 1988) or poem (Wells, 1990) or showing a videotape (Kowal, 2001). Such an event both connects to related events in students' lives and also provides an excellent basis for the forward-looking activities considered below that form the second part of the launch.

The aim of this 'recap' activity is to hear what ideas students spontaneously bring to the topic. Since personal experience tends to be emotionally charged, using it as a 'way in' is likely to provide positive motivation for further exploration of the topic. One possibility, which makes use of the 'solo' participant structure, is to ask students to jot down their ideas, including memories of actual events, in their journals or logbooks (D'Arcy, 1989). These can then be shared orally in small groups or in a whole class discussion. Another possibility is to ask students to work in small groups, listening to the contributions of all members and then preparing a list of key ideas generated within the group that will subsequently be presented to the whole class. An additional possibility that contributes further to student involvement is to designate a wall or table in the classroom on which students can display objects related to the topic that they bring from home, or pictures, books or writings of their own that they think will be of interest to their peers. These can then be referred to, as appropriate, as the unit progresses.

Brainstorm Possible Questions, Approaches, Procedures

Once student interest has been aroused, it is very worthwhile, in the interests of developing student ownership of the work they are embarking on, to elicit their ideas about questions and issues that would be important to explore. Once these have been listed and refined, suggestions as to the procedures and materials to be used can also be elicited and discussed. On this basis, students can then choose the issues or questions for their individual or group inquiries.

Plan: Goals, Procedures, Materials

Planning is a natural sequel to brainstorming, as it takes the outcomes of the latter and shapes them into a sequence of tasks to be carried out to reach the chosen goal(s). In part this will probably involve the whole class in deciding on how materials and equipment will be equitably shared and in setting timelines for the different steps. Part of the necessary protocol for a classroom that works as a community is that groups be ready to report and discuss their own and their peers' investigations at times agreed in advance. Planning also needs to be conducted in relation to the specific issues selected by the individuals or groups who are going to pursue them and it is important that a record be made of the outcomes of this activity, whether by the teacher or a designated member of each group, in a form that can be referred back to as the unit proceeds.

In a unit on technology in a Grade 4 class, for example, one of the DICEP teachers encouraged her students to see themselves as scientists or engineers and, instead of simply engaging in the practical aspects of the activity, to keep a written record of their ideas as well as their actions and results to which they added while engaged in the activity. This proved very helpful to two students whom I observed, as the writing provided a strong incentive to think carefully about what they were doing and why, and enabled them to make a well considered decision about what to make and ultimately to produce an effective working model of a land yacht (Wells, in press). In similar vein, another DICEP teacher insisted that students should make and record predictions about the outcomes of their science experiments before actually embarking on them (Wells, 1997). In both cases, the teacher's intention was to ensure that 'hands-on' work was complemented and enriched by thoughtful 'minds-on' work as well.

INFORMATION

Information is the basic material in relation to which the transactions of learning and teaching are organized. Information is not knowledge, however. Still less does the reception of information automatically lead to enhanced understanding. The problem with the traditional, 'delivery' model is that it tends to ignore – or at the very least to underestimate – the work needed to transform information into understanding. The activities to be described in this section are intended to prepare for, and encourage, this transformation.

Gather Information

Although by no means sufficient in itself, there are many occasions in the investigation of a topic when it is necessary to arrange for students to encounter substantial quantities of new information. The medium in which this occurs can vary from whole class presentations in the form of teacher exposition, through media presentation (video, audio) or visits to places of interest such as museums, field sites and workplaces, to individual reading of printed material of various kinds. Two things are likely to enhance both the intelligibility and the memorability of the new information: the first is for the information to be selected so that it relates to the questions and issues that were proposed during the preceding brainstorming; and the second is for the receivers of the information to have prepared 'pegs' on which to hang it. These pegs can take the form of a list of questions developed from the brainstorming activity or as the nodes in a preliminary topic web which groups or the whole class prepare. As is frequently done in relation to literature, students can subsequently be asked to write a response to what they took from the 'presentation'. This allows the teacher to get a good idea of what was most salient to the students and, where necessary, to take contingent action to correct individuals' misapprehensions or to clarify areas of confusion.

Obtain Evidence

Where curricular topics are approached through inquiry, students can be expected to take a more active role in searching out the information that they judge necessary to answer the questions they are researching, although they will probably need guidance in deciding where to look – which books, reference sources and internet sites to go to as being likely to provide the information they need in a form that they are able to deal with. While individual inquiries should not be ruled out, there are considerable advantages to students working in groups on the same, or related questions. First, when two or three students are searching for the same, or related, information, they can assist each other both in the more mechanical aspects of retrieving it and also in deciding which parts of what they find are most relevant to their purposes. Second, where there is a considerable amount of information to be sought out, the task can be divided among the members of the group, who will subsequently share what they have discovered with their peers.

Searching for information is only the first part of this activity, however. Making notes on the information found, or recording it in some other form, is absolutely essential. As with 'gathering information', it is important that students should prepare some kind of framework into which to fit the information they find; it is also beneficial if they respond to it in some form. (To carry out this phase successfully, students need to be helped to develop good note-taking and other study skills. This is an area in which direct instruction by the teacher may be very beneficial.)

In the Computer Supported Intentional Learning Environment (CSILE) project pioneered by Scardamalia, Bereiter and colleagues (1994), groups of students select their own sub-topics to research within a broad class theme, such as the functions of different parts of the human body or the opening up of the West (Canada or U.S.A.), and then post contributions based on their research to a central computerized class database. These notes are thus available for all to read and other students are encouraged to respond to them with notes that query or add to those of their peers, or propose theories or evidence of their own [6] A further feature of CSILE is that students can 'rise above' the individual contributions to investigate connections across sub-topics. This form of dialogic writing constitutes a mode of knowledge building, which is what CSILE is designed to facilitate (see 'Knowledge Building' below). A somewhat similar collaborative form of research characterizes the Learning Communities pioneered by Brown and Campione (1994), though in their case without the networked computers. Although the means of evidence collection are very similar, students in classrooms associated with the 'Communities of Learners' project typically take part in 'jigsaw' activities which are designed to ensure that the findings of individual groups are made available to the class as a whole.

Observe, Experiment

In many forms of inquiry, the gathering of evidence can go beyond library-based research. Most natural and social science topics, for example, lend themselves to investigations that involve empirical research. Such research can involve direct observation, as in the study of plants and other living organisms (see Gallas, 1995 for such investigations in Grade 1), experiments, as in chemistry or physics (see Van Tassell, 2001 for experiments in Grade 2), computer-based simulations, for example an investigation of gravity in Grade 6 (Cohen, 1995), or surveys of the experiences, beliefs or value judgments of others, as in the examples described by Roseberry et al. (1992).

As mentioned above, for information and evidence – however obtained – to lead to enhanced understanding, it needs to be transformed by being put to use in some way and the results evaluated and reflected on in relation to the question or issue that is motivating the investigation. This is the phase of Knowledge Building, to which we now turn.

KNOWLEDGE BUILDING

Agreement on the centrality of dialogic knowledge building in intellectual development is one of the most characteristic features of studies of learning and teaching undertaken from a social constructivist perspective (Bereiter &

Scardamalia, 1996; Brown & Campione, 1994; Lampert et al., 1996; Mercer, 1995, in press; Nystrand, 1997; Palincsar et al., 1998; Resnick, 1987). This holds both across grade levels and across subject areas. Two main reasons are given for this emphasis. First, it is argued that it is in and through collaborative knowledge building that students advance their understanding of the topics they are studying. This occurs as they review and evaluate the evidence obtained through the various inquiries they have carried out and attempt to arrive at a consensual description, explanation or solution of the phenomena or issues under investigation. However, while consensus is the goal, it is worked for, not imposed, and the voicing of ideas or experiences that go against the majority or 'official' position is encouraged rather than being treated as disruptive. Both interpersonally and cognitively, it is considered important that students should feel able to voice disagreement, since it is the expression of doubts and differences that advances the understanding of the group as a whole by forcing contributors to reconsider and, if necessary, to modify their own positions with respect to the issue under discussion (Matusov, 1996).

The second reason put forward for the emphasis on such discussion is that it provides the most effective means for enabling students to appropriate the genres in which meaning is made in the different academic disciplines that underlie the subjects of the school curriculum. As Lemke (1990) argues, students can only really learn science by having the opportunity to 'talk science' around topics that really engage them. Here the role of the teacher as model and coach of the relevant genres is crucial; the task is to build bridges between 'everyday' and specialist, or 'scientific', concepts over which students can cross as they develop their identities as members of the relevant discourse communities (Wells, 1999).

These two reasons are not independent, of course; rather they are complementary aspects of the purposeful nature of this form of discourse which, as Bereiter (1994) puts it, to be 'progressive', must lead to understandings "that the participants recognize as superior to their previous understandings" (p. 9). A similar position is expressed by Cobb & McClain (in press) with respect to the learning and teaching of mathematics:

> In our view, the value of such discussion is open to question unless mathematically significant issues that advance the instructional agenda become explicit topics of conversation. Conversely, students' participation in substantive discussions can serve as primary means of supporting their induction into the values, beliefs, and ways of knowing of the discipline.

The four activities in this group all contribute to these goals and, in a sense, they form a natural temporal progression. *Evaluate Evidence* and *Identify Patterns and Make Connections* would typically be activities carried out initially by the students addressing the various sub-topics under investigation. These activities are aimed at sifting and evaluating the information gained through their inquiries with respect to its significance and relevance for the specific questions under investigation The remaining two activities, *Formulate Solution, Explanation, Conclusion*, and *Present Interim/Final Results+Receive Feedback*, bring the investigations to an interim or final conclusion in order for the results to be shared with the class as a whole and responded to in a critical but supportive manner. In some cases, the feedback received may lead a group to return to the preceding phases of obtaining and evaluating evidence in order to answer the questions or criticisms leveled at their first report.

So far, we have considered the knowledge building activities in which the groups investigating sub-topics might engage. However, when all the groups have reported, the same knowledge building activities can be conducted by the class as a whole in order to evaluate the degree of fit between the conclusions of the different groups, to determine what conclusions of a general nature can be drawn about the topic as a whole, and to consider what further questions still need to be investigated. This, in fact, constitutes the first part of the final stage in the spiral, which addresses the understanding developed over the course of the unit.

UNDERSTANDING

By its nature, understanding is a criterion of learning that is extremely difficult to evaluate in any absolute manner. First, understanding is not an enduring state that can be reliably measured by decontextualized questions on a test. Understanding manifests itself in further action – in meeting a new challenge, whether in relation to a problem encountered in the world of material action or in the extension or modification of ideas in further dialogue. Perhaps the only clear evidence of an increase in understanding is the recognition that there are still further aspects of a situation or problem that one does not yet understand sufficiently clearly. The second feature of understanding is that it is only genuinely put to the test in specific situations. So, although one may think one understands such concepts as 'justice' or the principles of 'flotation', it is only when faced with a specific, situated problem to which one or more of these concepts seems to apply that one discovers the extent of one's understanding in terms of its utility as a tool in solving the problem. Thus, it is the participants rather than some external evaluator who can best decide whether they have increased their understanding of a topic and in what ways. Furthermore, the understandings achieved will almost certainly be different for different coparticipants in an activity, since individually they start from diverse experiential bases. Nevertheless, this does not mean that understanding is not a valid aim for learning and teaching. Indeed, as I argued earlier, it is only when understanding has been enhanced that true learning can be said to have taken place.

Given that understanding is a mental action rather than a state of mind, it is to action that we must look to observe its growth. Clearly, it can occur in solo settings, such as when an individual succeeds in solving a problem and recognizes what she/he has learned in the process, or when engaged in dialogue with self or with a text that she/he is writing. However, the situation in which an increase in individual understanding is most likely to occur, particularly in educational settings, is in the course of collaborative knowledge building. Each of the activities already considered in relation to Knowledge Building can lead to increased understanding. However, there is one, in particular, that in my opinion is most likely to achieve this effect.

Reflection on: Current Knowledge, Strategies Used, What Next?

In the DICEP model of inquiry, this activity is undertaken to bring a curricular unit to conclusion; however, it can also prove valuable at the end of any of the major constituent parts of a unit. Solo or group work may be undertaken in preparation, but the essential component is the whole class discussion, usually chaired by the teacher, in which an attempt is made to reach a consensus – a common understanding – about what the class knows as a result of the various investigations in which they have been engaged in relation to the overarching theme or topic. It also provides an excellent opportunity for participants to consider the practical and ethical implications of what they have come to know – in what ways they will act differently in future situations to which this knowledge applies. This may also be an appropriate moment to consider how far the group has come to understand the 'culturally accepted' way of thinking about the topic and, if they are in disagreement with it, why that might be the case.

As with all such discussions, while consensus is the goal, it is important to listen to divergent – or even contradictory – points of view and to attempt to see why the differences occur and whether they can be resolved. A key feature of Piagetian theories of intellectual development is the role played by 'cognitive dissonance' in pushing individuals to try to reach a better understanding. The same argument figures in sociocultural theory, where cognitive dissonance is seen as externalized in conflicting claims and points of view. Attempting to resolve them, or at least to recognize when and why more than one position is tenable, is an excellent way of enabling both the individuals involved and the class as a whole to achieve a better understanding of what is at issue.

A second purpose of this reflective activity is to "go meta", as Olson and Bruner (1996) call it – deliberately reflecting on the social and cognitive processes in which the group has been involved and on the status of the knowledge that has been jointly constructed. From a Vygotskyan perspective on intellectual development, this is the preeminent means whereby everyday ways of thinking are reconstructed in terms of "scientific concepts" (Vygotsky, 1987; Hasan, in press); it is also the means whereby advances in knowledge have been made and systematized in human history more generally (Dewey, 1974; Wartofsky, 1979).[7] Ironically, however, of all the activities identified in Table 1, this is the one that is least often observed in classroom practice (Nystrand et al., 2001). Yet, as I shall illustrate below, the benefits in terms of individual and community understanding can be very considerable.

PARTICIPANT STRUCTURES

It would be a straightforward matter to spell out and illustrate all the intersections between types of activity and structures of participation that are implied in Table 1, but it would be space-consuming and tedious to do so. Instead, I will reiterate the principles on which I believe pedagogic decisions about participant structure should be based and then present some actual examples of social constructivism in practice.

In general terms, CHAT conceives of development as occurring through transactions between individual participants and other members of the communities in whose activities they engage. In educational settings, there are thus two significant communities to be considered – that of the classroom and that of the wider society – and it is one of the teacher's major tasks as 'curriculum manager' to mediate the relationships between them.

In this respect, one of his or her most important responsibilities is to help students to develop their sense of responsible agency as lifelong learners who can actively participate in the construction of knowledge and its critique, and contribute to the betterment of the world they inherit. This is the rationale that Dewey advanced for the adoption of an inquiry approach to curriculum; it is also the rationale for the framework for selecting activities that was outlined above. By making 'understanding' the goal of each cycle of the spiral of knowing the teacher tries to ensure that students recognize that learning involves much more than memorizing information and that it has implications for action now and in the future .... As Barnes emphasizes:

> Learning is seldom a simple matter of adding bits of information to an existing store of knowledge ... Most of our important learning, in school or out, is a matter of constructing models of the world, finding how far they work by using them, and then reshaping them in the light of what happens. Each new model or scheme potentially changes how we experience some aspect of the world, and therefore how we act on it. Information that finds no place in our existing schemes is quickly forgotten. That is why some pupils seem to forget so easily from one lesson to the next: the material that was presented to them has made no connection with their pictures of the world (1992, p. 81).

Some of the most persuasive examples of adopting this approach can be found in reports, by the TERC group, of empirical investigations that have real life consequences carried out by English language learners in language minority classrooms. For example, one of their reports includes an account of a particularly successful investigation that centered around the quality of the water in various drinking fountains in the school (Roseberry et al., 1992). Other examples are described in the work of Brown and Campione (1994) with the Communities of Learners project, and in classrooms of 'at risk' students described by Dalton and Tharp (in press). As these authors show, emphasizing connections *between* curricular topics and the students' lives as members of communities beyond the school leads teachers to choose and organize the activities that make up the day by day life of the community *within* the classroom in such a way that they enact the relationship between learning and living that is one of the fundamental principles underlying the social constructivist conception of education.

The teacher's second major task is to organize the flow of activities so that, as well as participating as members of the classroom community – both contributing to and benefiting from joint activities in group and whole class structures – students have opportunities to engage in dialogue with self to clarify and develop their individual ideas, interests, and knowledgeable skills.

In introducing the different types of activity in the previous section, I placed the emphasis on joint activities of various kinds. However, there are also multiple opportunities for solo activities in relation to group and whole class activities. In particular, many teachers have discovered that starting in solo or small group participant structures both allows individuals the opportunity to put their thoughts into words and, thus prepared, enables them to contribute more fruitfully to the whole class discussion. For example, individual students can be asked to make entries in their journals or log-books on work in progress and on the tentative conclusions their group has reached. Alternatively, they can individually take responsibility for preparing reports of different aspects of their group's investigations in the form of brief texts in procedural or explanatory genres, or in tables, diagrams or three dimensional representations.

A particular advantage of writing of this kind is that not only does its production serve as a "thinking device" for the writer (Lotman, 1987), but it also allows the teacher to monitor and, if necessary, to intervene to assist individual students with the meanings they are making of the activities in which they are engaged. This sort of responsive intervention is what I earlier called the second level of teaching. In transmissionary classrooms, there is rarely time for teachers to work with individual students, as they spend the majority of the time that they are not lecturing in supervising seat work in which all students are working individually on the same teacher-selected task. By contrast, when activities are jointly undertaken, with groups sharing with the teacher the responsibility for determining their work schedules, controlling student behavior requires much less time and energy and the teacher is freed to observe and respond to individual and group efforts and to provide guidance and direct instruction when it is most needed, that is to say, when students are encountering difficulties and need assistance in completing the tasks they have chosen to undertake.

In sum, an inquiry approach to the curriculum accords equal value to solo, group and whole class participant structures and also accords a significant role to teacher supportive interaction with individuals and groups in which s/he provides assistance with problems encountered, offers constructive suggestions and critical comments on work in progress, and generally challenges students to "go beyond themselves" (Vygotsky, 1978) by extending and deepening the investigations they have undertaken and mastering the knowledgeable skills that are required to do so.

By now, it should be clear why I earlier cast doubt on the appropriateness of talking of social constructivist pedagogical methods. Where the curriculum is genuinely coconstructed in action, teaching methods are selected according to the needs of the moment and no methods in the teacher's repertoire are assumed, a priori, to be good or bad. Nevertheless, overall, the teacher's choice of method is made in relation to the superordinate goal of increasing understanding of the topic(s) under investigation. However, since this formulation is necessarily rather abstract, I should like, in the following section, to give some examples of what it might look like in practice.

APPLYING SOCIAL CONSTRUCTIVIST PRINCIPLES IN PRACTICE

Each of the following examples is taken from the collaborative action research database of the Developing Inquiring Communities in Education Project (DICEP) and in each case is based on videorecordings made by the author at the teacher's request and on discussions between the author and the teacher(s) concerned, as they investigated some aspect of their practice.

A GRADE TWO STUDY OF ENERGY

By the summer of 1995, Mary Ann Van Tassell and Barbara Galbraith had been coteaching Grade 2 science for a number of years. As they reflected on their experiences during the previous year, they recognized that, although they invited and recorded student questions about the topic at the beginning of each curricular unit, they were not using those questions in planning the sequence of activities through which the topic was subsequently studied. They therefore set this as a goal for the following year and decided to investigate their success in doing so during a unit on energy taught after the winter holiday.[8]

To launch the unit, the teachers first brainstormed with the whole class to discover what the children already understood about energy and they wrote this information on a large sheet of paper,which was hung on one of the classroom walls. They then proposed that they should start their investigation by making and testing elastic-powered rollers.[9] Each child was asked to bring from home a cylinder, such as a Coke tin or an empty plastic bottle; holes were then made in each end of the container, an elastic band threaded through the two holes, one end being secured to the exterior of the cylinder and the other threaded through a bead washer and then secured round one end of a length of dowel. As was explained, when the dowel was turned a number of times, the elastic inside the container became twisted and stretched and, when the roller was placed on a flat surface, the tension of the elastic would drive it for a considerable distance.

The children spontaneously – and competitively – became interested in how far their respective rollers would travel and some began to keep records of distance traveled for different numbers of turns of the dowel (Solo: Obtain Evidence). Unfortunately, though, a number of practical problems arose, the most frequent being the breaking of the elastic band when overenthusiastic children wound the elastic too tightly. These problems were reviewed in whole class discussions, in which not only did the class Recap Previous Experience and Brainstorm possible solutions, but they also began to develop explanations of underlying cause and effect relationships (Whole Class: Knowledge Building).

One of the most fruitful problems was presented by a child who had used an empty film canister for her roller. To her surprise, instead of travelling in a straight line, her roller persisted in following a circular trajectory. As this was demonstrated in a whole class meeting and possible explanations explored, another child saw an analogy in the effect of turning the steering wheel of a car. Although this did not really explain the observed phenomenon of the circling roller, it did prompt the teachers to suggest extending the investigation to the making and testing of elastic-powered cars.

After a variety of practical problems – such as the wheels failing to grip on the polished wooden floor – had been overcome (Whole Class: Brainstorm), the question jointly constructed for further investigation was: How far would a car travel for a given number of turns of the elastic round the axle when the car was pushed backwards? Together, the children designed an appropriate operational method of counting the turns and devised a chart for recording the results of increasing the number of turns and, working in groups, they began to carry out the necessary tests (Group: Obtain Evidence). In practice, most groups had some difficulties in making accurate measurements and benefited from assistance from one of the teachers (Group + Teacher: Gather Information). Whitney was in such a group and obviously gained from the teacher scaffolding. At the end of the session she came to show me her group's results: "Look, it goes up nineteen each time."

The next session started with a whole class meeting at which Whitney reported her results, which were written on the blackboard (Present Interim Results). One of the teachers then asked for suggestions as to how to explain the observed pattern. This proved to be a difficult problem for this group of seven-year-olds and, when this became obvious, various analogies were enacted at the suggestion of one of the teachers: walking along a tape measure and noting the regular pattern of increase in distance with each step, then putting a drop of ink on the rim of one of the driving wheels of Whitney's car and pushing it across a sheet of butcher's paper so that it left an inkmark for each revolution of the wheel. When the distance between the inkmarks was measured and proved to be 19 cm., one could see and hear 'the penny dropping'. One boy made a large clockwise circular gesture and several children simultaneously offered verbal explanations. Summing up this Knowledge Building discussion, one of the teachers orchestrated the conclusion that each class member could measure the circumference of one of the driving wheels on their respective cars and they would then be able to predict the results of further trials (Whole Class: Reflect on Current Understanding – with implications for action).

The practical work just described was accompanied by written journal entries in which the children recorded and reflected on their experiences (Solo: Reflection). Here is an example from Alexandra's journal during the mechanical problem solving phase:

> Today our group made sure we got acurat answers on how far our cars move. First we looked at Jansens car. After 2 minutes me and katie realizised that Jansons cars wheels

were rubbing against the box thats called friction. Then the car wouldent go very far because there was to much friction.

Entries such as these then provided material for whole class discussions. In the final discussion the value of this reflective writing was explicitly addressed (Whole Class: Reflect on Strategies Used) and this is what Alexandra had to say:

When you write stuff . . . . You can always remember it and then, when you share in groups you can write more stuff so . . . so whatever you share you learn more.

The teachers also made a practice of recording ideas that emerged in whole class discussion on large sheets of chart paper, the exact formulation being negotiated in collaboration with the children (Whole Class: Formulate Explanation). Here, the process of composing the written text helped the children to focus on what was happening, and why. The resulting text also provided a collective record of the group's emerging understanding, to which individual children could refer as they made their own entries in their science journals.

Thus, as can be seen, this curriculum unit involved students and teachers in activities from almost all of the rows and columns in the matrix. In terms of sequence, the spiral of knowing occurred at two levels. First it was apparent in the way in which the unit as a whole developed from experiential knowing, as the children built and tested their vehicles, to a community effort to construct more theoretical explanations of the substantive knowledge gained in the process. Second, the same pattern tended to occur in each phase of the unit where, on the one hand, there was a strong emphasis on understanding arising from and oriented to action, and on the other, it was very clear that the teachers believed that this understanding would be greatly enhanced through the knowledge building discussions that were a feature of each lesson.

However, in arguing for the quality of the knowing together demonstrated in this class, I am not claiming that all the children had achieved the same understanding by the end of the unit. From a social constructivist perspective on knowing and learning, such an outcome would be most unlikely, since the development of each individual's understanding builds on his or her prior understanding, which itself depends on the range and nature of previous relevant experience. As classes of children are rarely, if ever, homogeneous with respect to prior understanding, identity of outcome is not to be expected. On the other hand, it is reasonable to expect that each individual will extend or deepen his or her own understanding through the interplay of solo, group and whole class activity and interaction. And this, in the teachers' view, could be observed, over the course of the unit, in the changes in the children's manner of participation and in the quality of their contributions to the discourse.

RESOLVING CONFLICTING LAND CLAIMS IN WESTERN CANADA

My second example comes from a Grade 7 classroom in a multiethnic neighborhood in Toronto. Maria Kowal was the home-room teacher for this class and responsible for much of their program.[10] During the year she had engaged them in a number of social studies projects that took them out into various parts of the city, integrating first hand observation and data collection with library-based research, and concluding with presentations of the results of their inquiries using various modes of meaning making. In the last weeks of the year, she built on these earlier experiences with a short unit concerned with Native Land Claims in Canada, which was a prescribed social studies topic for this grade level. The outcomes specified for the course as a whole by the Toronto Board of Education required students to be able to: (a) outline different ways people are or have been involved in democratic process and change; (b) analyze relationships among bias, prejudice, stereotyping, discrimination and persecution; (c) analyze the struggle for basic human rights. Building on the class's previous work in social studies, Kowal decided to organize the unit around a simulation of a First Nations band's land claim. She also decided to invite the students to be coinvestigators with her of the manner in which the unit unfolded.

The unit started with two periods in which the students were introduced to the central issues through viewing a videotape and reading and discussing a text, both of which concerned the longstanding struggle between the Nisga'a band and the government of British Columbia, which had just become national news again. The teacher's purpose here was to ensure that the students became aware of and began to understand some of the key issues in these disputed land claims and, to this end, she stopped to ask questions about the material just viewed or read to ensure comprehension and to draw the students' attention to the subtlety of the points being made. At the most basic level, the activity was Guided Gather Information, but each discussion episode moved into Evaluate Evidence.

Kowal was a little concerned that this activity was painfully slow and might have been shutting down rather than arousing the students' interest. However, when asked later, the students validated her choice of a more direct form of instruction in this activity. As Jane, Keith and Richard said in the final joint interview I conducted with them:

> Keith: . . . well, when you read it by yourself you might think you understand it, but you don't really, but unless you discuss it then you –

Richard: – never would know if you have understood it.

Keith: Yeah, if you don't understand a part of it or get what's going on, when you like discuss it in a group you sort of get an understanding of what's going on.

Jane: If you discuss it then you understand it more because you're actually talking, you're like reading it in your mind (Kowal, 2001, p. 125).

In the next lesson, the teacher divided the students into two heterogeneous groups and introduced the major activity for the unit: to prepare and enact a simulation of a land claim dispute between two fictitious entities – the Wishga'a First Nations band and the Government of Province West – which would be heard before two judges in the Supreme Court. Kowal describes the preparatory activities as follows:

Drawing on past experience, I decided to provide a structure for the students to work with. Their first task was to work individually to list points for each side to support the respective claims to ownership of the land, based on information that had been introduced in previous lessons (*Brainstorm, Obtain Evidence*). After this, they were invited to share their thoughts and decide which side they wished to represent at our court hearing. The element of choice at this point was important. The brainstorming they had completed individually would help them to decide as a group which side they felt they could support more strongly, and I did not want them to be forced to make an argument that they did not really believe in. The students were being drawn closer to the center of the issues: they were beginning to develop a personal affinity with the subject matter and were being asked to reinterpret the facts and arguments they had heard to support a position that they wanted to support. (Kowal, 2001, p. 126; material in italics added.)

While the groups worked at developing, refining and organizing their arguments, the teacher met with each group to help them by making connections with them to other oral and written work they had done during the year and by focusing on the appropriate court-room register in which to express their points (Evaluate Evidence; Formulate Presentation). In this Group + Teacher participant structure, she was able to provide assistance in their zones of proximal development in relation to the knowledge and skills that they needed in order to present the case for their side as effectively as possible. At this point, the teacher decided that the whole class would benefit from a review of the nature and purpose of the simulation (Recap Relevant Knowledge) and so she spent the first part of one lesson Brainstorming in more depth the sort of concerns that individuals on both sides might have – for example, a Wishga'a fisherman with a family to support or a non-Native person who owned a business and sent his children to school in a small town in the disputed land. The groups then had two lessons in which to finalize and rehearse their presentations.

Two teacher colleagues played the judges' roles at the Supreme Court hearing and both sides made effective presentations. The following are speeches made by representatives of the two sides:

> Keith (Counsel for Province West): Good afternoon, your honors. My group and I are representing the Government of Province West. We feel strongly that the land that the Wishga'a are claiming to be theirs, although they FEEL that it is theirs, truly isn't. During this presentation, we'll, we will talk about economic issues, human rights issues, and other land claim issues. . . .
>
> Frank (Representative of the Washga'a Band): So in conclusion, I have to say that to me it is somewhat ridiculous that the government would even think that the land belongs to them. Our tradition has been broken, our bands have been separated, and our land has been taken. . . . Having our own government is a necessity because many problems have been inflicted on us. We believe that if we govern ourselves, we could give help that we are not getting right now. We are prepared to sign a treaty saying that we wouldn't evacuate non-natives from our land. We KNOW the land is ours and will ALWAYS be (Kowal, 2001, pp. 118–119).

Following the hearing, I interviewed both groups, showing them extracts from the videorecordings I had made and inviting their reflections. From the students' comments, it was clear that they felt that the simulation had enabled them to gain a much deeper understanding of the viewpoints of the contending parties than they would have done from simply reading about the topic and writing an essay about it. Asked about the relative value of the different activities in which they had been engaged, those representing the government considered all the activities to have made important contributions to the understanding they developed. The First Nations group, on the other hand, felt that the opening video was the most important as it was from watching it that the group had been able to develop their case. However, despite the obvious success of the unit overall, Kowal was less than satisfied as she reflected on all the evidence. In particular, she regretted that, because of limitations of time, there had not been opportunity for the groups to deepen their understanding by carrying out their own research in relation to the positions they chose to represent. As she wrote:

> I realize in retrospect that independent research is not something we do because it's a skill to be covered but because it is often an integral and motivating part of the learning process and, as such, should have been included in this unit. . . . In truth, as I now see, I wanted the students to perform for me so that I could evaluate how well they understood the issues I had put before them. My goals limited the opportunities for the students to follow through on points of significance and interest for them . . . a potentially important opportunity for knowledge building had been omitted from the planning (2001, pp. 132–133).

Thus, not only did the students gain greater understanding of the complexity of resolving the claims of First Nations' groups through engaging in the activities described, but they also increased their meta-understanding of the learning processes involved. Most importantly, however, through reflecting with the students and then later in her solo writing, the teacher also came to understand better how to organize both time and activities to maximize the students' learning and understanding.

COLLABORATING ON A UNIT ON SOUND

The third example is based on a report of an inquiry undertaken by Zoe Donoahue (in press) in collaboration with Janna Adair, one of her teacher colleagues, in order to explore how a science unit from the new and much more closely specified Ontario curriculum could be organized in such a way as to allow the students to share in its planning and to initiate their own inquiries. The unit in question was on the topic of sound and took place in a grade four class in a suburban elementary school in Toronto. In order to include the students as partners in the inquiry, Donoahue interviewed them in groups of six before the unit and asked them to complete a questionnaire at the end; she also designed a protocol for their written reflections which the students were asked to complete at chosen moments during a number of different types of activity.

The teacher started the unit by focusing on the prescribed "learning outcomes" for the unit. As Donoahue notes, "The children needed to understand that these were non-negotiables, but that they could have input as to *how* they would learn." The six outcomes were written on sheets of chart paper and pinned up around the room and, after the students had taken some time for *solo written brainstorming,* they wrote their chosen questions on sticky notes and posted them on the outcomes for which they judged them to be most relevant. The next day, the whole class reviewed the results with their teacher and decided how they could best answer their questions (Whole Class: Plan Goals, Procedures, Materials, etc.). The activities that they considered would be most appropriate were:

- doing experiments in groups
- studying books and other print resources (to find out what the ear looks like and how it works) and having a teacher guided lesson on the ear
- building a musical instrument
- researching a topic of interest relating to how we use sound in our everyday lives (Donoahue, op. cit.).

On the basis of this collaborative planning, the teacher decided to start with experiments and, specifically, with an experiment involving extending a ruler over the edge of the desk and observing what happened when they struck or pressed down and then released the free end. Before starting, though, the students were asked to write down their predictions, as the teacher considered that this practice "helped the children to focus and gave them something to think about as they worked with the materials." When the students had had sufficient time to complete their experiments (Solo: Observe, Experiment), they were invited to report their findings to the class (Solo: Present Interim Results + Receive Feedback).

All had found the work interesting and several students were inspired to continue experimenting on their own, in class or at home, in some cases using ideas from books that the teacher had made available in the classroom. Some worked out how to play songs with their rulers and some even figured out a way to record their songs, as music, on paper. One student, at home, made a bass with a box, a string and a meter stick. By pressing the string against different points on the meter stick and strumming, he found that the instrument made different sounds. Further experiments then followed, based on ideas suggested by the telephones that two students had made at home with plastic or Styrofoam cups and string. The final practical activity was to design and make a musical instrument of their choice, using the principles that they had been learning.

During the course of these experiments, the students were asked to complete the protocol described above. From what they wrote, Donoahue observed that "there was a good match between what [the teacher] hoped the children would learn and what they felt they were learning . . . [They] seemed to be very aware of the concepts she had in mind (sound, vibration, frequency, how sound travels, music and sound, the ear, and communication)." Asked in the protocol whether they thought experiments were a good way to learn, the majority were enthusiastic. The reasons they gave included that when experimenting, they "get more ideas", "have examples to help me " and "actually get to make sound"; several thought that they learned more about a topic by "doing things" than by "just reading about it." They also appreciated the opportunity to work in groups, both for social reasons and for the intellectual benefits of collaborative thinking.

Another practical activity carried out in groups involved solving one of two problems in which a plastic cup containing 15 pennies was taped to an empty shoebox. Both problems required choosing objects/materials to tape inside the box, in the first case to amplify the sound produced by shaking the assembly and in the second to dampen it. The groups' solutions were ingenious and, on the whole, effective and, as several insightfully observed in their comments on the in-process protocol, the problems were a good way of showing what they had already learned and how they could use this knowledge in action. One student commented "We must *know* how sound is amplified and absorbed" and another thought the task provided a "better way of using the words amplified and absorbed in a different way."

Many of the students continued their experiments at home and brought their work to show the class. Although this disrupted the teacher's planned schedule, she welcomed the evidence of their engagement with the topic of the unit and always made time for their efforts to be recognized and celebrated and to hear about what they had learned in the process.

Not all of the targeted outcomes were approached through group experiments, however. The concept of pitch was explored through a teacher demonstration that built on an activity that one student had initiated at home. Having filled a collection of bottles with differing amounts of water, the teacher showed the relationship between pitch and the volume of resonating air by blowing over the tops of the bottles. At the same time, the teacher encouraged discussion of the results, emphasizing the use of the register of scientific explanation, and taking the students' conjectures and hypothesis-based suggestions to guide how she proceeded with the demonstration.

Learning about the ear was also non-experimental, involving reading and a teacher 'lesson'. From their comments, it was clear that the students recognized the value of this approach, since, as one observed, "we can't look inside the ear"; another saw reading as a safer method of learning about the ear as "we can't do anything else without hurting ourselves." But they also recognized the value for their learning of being given information that was relevant to a topic of interest and importance to them (Solo and Whole Class: Gather Information), particularly when they had some input in the decision to learn in this way.

Toward the end of the unit, the students worked in pairs on a topic of their choice concerning sound in everyday life, researching their topic through reading, searching on the internet, and discussing what they were finding with others (Group: Obtain Evidence). Importantly, the goal of this activity was to present their findings to the rest of the class in whatever form they thought most appropriate. Once again, the element of choice added to their enthusiasm and a wide variety of modalities was drawn on, including speaking in role, demonstrating experiments and explaining displays mounted on bristol board (Group: Present Results + Receive Feedback). Of all the activities undertaken during the unit, presenting the results of their group's research on a self-chosen topic was rated most highly by the students, both as a mode of learning and for the pleasure and satisfaction of working toward the creation of their presentation.

In addition to what they learned about sound, much benefit accrued from the various forms of co-investigation that were included in the unit. A final questionnaire and a follow-up discussion showed that the students had reflected on *how* as well as *what* they were learning. They made some insightful comments about the pros and cons of groupwork and on the basis on which groups were constructed; they also explained the advantages they perceived in sharing in the planning of the variety of activities through which they investigated and learned about the topic of sound. Perhaps most important was their appreciation of having ownership of and a degree of control over how they worked. As one of them noted, "If you get to pick your own topic you're into it . . . and you want to get starting right at it because it's what you want to do."

In her paper, Donoahue (op. cit.) offers extensive reflections on all these features of the approach that was adopted in this unit, and suggests several ways in which she and Adair thought it could be improved. As she explains:

A benefit of asking the children if they enjoyed and were learning from various activities is that they developed a meta-awareness of their own learning styles. They came away from the unit with a better sense of how and under what conditions they do their best learning. We found that a benefit of co-researching with the students is that we were more explicit with them about the decisions we, as teachers, make during a unit and about our reasons for choosing certain types of activities to meet specific learning goals . . . .

The teachers came away from this unit with knowledge that will help them to plan science units that better meet the needs and interests of children. The children acquired a greater metacognitive understanding of the conditions under which they can learn with richness, depth and joy (Donoahue, op. cit.).

TEACHING ACCORDING TO SOCIAL CONSTRUCTIVIST PRINCIPLES: CLARIFICATIONS AND QUALIFICATIONS

The three examples just presented – and many more could have been included if space had permitted – reinforce some of the central points of the argument I have tried to develop in this chapter. In each case, it was various kinds of activity involving inquiry and exploratory talk that enabled students to become deeply engaged with the content of the unit and spurred them to learn the necessary skills and information. At the same time, these examples all illustrate the need for teachers to be flexibly responsive in selecting and organizing activities in the light of the affordances and constraints of their own specific situations: the characteristics of the students, the relationship of the current topic to the sequence of topics in the prescribed curriculum, the pressure of other, competing demands on the time available, and so on. In other words, these examples make clear that, from a social constructivist perspective, effective pedagogy requires a framework of general principles within which decision making can be emergent and strategic in each specific situation.

It is important to make clear, therefore, that my purpose in this chapter is not to argue that it is necessary – or even optimal – for every topic to be approached through a particular model of inquiry. As emphasized above, rather than being a 'method' for teaching certain types of topic, we see inquiry as a stance toward experience and information – a willingness to wonder, to ask questions and to attempt to answer those questions through the collection of relevant evidence by various means, both empirical and library-based, and to present the findings to one's peers for critical review and improvement. Moreover, its ultimate aims are to foster in each student the lifelong dispositions to be agentive in learning and to collaborate with others in seeking for understanding that enables effective and responsible action.

These aims are inherently dialogic. They cannot, therefore, be achieved through rigid adherence to a predetermined sequence of activities, however coherent and theoretically principled the overall plan may seem to be 'on paper'.[11] To be sure, these dispositions can be powerfully fostered when students engage in the full cycle of activities described above but, once dialogue and inquiry have become established as the norm, they can continue to permeate the life of the classroom, even when less open-ended approaches to a topic or unit are deemed more appropriate. Furthermore, it is not the case that topics for inquiry have to originate with the students in order to secure their engagement. Good questions can originate from many sources, including the teacher, a book, the internet, or a member of the wider community. Who originally proposes the question for investigation is much less important than that students invest in and take ownership of it.

A second clarification also seems necessary. It sometimes seems to be implied that it is working on group projects that is the essence of a social constructivist approach to learning and teaching and that, if students are not involved in 'group work', they are not constructing knowledge in collaboration with others. But 'group work' is not the only participant structure that advances the goals of a community of inquiry. As I hope the preceding examples have made clear, solo and whole class participant structures are equally appropriate – and indeed necessary – for the classroom community to benefit from the contributions of all members and to attempt to reach a shared understanding of the topic that they are addressing.

Nor should it be thought that, within this approach, there is not an important role for instruction and information giving, both by the teacher and by experts in the field, through their writing and other modes of communication.

There are certainly occasions when 'direct instruction' is necessary and desirable, particularly when it provides assistance that an individual or many students need in order to complete the activity in which they are engaged (Wells, 1998). In launching a new topic, too, it is often desirable to start with some form of 'presentation' by the teacher, a reading of a poem or story, or a current event on television or a drama recorded on film or video (see the second example above). Visitors to the classroom from the local community can also make very significant contributions of various kinds (Rogoff et al., 2001). Likewise, the practice of the teacher regularly reading aloud to the whole class – a serialized story (Donoahue, 1998), or a non-fiction book that is relevant to work in progress – can enable students at all grade levels to make contact with the work of artists, storytellers, historians and scientists in the wider world beyond the school.[12]

Effective pedagogy, therefore, involves appropriate selection from all the possible participant structures and all the activities I described earlier. What varies is the balance between them. Where depth of understanding is the goal, and time permits, allowing students to negotiate the topics for individual or group investigation and including whole class time for presentation and discussion of their findings is probably the ideal course to take. DICEP teachers' experience suggests that at least one unit should be approached in this way as early as possible in the school year in order to develop the ethos of a classroom community of inquiry. Open-ended, 'hands on' inquiry is also desirable when embarking on a completely new field of study so that students gain some first hand experience as a basis for making sense of information that is subsequently encountered largely through symbolic representations of what others have done and the conclusions they have drawn as a result. However, when the topic builds on one that has already been explored in some depth, and particularly when the time allowed for the topic is limited, it may be appropriate to devote a greater proportion of the time available to various forms of 'gathering information'.

However, in the latter situation – as in all those discussed – three principles remain paramount. The first is that the information presented should be related as far as possible to the concerns and interests that students bring from the world beyond the classroom.

The second principle is that students' questions and ideas should be welcomed and taken seriously, and opportunities provided for their discussion. Whether in group or whole class settings, such focused discussion is one of the most significant means for students to extend and deepen their understanding as they try to formulate their thoughts in a form appropriate to the emerging exchange of ideas (Wells, 1999). As Vygotsky emphasized, "Speech does not merely serve as the expression of developed thought. Thought is restructured as it is transformed into speech. *It is not expressed but completed in the word"* (1987, p. 251, emphasis added). If students raise more issues than there is time to take up during a particular lesson, one possibility is to invite them to post their questions or opinions on a 'knowledge wall' and to encourage written discussion of them by those who are interested (Hume, 2001, and above). Toward the end of the unit, a vote could be taken on which of these issues merited further whole class attention – perhaps as part of the final reflective discussion that, I would argue, should round off every unit, however short the time allotted to it.

But the most important principle is that of having a meaningful goal for the unit – an 'object' to be improved, both through and as a result of what is learned – whether this be the construction or modification of a material artifact, a problem to be solved pertaining to the students' own lives, a simulated situation in which they take on the roles of the participants, or the construction and public representation of their explanation of an event or phenomenon that is central to an understanding of the unit. As Vygotsky argued, it is in collaborative, goal-directed activity that knowledge has continually been created over the course of cultural history; and it is the same type of goal-directed activity that provides the most effective context for the creation of knowledge in each individual's development.

These principles were memorably captured by Ursula Franklin, a doyenne of Canadian science and an active feminist, when chairing a conference on the 'Ecology of Mind'. Knowledge, she argued, is created and recreated "in the discourse between people doing things together" (Franklin, 1996). In these words, she brought together three important features of the knowledge building that is the central concern of all communities of inquiry:

- it is an intrinsic part of "doing things"
- it is created between people
- it occurs in the collaborative meaning-making of their goal-directed discourse.

By the same token, therefore, in organizing the sequence of activities through which the members of the classroom community construct their understanding of the knowledge and skills involved in each curriculum unit, the teacher's prime aim should be to ensure that there is ample opportunity for this kind of dialogue of collaborative knowledge building.

CONCLUSION: MAKING IT HAPPEN

As will be clear from the preceding sections of this chapter, a social constructivist approach to learning and teaching does not fit easily with the contemporary emphasis on standardized outcomes and prespecified routes to their achievement. Truly to accept and welcome the diversity that exists in today's school population means abandoning the chimera of a universally effective way of teaching and, instead, encouraging teachers to take responsibility for negotiating with the students in their charge how best to address the curricular topics they must study in ways that engage the students in collaboratively constructing the relevant knowledge and skills in order to achieve goals that are of personal and social relevance to them as members of the communities to which they belong and to which they aspire to belong. It therefore follows that there can be no 'methods' that are universally suitable for all classrooms or for any particular curricular topic.

For those who seek to reduce teaching to 'delivery' of 'content' determined by others through the 'implementation' of a set of predetermined procedures, this must seem a very negative conclusion.. However, if – as Dalton & Tharp (in press) recommend – the standards are interpreted as a broadly-based "consensus about ideals and principles that must be enacted in local contexts through local participation," there is no fundamental incompatibility between goals to be aimed for and diversity in routes toward their attainment. Furthermore, it could very reasonably be argued that some variation in outcomes is unavoidable and, indeed, that it is a necessity if society as a whole is to retain the diversity that fosters creativity and originality in all fields of human endeavor (Lemke, in press).

On the other hand, for teachers who see learning as a lifelong endeavor – for themselves as much as for the students they teach – the challenge presented by the decision to organize their teaching according to social constructivist principles is both demanding and rewarding. It invites them, like other professionals, to be agents in determining, on the basis of their own experience and understanding, what courses of action are most appropriate in the situation and in the best interests of those for whose continued development they are responsible (Wells, 1999, Ch. 10).

There are many ways for teachers to meet this challenge of continuing to learn. Participating in supportive professional development activities and keeping abreast with relevant practice-oriented research are obviously important means. But, in line with the central arguments of this chapter, I should like to give particular emphasis to 'practitioner inquiry'. As is clear from the examples above, the inquiry approach that is so motivating for students can be equally energizing and productive for teachers. Since there are no universal solutions to the problem of how to effectively engage all students in learning what is specified in the prescribed curriculum, each class and each unit requires appropriate answers to be made as lessons and units are co-constructed by teacher and students together. However, when these processes are systematically investigated in collaboration with colleagues through the collection and interrogation of evidence from their own classrooms, teachers both achieve improvement in action and understanding themselves and provide a powerful model of learning for their students. In so doing, they also effectively demonstrate what it means to apply social constructivist principles of learning and teaching in practice.

NOTES

1. The research on which this chapter is based was largely carried out in conjunction with members of the 'Developing Inquiring Communities in Education Project' (DICEP). The group consisted of classroom teachers (Grades 1–8), two university teacher educators, a senior researcher, and a small number of graduate students. Between 1992 and 1998, with grants from the Spencer Foundation, the group attempted, through action research, to create communities of inquiry in their own classrooms, among colleagues in their schools, and in our own collaborative group, and to document the means that seemed most effective in achieving this goal. Accounts of some of their inquiries are collected in Wells (2001). Since I moved from Toronto, the group has been successful in obtaining a further grant from the Spencer Foundation to investigate the feasibility and benefits of involving their students as co-researchers.
2. A useful collection of articles that discuss this question is found in Guzzetti & Hynd (1998).
3. In a very interesting comparison of Dewey and Vygotsky, Glassman (2001) has recently shown that there are substantial similarities between the educational theories of these two writers, but also important differences. In the light of Glassman's argument, it is clear to me that, in the model presented here, I have modified the Marxist emphasis on cultural reproduction with a Deweyan emphasis on inquiry. From a classroom point of view, this leads to my advocacy for group inquiries on topics and issues that are negotiated between student(s) and teacher.
4. Mercer (in press) argues that discussion itself involves attitudes and skills that need independent attention and reports research that shows the improved quality and effectiveness of group discussion that resulted when preceded by a preparatory series of 'talk lessons'.
5. Although 'learning' is often treated as a unitary phenomenon, it seems clear that the term is habitually used to refer to the enhancement of relatively distinct forms of mental and physical activity. Most obvious is the distinction between 'knowing that' and 'knowing how to' (Ryle, 1949). While the sort of learning that I am concerned with combines both forms of knowing – hence the use of the phrase 'knowledgeable skills' – it is clear that much school learning has traditionally kept the two forms of knowing separate, both from each other and from situations of 'real-life' use. This is particularly apparent when the goal of learning is explicitly focused on being able to give correct answers to decontextualized items on tests.
6. Further information about CSILE can be found at the demonstration site: http://csile.oise.utoronto.ca/demo_csile.html
7. This argument is developed in greater detail in Wells, 1999, 2000.

8. A much fuller account of this investigation is included as Chapter 9 of Wells (1999). In addition to the teachers' focus on student questions, we were together also exploring what 'working in the zpd' might look like in contemporary classroom practice.

9. Instructions for making this elastic-powered roller can be found in Richards (1990).

10. For a much fuller account of this unit, viewed from the teacher's perspective, see Kowal (2001).

11. This argument is forcefully made in a recent case study by Christoph & Nystrand (2001), which traces the professional development of an experienced high school teacher of English as she attempted to become more 'dialogic' in her style of whole class interaction.

12. One of the most positive memories I retain of my own later years at school is of teachers of English and history who read aloud from works that they considered important for us to encounter.

ACKNOWLEDGMENT

I should like to acknowledge, with thanks, the grants received from the Spencer Foundation; however, the views expressed here are those of the author and not necessarily those of the Foundation.

REFERENCES

Bakhtin, M. M. (1986). Speech genres and other late essays (Y. McGee, Trans.). Austin: University of Texas Press.

Barnes, D. (1992). *From communication to curriculum*. Portsmouth, NH: Boynton/Cook Heinemann. (1st ed.: 1976) Harmondsworth, U.K.: Penguin).

Bereiter, C. (1994). Implications of postmodernism for science, or, science as progressive discourse. *Educational Psychologist, 29*(1), 3–12.

Bereiter, C., & Scardamalia, M. (1996). Rethinking learning. In: D. R. Olson & N. Torrance (Eds), *The Handbook of Education and Human Development* (pp. 485–513). Cambridge, MA: Blackwell.

Brown, A., & Campione, J. (1994). Guided discovery in a community of learners. In: K. McGilly (Ed.), *Integrating Cognitive Theory and Classroom Practice: Classroom Lessons* (pp. 229–270). Cambridge, MA: MIT Press/Bradford Books

Bruner, J. S. (1990). *Acts of meaning*. Cambridge, MA: Harvard University Press.

Cazden, C. (1988). *Classroom discourse: The language of teaching and learning*. Portsmouth, NH: Heinemann.

Chinn, C. A. (1998). A critique of social constructivist explanations of knowledge change. In: B. Guzzetti & C. Hynd (Eds), *Perspectives on Conceptual Change: Multiple Ways to Understanding Knowing and Learning in a Complex World* (pp. 77–115). Mahwah, NJ: Erlbaum.

Christoph, J. N. & Nystrand, M. (2001). Taking risks, negotiating relationships: One teacher's transition toward a dialogic classroom. *Research in the Teaching of English, 36*, 249–286.

Cobb, P., & McClain, K. (in press). Supporting students' learning of significant mathematical ideas. In: G. Wells & G. Claxton (Eds), *Learning for Life in the Twenty-first Century: Sociocultural Perspectives on the Future of Education*. Oxford: Blackwell.

Cohen, A. (1995). A culture of understanding: an examination of face-to-face and computer mediated environments. Unpublished Ph.D., University of Toronto, Toronto.

Dalton, S. S., & Tharp, R. G. (in press). Standards for pedagogy: research, theory and practice. In: G. Wells & G. Claxton (Eds), *Learning for Life in the Twenty-first Century: Sociocultural Perspectives on the Future of Education*. Oxford: Blackwell.

D'Arcy, P. (1989). *Making sense, shaping meaning*. Portsmouth, NH: Boynton/Cook and Heinemann Educational Books.

Dewey, J. (1974). *John Dewey on education: Selected writings* (R. D. Archambault, Ed.). Chicago: University of Chicago Press.

Donoahue, Z. (1998). Giving children control: Fourth graders initiate and sustain discussions after teacher read-alouds. *Networks, the Online Journal for Teacher Research, 1* (http://www.oise.utoronto.ca/~ctd/networks/).

Donoahue, Z. (in press). Science teaching and learning: Teachers and children plan together. *Networks, the Online Journal for Teacher Research* (http://www.oise.utoronto.ca/~ctd/networks/).

Egan, K. (1988). *Teaching as storytelling*. Chicago: University of Chicago Press.

Flanders, N. A. (1970). *Analysing teacher behavior*. Reading, MA: Addison-Wesley.

Franklin, U. (1996). Introduction to Symposium, *Towards an Ecology of Knowledge*. University of Toronto (unpublished presentation).

Freeman, W. J. (1995). *Societies of brains: A study in the neuroscience of love and hate*. Hillsdale, NJ: Erlbaum.

Freire, P. (1970). *Pedagogy of the oppressed*. New York: Herder and Herder.

Gallas, K. (1995). *Talking their way into science: Hearing children's questions and theories, responding with curricula*. New York: Teachers College Press.

Glassman, M. (2001). Dewey and Vygotsky: Society, experience, and inquiry in educational practice. *Educational Resewarcher, 30*(4), 3–14.

Guzzetti, B., & Hynd, C. (Eds) (1998). *Perspectives on conceptual change: Multiple ways to understanding knowing and learning in a complex world*. Mahwah, NJ: Erlbaum.

Hasan, R. (in press). Semiotic mediation and mental development in pluralistic societies: Some implications for tomorrow's schooling. In: G. Wells & G. Claxton (Eds), *Learning for Life in the Twenty-first Century: Sociocultural Perspectives on the Future of Education*. Oxford: Blackwell.

Holzman, L. (1995). Creating developmental learning environments. *School Psychology International, 16*, 199–212.

Hume, K. (2001). Seeing shades of gray: Developing a knowledge-building community through science. In: G. Wells (Ed.), *Action, Talk, and Text: Learning and Teaching Through Inquiry*, (pp. 99–117). New York: Teachers College Press.

Kowal, M. (2001). Knowledge building: Learning about native issues outside in and inside out. In: G. Wells (Ed.), *Action, Talk, and Text: Learning and Teaching Through Inquiry* (pp. 118–133). New York: Teachers College Press.

Kress, G. (1997). *Before writing: Rethinking the paths to literacy*. London: Routledge.

Lampert, M., Rittenhouse, P., & Crumbaugh, C. (1996). Agreeing to disagree: Developing sociable mathematical discourse. In: D. Olson & N. Torrance (Eds), *The Handbook of Education and Human Development* (pp. 731–764). Cambridge, MA: Blackwell.

Langer, J., & Applebee, A. (1987). *How writing shapes thinking: A study of teaching and learning* (Research Monograph Series 22). Urbana, IL: National Council of Teachers of English.

Lave, J., & Wenger, E. (1991). *Situated Learning: Legitimate peripheral participation.* New York: Cambridge University Press.

Lemke, J. L. (1990). *Talking science: Language, learning, and values.* orwood, NJ: Ablex.

Lemke, J. L. (in press). Becoming the village: Education across lives. In: G. Wells & G. Claxton (Eds), *Learning for Life in the Twenty-First Century: Sociocultural Perspectives on the Future of Education.* Oxford: Blackwell.

Leont'ev, A. N. (1978). *Activity, consciousness, and personality.* Englewood Cliffs, NJ: Prentice Hall.

Leont'ev, A. N. (1981). The problem of activity in psychology. In: J. V.Wertsch (Ed.), *The Concept of Activity in Soviet Psychology* (pp. 37–71). Armonk, NY: Sharpe.

Lotman, Y. M. (1988). Text within a text. *Soviet Psychology, 26*(3), 32–51.

Matusov, E. (1996). Intersubjectivity without agreement. *Mind, Culture, and Activity, 3*, 25–45.

Maybin, J., Mercer, N., & Stierer, B. (1992). 'Scaffolding' learning in the classroom. In: K. Norman (Ed.), *Thinking Voices: The Work of the National Oracy Project.* London: Hodder & Stoughton

Mercer, N. (1995). *The guided construction of knowledge.* Clevedon, U.K.: Multilingual Matters.

Mercer, N. (in press). Developing dialogues. In: G. Wells & G. Claxton (Eds), *Learning for Life in the Twenty-first Century: Sociocultural Perspectives on the Future of Education.* Oxford: Blackwell.

Nystrand, M. (1997). *Opening dialogue: Understanding the dynamics of language and learning in the English classroom.* New York: Teachers College Press.

Nystrand, M., Wu, L. L., Gamoran, A., Zeiser, S., & Long, D. (2001). *Questions in time: Investigating the structure and dynamics of unfolding classroom discourse.* National Research Center on English Learning and Achievement (CELA), The University of Wisconsin-Madison.

Olson, D. R., & Bruner, J. S. (1996). Folk psychology and folk pedagogy. In: D. R. Olson & N. Torrance (Eds), *The Handbook of Education and Human Development* (pp. 9–27). Cambridge, MA: Blackwell.

Palincsar, A. S., Magnusson, S. J., Marano, N., Ford, D., & Brown, N. (1998). Designing a community of practice: Principles and practices of the GIsML Community. *Teaching and Teacher Education, 14*(1), 5–20.

Resnick, L. (1987). Learning in school and out. *Educational Researcher, 16*(9), 13–20.

Richards, R. (1990) *An early start to technology.* London: Simon & Schuster.

Rogoff, B., Goodman-Turkanis, C., & Bartlett, L. (Eds). (2001). *Learning together: Children and adults in a school community.* New York: Oxford University Press.

Roseberry, A., Warren, B., & Conant, F. (1992). Appropriating scientific discourse: findings from language minority classrooms. *The Journal of the Learning Sciences, 2*, 61–94.

Ryle, G. (1949). *The concept of mind.* London: Hutchinson.

Scardamalia, M., Bereiter, C., & Lamon, M. (1994). The CSILE project: Trying to bring the classroom into World 3. In: K. McGilley (Ed.), *Classroom Lessons: Integrating Cognitive Theory and Classroom Practice* (pp. 201–228). Cambridge, MA: MIT Press.

Smagorinsky, P. (1995). Constructing meaning in the disciplines: Reconceptualizing writing across the curriculum as composing across the curriculum. *American Journal of Education, 103*, 160–184.

Stetsenko, A., & Arievich, I. (in press). Teaching, learning, and development: a post-vygotskian perspective. In: G. Wells & G. Claxton (Eds), *Learning for Life in the Twenty-First Century: Sociocultural Perspectives on the Future of Education.* Oxford: Blackwell.

Van Tassell, M. A. (2001). Student inquiry in science: Asking questions, building foundations, and making connections. In: G. Wells (Ed.), *Action, Talk, and Text: Learning and Teaching Through Inquiry* (pp. 41–59). New York: Teachers College Press.

Vygotsky, L. S. (1978) *Mind in society.* Cambridge, MA: Harvard University Press.

Vygotsky, L. S. (1981). The genesis of higher mental functions. In: J. V. Wertsch (Ed.), *The Concept of Activity in Soviet Psychology* (pp. 144–188). Armonk, NY: Sharpe.

Vygotsky, L. S. (1987). Thinking and speech. In: R. W. Rieber & A. S. Carton (Eds), *The Collected Works of L. S. Vygotsky, Volume 1: Problems of General Psychology.* New York: Plenum.

Wartofsky, M. (1979). *Models, representation and scientific understanding.* Boston: Reidel.

Wells, G. (1990). Talk about text: Where literacy is learned and taught. *Curriculum Inquiry, 20*(4), 369–405.

Wells, G. (1997). From guessing to predicting: Progressive discourse in the learning and teaching of science. In: C. Coll & D. Edwards (Eds), *Teaching, Learning and Classroom Discourse: Approaches to the Study of Educational Discourse.* Madrid: Fundación Infancia y Aprendizaje. (Reprinted in Wells, 1999.)

Wells, G. (1998). Some questions about direct instruction: Why? To whom? How? and When? *Language Arts, 76,* 27–35.

Wells, G. (1999). *Dialogic inquiry: Towards a sociocultural practice and theory of education.* Cambridge: Cambridge University Press.

Wells, G. (2000). Dialogic inquiry in the classroom: Building on the legacy of Vygotsky. In: C. Lee & P. Smagorinsky (Eds), *Vygotskian Perspectives on Literacy Research* (pp. 51–85). New York: Cambridge University Press.

Wells, G. (2001). The case for dialogic inquiry. In: G. Wells (Ed.), *Action, Talk, and Text: Learning and Teaching Through Inquiry* (pp. 171–194). New York: Teachers College Press.

Wells, G. (in press). The role of dialogue in activity theory. *Mind, Culture, and Activity.*

Wood, D., Bruner, J. S., & Ross, G. (1976). The role of tutoring in problem-solving. *Journal of Child Psychology and Child Psychiatry, 17,* 89–100.

SOCIAL CONSTRUCTIVIST TEACHING AND THE SHAPING OF STUDENTS' KNOWLEDGE AND THINKING

Graham Nuthall

INTRODUCTION

Because so much has been written about social constructivist teaching, it is impossible to identify any single description or underlying theme that can be said to define its essential nature. More often than not social constructivist teaching is described in opposition to a simple transmission model of teaching in which what a teacher or text says becomes what the student learns.

Perhaps the best way of defining the social constructivist model of teaching is to say that it represents a set of pedagogical intentions that can be realised in a variety of forms. These intentions focus on the need to bring about intellectually significant changes in the minds of students through social processes. They are concerned with producing students who are skilled participants in the processes of creating and evaluating new knowledge, using evidence and reasoning in ways that characterise the academic disciplines.

Underpinning these pedagogical intentions is the belief that knowledge and the cognitive processes that produce, elaborate and evaluate knowledge develop through social experience. The content and processes of the mind reflect the cultural and social contexts in which they develop.

Social Constructivist Teaching, Volume 9, pages 43–79.
Copyright © 2002 by Elsevier Science Ltd.
ISBN: 0-7623-0873-7

Research on social constructivist teaching has focused on three different kinds of classroom contexts. First, and perhaps most often studied, is the teacher-managed (or facilitated) whole-class discussion in which students and teacher together engage with significant issues or problems in mutually constructive and reasoned ways (cf. O'Connor & Michaels, 1996; Varelas, Luster & Wenzel, 1999). Second, researchers have studied the way students working in small groups engage with academic problem solving activities as they manage their interactions with each other and with relevant materials (cf. Anderson et al., 2001; Hogan, Nastasi & Pressley, 2000). Third, there are studies that focus on the ways students engage in physical activities (such as science experiments) or use resources (such as computers) in ways that facilitate or constrain intellectual processing and knowledge construction (cf., Roth, McGinn, Woszczyna & Boutonné, 1999). Although not ostensibly social, these physical activities and resources are described as sociocultural tools that have embedded in them their cultural history. Becoming expert in their use involves the internalisation of this sociocultural history.

Much of the writing on social constructivist teaching claims to have its theoretical basis in two general views of the nature of learning. One is the view that students must construct knowledge for themselves. No matter how well a teacher uses language to explain something, each student must make their own sense of what the teacher is saying based on their previously acquired knowledge and experiences. Second, is the view that learning is a by-product of participation in a community. What is significant in any learning activity is that the learner is primarily concerned with playing a role. As Lave (1992, April) puts it: "Learning is, in this purview, more basically a process of coming to be, or forging identities in activity in the world" (p. 3). There is, however, an uneasy and unresolved relationship between descriptions of social constructivist teaching methods and the kinds of learning that it is intended to produce. A number of writers have pointed out that these general views of learning do not, in themselves, logically entail any particular method of teaching (cf. Bentley, 1998; Driver, 1997). But the justification for a particular method of teaching does lie in the kinds of learning it is intended to produce (O'Connor & Michaels, 1996). Exactly what kinds of learning social constructivist teaching methods are intended to produce is something that researchers have remained somewhat ambiguous about.

Although we assume individuals experience cognitive growth during group discourse, our analysis does not attempt to make claims about the shift in knowledge of individuals, or about individuals' competencies . . . (Hogan, Nastasi & Pressley, 2000, p. 381).

I would like to argue in this chapter that without a more explicit understanding of the relationship between social constructivist teaching and the learning it is intended to produce, it is not possible to evaluate the relative significance of social constructivist teaching, determine when it can be most fruitfully used, or adapt it successfully to the different contexts in which it might be useful. One of the dangers of any defined method or type of teaching is that it will become a fashionable part of the standard culture of teaching, advocated and applied without understanding how it might need to be adapted to the needs of specific students or the constraints of particular contexts.

The purpose of this chapter will be to try to clarify the rationale for using social constructivist methods of teaching so that we can get a better understanding of how and why it works and consequently develop a better idea of when, how, and with whom, it should be used.

In the first part of the chapter I will draw on a number of recent excellent studies of social constructivist teaching in order to outline its most important characteristics. These studies have all involved researchers working closely with teachers in "design experiments" (de Corte, 2000) to develop the theory and practice of this kind of teaching. In the next part of the chapter, I will examine the kinds of learning that social constructivist teaching is intended to produce. The purpose of this part is not to go deeply into the learning process itself but to try to clarify the different ways in which social constructivist teaching shapes students' knowledge and ways of thinking. This will provide the basis for the third part of the chapter which looks at where and how social constructivist teaching fits within the larger units of work that make up the curriculum in areas like science and the social studies.

In addition to drawing on the work of other researchers, I will make use of data from a series of studies carried out at the University of Canterbury (Nuthall, 1999b; Nuthall & Alton-Lee, 1993). Each study involved the detailed observation and recording of the experiences of individual students during the course of a unit in science, technology or social studies in elementary and middle school class-rooms. Some of the units also integrated related mathematics and literacy tasks.

In each study, the teacher taught the unit using the style of teaching with which they were most familiar. All were highly experienced teachers who used a mixture of whole-class, small group, and individual activities. None of the teach-ers believed in a transmission or text-book based model of teaching. Some used formally structured tasks and had established routines in which students knew what was expected of them. Others gave students a choice of alternative activities and allowed students to work out for themselves how they would carry out the tasks. A description of the content of the units is contained in Table 1.

Table 1. Characteristics of the Curriculum Units and the Individual Students Observed and Interviewed in the Eight Studies Referred to in this Chapter.

Topic of unit and hours of recorded time per student	Students (gender)	Age (years)	Achievement (percentile)[a]
Study 3. Social Studies: New York – A study of cultural differences (6.4 hours over 5 days).	Ann (f)	12.5	55
	Mia (f)	12.4	96
	Jon (m)	11.8	97
	Joe (m)	12.2	55
Study 4. Science: Weather – observation and forecasting. (7.1 hours over 8 days).	Rata (f)	10.4	68
	Pam (f)	10.4	21
	Jan (f)	10.4	70
	Tui (m)	10.4	11
Study 5. Science and Social Studies: Antarctica – Living in a harsh environment. (11.8 hours over 6 days)	Claire (f)	12.7	43
	Teta (f)	12.8	9
	Bruce (m)	12.4	94
	Peter (m)	12.10	50
	Ross (m)	13.1	13
	Linda (f)	12.11	79
Study 6. Science and Social Studies: Antarctica – Conditions, people, animals, and plants. (13.4 hours over 6 days)	Paul (m)	12.2	89
	Jane (f)	11.5	83
	Joy (f)	11.10	70
	Jim (m)	11.9	56
	Teine (f)	11.4	34
Study 7. Social Studies: Ancient Egypt. (10.3 hours over 8 days)	Alice (f)	10.7	68
	Jerry (m)	9.10	73
	Kent (m)	10.0	25
	Verity (f)	9.5	28
Study 8. Social Studies: Ancient Egypt. (13.2 hours over 8 days)	Amity (f)	10.5	32
	Dean (m)	10.0	35
	Julie (f)	9.9	68
	Kirk (m)	10.5	81
Study 9. Science: Light and color. (7.4 hours over 8 days)	Austin (m)	10.9	85
	Karin (f)	10.11	64
	Shaun (m)	9.9	46
	Sonya (f)	11.1	26
Study 10. Science: Light and color. (8.9 hours over 6 days)	Eleanor (f)	11.4	95
	Jordan (m)	10.3	55
	Seth (m)	11.2	36
	Sylvia (f)	9.8	41

[a] Average age-related percentile on at least three school-administered standardized achievement tests, including reading comprehension.

During the course of the unit in each classroom, each student wore a miniature wireless microphone and 6–8 small ceiling mounted videocameras with zoom lenses were used to record the language and behaviours of selected students. In addition, observers kept continuous running records of the behaviours of the selected students and the way the students used resources and equipment. The students were also helped to keep records of all their relevant out-of-class experiences and activities.

In each study an achievement test was developed based on interviews with the teacher and analysis of the resources the students used in the unit. This test covered all the concepts, principles, explanations and other knowledge-related outcomes that the teacher intended the students to learn. It was administered orally to the students before the unit began and again after the unit was completed. In some studies it was administered again 8 to 12 months after the unit. In addition, students were interviewed about what they had learned during the unit. They were asked to talk about their understanding of every concept, principle, or explanation included in the test, how they thought they had learned it, their recollections of all relevant in-class and out-of-class experiences, and their beliefs about their own learning and memory processes.

In each study, full observational, recorded and interview data was obtained on a sample of 4–6 students. Table 1 details the pseudonyms, ages, and levels of ability of these selected students. They were randomly selected from within categories representing differences in gender, ethnic background, and ability level as measured by standardised academic achievement tests.

The data from these studies was analysed by creating a "concept-file" for each concept, generalisation, or explanation covered in the achievement test for each student. Each concept-file for each student contained all of the data from all sources that was in any way related to whether the student learned that concept or not. These concept-files brought together both the objective and subjective data to create a narrative account of how the student experienced and was affected by all events relating to a specific concept (see Nuthall, 1999a; Nuthall & Alton-Lee, 1993, for further details)

THE NATURE OF SOCIAL CONSTRUCTIVIST TEACHING

Perhaps the most extensively researched form of social constructivist teaching is the teacher-facilitated discussion involving the whole class or a signifi-cant group of students. This discussion is seen as the arena in which significant knowledge and ways of thinking are produced and assimilated. The role of the teacher is to engage with the existing knowledge, beliefs, and skills of the students and by setting challenging problems or posing significant questions to engage those cognitive processes in the minds of the students that are seen as central to the knowledge building practices of the academic disciplines.

This requires the teacher to be constantly monitoring the ways in which the students are interacting with each other and with the content of the discussion (Howe & Berv, 2000). It involves what Confrey (1998) has called "close listening" in which the teacher treats every student idea seriously, especially unusual and innovative ideas. It also involves a constant focus on the ways students use reasons and evidence to support their views (Cobb, Perlwitz & Underwood-Gregg, 1998). The students' knowledge, beliefs, and ways of thinking have been described as the intellectual capital that the teacher must develop and elaborate (Tobin, 1998).

Part of the role of the teacher is to avoid providing students with knowledge or solutions when it is possible for them to work them out for themselves. Several researchers have identified this as one of the most significant and difficult aspects of the teacher's role (cf. Herrenkohl et al., 1999; Hogan, Nastasi & Pressley, 2000).

The student role is not just to give answers but to express genuine beliefs or make serious claims and to support them with evidence or reasons. This requires the teacher to focus the discussion around a significant problem or issue that is central to the discipline and that students find challenging and worth debating. This means selecting from the curriculum, elements that connect directly to the lives and concerns of the students and involve the knowledge and procedures typical of the academic discipline (Brophy & Alleman, in press). It also means that the teacher does not stand between the student and the curriculum but works to facilitate a direct engagement between the student and these critical issues and problems. Hogan, Nastasi & Pressley (2000) identify this selection of the problem or issue as the single most important factor in determining the quality of the discussion.

Achieving this kind of teaching involves managing a discourse that has a number of distinctive characteristics. Several researchers have noted that there are, in fact two distinct types of discourses (or layers of discourse) that are involved (Cobb, Perlwitz & Underwood-Gregg, 1998). At one level, there is the talk about the curriculum content in which teacher and students exchange and debate beliefs, reasons and evidence. At the other level there is talk about the kind of talk that is occurring at the first level. Varela, Luster and Wenzel, (1999) refer to the first level as the "intellectual-thematic dimension" and the second level as the "social-organisational dimension". In general, the teacher participates more actively in the second level because this is the discourse in which the rules of participation, the defining of roles and permissible topics and ways of talking and debating in the first level are worked out.

Developing the Intellectual-Thematic Dimension

The teacher's role in the intellectual-thematic dimension is to develop and sustain genuine debate and argumentation about significant ideas in which the students are full and active participants (Ball & Bass, 2000). There are a number of tactics the teacher can use to sustain the kind of discussion in which students' ideas have central place. For example, the teacher can stay with the same topic for several turns, involving several students in elaborating or evaluating the same idea or argument (Hogan, Nastasi & Pressley, 2000). The teacher can hold together the threads of the discussion by relating students' new statements to their previous statements, helping them to link their ideas and through this to see the logical connections between them (Varelas & Pineda, 1999).

The following excerpt from a study by Hogan, Nastasi & Pressley (2000) illustrates some of these tactics. The students (in an 8th grade science class) had been asked to work on creating a mental model of the nature of matter. The teacher is talking with a small group:

Teacher: Okay, now what would a liquid look like if you magnified it millions of times?
Student 1: Probably the same thing . . . Because we thought atoms are probably the basics, the smallest things.
Teacher: So the liquid would look exactly the same?
Student 2: I thought it was kind of like . . .
Student 3: Maybe, like spread out more, not exactly the round shape.
Student 1: Err, and they may not be stuck together, they may be free floating.
Teacher: Draw me a picture of what you think you'll see.
Student 2 (drawing): So they'd just be kinda like, they'd lose their definite shape . . .
Student 1: Yeah, they'd lose their . . .
Teacher: So you're going to have molecules having kind of different shapes?
Student 2: Yeah.
Student 1: Yeah, and not being stuck together as much as solids.
Teacher: Okay, now he is sticking them together, though (refers to a student working on the drawing) . . . (Hogan, Nastasi & Pressley, 2000. p. 405).

The teacher's use of questions is typical of this kind of discussion (Solomon, 2000). He uses them sparingly, and then to show that he is genuinely interested in the students' ideas. As he seeks clarification, he helps the students to clarify their thinking and become more explicit and consistent. During the interaction, the students minds are focused on the problem as they talk and try to draw a picture of their ideas. At the same time, they are engaged in listening to, co-ordinating, and supplementing each other's ideas. According to Varelas and Pineda (1999), one way of determining the quality of the discussion is the degree to which one statement is linked to or integrated with the next. For example, in the excerpt above, Student 2 and Student 3's answers to the teacher's clarification question ("So the liquid would look exactly the same?") overlap with each other as though Student 3 was completing the thought of Student 2. Varelas and Pineda refer to this as "intermingling" and describe it as the "discursive aspect of the meeting of minds" (1999, p. 27).

One aspect of the teacher's role that has received considerable attention has been the way in which the teacher responds immediately following a student's statement. This is illustrated in the following excerpt from a 7th grade social studies class. The class was discussing the deforestation of the north of New Zealand.

Teacher: Why do you think perhaps they cut down all the kauri trees before? What was the reason for this?
Trevor: Building houses and homes and things like that.
Teacher: Yes, they wanted to do that with it. Yes?
Brian: Um, cut it down and put in place of it pine trees. It's a little bit faster.
Teacher: They cut down the kauri trees so that they could replace them with pine trees because they grow faster? Mmmm. I don't think so.
Warwick: Kauris are timber that doesn't take so long to rot and it would be good for housing and that.
Teacher: Yes. But there's another reason why the kauris were cut down. Can you tell me? Do you think they might have been wanting something else?
Murray: Farmland?
Teacher: Yes, perhaps they wanted to cultivate land. Yes.
Student: The gum.
Teacher: Yes. They wanted to get the gum underneath, so they went around and rather recklessly destroyed those great kauri forests. But, as I said before there's still a lot of kauri there.

As each student contributed to the discussion, the teacher appropriated and reworded each of the students' responses, usually adding information to them. For example, Brian's suggestion that they had "cut it down and put in place of it pine trees. It's a little bit faster" is reworded by the teacher as "They cut down the kauri trees so that they could replace them with pine trees because they grow faster". The teacher's rewording of Brian's recollection added the linguistic markers of a reason ("... so that they ...", "... because ..."). Later a student provided a significant explanation, but it was only a single word ("gum"). The teacher took this response and turned it into a complete explanation ("They wanted to get the gum underneath, so they went around and rather recklessly destroyed these great kauri forests").

Several researchers have identified this "reformulating" or "revoicing" as a way in which teachers can acknowledge the significance of what the student says, expand the student's contribution to the class discussion, help the student clarify their own reasoning, and connect the student's contribution to the argument structures of the discipline by using the terms and concepts of the discipline (cf. Cobb, Perlwitz & Underwood-Gregg, 1998; O'Connor & Michaels, 1996; Varelas, Luster & Wenzel, 1999) In the example above, it is the linguistic form of an explanation that the teacher modelled in her reformulations.

A further aspect of the teacher's role is the way the teacher uses questions. Much has been made of the fact that in most classrooms, teachers use questions to direct the content of the discussion and to evaluate the students' knowledge and engagement. The teacher is the person who knows the answers and is interested primarily in making sure the students' answers match hers. In social comstructivist teaching, the teacher's use of questions changes. Center stage is taken by the problem or issue being discussed. The teacher's role is to facilitate the students' direct engagement with this problem or issue. Consequently, the teacher uses questions to help students clarify and organise what they are saying and thinking (Chinn & Anderson, 1998; Herrenkohl, Palincsar, DeWater & Kawasaki, 1999).

Behind these techniques, the major concern of the teacher must be with focusing the discussion on the use of evidence and reasons. Students must progressively become skilled at expressing and justifying their beliefs using the procedures and logical structures that characterise the disciplines. This means scaffolding, modelling and fading, and building expectations that the classroom is the place where serious intellectual work is the norm (Ball & Bass, 2000; Driver, Asoko, Leach, Mortimer & Scott, 1994; O'Connor & Michaels, 1996).

Developing the Social-Organisational Dimension

It is generally accepted that this kind of discourse is not common and that teachers need to work hard to establish with their students the rules by which it can operate. In an extensive observational study of teaching in high school science classrooms in Britain, Newton, Driver and Osborne (1999) found that the proportion of the time that students engaged in serious intellectual debate was as little as 1–2%. Stigler and his colleagues (Stigler et al., 1999) found, from their detailed video study of the teaching of 8th grade mathematics, very little evidence in classrooms in the United States of the reasoning, formulation of alternative solutions, or use of evidence, characteristic of social constructivist mathematics teaching. As Stigler and Hiebert (1999) concluded from their data, teaching appears to be a remarkably stable cultural ritual that we all learn through many years of observation and participation as students if not as teachers. Despite changing teacher education programs, changing forms of classroom organisation, and many attempts to reform teaching methods, the ritual in which teachers do most of the talking and students do most of the listening remains largely unchanged, sustained by a "stable web of beliefs and assumptions that are a part of the [wider] culture" (Stigler & Hiebert, 1999, p. 87).

For this reason, researchers involved in developing social constructivist teaching practices emphasize the need for teachers to progressively create new roles for the students as well as for themselves. They point out that students will try to pull the teacher back into more traditional forms both because of well-established expectations and because students can be skilled at negotiating downwards their level of cognitive ambiguity and effort (Varelas, Luster & Wenzel, 1999; Yerrick, 1999).

The aim of the teacher is to create a community in which the active cognitive participation of all students is promoted and valued. This means that the exploration of ideas is accepted as more important than getting through the set curriculum, that students are not only expected to contribute their ideas but also to give reasons in support of them, and that, where appropriate, students should commit themselves to the discussion rather than remain indifferent and outside the debate. For example, in the "collaborative reasoning" model developed by Anderson and his colleagues (Anderson et al., 1997) the teacher is expected to develop, with the students, a set of rules which require the students to listen carefully and evaluate each other's arguments, disagree by challenging with counter-arguments, and to change their position by weighing the evidence and arguments put forward by others. The discussion is initiated by getting all the students to declare their position on the central issue. As the discussion progresses, the teacher helps the students to develop an "open participation" structure in which the students respond directly to each other, without asking permission, and without interrupting each other or speaking simultaneously. In the formative stages, the teacher uses the language of critical and reflective thinking, models reasoning by thinking out loud, and challenges the students with ideas they have not thought of.

WHAT KINDS OF LEARNING ARE INVOLVED IN SOCIAL CONSTRUCTIVIST TEACHING?

The rationale for social constructivist teaching is based on a set of inter-related theories about the nature of classroom discourse, the nature of meaning, the nature of the learning process, and the nature of the knowledge, beliefs and skills that are the intended outcomes.

Many writers refer to classroom discussion as "discourse" in the sociolinguistic or sociocultural sense of that word (Gee, 1989; Roth, McGinn, Woszczyna & Boutonné, 1999; Yerrrick, 1999). In this sense, discourse has a broader meaning than just talk. It also refers to the activities, ways of thinking and relating to others that go with the talk within a specific community. It is what people in a community expect to do, feel and think when they interact with each other in familiar ways. In this view, acquiring a particular discourse is a consequence of becoming a member of a "community of practice" (Lave, 1991). From this perspective, learning is seen as an apprenticeship in which the novice assimilates or appropriates the expectations, beliefs, and skills of the more experienced members of the community by participating with them in the activities that define the community (Rogoff, 1994, 1995). By defining the classroom as such a community of practice, students can be seen as apprentices in the process of acquiring the discourse of an academic discipline.

Behind this view of the classroom as a community of practice, are two differing views of the nature of mind and cognitive processes. There are those who distinguish the surface features of classroom discourse from the cognitive processes and learning that lie behind those surface features. They see the acquisition of the discourse as shaping the knowledge and forms of thinking that students acquire, but still view these as individual processes that depend on individual prior knowledge and skills. The research of Anderson and his colleagues on collaborative reasoning in literacy classes (cf. Anderson et al., 2001) and of Hogan and her colleagues in science classes (Hogan, Nastasi & Pressley, 2000) are based on this position.

Against this there are those who argue that you cannot distinguish cognitive processes from discourse. Such a dualism between mind and behaviour is not philosophically tenable or of any practical significance (Lemke, 1990). Changing what students know and the ways in which they think is entirely contained in changing the ways they talk and act (Rogoff, 1995; Roth et al., 1999). For example, as students learn to discuss mathematical problems like mathematicians they are, by definition, learning mathematics and learning to think like mathematicians. Allied to this view is the claim that cognition and knowledge are not the properties of individuals but of groups or communities. Cognitive activities, like the solving of problems or the recollection of past activities, are shared between individuals and between individuals and the artefacts (such as computers, texts, pictures) that they interact with when carrying out these activities.

The distinction between these two views can be seen more clearly by looking closely at the different kinds of learning that are involved. First there is the learning, or acquisition of meanings. Through participation in classroom discourse students learn the meanings of the terms and phrases that constitute the academic discipline. Second, there is the acquisition and modification of well-thought-out knowledge. As the teacher and students talk together, new knowledge is created through the interplay of their individual contributions. Ideas are clarified, elaborated, and differences resolved through the use of supporting evidence and reasons. Third, there is the acquisition of new ways of thinking and solving problems. Within each of the academic disciplines, there are characteristic ways of developing, verifying, and structuring knowledge. By confronting and working though significant issues and problems, these characteristic ways of thinking and reasoning are acquired.

The Acquisition of Meanings

One way of understanding the significance of acquiring the discourse of a discipline is to claim that it involves the acquisition of the meanings that underlie the discourse. This is based on the view that language shapes how we perceive and think about the world both explicitly and implicitly.

Language embeds implicit assumptions about the world that constitute common ground or mundane knowledge that does not need expression because it is self-evident. (Roth et al., 1999, p. 297)

Without becoming entangled in a technical analysis of the nature of meaning, it is possible, for practical purposes, to identify a continuum of kinds of meaning that are involved in the use of language in classrooms.

At one end of the continuum are the general public meanings that words and terms have when they are in common use. These are the dictionary definitions that a speaker can assume almost all native users of the language will understand.

At the other end of the continuum are the meanings of words and terms that are specific to an individual. These are the private meanings that arise from the unique experiences of the individual and are unlikely to be shared by any other person.

Between these two extremes are the meanings that words and terms acquire when they are used within the context of a social group or personal relationship. When words or terms are used within the group or relationship they refer to the activities, beliefs, and theories that make up the expertise and common experiences that are unique to that group or relationship.

Mathematicians, scientists, historians, writers, sororities, families are examples of such social groups or relationships.

During the course of conversation with friends or strangers, the words or terms used will elicit common public meanings, meanings associated with participation in more or less intimate groups, and meanings that are unique to the individual experiences of the participants (Grice, 1989).

Those who see the acquisition of meanings as an important outcome of social constructivist teaching view the classroom as a community (Lemke, 1990; Varelas & Pineda, 1999). By engaging in discipline-specific activities and talking about those activities in discipline-specific ways, students come to use words and terms with the appropriate discipline-specific meanings. This kind of learning is a process of language acquisition within a community of shared experiences (Brown & Campione, 1994; Rogoff, 1995).

From research on language acquisition, we know that there are two ways in which the meanings of words are acquired (Pinker, 1999). First, the meaning of a word comes to be understood as it is used in association with the objects or activities it refers to. Using the word is initially part of the activity itself so that its meaning is contained in the experience of the activity. Because of this association, the word can later be used to represent or refer to the activity. Second, the use of words can be acquired through interaction with a more expert language user. The expert models the use of the word and reformulates inappropriate usage. This is what happens when teachers "revoice" students' contributions to classroom discussions (O'Connor & Michaels, 1996, see above)

The following example illustrates how words can acquire specific meanings within the context of a classroom activity. It is taken from recordings of a 6th grade class studying a science topic on "light" (Study 9, Table 1). The teacher used a set of activity cards that contained instructions (with diagrams) for experiments with light. Each card provided the instructions for carrying out an experiment, some relevant background information, and a list of questions to focus student thinking on the physical principles underlying the experiment. At the bottom of the card, under the heading "Find out about" there were additional questions designed to show how the principle applied to aspects of ordinary life.

The students worked together in groups and during the first day, the teacher spent time with each group, helping them follow the instructions. During this process, the heading "Find out about" on the instruction card came to be used as a marker of how far the students had got in completing their experiments.

Teacher: ... It might be that you don't write your refraction comment until you've done your "find out about" ... If you've finished the "find out about", you'll need to use the books at the back of the room ...

Later as the teacher moved around the groups, she used the term as a way to check how far the students had gone.

Teacher: Have you finished your find out abouts?
Kelly: We have.
Teacher: Okay you've finished them?
Teacher: Ok, if you're on the find out about, the sheets are at the front on the desk. Come on, you need to get going, you need to be almost at the find out about, thank you.

The students also started to use the term in the same way:

John: Have you done "what are the colours"?
Austin: Me? Yeah, I'm on to find out about.
Shaun: . . . No, now we gotta do find out about.
Patrick: No but, see – I thought that was the find out about.
Shaun: No that wasn't, no that wasn't the find out about.
Patrick: But it's, but it's only two questions for find out about.

By the sixth day of the unit, the term was so commonly used that it became shortened to "find out".

Rowena: Hey, you haven't done find out.
Sonya: Yes I have.

This example illustrates the way in which a term, used as part of the talk that accompanies an activity, comes to take on the meaning of the activity. To an outsider, Rowena's statement ("Hey, you haven't done find out") would have no meaning. To the students in the class, it had a precise and complex meaning that related to their developing understanding of the things you do in science.

A different process of acquiring meaning occurs for the technical terms that refer to scientific concepts. In this same class, the term "refraction" was used in some of the experiments. At the beginning of the unit, none of the students could explain what the word meant, but at the end each knew what it meant in the sense that they had learned how to use it. On the last day of the unit, the teacher asked each group to write a completion of the sentence "Refraction is . . . " All the students wrote ". . . the bending of light".

It is possible to trace how the students acquired this definition. It came up several times in the material the students read about their experiments.

Mary (reading aloud to her group an information card explaining the bent appearance of a pencil standing in a glass of water): . . . Light travels more slowly through glass or water than it does through air. If light hits glass or water at an angle this slowing down makes it change direction. The bending of light is called refraction.
Derek: Ah, now we know what refraction is . . . .

It also came up in the frequent discussions that the teacher had with the students as they worked in their groups.

Teacher: ... Binoculars; what do binoculars do?
Patrick: They make you see.
Shaun: They make you see further and it looks closer.
Teacher: Okay so does refraction, bending of light, help that?
Patrick: Um, by ...
Teacher: Okay what is refraction?
Patrick: When light bends off the ...
Teacher: Perfect. No, no, don't need anymore. What is it?
Shaun: When light bends.
Teacher: That's all you need isn't it. Excellent.

Frequent repetitions of the phrase "light bends" resulted in all the students being able to describe refraction as the "bending of light". But many of the students found this definition did not help them make sense of their experiment. Many connected it, through references to water, glass, and lenses, to "reflection", a term they did understand.

Shaun (reading questions from the instruction sheet): "What causes the bending of light?" Refraction. "Where do you see this?"
Patrick: Um on a crystal. On houses and trees.
Shaun: No it doesn't work on trees. Crystals, water, windows. 'Cause when it hits something shiny it always bends.
Patrick: Metal.
Shaun (shaking his head): No 'cause that's not like water.
Patrick: 'Cause that is shiny.
Shaun (preparing to write his answer): Yeah. What causes the bending of light, refraction. Anything that's silver, 'cause it's shiny.

Later when Shaun was asked in an interview to talk about refraction he explained:

Shaun: It's about when um, when it hits something shiny and that. It goes more slower and it causes it to bend. . . . It goes slower because when like the sun hits something shiny and that, it makes it slow down.
Interviewer: Oh right. Because it's shiny you think?
Shaun: Yeah.
Interviewer: So that's something you've seen for yourself do you think, or did somebody tell you that?
Shaun: Oh, I saw it for myself. 'Cause where I live there's a lake and I went fishing one time when the sun was out and it, and like, here's the light here, the sun's way over here and, yeah.
Interviewer: So you the see the light on the water.
Shaun: Yeah.
Interviewer: Kind of reflection. And from that you work out that the light would move more slowly in the water?
Shaun: Yeah.

What this example highlights is the distinction between meanings that are generated in the public arena of teacher-managed discussions and the more

as a consequence of recording?

personal meanings that emerge as students interact with each other or with specific problems or resources. Terms like "find out about" come into common use through their association with shared activities and reflect the students' developing understanding of the science activities they are engaged in. Terms like "refraction" may develop one meaning through repetition of a definition and a different meaning as students struggle to relate it to their existing knowledge and individual experiences.

Classroom discussions are public performances and students are capable of learning and saying what they believe teachers want them to say without understanding or believing what they say. Despite the claim that the acquisition of terms implies the acquisition of their meanings, it is possible, especially with technical terms, for students to learn to use words without understanding. Acquiring the meanings of technical terms is a more complicated problem solving process.

The Acquisition of Knowledge

The second kind of learning that results from classroom discourse is the acquisition and modification of individual knowledge. Researchers are divided as to whether they see this learning occurring as part of the discussion, or as a consequence of the discussion. According to Varelas and Pineda learning occurs as students and teacher work together ". . . to clarify ideas, to differentiate concepts, to organise ideas in a coherent whole, to extend ideas further, and/or to make sense of new ideas with the ultimate aim of reaching accepted scientific knowledge" (1999, pp. 44–45). In this view, prior beliefs are modified and elaborated and new knowledge is created in the process of engaging with others in the classroom.

Others are, however, less certain of the role that classroom discourse plays in the acquisition of knowledge and the changing of beliefs. O'Connor and Michaels (1996) in their study of thinking practices in group discussion say they assume that "each instance of student participation, fostered and scaffolded by the teacher, represents an opportunity for an increment in learning, however small" (1996, p. 64). Students may not, however, make use of these opportunities.

There are two issues underlying this problem. The first is that in most classroom discussions, only some students participate more than occasionally. A larger number participate a little and the majority are, ostensibly, passive listeners. Sahlström (1999) has shown that student participation needs to be understood as a kind of economy. Opportunities for participation are limited, consequently in most classrooms there is an underlying (usually unconscious)

competition for participation. This competition is organised according to the social system underlying classroom activities. Erickson (1996) refers to this as the "social ecology" of the classroom. Most of the research on social constructivist teaching seems to be based on the assumption that the discussion takes place between the teacher and a collective student or small set of collective students who somehow represent all students. As Sahlstrom and Lindblad's research shows, this is more than just a matter of different levels of participation. Seen through the lives of individual students, different types of participation reflect quite different perspectives on the nature of the curriculum and the purpose of schooling (Sahlstrom & Lindblad, 1998; Yerrick, 1999).

The second issue concerns the role that classroom discussion plays in the acquisition of knowledge by individual students. Ball and Bass, for example, point out that effective classroom discussion depends on a base of taken-for-granted knowledge that can be referred to without explanation or elaboration. ". . . this base of public knowledge comprises the expanding set of publicly expressed ideas and shared knowledge which can be used by the class in explanation or justification" (2000, p. 202). Without this common base, arguments and references to evidence will not be understood. As Ball and Bass go on to point out, participants in a discussion must proceed as though everyone shared their knowledge and understanding of the evidence, and listeners must act as though they share the same knowledge and understanding in order not to derail the discussion.

Our research studies have shown that mutually shared knowledge is relatively uncommon unless the knowledge relates to an experience that all students in the class recently shared (Nuthall, 2000, September). When students are assessed before a typical science or social studies unit, they know or understand, on average, about 40–50% of what the teacher intends them to learn during the unit. However, the amount of this prior knowledge that all the students in a class share in common is about 10–20%. This climbs to about 30-40% during the course of a 3–4 week unit. These figures are approximate because our tests and interviews only covered the intended focus of the units and not everything that the students might have learned. However, it does seem clear that the assumption that all or most of the students share the same prior knowledge or acquire the same understandings, is not true. Only within those areas of the curriculum that have already been thoroughly talked about and understood is there likely to be a convergence of shared knowledge and understanding.

Taken together, these two issues mean that the experiences of individual students within the same class discussion are likely to be more different than the same. This is further exacerbated by the fact that student experience in the classroom is determined by their simultaneous participation in three distinct, but interactive, contexts (Nuthall, 2001, April). The first is the public context of the teacher-managed discussion which is the focus of research on social constructivist teaching. The second is the ever-present semi-private context of peer interactions and relationships. This context is continuous across most in-school and out-of-school activities where students are interacting with each other. The third is the internal, cognitive and affective context of the student's individual mental and emotional life. This context is continuous across all of a student's life. Any event or activity is experienced through the role it plays in each of these three contexts. To understand both how the event or activity is interpreted and experienced, and what effect it might have on a student's knowledge, beliefs, or skills, you need to understand what these three roles are and how they interact with each other. For example, Sahlström and Lindblad (1998) have shown that the participation of individual students in science activities is partly determined by the role that they see achievement in science playing in their lives.

Opposite is a transcript of a class discussion that illustrates the way simultaneous participation in the three contexts shapes the way students interact with the curriculum content. The class were discussing what a diagram of the compass points would look like on a map of Antarctica (Study 5, Table 1 above). Phillip was asked to draw a diagram of the compass points on a wall map of Antarctica. In this transcript, the public discussion is in the left hand column, and what Bruce and Ross were whispering to themselves, each other, and another student (Phillip) at the same time, in the right hand column. This private talk was recorded on the individual wireless microphones that the students were wearing (see Nuthall, 1999a, b, for further examples).

What this transcript illustrates is that when students become actively involved in a problem posed by the teacher, many alternative discussions erupt in parallel with the public discussion. This largely invisible private talk slips between self-talk and talk to neighbours. Sometimes it is like thinking aloud, sometimes like a parallel class discussion. How Bruce and Ross interact privately is simultaneously a function of the way the teacher manages the class discussion (and Phillip's publicly visible drawing of the compass points), of the nature of Bruce and Ross's relationship, and of their individual knowledge and understanding of the problem. For example, Bruce believed he knew more than the others and liked to demonstrate this by explaining things even when others already knew them. To understand how students experienced and consequently learned from an episode like this, you need to take into account these three contexts.

Transcript A.

Teacher-managed public discussion	Ross and Bruce talking privately (to self and peers)
Teacher: Phillip, can you put it on the map? (Phillip starts to draw a direction finder [compass] on the map) That's good. OK. Terry: Mr G, if it's the South Pole everything faces north. Doesn't that sort of muck it up a bit? Teacher: Let's have a look and see what Phillip does. Girl: It shouldn't be like that. That's not right. Teacher: Hang on. Let's wait and see. It's not wrong yet. Charles: Not right either. Teacher: Oh, it's a beautiful one . . . . . . OK. Complete it. Ross: Doesn't have to be that good Phillip. Misa: (inaudible) Teacher: Well done except that it's got one small problem with it or three small problems with it. Sit down please Phillip. What do you think the problem is with his little directional thing here? What do you reckon Jessica? Jessica: It might be in the wrong place. Teacher: Well, yes, you can put it there basically. Cain? Cain: Well I don't know, it's, I know it's um, when you're in the South Pole, all the directions are mucked up. Charles: No, that depends where you are. If you're standing where that dot is then you (inaudible) mucked up (inaudible) Teacher: OK. If you're at the South Pole. Terry: That's the South Pole isn't it? . . . Teacher: OK. Imagine that that's right there, right at the south. What will all the directions be from there? Students: North. Terry: All pointing north then? Teacher: OK. So we could put that in there (adds "Ns" to direction finder points on map). Every direction would have to be north. 'Cause let's have a look at where Antarctica is. This side (of map on wall) shows Antarctica in relation to world.	Ross (to self) I don't think I do. Ross (to self) Phillip! Bruce (to Ross) Everywhere faces north . . . Everywhere faces north if you're on the direction finder. Ross (to Bruce): Mm. What's he writing? Bruce (to Ross): North, South (laughs) Ross: Eh? Ross (to self) That's Phillip. Bruce raises hand Ross (to self as raises hand) North, South and East and that. It's in the wrong place. Bruce (to self) Oh, oh . . . Bruce (to self) Oh. Gee . . . (raises other hand, to self) Oh! Phillip: (inaudible) Bruce (to Phillip) Mm? So if you've got a globe, Antarctica's there see (demonstrates position of Antarctica at bottom of imaginary globe). Ross (with others) North. Ross (to self) Can't see the stupid thing.

In addition to the diverse backgrounds and the diverse experiences of individual students, there is diversity in the ways in which students interpret and remember the content of their experiences. It seems to be assumed in research on social constructivist teaching that the knowledge that is generated through the interactions of teacher and students becomes what students know. However, everything that we have been able to ascertain from our studies of students' classroom experiences points to the fact that learning is a sequential process constantly subject to the transforming effects of forgetting (Nuthall, 1999a, 2000a, b; Nuthall & Alton-Lee, 1993). In order for a concept or idea to become part of the established knowledge of a student that can be used in subsequent learning or problem solving activities, the student must engage with that concept or idea on several different occasions. Without these multiple exposures, even the most significant concepts or ideas will be forgotten or transformed and assimilated back into previously held beliefs.

This analysis of the relationship between social constructivist teaching and the acquisition of knowledge suggests that we need to be very cautious about claiming that, in a well-managed discussion, teacher and students construct knowledge together. New understandings and insights may be expressed and new ideas generated by some of the participants, but it is unlikely that these are shared by all the students in the class, nor that they will become an established part of the knowledge of even those students who participate in the discussion. If the aim is that the new understandings and ideas that are expressed in the discussion should become part of the knowledge of all the participants, then the normal participation structures characteristic of whole-class discussions need to be changed and the discussions located in a larger context of related and contributory learning activities. How this might be done is taken up in the last part of this chapter.

THE ACQUISITION OF NEW WAYS OF THINKING AND SOLVING PROBLEMS

The third, and most commonly implied justification for the significance of social constructivist teaching is that it shapes the development of thinking and problem solving skills. There are three approaches to explaining how this occurs. Some, such as Rogoff (1994, 1995) see the development of thinking and problem solving skills as occurring in the interactions between teacher and students. Students take on the roles that involve these skills as they participate in the classroom community. They learn what they must do to play their part in relation to others. In this view, problem solving and thinking are seen as community practices, activities that people engage in together in order to achieve community goals. Developing the thinking skills of students is a matter of developing a community in which these practices are commonly understood and habitual ("It is what we do in this class"). According to Rogoff (1995), this role learning consists of "appropriating" both the practices and the goals of the more expert members of the community. The influence of previous participation on subsequent participation defines learning.

Others such as Cobb and his colleagues (cf. Cobb, Perlwitz & Underwood-Gregg, 1998; Cobb & Yackel, 1996) have argued that there is a "reflexive" relationship between the discussion that goes on as students work on solving significant problems and the thinking process that guides their joint problem solving. "[O]ne does not exist without the other" (Cobb, Perlwitz & Underwood-Gregg, 1998, p. 74). What students say and do with the teacher or with each other is a product of what they know and how they think. As the interaction occurs their knowledge and thinking is shaped by what they say and do and how others respond to what they say and do. This, in turn, changes what they say or do next. Because of this reflexive or twinned relationship, changing the quality of the public discussion changes the quality of the thinking processes that students use. A similar approach is taken by Hicks (1996). She bases her analysis on Bakhtin's claim that all thought, even when the thinking person is alone, is inherently social or dialogic (Bakhtin, 1981). Thought is internalised speech with another who is either playing the role of audience or antagonist. In Hicks' interpretation, thinking is a "boundary" phenomenon that is neither in the head, nor in the social context, but in between. Talking and thinking are alternative versions of the same activity.

Behind this view is the concept of "internalisation" as the relationship between the external social activity and the internal, parallel cognitive activity. According to Vygotsky (1978, 1981), the higher mental processes develop out the internalisation or "interiorisation" of social activities, retaining the essential form or structure of the social activities, but not their detail.

The most detailed and convincing accounts of the process of internalisation come from the later research of Piaget (e.g. 1978) and of Vygotsky's follower Gal'perin (Arievitch & van der Veer, 1995; Haenan, 1996, 2001). Both demonstrate that internalisation occurs as a function of habituation. Repeated enactment of an activity leads progressively to control being transferred from the external world to the conscious and later to the unconscious mind. The basic structure of the activity becomes so familiar that its essential components can be imitated or replayed independently of the contexts in which they were originally experienced. Thinking is described as a kind of internal imitation that can be carried out in the head for the purposes of planning or calculating the consequences of the activity. When internalisation is complete, the activity can be managed in the mind without awareness and can become a component of larger cognitive structures (Lawrence & Valsiner, 1993; Piaget, 1978).

Producing evidence for either the assimilation or internalisation of the patterns of argumentation or reasoning that students experience in the classroom is an extraordinarily difficult task. Few researchers have discussed the problems involved in trying to do it, let alone carried out research designed to demonstrate it. What is at stake is not just training students to carry out specific information processing activities of the kind that are said to make up problem solving skills (cf. Bransford, Sherwood, Vye & Reisser, 1986) because there is no evidence that they become, or could become, habits of the mind.

The exception is the work of Anderson and his colleagues who have developed a program for "inculcating the values and habits of mind of reasoned discourse as a means for choosing between competing ideas" (Anderson, Chinn, Waggoner & Nguyen, 1998, p. 172). They created a model of argumentation (which they refer to as "collaborative reasoning") to be used in story discussion in the literacy curriculum. Prior to a collaborative reasoning discussion, students read a story that contains a significant issue or moral dilemma faced by one of the story characters. The discussion is initiated by the teacher posing a question about the central dilemma and getting the students to declare their position on the dilemma. The students are then expected to try to resolve their differences by developing arguments with supporting evidence from the story to support their position. They are expected to listen carefully to each other's arguments, and where appropriate challenge with counter-arguments or alternative evidence. The teacher's role is to sustain this discussion by initially modelling appropriate arguments and use of evidence and progressively handing control of the discussion to the students.

In their analysis of a sequence of 48 collaborative discussions (using different stories and dilemmas) from four different classrooms, Anderson and his colleagues found that students made increasing use of specific ways of arguing and using evidence by imitating each other. For example, they identified 56 instances of students using the "what if . . ." form of hypothetical reasoning (e.g. "what if some of them got sick and they couldn't . . ."). They found that after the initial occurrence of this form of reasoning there was an increasing use of the form, with shorter and shorter gaps between each occurrence. In addition, the percentage of students in each group using each form increased. They argue that this "snowball" effect is a consequence of the mutual experiences of group members. When one student uses a stratagem to good effect, the others are increasingly likely to use the same stratagem.

This study provides evidence that in effectively managed group discussions, language and argument forms, once introduced and shown to have good effect, become part of the common practice of group members. Whether they also become part of the way in which group members think is the more difficult question to answer. Common sense would suggest that students who use argument forms in a discussion must, in some sense, know them. Imitating other's use of them involves, at least, learning when and how they can be appropriately used.

Some would argue that this kind of appropriation is all there is to it. To participate effectively in a reasoned debate is all there is to developing the "higher mental processes" (Lemke, 1990; Roth et al., 1999; Walkerdine 1997). The problem with this view is that you cannot distinguish between mindless imitation and purposeful use. For genuine internalisation to have occurred, there needs to be evidence of the use of argument structures in different contexts, in which direct imitation is not possible. Anderson and his colleagues have also obtained evidence that students who have been involved in collaborative reasoning groups use more argument forms in their later writing than students who have not had this experience (Reznitskaya et al., in press).

What seems critical from the Anderson studies is that for appropriation and/or internalisation to occur from within a group or class activity, the participants must share, and be committed to, the same goal. For students to want to imitate a model provided by teacher or peers, they must be convinced of the functional utility of the model for their own purposes (Schunk, 1998).

IN WHAT CONTEXTS IS SOCIAL CONSTRUCTIVIST TEACHING MOST EFFECTIVE?

There is no doubt about the appeal of social constructivist teaching. When it is contrasted with a model of teaching where the teacher stands in front of the class doing most of the talking and the students sit passively listening, occasionally answering simple questions, reading aloud or copying notes off the blackboard, it seems a much more exciting, motivating and intellectually stimulating model. But it should be clear from this analysis that it does not necessarily solve all of the problems of transmission teaching.

It is true that the social construction of meaning does take place for words and terms that are used in association with shared activities (Wells, 1993). Words and terms that refer to experiences or activities that are not commonly shared, experienced, or understood in the same ways, do not acquire mutually understood meanings.

It is also true that knowledge can be mutually created, clarified, structured, and organised, through joint participation in teacher managed discussions. But for this knowledge to become an established part of the beliefs and understandings of all the participants requires a number of conditions. The participants must share a substantial body of prior knowledge and they must experience the discussion in essentially the same ways. This means they must all share the same interpretation of the purposes of the discussion. This, in turn, means that the social context and patterns of participation must not favor some students over others or interfere with the free exchange of beliefs and ideas. Finally, the knowledge and reasoning that is achieved during the discussion must occur in a context in which it is revisited on at least three or four different occasions if it is to become part of the established knowledge of all of the students (Nuthall, 1999b; Nuthall & Alton-Lee, 1993).

If the most important outcome of social constructivist teaching is to change the ability of students to think and solve problems in ways that match the characteristic methods of the academic disciplines, then ensuring this outcome is much more problematic. Getting students to imitate strategies modeled by the teacher or peers is not difficult. As Anderson and his colleagues have found "children appropriate an argument stratagem when they judge that the stratagem is a useful tool for advancing understanding or adding to the persuasive force of an argument" (Anderson et al., 2001, p. 4). But such imitative appropriation is almost always situation specific. Of more importance is internalisation in which the underlying logical structures of reasoning or argument become deeply embedded and more generally applicable ways of thinking or tackling problems. Here it seems, frequent use allowing the essential or underlying structure of the reasoning or argument to be separated from the particulars of its use in a specific context, is an important prerequisite. While it seems obvious that scaffolded participation in reasoning discussions (as they occur in social constructivist teaching) must be better than the lack of such experience (as in transmission teaching), it is still not clear how participation leads to internalisation, and how, for example, a teacher might monitor its progress in individual students.

THE CONTEXT FOR USING SOCIAL CONSTRUCTIVIST TEACHING

In this final part of the chapter, I would like to examine the teaching contexts in which social constructivist teaching is likely to be most useful and effective. The discussion will narrow to a focus on the teaching of science and the social studies because teaching contexts vary significantly with curriculum areas.

First, there are two preliminary points that follow from the analysis so far. The first is that social constructivist teaching seems to work best in the context of activity-based teaching in which the focus of the discussion is on experiences that the students have shared with each other. When students are doing things together (carrying out a science experiment, constructing a model village, visiting a museum) the referents of their language are mutually accessible. The activity and the language are mutually supportive and shared meaning is not a problem. When the focus of the discussion is on material that has been read or reported and refers to phenomena the students have not mutually experienced, the possibilities of creating and sharing new knowledge are severely restricted (see, for example, the activities studied by Hogan, Nastasi & Pressley, 2000; Veralas, Luster & Wenzel, 1999; Herrenkohl, Palincsar, De Water & Kawasaki, 1999).

Second, the aims of social constructivist teaching are more achievable in small groups than with a whole class. The possibility of students sharing the same goals, the same meanings and understandings, and fully participating in the group process are much reduced when a whole class is involved. Similarly, it is impossible for a teacher to be sensitive to student backgrounds, to their the changing understandings, and to the implicit meanings in the discussion, when there is more than a small number of students. In addition, because students' participation and experiences of an activity are determined as much by their on-going relationships to other students as they are to the teacher, the possibility of developing the mutually responsive and respectful relationships that sustain open discussion is much greater in smaller groups. This implies a much greater involvement of the teacher in the personal relationships between students than is normally seen as part of the teacher's responsibility. Evidence from the studies of Anderson et al. (2001) and Hogan, et al. (2000) show that once students are capable of running their own groups, the quality of their participation, the frequency with which they provide reasons and explanations increases.

In this regard, it is instructive to consider the analogy to an orchestra that is often used in describing social constructivist teaching. For example, Varelas, Luster, and Wenzel (1999) describe the teacher as an orchestra leader who "pulls together children's individual voices and individual ways of thinking" (p. 229). If that analogy has any validity, it is an impossible task with more than a small number of students. Better for the teacher to be the leader of a quartet or quintet where every player's contribution is continuously essential to the whole performance.

THE SOCIAL CONSTRUCTIVIST DISCUSSION AS PART OF A UNIT OF WORK

In order to examine the role of social constructivist teaching in the wider context of a complete unit of work, I will draw on the work of one of the teachers in our studies who provided hands-on activities for students working together in small groups.

All of the teachers in our studies made use of activities that were designed to engage students both in discovering and thinking about the content of the unit. In the science units the activities included experiments (e.g. splitting white light into its component colours) and the construction of models or equipment. In social studies units the activities included searching library or computer resources for information (e.g. about the roles of women in ancient Egypt) or constructing models or simulations of events (e.g. preparing for an expedition in Antarctica). As a general rule, the activity was contained within a sequence of preparatory and concluding events. This larger activity format consisted of four stages.

(1) *Instructions*. At the beginning of the activity, the teacher provided instructions about what the students were expected to do. These might have been spoken by the teacher, discussed with the students, printed on an instruction or worksheet, or some combination of these. They usually related both to the specific activity and to the general rules and procedures expected for activities of this type.

(2) *Carrying out the activity*. The students engaged in the activity on the basis of their understanding of the instructions, their knowledge of what was usually expected in such activities, and their awareness of the consequences of following or not following the instructions and conforming to the implied expectations. In addition, students' behaviour was constrained by the availability and usefulness of the resources and their ability to negotiate and manage the social context in which the activity was carried out.

(3) *Preparing a report*. Almost always teachers required the students to record or report (as in a class presentation) on the outcomes of the activity, or show some evidence of what they had done. Since this aspect of the activity was the most likely to be noticed or evaluated, it exerted a continuously controlling influence on the way the activity was carried out.

(4) *Discussing the results*. During, or at the end of the activity, the teacher usually discussed the activity or its outcomes with the students. These discussions served several purposes. They provided the students with an account of what the activity and its outcomes were intended to mean or achieve. They were occasions when the teacher related the physical aspects of carrying out the activity to the intended curriculum purposes and processes. The teacher made connections to previous activities, to previous knowledge, and to the implications implicit in the outcomes. Even if the students had no idea why they were doing the activity, had interpreted its

purposes quite differently from the teacher, had not completed the activity, or obtained the wrong outcomes, this discussion served to tell the students what they should have done, how they should have understood it, and what they should have concluded (Wells, 1999).

Depending on the nature of the activity, the occasions for reasoning about the content of activity occurred during the time when the students were carrying out the activity, as part of creating a report or record, or when the teacher was discussing the results with the whole class.

These four stages are an idealised description of what happened in each class. In practice the stages over-lapped and intermingled with each other. For example, the instructions could never be complete and fully explicit (Amerine & Bilmes, 1988). Problems and unexpected difficulties arose that needed to be resolved. The meaning of the instructions depended on the mutual understandings and expectations that the teacher and students had developed through previous activities. Some students needed to be explicitly reminded of these. Similarly, what counted as having carried out the activity was never entirely clear. Students would move on to preparing a report before they had finished an experiment or obtained adequate information. The teacher would join a group and provide additional scaffolding for the discussion they were supposed to be having about the reasons for their results. The effect was that students were constantly, independently or under teacher guidance, moving backwards and forwards between the different stages of the activity.

The following example illustrates the way in which one teacher tried to create the context in which the students could independently discuss a scientific explanation. The class (Study 9 in Table 1 – the same class described in the example of "find out about" and "refraction" above) were doing a series of experiments on light. In this excerpt, the students were working in groups looking at the magnifying effects of water. The experiment required them to look at the print on a printed page through different sized drops of water. When they had recorded their results they were to create, as a group, an explanation for the effect.

Austin's group (like most of the other groups in the class) had made several attempts to carry out the experiment but could not agree on the results. The teacher wanted them to leave enough time to work on an explanation so she joined the group to help them produce the results they needed to use in their explanation.

Teacher (working with Austin's group): Okay, which drop was bigger, which drop magnified better, the small drop or the big drop? Probably you're guessing. Okay, put a little drop on for me, please, one of you. On these letters here, so we can have a look . . . Okay, that's

it. Just stop . . .. Right have a look. Stand up and have a look at it so you can see how it
magnifies, okay . . .
Austin: It doesn't magnify very much.
Teacher: Okay, right. Now I want you to put a big drop on, on the same print somewhere
close – not too close to it . . .. Okay, there's your big drop, there's your little drop, compare
the two. Which is bigger?
Paul: The big one makes it go small.
Teacher: Which one makes it go bigger, the big drop or the little drop?
Paul: The little.
Austin: The little one, cause it . . .
Teacher: Okay, why? Have a look at the shape of the little one, have a look at the shape
of the big one and think about something you've done a couple of days ago.
Austin: The big one, um, is bigger so you can see it all or something?
Teacher: Think about, think about the shape of the little one, what's it doing?
Rowena: It's spread out more.
Austin: It's curving.
Teacher: Okay. And this one here's not as curvy is it? It's flatter isn't it?
Austin: Yeah.
Teacher: So think about curving, which is it, which curve was it?
Rowena: Concave.
Paul: Concave.
Austin: Convex.
Teacher: You can have that discussion amongst yourselves and work it out which one. I'm
not going to tell you, but you think about that, okay.

There are two significant things the teacher did during the excerpt. First, she was
aware that being able to create an explanation depends on the students sharing the
same experiences and understanding of the results of the experiment. To ensure
this, she worked through the experiment again with the students, getting them to
agree on the results. This discussion is far from the model of a constructivist
discussion. Each question is a leading question, focusing their attention on what
they need to know. Second, she cued them in to the related information they
needed to consider in their explanation ("Have a look at the shape . . . and think
about something you've done a couple of days ago . . .. So think about curving").

The students went on to debate the explanation between themselves. They
wrote a report of their results and their explanation in their individual report
books. At the end of this day's activity, the teacher reviewed the work each
group had done in a whole-class discussion.

Teacher: When you were making a hypothesis, you were guessing intelligently about which
drop would be – would have the most magnifying effect. Who thought that the big drop
was going to make it bigger? (Most of class raise their hands)
Teacher: I would have thought that too. Who found out that the big drop did make it bigger?
(no one raises hand) Good, mmm. (laughs). Okay, so you all discovered why. Who can tell
me which drop magnified best?

Nellie: The small drop.

Teacher: Why do you think that was? Got any ideas why that was? Okay, why do you think it was, please, Bettina?

Bettina: 'Cause it was rounder.

Teacher: Right, okay. The small drip had a more rounded finish to it. When you put more water on, it sort of went flatter didn't it? And what did we, what do we know about round things, round lenses, Karin?

Marcus: Makes things look bigger.

Teacher: Okay. Right, so that was the way it [the drop] was magnifying, so that was excellent.

Nina: Oh, and on one magnifying glass you got a wee one and it magnifies better than the big one. I had one with . . .

Teacher: Oh, on one of the magnifying glasses it's got a small one inside it, yeah.

At the end of this day, the constructivist discussions occurred (more or less successfully) in the students' groups, sandwiched between tightly scaffolded experiments, report writing, and a brief whole-class discussion at the end. All the final discussion did was refer to two key concepts ("rounded", "magnifying") that the students had used when they developed their own group explanations, and which they had recorded in their report books.

However, at the end of this unit, after a series of these experiments, the students were more familiar with the nature of scientific explanations, and in subsequent interviews were able to recall and discuss appropriate evidence and reasons for the phenomena they had been studying. For example, Austin explained about the drop experiment in an interview several weeks after the unit was completed.

Austin: And we, like, got some [plastic sheet] and put a drop of water on it and we experimented with little drops and bigger drops. and the little drop made it, magnified it more.

Interviewer: Did it?

Austin: 'Cause it was more rounded than the big one.

Interviewer: So it makes it look bigger because it's more . . . ?

Austin: Yeah the little drops are more rounded and bigger ones are . . .

Interviewer: Are flatter?

Austin: Yeah.

Interviewer: Isn't that interesting. So why if it's rounder does it make things look bigger?

Austin: 'Cause it magnifies it. It's yeah, it magnifies it.

Interviewer: Yeah, so what makes it magnify?

Austin: No, I don't know like if it's curved how, how it would make it magnify. I just know that if it's like curved outward it would make it magnify.

Interviewer: And are you sort of puzzled why that would be like that?

Austin: Yeah. Probably like 'cause it's a . . . . Probably 'cause it's like a mirror and like it's curved outwards. So would make it look a lot bigger.

To understand how this unit had been effective, you need to take into account two things. First, the accountability system that the teacher had set up, and second, the extent to which the students had practiced or repeated both the content and structure of the scientific explanations they had created.

(1) *The accountability system.* In this class, the report book in which the students recorded the results of experiments and the answers to the questions the teacher had set for each activity (the "find out about" questions in the example above), was the core of the accountability system. It was here that the students recorded their evidence and their explanations. The teacher read these books regularly and wrote her comments on what the students had written. The students also took these books home for their parents to see. This was the publicly visible record of their science. It was clear from the way the students worked on these report books that they took them very seriously. It was also clear from the nature of their group discussions that they knew they needed to resolve any ambiguities and arrive at satisfactory explanations so they would have something significant to write in their reports.

(2) *The sequencing of experiences.* This teacher revisited the results of group discussions several times. In the example given above, the whole-class discussion does not repeat the whole of the explanation that the students created in their groups. Using terms that stood for key concepts, the teacher re-instated in the minds of the individual students, their previous discussions. The teacher repeated this process the next day, reminding the students about the shape of lenses and the way light is bent when it passes through a "rounded" surface. This had two effects. First, it ensured that the students remembered the content of their explanations and had this content readily available when it was needed in subsequent discussions. Second, it stimulated continued informal discussions of the topic among the students in and out of school. Repeated references throughout the unit enhanced the significance of the explanation (and its key concepts) relative to the other activities that the students were engaged in during the same time span.

Throughout this science unit on light, the teacher constantly interacted with the students when they were working in their groups, participating in their discussions by modelling and scaffolding the use of evidence and the creation of explanations. By the end of this unit, the students were familiar with a routine of activities that made up their experiments. The time spent on instructions decreased. The time spent on discussing and explaining the results increased and was more focused, except on those occasions when the experiments were more difficult to carry out. And because of the overlap of the content of each experiment, the students knowledge and understanding of the significant concepts in the unit was progressively extended and elaborated.

There is not space in this chapter to explore the many different ways reasons, explanations, and evidence, were woven through the activities that made up the work done by the teachers in our studies. The example described above should, however, give a sense of the significance of the context within which social constructivist discussions occur.

Implementing Social Constructivist Teaching

In order to formalise this context, the following principles for the implementation of social constructivist teaching have been developed from our analysis of the work of the teachers in our study. They also incorporate our evolving understanding of the ways in which students learn from their classroom experiences (Nuthall, 2001, April).

(1) *Developing a an activity framework* The first concern must be with developing a sequence of activities that form a coherent learning system. In our studies, the teachers used a system, described above, of encasing the primary learning activity within a sequence of instructions, report writing and concluding discussion. In their development of a community of learners, Brown and Campione (1994) created an elaborate system of interdependent activities, each with its special purpose and design characteristics. Behind the social constructivist discussions reported by Herrenkohl, et al. (1999) was a sequence of physics experiments that provided the basis for the discussions. If social constructivist discussions are to produce the outcomes that are claimed for them, they must be located within a system of carefully constructed related activities each of which has an essential role to play in the learning process.

(2) *Establishing an accountability system* Several writers have noted that students are responsive to the underlying accountability system that teachers establish within their classrooms (Doyle, 1983; Doyle & Carter, 1984; Newton, Driver & Osborne, 1999; Yerrick, 1999). Students will avoid those activities or aspects of activities that they are not held accountable for either individually or as part of a group. Teachers frequently ask or promise to reward students for behaviours that they want them to carry out, but do not follow-through or build the reward system into the activity. The result is that the intentions of the teacher are undermined by hidden or implicit reward systems that the teacher is unaware of. In the example given above, the students discovered that the written report was all that they were ultimately held accountable for. The instructions, admonitions, or passing praise of the teacher counted for little by comparison, and even the

requirements of the written report could be subtly negotiated downwards. Consequently it is essential that the general and the activity-specific reward systems be carefully built into the larger activity structure.

(3) *Developing monitoring procedures.* Closely related to the second principle is the necessity for the teacher to establish a way of constantly monitoring how students are carrying out the activities that make up the larger activity structure. In the example given above, the teacher moved constantly from group to group monitoring their activities and where appropriate intervening by suggesting, modelling, and scaffolding. The underlying principle is that instructions are never completed until the activity is finished. The success of the monitoring depends on the ability of the teacher to anticipate what will happen in each group and be ready to intervene at critical moments.

(4) *Setting up common experience.* I have already noted that effective social constructivist discussions depend on the participants sharing a common base of knowledge and experience. This is most easily created by having the students engaged, in relatively small groups, in a co-operative activity that produces the data, knowledge, or experience, that will be the focus of the discussion. Several writers have noted that the quality of this activity is a critical factor in determining the quality of the subsequent and concurrent discussion (cf., Brophy & Alleman, in press; Hogan, Nastasi & Pressley, 2000). This means creating a focal activity that involves issues that: (i) the students can identify with and believe are worth resolving, and (ii) relate to concepts or principles that are significant in the academic discipline.

(5) *Ensuring frequent repetition.* Because internalisation depends on habituation, students need frequent practice in those reasoning activities that are intended to become habits of mind. It would seem desirable to keep the activity structure relatively small and uncomplicated. Rather than have the students spend, for example, considerable time developing shared background knowledge and little time engaged in constructivist discussions, more frequent activities that follow a predictable format including frequent discussions, would seem desirable. For example, one of the teachers in our studies developed a format, based on the use of instruction cards, in which the students carried out a small science activity each day. These activities became routinized so that less and less time was spent on instructions and finding out what to do, and more time was spent on constructive discussion and debate of the issues. There is extensive evidence that without the establishment of effective routines, students will spend most of their time on organisational activities to the exclusion of more content-focused activities (Hogan, 1999; Newton, Driver & Osborne, 1999).

(6) *Critical content is repeated.* Research on the classroom experiences of students makes it clear that, as a general rule, learning is a function of repetition. Even when a discussion leads to a substantial change in students' beliefs or understanding, the results of the discussion will be forgotten, or substantially changed by the forgetting process, unless the new beliefs or understandings are re-visited on several occasions (Nuthall, 2000a, b; Nuthall & Alton-Lee, 1993). Probably the most efficient way of doing this is to ensure that the understandings developed on one occasion become the foundation for further understandings on subsequent occasions. In this way the recollection of a previous discussion is not only required, but given an obvious purpose. Achieving this kind of co-ordination between successive activities requires considerable planning and sophisticated analysis of the potential connections between topics.

(7) *Training in group interaction procedures.* It is now well established that the ways in which students participate in, and learn from, constructivist discussions is as much a function of their relationships with other students as it is of the teacher's management of the discussion (Cobb, Perlwitz & Underwood-Gregg, 1998; Linn & Barbules, 1993; Nuthall, 2001, April; Solomon, 2000). This implies that the effective management of discussions is dependent on the effective management of the social relationships between students in the classroom. Yerrick's study of his attempts to introduce social constructivist teaching of science in a class of students from impoverished backgrounds, details some of the ways in which the culture of the students cut across and undermined his teaching (Yerrick, 1999). He found that differences of opinion were automatically interpreted as status conflicts and evoked cruel and darkly sarcastic reactions. The way students contributed to discussions reflected their deep-seated hostility to the school and teacher and their fear of constant rejection by the school system. Most of those who have described design experiments in which they have worked with teachers to develop and sustain effective constructivist discussions in their classrooms talk of the need to develop rules of participation that change the ways students routinely relate to each other (cf. Anderson, et al., 2001). Again, it would seem most effective if these rules of participation were built into the larger activity structure rather than coming into operation only when discussions were occurring.

CONCLUSIONS

I have attempted in this chapter to describe the nature of social constructivist teaching by drawing on a number of research studies in which researchers have worked alongside teachers as they tried to implement this kind of teaching. I then examined the kinds of learning that social constructivist teaching is intended to produce. This led to a critical appraisal of the limitations of the claims made about social constructivist teaching and the conditions under which it is likely to be most effective. Finally, I have attempted to identify the design principles that would place social constructivist teaching within an effective supporting context.

My major concern has been that, without a critical appraisal of the learning outcomes of social constructivist teaching, its performance would become idealised as the way to run a model classroom. There is always a danger that a method of teaching will be seen through the eyes of the teacher without serious regard for how it is experienced by students. It would seem common sense that a classroom in which the students are actively engaged in a well-reasoned discussion is better than a classroom in which the students sit passively while the teacher talks at them. But such common sense is a cultural artefact that requires careful analysis of what is being taken for granted as well as systematic research to evaluate its practicality and effectiveness.

REFERENCES

Alton-Lee, A. G., Nuthall, G. A., & Patrick, J. (1993). Reframing classroom research: A lesson from the private world of children. *Harvard Educational Review, 63*(1), 50–84.

Amerine, R., & Bilmes, J. (1988). Following instructions. *Human Studies, 11*, 327–339.

Anderson, R. C., Chinn, C. K., Chang, J., Waggoner, M., & Yi, H. J. (1997). On the logical integrity of children's arguments *Cognition and instruction, 15*(2), 135–167.

Anderson, R. C., Chinn, C. K., Waggoner, M., & Nguyen, K. (1998). Intellectually stimulating story discussions. In: J. Osborn & F. Lehr (Eds), *Literacy For All* (pp. 170–196). New York: Guilford.

Anderson, R. C., Nguyen-Jahiel, K., McNurlen, B., Archodidou, A., Kim, S. Y., Reznitskaya, A., Tillmanns, M., & Gilbert, L. (2001). The snowball phenomenon: Spread of ways of talking and ways of thinking across groups of children. *Cognition and Instruction, 19*(1), 1–46.

Arievitch, I., & van der Veer, R. (1995). Furthering the internalisation debate: Gal'perin's contribution. *Human Development, 38*, 113–126.

Bahktin, M. M. (1981). *The dialogic imagination: Four essays by M. M. Bakhtin* (M. Holquist, Ed.). Austin: University of Texas Press.

Ball, D. L., & Bass, H. (2000). Making believe: The collective construction of public mathematical knowledge in the elementary classroom. In: D. C. Phillips (Ed.), *Constructivism in Education: Opinions and Second Opinions on Controversial Issues* (pp. 193–224). 99th Yearbook of the National Society for the Study of Education, Part I. Chicago: University of Chicago Press.

Bentley, M. L. (1998). Constructivism as a referent for reforming science education. In: M. Larochelle, N. Bednarz & J. Garrison (Eds), *Constructivism and education*, (pp. 81–103). New York: Cambridge University Press.

Bransford, J., Sherwood, R., Vye, N., & Reisser, J. (1986). Teaching thinking and problem solving: Research foundations. *American Psychologist, 41*, 1078–1089.

Brown, A. L., & Campione, J. C. (1994). Guided discovery in a community of learners. In: K. McGilly (Ed.), *Classoom Lessons: Integrating Cognitive Theory and Classroom Practice* (pp. 229–270). Cambridge MA: MIT Press/Bradford Books.

Brophy J., & Alleman, J. (in press). Learning and teaching about cultural universals in primary-grade social studies. *Elementary School Journal*.

Chinn, C. A., & Anderson, R. C. (1998). The structure of discussions that promote reasoning. *Teachers College Record, 100*, 315–368.

Cobb, P., Perlwitz, M., & Underwood-Gregg, (1998). Individual construction, mathematical acculturation, and the classroom community. In: M. Larochelle, N. Bednarz & J. Garrison (Eds), *Constructivism and Education* (pp. 63–80). New York: Cambridge University Press.

Cobb, P., & Yackel, E. (1996). Constructivist, emergent, and sociocultural perspectives in the context of developmental research. *Educational Psychologist, 31*(3/4), 175–190.

Confrey, J. (1998). Voice and perspective: Hearing epistemological innovation in students' words. In: M. Larochelle, N. Bednarz & J. Garrison (Eds), *Constructivism and Education* (pp. 104–120). New York: Cambridge University Press.

De Corte, E. (2000). Marrying theory building and the improvement of school practice: A permanent challenge for instructional psychology. *Learning and Instruction, 10*, 249–266.

Doyle, W. (1983). Academic work. *Review of Educational Research, 53*, 159–199.

Doyle, W., & Carter, K. (1984). Academic tasks in classrooms. *Curriculum Inquiry, 14*(2), 129–149.

Driver, R. (1997). The application of science education theories: A reply to Stephen P. Norris and Tone Kvernbekk. *Journal of Research in Science Teaching, 34*(10), 1007–1018.

Driver, R., Asoko, H., Leach, S., Mortimer, E., & Scott, P. (1994). Constructing scientific knowledge in the classroom. *Educational Researcher, 23*, 5–12.

Erickson, F. (1996). Going for the zone: The social ecology of teacher-student interaction in classroom conversations. In: D. Hicks (Ed.), *Discourse Learning and Schooling* (pp. 29–62). New York: Cambridge University Press.

Gee, J. (1989). What is literacy? *Journal of Education, 171*, 18–25.

Grice, H. P. (1989). *Studies in the Way of Words*. Cambridge, Mass: Harvard University Press.

Haenan, J. (1996). *Piotr Gal'perin: Psychologist in Vygotsky's Footsteps*. New York: Nova Science Publishers.

Haenan, J. (2001). Outlining the teaching learning process: Piotr Gal'perin's contribution. *Learning and Instruction, 11*(2), 157–170.

Herrenkohl, L. R., Palincsar, A. S., DeWater, L. S., & Kawasaki, K. (1999). Developing scientific communities in classrooms: A sociocognitive approach. *The Journal of the Learning Sciences, 8*(3 and 4), 451–493.

Hicks, D. (1996). Contextual inquiries: A discourse oriented study of classroom learning. In: D. Hicks (Ed.), *Discourse Learning and Schooling* (pp. 104–141). New York: Cambridge University Press.

Hogan, K. (1999). Assessing depth of cognitive processing in peer groups' science discussions. *Research in Science Education, 29*(4), 457–477.

Hogan, K., Nastasi, B. K., & Pressley, M. (2000). Discourse patterns and collaborative scientific reasoning in peer and teacher-guided discussions. *Cognition and Instruction, 17*(4), 379–432.

Howe, K. R., & Berv, J. (2000). Constructing constructivism, epistemological and pedagogical issues. In: D. C. Phillips (Ed.), *Constructivism in Education: Opinions and Second Opinions on Controversial Issues* (pp. 19–40). 99th Yearbook of the National Society for the Study of Education, Part I. Chicago: University of Chicago Press.

Lave, J. (1991). Situated learning in communities of practice. In: L. B. Resnick, J. M. Levine & S. D. Teasley (Eds), *Perspectives on Socially Shared Cognition* (pp. 63–82). Washington, D.C.: American Psychological Association.

Lave, J. (1992, April). Learning as participation in communities of practice. Paper presented at the annual meeting of the American Educational Research Association, San Francisco.

Lawrence, J. A., & Valsiner, J. (1993). Conceptual roots of internalisation: From transition to transformation. *Human Development, 36*, 150–167.

Lemke, J. (1990). *Talking Science: Language, Learning, and Values.* Norwood, NJ: Ablex.

Linn, M. C., & Barbules, N. C. (1993). Construction of knowledge and group learning. In: K. Tobin (Ed.), *The Practice of Constructivism in Science Education* (pp. 91–119). Hillsdale, NJ: Lawrence Erlbaum.

Newton, P., Driver, R., & Osborne, J. (1999). The place of argumentation in the pedagogy of school science. *International Journal of Science Education, 21*(5), 553–576.

Nuthall, G. A. (1999a). Learning how to learn: the evolution of students' minds through the social processes and culture of the classroom. *International Journal of Educational Research, 31*(3), 139–256.

Nuthall, G. A. (1999b). The way students learn: Acquiring knowledge from an integrated science and social studies unit. *Elementary School Journal, 99*, 303–341.

Nuthall, G. A. (2000a). The role of memory in the acquisition and retention of knowledge in science and social studies units. *Cognition and Instruction, 18*(1) 83–139.

Nuthall, G. A. (2000b) The anatomy of memory in the classroom: Understanding how students acquire memory processes from classroom activities in science and social studies units. *American Educational Research Journal, 37*(1), 247–304.

Nuthall, G. A. (2000, September). Understanding how classroom experience shapes students' minds. Paper presented at 17th Kongress der Deutschen Gesellschaft für Erziehungswissenschaft, Göttingen, Germany.

Nuthall, G. A. (2001, April). Student experience and the learning process: Developing an evidence based theory of classroom learning. Paper presented at the annual meeting of the American Educational Research Association, Seattle.

Nuthall, G. A., & Alton-Lee, A. G. (1993). Predicting learning from student experience of teaching: A theory of student knowledge construction in classrooms. *American Educational Research Journal, 30*, 799–840.

O'Connor, M. C., & Michaels, S. (1996). Shifting participant frameworks: Orchestrating thinking practices in group discussion. In: D. Hicks (Ed.), *Discourse, Learning and Schooling* (pp. 63–103). New York: Cambridge University Press.

Piaget, J. (1978). *Success and understanding.* London: Routledge & Kegan Paul.

Pinker, S. (1999). *Words and rules: The ingredients of language.* London: Wiedenfeld & Nicolson.

Reznitskaya, A., Anderson, R. C., McNurlen, B., Nguyen, K. T., Archodidou, A., & Kim, S. (in press). Influence of oral discussion on written argumentation. *Discourse processes.*

Rogoff, B. (1994). Developing understanding of the idea of communities of learners. *Mind, Culture, and Activity, 1*, 209–229.

Rogoff, B. (1995). Observing sociocultural activity on three planes: Participatory appropriation, guided participation, and apprenticeship. In: J. V. Wertsch, P. del Rio & A. Alvarez (Eds), *Sociocultural Studies of Mind* (pp. 139–164). New York: Cambridge University Press.

Roth, W-M., McGinn, M. K., Woszczyna, C., & Boutonné, S. (1999). Differential participation during science conversations: the interaction of focal artefacts, social configurations, and physical arrangements. *The Journal of the Learning Sciences, 8*(3 and 4), 293–347.

Sahlström, F. (1999). Up the hill backwards: On interactional constraints and affordances for equality-construction in the classrooms of Swedish comprehensive school. Unpublished Ph.D. dissertation, University of Uppsala, Uppsala.

Sahlström, F., & Lindblad, S. (1998). Subtexts in the science classroom – An exploration of the social construction of science lessons and school careers. *Learning and instruction, 8*(3), 195–214.

Schunk, D. H. (1998). Peer modeling. In: K. Topping & S. Ehly (Eds), *Peer-Assisted Learning* (pp. 185–202). Mahwah, NJ: Lawrence Erlbaum.

Solomon, J. (2000). The changing perspectives of constructivism: Science wars and children's creativity. In: D. C. Phillips (Ed.), *Constructivism in Education: Opinions and Second Opinions on Controversial Issues* (pp. 283–307). 99th Yearbook of the National Society for the Study of Education, Part I. Chicago: University of Chicago Press.

Stigler, J. W., Gonzales, P., Kawanaka, T., Knoll, S., & Serrano, A. (1999). *The Timms videotape classroom study: Methods and findings from an exploratory research project on eighth-grade mathematics instruction in Germany, Japan and the United States.* Washington: National Center for Education Statistics, U.S. Department of Education, NCES 99–074.

Stigler J. W., & Hiebert, J. (1999). *The teaching gap: Best ideas from the world's teachers for improving education in the classroom.* New York: The Free Press.

Tobin, K. (1998). Sociocultural perspectives on the teaching and learning of science. In: M. Larochelle, N. Bednarz & J. Garrison (Eds), *Constructivism and Education* (pp. 195–212). New York: Cambridge University Press.

Varelas, M., Luster, B. & Wenzel, S. (1999). Making meaning in a community of learners: Struggles and possibilities in an urban science class. *Research in Science Education, 29*(2), 227–245.

Varelas, M., & Pineda, E. (1999). Intermingling and bumpiness: Exploring meaning making in the discourse of a science classroom. *Research in Science Education, 29*(1), 25–49.

Vygotsky, L. S. (1978). *Mind in society: The development of higher psychological processes* (M. Cole, V. John-Steiner, S. Scribner & E. Souberman, Eds). Cambridge, MA: Harvard University Press.

Vygotsky, L. S. (1981). The genesis of higher mental functions. In: J. V. Wertsch (Ed.), *The Concept of Activity in Soviet Psychology* (pp. 148–188). Armonk, NY: Sharpe.

Walkerdine, V. (1997). Redefining the subject in situated cognition theory. In: D. Kirschner & J. A. Whitson (Eds), *Situated Cognition: Social, Semiotic and Psychological Perspectives,* (pp. 57–70). Mahwah NJ: Lawrence Erlbaum.

Well, G. (1993). Working with a teacher in the zone of proximal development: Action research on the learning and teaching of science. *Journal of the Society for Accelerative Learning and Teaching, 18,* 127–222.

Wells, G. (1999). *Dialogic inquiry: Towards a Sociocultural Practice and Theory of Education.* New York: Cambridge University Press.

Yerrick, R. (1999). Renegotiating the discourse of lower track high school students. *Research in Science Education, 29*(2), 269–293.

A DIVERSITY OF TEACHING AND LEARNING PATHS: TEACHING WRITING IN SITUATED ACTIVITY

Carol Sue Englert and Kailonnie Dunsmore

INTRODUCTION

The fundamental enterprise of education is to enhance the knowledge, expertise and competence of students. One question that arises is how knowledge acquisition can be situated in classroom activity in ways that give rise to the acquisition of the formal discourses, tools and practices of the academic discipline in which it is embedded. This is especially challenging in settings where students with disabilities are fully included for the entire day, widening the gap between the performance of the individual and that of the collective.

The purpose of this chapter is to explore several ideas related to a research program designed to enhance students' knowledge about literacy. This program, the Literacy Environments for Accelerated Progress (LEAP), was a multi-year intervention that focused on providing access to the discourses, social practices, tools, and artifacts of readers and writers. On the LEAP project, it was our goal to construct and investigate effective teaching practices that served students with disabilities in both resource room and inclusion settings. Students with disabilities are a group for whom educational progress and success have been

Social Constructivist Teaching, Volume 9, pages 81–130.
ISBN: 0-7623-0873-7

particularly problematic, thus, necessitating the importance of developing effective teaching to support those students most at-risk for school failure. In this chapter, we present three instructional snapshots to illustrate what we mean by "best practices" within a sociocultural perspective, the nature of discourse and artifacts in different instructional arrangements, and the dilemmas and issues that arise from employing the teaching practices of a sociocultural model. Our intention for presenting these instructional snapshots is to explore what social constructivist teaching means for the teaching of writing, and especially, what forms that these methods can take for the effective instruction of students with disabilities.

Emphases on cognitive apprenticeship provided the basis for the design and implementation of the intervention that constituted the Literacy Environments for Accelerated Progress Project. Our notion of cognitive apprenticeship was grounded in the sociocultural literature, most notably, Vygotsky's (1978) work. Vygotsky (1978) suggested that the mechanism that supports the transfer of responsibility from the social level (cognitive processes shared by participants) to the individual level (processes directed by individuals) resides in the mediation of activity through verbal or nonverbal signs modeled by an adult or more knowledgeable other (Stone, 1993). This sociocultural model has been elaborated with recent emphases on the role of cognitive apprenticeships in a community of practice that helps novices acquire, participate in, and contribute to the values, attitudes, discourses and practices shared by and lived out by members of the community (Gee, 1995; Lave & Wenger, 1996; Rogoff, 1995). There were five central ideas that framed the core of the project's literacy approach, and that informed our assumptions about teaching and learning.

First, we viewed artifacts and tools as mediators of human thought and behavior in the context of human activity (Nardi, 1996). Mediational tools include language, written symbols, diagrams, writing implements, signs, procedures, rules of thumb, and any tool used in the transformation and construction process (Wetsch, 1995). A person's mental process is influenced by such mediational tools, and simultaneously, the nature of tools is shaped by the history of the individual's use of such tools. Examination of learning, therefore, requires attention to ways in which the broader culture promotes the acquisition, adaptation and transformation of the cognitive, physical and symbolic tools associated with literate activity.

Second, we emphasized the role of teachers in providing cognitive apprenticeships in the context of situated writing activity. Tools cannot be understood in isolation from the social activity which give meaning to their function within a specific set of events (Nardi, 1996). The meaning of the writing tools, the mental and physical actions related to the tools, and their integration in a larger task are brought into focus in the context of their goal-directed use in the performance of an activity (Hutchins, 1997; Roth, 1998). There is both an external and internal side of activity in which overt actions are directed and informed by covert thought processes. The internal aspects of writing entail a planfulness and a set of executive routines that help writers identify, coordinate, monitor and make explicit to a distant audience the connections, organization, meaning and cohesion among ideas embedded in extended and lengthy utterances. Such collective practices are not reducible to sums of individual acts, but must be rooted in the situated context of the full activity in order to be understood and mastered in their entirety (Engestrom, Miettinen, Punamaki, 1999). Therefore, an examination of cognitive apprenticeship must examine how teachers orchestrate the cognitive and social learning environments, and the mediational resources they bring to bear on the activity setting.

Correspondingly, our approach to literacy teaching encompassed ways in which teachers might make explicit the way language and tools work to create texts and meanings. The failure of schooling might be conceived as lack of opportunities to co-participate in the practice, to hear the discourse and inner speech associated with tool use, to see practice-related principles and tools in action, including the false starts, waverings, impasses and renunciations, and to observe the corrections that address situated problems in the ebb and flow of constructive activity (Roth & McRobbie, 1999). This is especially true for written language, which requires a considerable degree of abstraction, metalinguistic awareness, self-monitoring, problem-solving and directing of one's thought processes (Wells, 1999). We sought to devise a teaching approach that would make visible these written language practices and conventions, showing what kinds of social situations and discourses produced written artifacts, the interactive play between mental and physical actions with respect to the construction and revision of artifacts, and the relationship between various text forms and the communicative or social functions for which they were intended (Kress, 1993). Teacher modeling of deliberate analytical action (Vygostky, 1978), and conscious attention to the craft, tools, resources, symbols, actions, discourses, text genres, inner speech, and mental operations that built the written texts lay at the core of the project's instructional framework (Englert & Mariage, 1996). Simultaneously, the process of constructing textual artifacts provided instructional obects-to-think-with and objects-to-talk-with as young writers were apprenticed in the language functions and codified procedures associated with print (Roth, 1998).

Third, the teaching of writing entailed the creation of and participation within a community of practice composed of several interrelated layers. One layer encompassed the classroom culture with the norms, rules and relationships that defined what it meant to participate as a member in the community, and the various ways in which the members coordinated and distributed their individual cognitions and abilities to achieve a collective or shared goal related to writing (Bellamy, 1996). The second layer encompassed the participation of the members in a broader collective of writers and readers in the culture at large, with the system of interpersonal involvements and arrangements in which people engage in any culturally organized activity (Rogoff, 1995). There exists an inherent and reciprocal connection between individual and collective activity within the local context, and the broader literate culture and systems of relations within which the activity is valued and expressed. This attention to social configuration and shared forms of life within the local and broader sociocultural contexts supports the establishment of a learning environment in which teachers seek to help individuals fashion their personal and academic identities in the local community, and by extension, positioning themselves and their texts with respect to the knowledge, texts, and practices of others outside the group.

Fourth, a cognitive apprenticeship model requires teacher attention to the flux of ongoing human activity and the manner in which learners acquire problem-solving processes within a responsive and developmental process of knowledge acquisition (Nardi, 1996). Beginning writers, like other novices in an apprenticeship situation, are enculturated into the social practices of a sociocultural group in ways that ensure that they have their attention focused on the right aspects of the task through interaction with "more knowledgeable members or masters" (Gee, 1992). What initially is too difficult for novices to accomplish alone is gradually acquired working side by side with more knowledgeable members as beginners move from peripheral participation to central participation in the performance of the various events, tools, and processes associated with an activity (Bellamy, 1996; Wenger, 1998). With their movement to perform more central roles and tasks, novices assume greater responsibility for the social languages and practices previously practiced and modeled by experts or more knowledgeable others.

What is considered as part of one's mental life, therefore, is actually part of one's "social life" (Toulmin, 1999), constructed and shared in the collective activities experienced by individuals as part of their social interactions with others in the public domain (Toulmin, 1999). There exists an inherent reciprocity in an apprenticeship model, involving finely tuned and scaffolded adjustments by teachers as they step in to provide additional information when it is necessary for a learner to extend his/her behavioral repertoire, while stepping-back and removing support when a student is able to accomplish facets of the task unassisted. Through the collective participation of all members in the activity, communication and coordination of the writing activity is stretched among the various participants to reflect a heteroglossia of languages and distributed practices available to all members through interactions with others. In these interpersonal and collaborative arrangements, students work at the outer edges of their competence while receiving the social mediation and support that ensures their increasing mastery of the discourse and higher psychological processes associated with written literacy. Mental thought and literate practices are always reflective of the dialogic and social processes in which they originated.

THE LITERACY ENVIRONMENTS FOR ACCELERATED PROGRESS PROJECT

To summarize, the implications of the sociocultural literature led the research team to develop teaching emphases and teaching-learning contexts that provided:

- cognitive apprenticeships that supported novices in the participation and performance of a discipline, including the acquisition of the discourses, tools, and actions;
- collaborative arrangements and activity spaces that allowed students with disabilities to develop greater mastery, control and ownership of the conventions, discourses and practices of the community;
- scaffolds and mediational tools that supported learners in advance of independent performance while allowing students to outgrow the supports over time (Stone, in press);
- explicit instruction and the modeling of reasoning and metacognition in the situated problem-solving context of a content area subject (as opposed to decontextualized skill or strategy instruction).

We felt that these principles were especially valuable in special education contexts because students with disabilities are thought to benefit from ongoing interaction in which an adult provides carefully calibrated assistance at the child's' leading edge of competence (Stone, 1998). However, the process of providing such calibrated assistance requires a great deal of expertise on the part of the teacher in several respects (Stone, in press), including their mastery and competence in three interrelated areas: (a) expertise in modeling the curriculum, tools, practices and abstract processes of writing; (b) expertise in creating instructional dialogues that both challenge and support students in the construction of written texts; and (c) ability to responsively instruct students and to provide graduated assistance with respect to their evolving writing knowledge. These complexities take time for teachers to accomplish, particularly in light of the challenges of making moment-to-moment instructional decisions based upon the dynamic assessment of both individual and collective knowledge.

The purpose of this chapter is to investigate the complexities and dilemmas related to teaching within a sociocultural perspective that featured cognitive apprenticeship. We undertook an exploration of instructional discourse in three situational contexts to investigate the complexities and dilemmas related to teaching within a sociocultural perspective that featured cognitive apprenticeship. Given the six year nature of the LEAP project, we exploited this longitudinal feature to explore the changing nature of a teacher's participation in the instructional discourse, the changing nature of lesson artifacts over time, and the role of student participation in peer collaborative discourse. We focused on writing instruction because of its prominent role in the LEAP curriculum. There were four questions that informed our exploration: (1) How does an effective teacher apprentice her students in the discourses and tools of skilled writers, and to what extent does the apprenticeship reflect transformation of the teacher's and students' roles across time? (2) How does the teacher's content coverage, instructional practices, and discourse moves reflect her deepening awareness of the apprenticeship and scaffolding process? (3) What is the nature of discourse in whole class and peer-mediated collaborative spaces, and how do these instructional spaces influence student participation and knowledge acquisition? (4) How does the teacher support students with disabilities in the unfolding discussion? In answering these questions, it was our intention to expose the teaching practices associated with constructivist teaching, the ways in which these methods are implemented during writing instruction, and what might be involved in implementing them successfully with diverse learners.

BACKGROUND OF THE ACTIVITY CONTEXT

The exploration of the dilemmas of cognitive apprenticeship was undertaken in an activity called Morning or Personal News, which afforded a unique vantage point for the study of the balance between leading development and transferring control of skills to students, as well as the role of scaffolds and collaborative arrangements. In Personal News, a student recounts an experience or event, which is then jointly transformed and composed by the class into a written text.

The content comprising the news stories are drawn from personal activities and experiences (Christie, 1993), which are often elicited by questions to the author presented by student audience members. The power of the personal news genre lies in its capacity for teachers to model the use of language to represent and reconstruct experience for the benefit of people not present when the events occurred (Christie, 1993). This representational function is a unique feature of written language that is important for school learning, and that develops through the guided intervention or scaffolding on the part of adults (Christie, 1993).

Throughout the Personal News activity, the teacher acts as a scribe for the class in recording the group's ideas, although the group jointly negotiates and collaborates to transform the narrative or spontaneous form of oral language related to one's personal experience into the "language of written text." Teachers and students progressively refine the ideas, as they gradually construct forms of literacy progressively more distant from the immediacy and informality of the grammar of speech (Cope & Kalantzis, 1993). Important to make visible in this process is the set of mental and linguistic transformations by which inner speech and thought are generated from experience, and the transformations in the opposite direction, by which private thought and speech for oneself become publicly communicable through linguistic, symbolic, and codified transformations associated with written language (Cazden, 1996). The juxtaposing of oral and written texts can help students see the characteristic features and functions of each, and how a type of text might exploit the conventions of a particular genre (Morgan, 1997). The process of recording experience and ideas in a written artifact congeal and reify the experience and related practices into "thingness" (Wenger, 1998). Simultaneously, teachers make the rules of discourse and inquiry explicit and visible to students as oral texts are negotiated and transformed into written texts in front of students.

There are added benefits to participating in the social discourse related to writing in the Personal News activity. Reading and writing, especially, are inherently social activities since writers and readers are in relationships with each other (Luke & Freebody, 1997). Likewise, through repeated participation, speakers and listeners enter a dialectical relationship which can lead them to begin to anticipate another's utterances, questions, and perspectives, paralleling the interactions between the author and reader or audience. Experiencing first-hand the responsive dialogue between speakers and listeners lays the foundation for turning the social discourse inward to mediate their own writing actions and thoughts as they construct a dialogic sphere with their text and their envisaged audience. Ultimately, the collaborative progressive discourse is essential since the internalization and transformation of this discourse enables the writer to dialogue with his/her emerging text as well as with the distant 'posited' audience and reader, interfacing in a symbolic and dialectical way with the community for whom the text is intended (Wells, 1999).

Finally, the emphasis on the oral discourse lends itself to another feature of Personal News that renders it a rich site for the study of apprenticeship. The public nature of texts and language makes visible to teachers their individual students' zones of proximal development – the distance between what students can accomplish alone and that which can be accomplished through the joint and inter-mental interaction of learners and other people cooperating in the activity (Wells, 1999). The degree of support provided by the teacher depends on the level of competence demonstrated by students, and teacher's responsive assistance must foster students' participation in the discourse by improving students' instrumental knowledge (e.g. knowledge of the use of tools or conventions to mediate their activity), procedural knowledge (e.g. the specific actions or sequence of steps related to instrumental knowledge), and substantive knowledge (e.g. the ability to explain, justify, and coordinate one's actions through explanation) (Wells, 1999). This type of 'metaknowing' is assessed and promoted when teachers investigate what children reflect on when they act, and why they think as they do.

CONTENT COVERAGE: WHAT IS TAUGHT

As was mentioned, a central feature of a sociocultural model of cognitive development is that all thinking is rooted in the physical, mental and symbolic tools of the collective as they engage in goal oriented activity. It is important, therefore, to attend to the ways in which teachers construct discourse communities within their classroom where linguistic tools and social interaction patterns mediate the participation of individuals within the collective activity. Assuming that cognitive apprenticeship is a challenging task, we expected that there should be changes in the instructional discourse as teachers on the project progressed from being a novice in the teaching practices to being an acknowledged expert in the discourse. By studying a 'master teacher's' instructional profile at two points in time (early and late in the project), we hoped to gain insight into what apprenticeship means in practical settings, what curricular content is encapsulated in the instructional discourse, what teaching practices characterize expertise, and how expertise is reflected in the nature of teacher and student talk. A central goal of this section is to analyze the relationship between a teacher's developing expertise at using talk strategically and the extent to which her students with disabilities were more fully supported in a wider range of discursive roles and cognitive routines. Such an investigation would shed light on the question of to what degree the social constructivist methods might be used by a novice teacher, and how a teacher's deepening knowledge might be reflected in changing teaching forms and methods.

In the first exploration (Englert & Dunsmore, 2000), we examined the curriculum content coverage of a special education teacher in her first year of participation in the project, and then six years later, when she had become an expert and master in the instructional routines, as acknowledged by her peer teachers and project leaders. In both years, there were the same approximate number of special education students (e.g. 12–15 students) in her classroom, although in the sixth year she was teaching in a multi-age classroom with 34 general and special education students. We transcribed the videotapes and coded each interaction according to the specific curricular objectives that were addressed within the writing lesson.

When we coded the teacher's curricular coverage during the two lessons, the results revealed a decided expansion of the content coverage across the teacher's years of participation on the project. Figure 1 shows the results of this analysis.

In her first year of participation, the teacher covered 6 content categories using 22 content-related moves, whereas in the sixth year, the teacher covered 18 content categories using 76 content-related moves. Moreover, the teacher had progressed from an early emphasis on the basic mechanics of writing (e.g. editing, periods, grammar, and genre) to a more complicated set of instructions

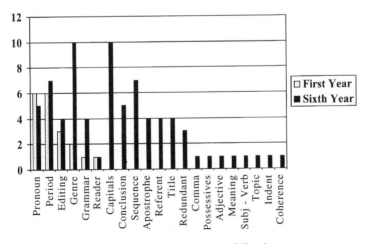

Fig. 1. Content Coverage of Teacher.

related to the conventions and the codified features of written language (e.g. apostrophes, possessives, title), as well as to the writing practices entailing the development of structurally- and topically-developed written texts (e.g. referents, sequencing, genre, conclusion, redundancy, coherence, topic sentence). Clearly, the teacher had expanded her content coverage threefold as her expertise in teaching writing had deepened.

The two instructional texts produced during the two lessons illustrate the expansion in the teacher's content coverage, as shown in Figs 2 and 3. Both instructional texts are nine sentences in length, but the earlier Lemoy Story (Fig. 2) shows a fairly narrow focus on the replacement of first-person pronouns with third-person impersonal pronouns or proper names. The teacher adds a topic sentence to the Lemoy Story, but the story does not adhere to this focus, as illustrated by an abrupt shift in topic from Lemoy's new toys (beginning of story) to his desk (end of story).

In contrast, the later text is filled with genre features that provide attentional devices that point the readers forward to the elements of the story, including the teacher's and students' attention to the story title, topic sentence, concluding sentence, sequencing and redundancy. Interestingly, it is apparent that the class generated multiple titles and concluding sentences, and the students are engaged in process of decision making with respect to these alternatives as indicated by the circling of a specific choice. At the top of the paper, the teacher and students listed question words that guided their social interactions during the activity and that represented a rubric for the personal experience genre: "Who, What, When, Where, How, Why." The story adheres to this genre through the group's specific reference to who ("Annie, David, Shamaque, cousins, Annie's family);

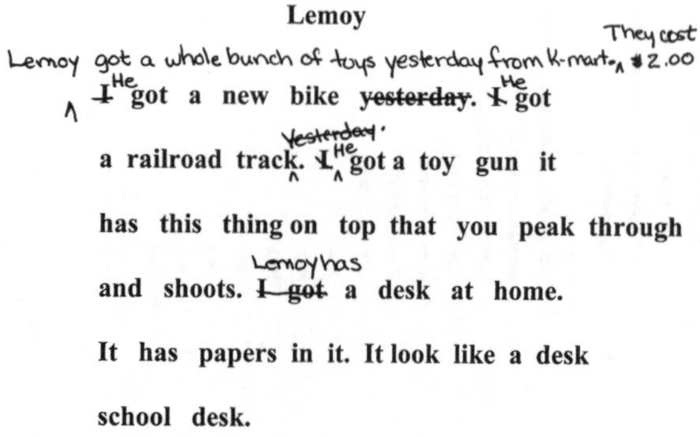
Lemoy

Lemoy got a whole bunch of toys yesterday from K-mart. They cost $2.00

~~I~~ He got a new bike ~~yesterday~~. ~~I~~ He got

a railroad track yesterday. ~~I~~ He got a toy gun it

has this thing on top that you peak through

and shoots. ~~I got~~ Lemoy has a desk at home.

It has papers in it. It look like a desk

school desk.

Fig. 2. First Year Personal News Story.

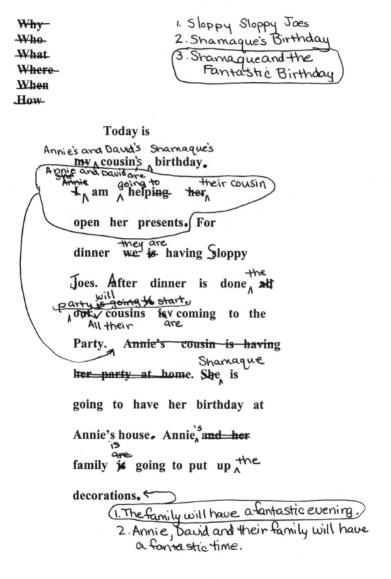

Fig. 3.   Whole Class Personal News.

what (birthday party, open presents, eat dinner); where (Annie's house); and How (family, putting up decorations). They also have addressed specific problems related to sequencing and redundancy, as indicated by the fact that they have rearranged and deleted sentences to conform to the evolving text structure. As a collective, therefore, the students seem to be exhibiting a growing greater sophistication in constructing a "situation" that they convey through the whole text and through the deliberate structuring of language (Scribner, 1997) to communicate the situation to their audience. Nevertheless, the class does not neglect the basic skills, as reflected in their attention to apostrophes, periods, capital letters, and commas.

Simply looking at the visual features of the stories suggests differences in the extent to which the teacher was able to represent a wider breadth of actions that writers take with respect to the codification process related to the transformation of oral speech into written text. There are 10 transformations to the earlier text, whereas there are 43 changes or manipulations to the later text. Thus, there is a greater exploitation of the features of written language and there is evidence of a process of instrumentality through which the members have worked to pursue specific language ends. If thought is expressed in language and language is objectified in writing (Scribner, 1997), then it seemed that the teacher had become more proficient in guiding her class to "stand back" as authors to subject their ideas to a critical "second look" (p. 167).

TEACHING PRACTICES: HOW IS WRITING TAUGHT?

Written artifacts, as an instrumental entity created in social contexts, are fundamentally the result of a dialogic process. That is, changes to the text should be reflective of a dialogic process (Artiles, Trent, Hoffman-Kipp & Lopez-Torres, 2000). Thus, we sought to examine the frequency and nature of the types of discourse moves, as well as to apply classification schemes that featured the apprenticeship positions of students and the teacher in the activity. We were interested in exploring whether the nature of their participation changed over time.

In the first part of this examination, we counted the number of teaching moves that indicated the teacher's leadership and expert status in the activity, as indicated by the occurrence of teaching events where the teacher modeled, offered explanations, or prompted students following incorrect or partly correct answers as part of a process of teaching or scaffolding students' knowledge about writing. These moves signified occasions when the teacher took the lead, demonstrating her authority over the information, process, or knowledge, and responsively interacting with students to form more complete knowledge. These were called "step-in" moves.

Simultaneously, we examined "step-back" moves – moves that repositioned the students in central roles where they were asked to assert their authority or mastery over the content. These included moves in which the teachers asked students to explain (e.g. what to do, how to do it, when it should be done, and why), to offer opinions about what to change or revise, to engage in decision making about the text, or called upon students to direct the writing process. These moves entailed the teacher's efforts to transfer control of the writing tools, practices, and discourse to students.

The two categories of moves were applied by coding their occurrence in the lessons corresponding to the texts in Figs 2 and 3. The results revealed striking differences in the apprenticeship positions of the teacher and students over time, as shown in Fig. 4 (Englert & Dunsmore, 2000). Summing across all separate teaching moves, the number of step-in moves increased from 11 to 30 over time. At the same time, the number of step-back moves increased from a total of 7 in the first lesson, to a total of 62 in the lesson six years later. Clearly,

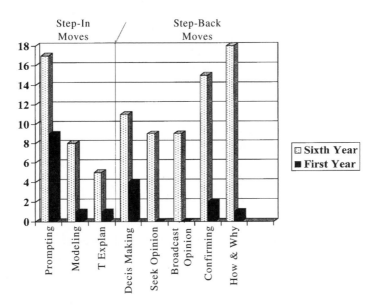

Fig. 4.

the greatest change in practice was that which involved the teacher stepping back from leadership roles that she had formerly occupied to allow her students to assume more central roles of participation and authority. With this conferral of authoritative status and regulatory functions to students, the teacher seemed to reposition students as central players in the activity corresponding to the position of "experts and master craftsmen".

Before describing the nature of the apprenticeship process, it is helpful to examine the instructional transcripts of the Personal News lessons at the two points in time. In the earlier lesson, the teacher steps in to cue students, for example, to add symbolic marks to their written texts (e.g. period), but the rhetorical nature of her questions does not require students to use the discourse, tools, or practices of writers to name the event or to utilize the decisions implemented by writers as they participate in the written language events.

T: (*Recording and reading the text provided by the author aloud*) "I got a new bike yesterday. I got a railroad track". (*To class*) Now, do we need to add a period (pointing to the end of the words "railroad track")?
Ss: Uh-huh.
T: (*Adds a period*). Do we need to add a period after: "*I got a new bike yesterday*"?
Class: Yeah.
T: Yeah. That's the end of our sentence. (*Reads what she has written down for the MM so far*) I got a new bike yesterday. I got a railroad track. (*Some students have their hands in the air*) Put your hands down until we're ready for questions.
Lemoy: I got a toy gun and it has this thing on it.
T: (*Writing*) I got a toy gun, what else did you say I got a toy gun . . .
Lemoy: and it has this thing on the top of it that you spy through to shoot.
T: (*Writing and saying the words aloud*) . . . and it has this . . .
.
.
.
Lemoy: thing you peak through and it shoots.
T: (*Teacher recording the text*) and it shoots. Boy that's a long sentence. Do we need a period?
Lemoy: no a caret.
T: Are we going to add anything on top right now? (*Pause*)
T: No so we need to put in our . . .
Lemoy: period.

In this segment, the teacher undertakes the preponderance of the intellectual work of the actions and language associated with writing, as she names the writing tools and practices (e.g. period) and the associated conditions associated with it (end of the sentence). In essence, she performs the aspects of the process associated with the "knowing" and "doing of writing", as she cues students to the "what they need to do, when they do it, how they do it, and why". However, the features of the text that qualify a particular segment as a "sentence", and the situational conditions under which periods are employed are not fully explained or modeled by the teacher. Similarly, when students suggest changes, she simply adds the information to the text without modeling or asking students to think aloud about the mental process involved behind the actions. Thus, the internal aspects of mental thought associated with external actions were not revealed through the teacher or student talk. Overall, the character of her Step-in moves were less effective than what they might be under different teaching circumstances, and there were few Step-back moves that required students direct and monitor the writing process. Not surprisingly, Lemoy does not understand the elements in their entirety, as suggested by the fact that he suggests to the teacher that she add a caret to the text rather than a period – an action that he mistakenly suggests at another point later in the lesson.

Another goal for teacher talk is to lead students' zones of proximal development within the context of problem-solving activity. Students need opportunities to take up the communication and coordination of activity within the context of the teacher-directed lesson. In this lesson, the teacher actually discourages the spontaneous moves of students who bid for the floor to offer suggestions and feedback within the context of the evolving text. Thus, she doesn't respond to students' zones of proximal development that emerged during the course of the lesson. She tells the students early in the segment to hold their ideas ("Put your hands down until we're ready for questions"), and for the remainder of the segment, she does not invite them to offer their ideas. Inadvertently, by trying to control the timing of student talk, she diminishes the spontaneity of problem-solving in the context of generating and rereading text, which is one of the quintessential characteristics of teaching writing in an apprenticeship model. This is especially problematic for students with disabilities, who often need to make immediate changes to text when they hear discordant or unclear ideas. To delay the problem-solving process for such students may cause them to lose track of the text problem and their suggested text remedies. To work in the zones of proximal development of students is to respond to their ideas and create deeper levels of understanding at the sites of students' confusions and questions. Thus, she does not model writing practices and tools in the context of situated problem-solving activity.

Finally, it is apparent that she does not allow students to articulate the reasoning and explanations required for the various actions made to the text. In her zeal to foster errorless learning, she overprompts the students to the point where they do not need to understand the principles of the various writing conventions (e.g. periods) in order to answer the teacher's questions. She seems uncomfortable with the possibility of student errors and how she might respond in the context of their mistakes. Several studies point to low expectations of educators for the future accomplishments of students with learning disabilities, which can be related to teaching interactions which are more directive and less challenging (Bryan, 1998; Stone, in press; Stone & Conca, 1993). Yet by not engaging students in the meaning of the writing tools through the advancement of both the external and internal sides of writing activity, the teacher does not promote the development of executive routines that might help students learn to coordinate, monitor and construct the meaning and cohesion among ideas.

Six years later, the character of personal news had changed dramatically, shaped by the altered quality of teacher and student interactions. The segment below was taken from a transcription of the personal news lesson corresponding to the written artifact shown in Fig. 2. Annie, the author, is recounting a birthday party for her cousin.

T: Let's re-read it. (Class reads text as teacher points to each word: "Today is my cousin birthday").
T: Barb has a thumbs down.
Barb: It's not my cousin. It's Annie's cousin.
T: So what should we do?
Barb: Cross out my and put Annie's.
T: You said Annie's? How do I change Annie into Annie's?
Barb: Put apostrophe s
T: *Because her cousin belongs . . . ?*
Barb: Belongs to Annie.
T: *(Re-reading text and pointing to words)*: Today is Annie's cousin birthday.
Nem: Put an apostrophe s on cousin.
T: *Why?*
Nem: Because . . . . It's Annie's cousin.
T: So whose birthday is it?
Nem: Her cousin, Shana.
T: Today is Annie's **cousin's** birthday. So you want me to add something right here? *(points to location in text)*. How do I add something to our writing? *(re-reading)*.
.
.
.
T: *(re-reading with class)*. I am helping her open her presents. Amy.
Amy: Annie is going to help her open her presents.
T: So what do I need to do?
Amy: Cross out 'I am', put a caret, and put Annie is going to help . . .
T: [Records changes and then rereads the revised sentence]. Annie is going to help helping her open her presents.
Amy: No. No 'ing' . . .
T: (No) 'ing' on 'go'?
Amy: Annie is **going** to **help**.
T: So I need the word "to" [adds the word to the text]
T: Annie is going to help . . . I need to take off the "ing" (from help). Annie is going to help her open her presents. Confusing, isn't it? What do you think, Dan?

Dan: [inaudible] Cross out. . . [Inaudible] It sounds like Annie is going to open her own presents.
T: How can we clear that up? 'Cause I'm thinking the same thing.
Dan: Cross out "her" and the other "her" and put Annie.
T: So it says, "Annie is going to help . . .
Dan: her cousin.
T: You want me to add "her cousin"? Since we have space, I'll add it right there. Annie is going to help her cousin open her presents.
T: Two thumbs up. Jack, you don't think so.
Jack: It's two Annies. Cross out the second one and put "she".

In this lesson, the text serves as a critical site for apprenticing students in the problem solving realities of generating and monitoring text production. The continual rereading of the text by the teacher allowed students to participate in a process of interrogating the text (Morgan, 1997), coordinating the reciprocal processes of reading and writing within a recursive process of text production, comprehension and revision. Students self-identified text breakdowns or problems and based upon their evaluations, prompted the group to coordinate the process of text repair. Text, therefore, served a dialogic function, becoming what Lotman (1988) called a "thinking device" and a "generator of meaning" (Wells, 2000), linking and mediating readers' and writers' talk, thoughts, gestures, and actions. Their problem-solving activities in the construction of the written artifact provided a critical site for synchronizing the joint cognitive, dialogic, and social activity of the participants, providing constraints and opportunities that shaped their collective behavior, thoughts and responses. The activity takes on a unique rhythm, moving between the personal ideas and texts contributed by Barb, Nem, Annie, Dan, and Jack. The end result is a text filled with notes and representational devices that reified the repairs undertaken to address the misalignment of meaning and that served as a record of the history of students' participation (Wenger, 1998). This is an especially important process for students with learning disabilities, who often fail to detect comprehension failures, fail to ask for clarification of ambiguous statements, and who lack fix-up strategies (Donahue, 1984; Wong, 1979; 1980).

The step-back moves of the teacher were another interesting technique that the teacher employed to apprentice her students in the sociocultural practices of the community, and which might have provided the backdrop that provoked the self-initiations of students. One example of a teaching move was the direct request of the teacher for students to *direct the writing process*. When students identified a problem, the teacher responded by saying "So what should I do?" or "How do I . . ." or "How can we clear that up?". This multi-faceted doublemove created reversible role relations: it simultaneously positioned the teacher in the role of the apprentice or novice, and repositioned her students as the experts who provided direction to the group's actions (Mariage, 1995). By so doing, the teacher inducted her students into the "doing" or "performing" of specific writing practices, and transformed their inner speech and covert writing practices into a public context where other students might access information about the external and internal sides of writing activity. When the student above, for example, responded by saying: "It sounds like Annie is going to open her own presents . . . . Cross out "her" and the other "her" and put "Annie"", not only was the student appropriating the discourse and forms associated with "being a writer", she served to apprentice others by making the questions, language and practices of the writing community transparent (Mariage, 1995). Many of the students who offered explanations were students with learning disabilities, which further deepened their knowledge of the writing process and provided opportunities for them to exercise the self-directive employment of academic talk and skills (Biemiller & Meichenbaum, 1998).

The teacher's provision of opportunities for her students to construct their own ways of attacking problems which then were shared with the rest of the class, revealed that there were multiple ways for reaching problem resolutions (Jukubowski, 1993). Rather than simply 'tell students about writing', the teacher used a discourse and participation structure that involved students directly in the doing of the writing enterprise and that initiated them into the specialized forms of writing discourse (Roth, 1993, 1998). Forman and Cazden (1985) argue that for optimal learning, students must have opportunities to reverse the interactional roles so that they teach, give directions, and ask questions. Scribner (1997), too, suggests that for the acquisition of written language, children must assume roles in which they "direct the writing process, participate in it actively and intentionally, and keep it under conscious control" (p. 170). Although several authors suggest that the primary context in which this goal can be attained is working with peers or working one-on-one with the teacher (Stone, 1998; Roth, 1998), this instructional episode suggests that teachers can design whole class activities that offer apprenticeship opportunities for constructing meaning and that transform traditional teachers' and students' participation roles. Simultaneously, the students' collective contributions can push and position the teacher to bring increasingly more sophisticated writing forms and tools into the writing curriculum.

A related type of step-back moves involved teacher solicitations for explanations or justifications of students' positions (e.g. "Why do we indent?" "Why do we need to capitalize?)". Although these moves might have sounded like the teacher was testing knowledge, in actuality, these moves represented opportunities for students to communicate their command of the writing discourse and to engage in a type of metatalk related to the conditional or executive knowledge about when writers use specific tools and why. In fact, a parallel type of talk occurs between apprentices and experts when the apprentice presents the expert with questions pertaining to "why" a particular tool or practice is used. The answers to such questions provides local access to the embodied knowledge of the experts in the community (Roth, 1998). Envisioning expertise as an intellectual endpoint, the teacher used the evolving text, artifacts, and discourse to ask questions that supported students' participation in a type of 'shop talk' or 'laboratory talk' that brought them more deeply into an understanding of their writing craft (Roth, 1998). In the resultant dialogue, the teacher could make more explicit how texts and writing tools work; how texts situate and manipulate readers; and why linguistic techniques can be used by writers for different effects and purposes.

Simultaneously, student discourse afforded the teacher the opportunity to study how writers went about writing tasks, and by what operations they solved writing problems. As Leont'ev suggests, (1981, p. 76), "If the persons training a child see themselves the goal of imparting knowledge and pay little attention to how the child itself goes about it, by what operations it solves the school problems it has been set, and does not check whether a further transformation is taking place at the proper time in these operations their development can be disturbed!" To study 'how the child goes about a task', is to reveal the actual nature of the underlying process and the situations that might provoke further development. This type of metaknowing is assessed and promoted when teachers investigate why writers think as they do and what writers reflect on when they act. The participation structure of the activity provided teachers with on-going information about children's knowledge and skills. At the same time, the types of teaching moves that support this knowledge construction process are applied differently for different students, and are not known by teachers a prioi. This is why the creation of zones of proximal development and related dynamic opportunities assessment is a challenging and complex task for teachers.

Through these various types of step-back moves (asking students to direct, calling for explanations), the teacher accomplished six critical teaching-learning objectives aligned with cognitive apprenticeship and social constructivist models of teaching: (1) inducted students into talking about writing practices and using their knowledge authoritatively in the situated writing context; (2) positioned students to defend their ideas and articulate their thinking, thereby transferring control to students for explaining, describing, and doing; (3) created opportunities for students to apprentice others by providing them occasions to provide labels and conventionalize writing practices; (4) supported self-regulation by fostering a type of 'metatalk' and 'metaknowledge' that helped students articulate and understand the "what", "how", "when" and "why" that would enable them to employ skills as strategies (Duffy & Roehler, 1987a, 1987b); (5) created sites for the assessment of students' knowledge and understanding of the social language and practices of writers; and (6) challenged students to think for themselves, and promoted their understanding of writing as a problem-solving endeavor in which all members can participate. These objectives are of particular importance for students with learning disabilities given their potential to alter the learner's executive responsibility for his/her employment of the discourse, skills and strategies of writers, and to budge learners from passive to active positions in the text construction process (Biemiller & Meichembaum, 1998).

Within a social constructivist model of apprenticeship, however, explicit instruction by experts are central tools for mediating learning. In this lesson, the teacher assumed an active role as coach and facilitator when students experienced difficulties by stepping-in to provide assistance in ways that were calibrated to students' developmental needs. Thus, the teacher was always adjusting her instructional methods and the writing curriculum in order to satisfy the limitations exposed to her by the students' problem-solving actions. The teacher also scaffolded in more direct ways through the provision of graduated assistance that was specifically calibrated to an individual student's confusion or difficulty. When students struggled with new concepts during the Personal News activity, the teacher did not turn the problem over to another student, but instead, supported that student until some successful conclusion was reached that was within the reach of the student's developmental abilities. This type of floor-holding created an important message to students that conveyed her high expectations for them, as well as promoted their academic self-efficiency and persistence. In the segment below, for example, the teacher struggled to support Stan, a first-grade student with learning disabilities, who had mistakenly appropriated the notion of apostrophe as he tries to understand its use. When he offers the explanation that the apostrophe should be added because it's the name of a food, the teacher artfully orchestrates a series of interactions to resolve the dilemma in a way that will respect Stan's contributions and advance his knowledge.

> T: (Re-reading). For dinner they are having sloppy joes. Stan?
> Stan: Put an apostrophe s behind the sloppy joes because it is the *name* of a food.
> T: That's interesting. If it's a *name*, it needs a what?
> Stan: Apostrophe s.
> T: Hmmm .... When you write your *name*, what do you do at the beginning of yours?
> Stan: S.

T: What kind of an S.
Stan: Capital s.
T: 'Cause *names* need . . .
Stan: [No answer].
T: Cause names need . . . *What kind of letter? Apostrophe s is if you belong to somebody.*
Do the sloppy joes belong to somebody?
Stan: No.
T: So we don't need an apostrophe s. (*Speaking to another child*) That would be your
warning. We don't laugh at anybody else in the classroom. So it doesn't need an
apostrophe s, Stan, but it is the name of a food and names need.
Stan: Food? (softly).
T: No, not food. But *names need . . . What does your name need?*
Stan: Stan. S-T-A-M.
T: "What kind of 's' does it need?
Stan: Capital S?
T: So *names need capital letters.* So, this *name needs . . .*
Stan: A capital letter.
T: Yes, so we'll put . . . a capital s on "sloppy" and a capital 'j' on "joes." Thank you, Stan
. . . . Good job! For dinner, they are having sloppy joes.

What was interesting about this set of interactions was that Stan seemed to
have appropriated the discourse stance of offering an explanation because he
automatically provided an explanation at the outset ("put an apostrophe s behind
the sloppy joes because it is the *name* of a food.") The teacher moved
to legitimate his suggestion through a series of moves. Recognizing that
apostrophes were beyond his developmental grasp, she began to shape his
understanding and the subsequent revision of the text at the level where he
could develop new writing understandings (capitalization of names). She
calibrated her instruction at a level close enough to his understanding to capture
his interest and participation (Stone, 1998). First, she started by simply asking
Stan "If it's a name, it needs a what?" When Stan continued to misapply the
concept (apostrophe s), the teacher hesitated while she thought (e.g. Hmmmm),
then she discovered a way to link his concept to something familiar (his own
name), by asking him: When you write your name, what do you do at the
beginning of yours?" When this question did not elicit the correct response,
she narrowed the range of responses through a specific prompt ('Cause names
need . . .) and by specifically distinguishing the case from possessive cases
(Apostrophe s is if you belong to somebody). Finally, she constructed a series
of prompts to elicit the type of information that could be used to amend the
text and that would enable him to take part in the task (Holzman, 1996): "What
does your name need? . . . What kind of "s" does it need . . . . So names need
capital letters. So, this name needs . . . ." In this manner, the teacher provided

a titration of assistance that was associated with genuine scaffolding (Stone, 1998) to help him accomplish the goal (Stone, 1998). The teacher sensitively geared demands and instruction to the child's abilities and achievements, by staying one step ahead and focusing on aspects of the task that lay just beyond the level that the child had attained (Schaffer, 1996).

The segment also reveals a type of teaching discourse used to support students in what might be referred to as a joint involvement episode (JIE) (Schaffer, 1996). There is the quality of an interlocking discourse in which the teacher provided the first half of the discourse, and the student provided the second part. Like a dance, their understanding was constructed interpsychologically (Roth, 1993; Stone, 1998), arising from the joint involvement and moment-to-moment interactions between the two participants. With his teacher's assistance, Stan was involved in the active process of constructing new knowledge at the precise moment of his confusion. The support was scaffolded insofar as it was contingent on his current understanding, it afforded him a hierarchy of prompts that were minimally discrepant from the previously provided prompt, and prompts became more specific in response to failure or confusion (Stone, in press). Although this graduated assistance was a regular feature of the participation structure constructed by the teacher in her writing lessons, ordinary classrooms do not typically present such one-on-one learning opportunities within a whole class lesson (Roth, 1993).

What made this episode especially unique was that many other teachers would not have allowed the 21 turns that this interaction took to negotiate a relatively small change to the text. Yet the teacher's actions suggested her belief that the concept of capital letters was within Stan's grasp, and she considered his participation to be vital. Without such participation, Stan's learning in the current situation and his willingness to take future risks might be jeopardized, since participatory appropriation is at the heart of learning and apprenticeship (Rogoff, 1993; Stone, 1998). Too often, however, teachers become more directive in the face of such learning challenges or call on another student to provide the answers. Unfortunately, this may cause a student with learning disabilities to develop a sense that the "writing process is beyond his capacities", contributing to a low self-efficacy and a diminished desire to participate.

In fact, Stan remained highly motivated and excited to participate in personal news. Although he was a nonreader and nonwriter on conventional measures, his participation became more self-assured during the remainder of the personal message activity. At one point, when the text read: *Annie's cousin is having her party at home*, the following exchange occurred related to Stan's observation that the text was unclear about where the party will take place:

Stan: Where's home? Annie?

A: AT MY HOUSE, they live with us.

T: So would that be important information to have?

S/Ss: Yeah (*said with others*).

T: Any ideas?

Stan: Annie. Listen. Annie's ... Um ... Annie cousin's birthday going to be at .... What about ... ? No! Annie's cousin's birthday is going to be at ... her house .... At Annie's .... What about .... Wait. She is going to have a birthday at Annie's house.

T: Oh, okay. Say that again, Stan.

Stan: (*louder*) She is going to have a birthday at Annie's house.

T: Do you like that? (*Before writing*) Yeah? Okay, let's just put it in then. Let's get this one out there. Say it again, Stan.

Stan: She is going to have a birthday at Annie's house.

T: She is going to have her birthday at Annie's house. What do we need at the end? (Writes she is going to have her birthday at Annie's house ...)

Stan/Ss: Period!

Yvonne: Put a capital on she.

T: (*Interruption.*) Put a capital on "she" I have to switch colors.

S: Cross out "she" and put her name.

T: Would you like it, Annie, to have "**she** is going to have her party at Annie's house" or "Shana is going to have her party at Annie's house"?

Stan: (*Under his breath*). Shana.

A: Shana.

Stan: (*Reading aloud*) Shana is going to have her birthday at Annie's house.

T: Shana is going to have her birthday at Annie's house. Thank you.

Stan: (*Saying aloud*) Good job!

In this set of interactions, Stan was highly successful in negotiating the meaning of the text. Among the student members, Stan was the participant to point out the lack of clarity about whose home was to be used to host Shana's birthday party. The fact that he was engaging in metacognitive and exploratory thought was suggested by the number of hesitations, half-starts, and repetitions in his speech. He was working at the outer edges of his language abilities, yet this is the site where it is more likely that Stan could acquire new knowledge and competencies. Stone (in press) suggests that the notion of challenge is an essential aspect of effective scaffolding for students with learning disabilities.

Though Stan would have been unable to perform the text construction and revision process alone, the group collaborated and problem-solved in co-constructing a sentence that included capital letters, referents, and periods. His pride in the result was evident in the self-praise he administered at the end, when he said "Good job!" Later in the lesson, he echoed the praise of the teacher "Good work!" after the group successfully selected a closing sentence to finish the message. Although Stan was one of the lowest performers in the classroom, he clearly displayed a sense of ownership and agency in the activity context.

As Stone (1998) and Biemiller and Meichenbaum (1998) have suggested, Stan's attitude seemed to reveal a quality of effective teacher scaffolding, which is the retention of student ownership of the activity, that is "our task, engaged in by us" rather than "your task, performed by me" (Biemiller & Meichenbaum, 1998, p. 366). Though some have pointed out the dilemmas of providing scaffolded instruction in whole-class lessons (Stone, 1998), Stan's case suggested that such scaffolding can occur in general education inclusion classrooms. Personal News not only provided opportunities for the most advanced students to assume task responsibility, but afforded students who might be marginalized in many classrooms by virtue of their low skills, the opportunity to assume monitoring and regulating functions (Biemiller & Meichenbaum, 1998, p. 366). To summarize, the teacher had increasingly grown capable of sharing her *authority for knowing* with her students. In this specific case, the teacher strategically assigned her students more dominant roles by using a participant structure that positioned her students to teach and explain. Across time, student talk was transformed from largely teacher-initiated to student-initiated interactions, and from responding to textual features pointed out by the teacher to initiating their own critical and evaluative remarks about the text. The teacher accomplished this through step-back and step-in moves. By stepping back into an apprentice role and asking questions about how and why, her students were positioned to experience firsthand the problem-solving process and the constructive dialogue that arose in the dialogical relationship between authors, texts, and readers. These moves served as rich instructional devices that were designed to teach and develop students' proficiency in written language functions and practices. Simultaneously, she stepped into more directed teaching roles to advance and scaffold knowledge when students demonstrated incomplete knowledge.

One outcome was an increase in the density of students' appropriation of and participation in the social languages, practices, and tool use of writers. Figure 5 summarizes the frequency of student use of the social languages, practices, and tools, as well as the frequency of student-initiated talk, breakdown bids related to problems in the text, and student involvement in the situated doing of the craft of writing. Social Practices, for example, was defined as a student move that showed their use and demonstration of the tools, actions and conventions of writing (e.g. "It's two Annie's. *Cross out* the second one and *put* 'she'; "Put a *circle* around that and then *show the arrows*"). Social language encompassed student moves that demonstrated their ability to use the talk associated with writing practices and processes, that is, the language that constitutes being a writer (e.g. "caret"; "apostrophe").

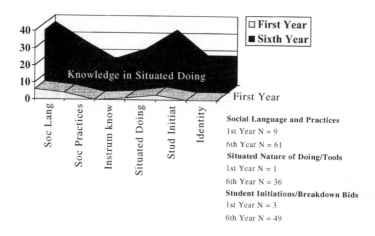

Fig. 5. Number of Student Moves Related to Knowing and Doing.

In the first year, there were only nine occurrences of student use of the social language and writing practices of the classroom in the writing lesson, whereas there were 61 occurrences of such deployment by students in the last year. Likewise, there were only three student-initiated responses to the text when the teacher was a novice to the project, compared to 49 student-initiated responses to the text when the teacher was the content and pedagogical expert on the project. These data suggest that there were large shifts in the participation of the students. As the teacher developed her instructional expertise, her students progressed from peripheral roles in the discourse (e.g. answering questions) to dominant central roles (e.g. directing the writing activity and employing the social languages and practices of writers). Although it might be assumed that students' appropriation of talk and tools might come in the context of small group or independent activity, the data suggested that the teacher became more proficient in apprenticing students in the internal and external facets of writing in the context of whole-group lessons. Working side by side in the text construction and revision process, she helped young writers move from peripheral participation to central participation in the performance of the various events, tools, and processes associated with an activity (see Bellamy, 1996; Mariage, Garmon & Englert, 2000). Thus, the participant structure and instructional discourse seemed to be pivotal in the accomplishment of apprenticeship goals (Mariage, 1995). The teacher focused on students' interaction and coparticipation in order to facilitate the emergence of new knowledge (Larochelle & Bednarz, 1998; Mariage, 1995).

The professional development that undergirded this project was based upon an apprenticeship model itself where talk about practice supported teachers' deepening understanding of how their own pedagogical tools and practices were consequential to the literate worlds constructed in their classroom (see Englert, Mariage & Raphael, 1998 for a discussion of the teacher-researcher community and a theoretical analysis of the intervention principles). Combined with the analysis of her content coverage, this view of teacher development suggests that the teacher's actions to assimilate her students as coparticipants in the text construction process provided multiple ways for a diverse range of learners to enter the activity, ranging from the beginning writers who could offer simple changes to the text (e.g. periods and capital letters), to the inclusion of sophisticated writers who monitored the text for topical coherence and redundancies. As Artiles et al. (2000) have suggested, the teacher had grown in her ability to capitalize on the interplay between the lower and upper ends of the collective zones of proximal development represented in her classroom. Personal News represented a "collective, multivoiced construction of its past, present, and future zones of proximal development" (Engestrom & Miettinen, 1990, p. 10). This mastery of the principles of classroom discourse involved a complicated set of dialogic interactions set in a moment-to-moment discursive context that took time for the teacher to master and understand. We suggest, then, that teachers' own understanding of and facility in constructing cognitive apprenticeships for their students is consequential to the nature and trajectory of students' participation and subsequent development. Analysis of changes in this teacher's discourse moves indicates that the construction of discourse communities such that student and teacher talk provides ever deepening entry into literate practices is contingent upon the ability of the teacher to strategically reposition herself and her students with respect to the tools and conventions represented in the collective activity.

COLLABORATIVE WRITING

Analysis of changes in one teacher's practice indicates the difficulty involved in using discourse to support student tool acquisition and use. The data above, however, do support the theory that there is a dialogic relationship between the cognitive roles which students assume and the patterns of discourse supported by the teacher's practices. The question that we have yet to address is the unique contribution of collaborative tasks in learning. It is not sufficient for teachers to guide students through the process of writing in teacher-directed and mediated lessons, there must be collaborative spaces for students to appropriate the discourse and strategies for personal use. Vygotsky's (1978) work suggests that there are three planes of cognitive development: other-directed (e.g. teacher modeling), collaborative and intermental (e.g. teachers and students as coparticipants working side by side), and inner-directed or intramental (e.g. students working alone). In other words, each participation space (whole group, small group, individual) differentially supports the individuals' acquisition of the mental practices of the collective activity.

In much of the research literature, the attention of researchers have focused on the collaborative spaces where students are working as coparticipants with peers. In this chapter, thus far, we have seen the powerful role of the teacher as a coparticipant in an instructional process that involves the participation of all students in the personal news activity. However, what is the value of peer collaboration?

In an exploration of collaborative writing, we reported (Englert, Berry & Dunsmore, 2001) several key findings from this research that are relevant to this discussion. First, we found that peer collaborative spaces afforded unique types of learning opportunities. For students with disabilities, collaborative spaces allowed them to implement cultural practices at levels that exceeded what they could accomplish in independent or solitary writing activities. Peer collaboration opened up zones of possibilities that facilitated the development of higher mental functions, and allowed low-achieving students to be coparticipants in a process that they could not perform otherwise. Second, peer collaborative environments seemed to foster participatory appropriation by providing a mechanism for transferring control to learners for cultural practices and languages in situated problem-solving activity. Students in collaboration with peers were immersed in the use of cultural language and practices in ways that were more intense and frequent than what was possible in teacher-directed lessons or independent writing arrangements, while still receiving support from their peers. Third, peer collaborative writing arrangements provided an important context for understanding children's developmental capabilities. Peer collaboration provided opportunities for teachers to investigate children's emerging thought processes and capacities by listening to the collaborative discourse and actions. Such open displays of talk and actions were not accessible to teachers in the solitary and independent writing activity of students. Fourth, the study revealed the importance of mediating artifacts and practices that helped students coordinate their talk and activities.

To study the nature of collaborative spaces as a context for supporting individual literacy development, we focus in this section on the collaboration of one small group of students who were constructing a personal news story within the classroom of the teacher we analyzed above. The data emerges from an activity which occurred during year six of the teacher's participation in this study and thus is concurrent with the instructional practices analyzed above. We videotaped and transcribed a small group in which Annie was a participant within one month of the time of the personal news lesson discussed above. In this small group, there was one general education student (Yvonne), and three students with disabilities, including two students with learning disabilities (Jack, Jordie), and one student with a mild cognitive impairment (Annie). Of particular interest to our analysis here is the nature of the participation of a first grader in this group named Jordie. Of all the members of the group, he problematized the meaning and nature of apprenticeship both because of his lack of experience with the tools and language of the activity as well as of the complexity that he presented to his peers as his zone of proximal development was the most distant from those represented by his peers. The question raised, then, is of the value to Jordie of participating in a collaborative activity with peers who were both more facile with the literate practices embedded with the Personal News activity as well as less competent to provide instructional support for or access to participation. Thus, how does the discourse within a small group setting provide cognitive apprenticeship opportunities for a diverse range of students?

We repeated the same analyses with the data discussed here as we conducted for the analysis of the teacher-directed whole class lessons. First, we examined the nature of the content coverage of the small collaborative group. The results are shown in Fig. 6.

Whereas, students covered 6 and 22 content categories in the teacher-directed lessons in the first and last lesson six years apart, respectively, the students in the small collaborative group covered 14 content categories. They covered more content categories than the lesson when the teacher was a novice, but fewer content categories than the lesson when the teacher was an expert. This suggested that, when the teacher possessed the greatest expertise, she provided the greatest content coverage, and potentially, the greatest access to the conventions and practices of writing. Nevertheless, the small group activity yielded possibilities for students to appreciate and use the discourse and practices of the writing curriculum.

In fact, when we examined the personal news story constructed by the students in the small group, there were close similarities between their text and the text produced in the whole-class lesson. As shown in Fig. 7, the students have generated multiple alternatives for the title and several alternative concluding sentences. They also use the Wh- question words to ask questions of the author, and completed a plan sheet corresponding to the information represented by these categories (Who, What, How, When, Where, Why). The arrow at the beginning of their paragraph is a convention that had been introduced by their teacher in the whole-class lessons. Although the text is not as complicated in terms of the incorporation of revision practices relative to

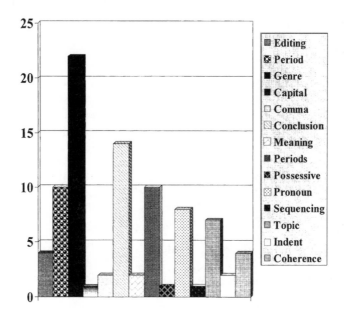

Fig. 6.   Small Group Content Coverage.

the teacher-guided text in the sixth year, it shows a greater consideration of the genre and written language features than the text produced by the class in the teacher's first participation year. Thus, students in the small collaborative activity were appropriating the writing practices of the collective for their own writing purpose in text construction.

When we examined the frequency of participation of the four individual students in the teacher-directed and small group lessons, there were substantial differences. In the teacher-guided lesson, Yvonne participated 6 times, whereas she participated 118 times in the small group activity. Jack and Jordie both participated 1 time in the teacher-directed lesson, whereas they participated 62 and 69 times, respectively, in the small group activity. Finally, Annie participated 29 times in the teacher-directed lesson since she was the subject of the personal experience story, but she participated 23 times in the small group activity. Overall, this suggested that the sheer amount of participation significantly increased in the context of the small group collaborative problem-solving activity (Roth, 1993). If the teacher-directed lesson is the site of content introduction, then the small group activity offers a site for increasing the participation of students in the use and application of those content practices.

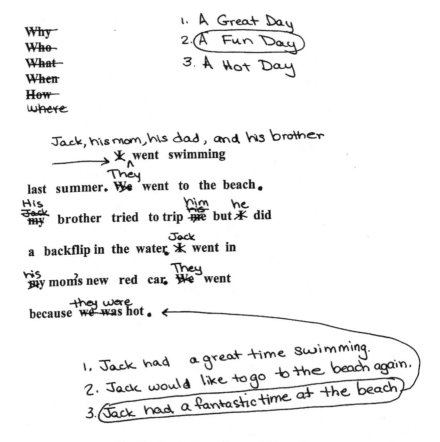

Fig. 7. Small Group Personal News Story.

Next, we considered the nature of the students' use of the social languages and practices. The results were striking. In the first teacher-directed lesson, there were a total of 12 instances of the students' appropriation of the language and practices of the community; six years later, there was a total of 61 occurrences of students' appropriation of the language and practices of the community; but in the small group collaborative activity, there were a total of 142 instances of students' appropriation and employment of the social language and practices. The collaborative group offered substantial opportunities for students to step into the language and practices that had been introduced and modeled by the teacher, although the entry points of the small group seemed to provide more abundant literacy opportunities for the lowest performing writers.

To illustrate some of the themes the emerged in our analysis of the collaborative group, we have extracted some segments from the activity's transcription. In the segment below, Jack is dictating text for his personal experience story about his family's trip to the beach. Annie, who is an emergent reader, has assumed the role of guiding the group in rereading the printed text as she points to each of the words, and she serves as the group's editor who makes changes to the text recommended by the group. Yvonne is the group's leader, writing the text dictated by Jack and serving as the self-appointed coach for the group during the problem-solving process. Jordie is assigned the role of putting in the periods at the end of the sentences.

> Jack: We went to the beach.
> Yvonne: [Starts to write] . . . . Just say the whole sentence (again)
> Jack: We went to the beach.
> Yvonne: [Beginning to write dictated sentence].
> Annie: We (points to spaces where words will be written with her marker) went (touches with marker) to (touches) the (touches) beach (touches). Repeats it again after all the words are written: We went to the beach.
> Jordie: (speaking softly to Annie) period.
> Annie: Period! (Jabs at end of sentence to show Jordie where to put period)
> Jordie: [reaches for marker from Aisha. Takes it. Puts in period.]
> Yvonne: Right here. At the end of the sentence (touches place on the page).
> Jordie: There!
> Annie: You put two.
> Yvonne: It doesn't matter. (It's) just a draft. It doesn't (matter) how it looks.

In this episode, the students are successful in using the participation structure and their assigned roles to respond to the zones of proximal development of the other members. Annie is able to develop her print awareness by rereading and pointing to the words, and Jordie is successful in putting in periods with the coaching and support of his peers. In the teacher-directed lessons, this level of engagement and participation in the activity at their appropriate levels of literacy knowledge might not be easily possible without a restructuring of the activity to develop emergent literacy skills. Yet in this brief episode consisting of 12 interactions, Annie participates three times, Jack two times, and Jordie three times. Further, there exists opportunities in the transactions for students to use the functions or tools of literacy associated with written text, as well as to deepen and test their understanding of the revisionary capacities of the editing process. Jordie, for example, receives scaffolded support from Annie, who cues him where to locate his period, and likewise, Annie is reminded by Yvonne that the edited version is merely a draft, reinterpreted by Yvonne to mean that the appearance of the text is irrelevant. Social mediation and assisted performance were key elements of learning and development (Rueda, Gallego & Moll, 2000), and students served as resources for one another in exploring, aiding, and nudging each other's understandings (Rogoff, 1990).

Problem-solving by the individual members of the small group did occur directly and frequently. In the segment of transcript below, Yvonne addresses the confusion surrounding the question of 'who went the beach', pointing out and then undertaking the recovery work to address the problem represented in the portion of the text that reads: "They went to the beach".

Yvonne: Do we have any more editing to do? (Pause) First it was talking about Jack, then it was talking about "they" .... We don't know who "they" is.
.
.
.
Yvonne: No, no, no, no, no. Not "WE" went. Again. We are talking about last summer. And this .... You said "Jack went swimming. They went to the beach. "We don't know who "they" is.
Jack: Lucy and [seems to be dictating a section of the text to address Yvonne's question].
Yvonne: We aren't starting a new sentence. We're going back up here (points to the previous sentence containing the word "they")
Jack: Okay. Jack and Lucy ... (dictating in third person)
Yvonne: We don't know who Lucy is.
Annie: Lucy is his mom.
Yvonne: We don't know that. We don't.
Annie: All it says is this. Jack went swimming last summer. They went to the beach.
Yvonne: It says Jack.
Annie: [re-reads again] Jack went swimming last summer. They went to the beach.
Yvonne: No. Jack's mom ...
Jack: Jack's mom ... (inaudible)
Yvonne: Is like this (takes editing marker from A and makes insertion to the first sentence).
Jack, comma.
Annie: Jack, comma.
Jordie: You're not supposed to put a period. I put a period.
Annie: It's not a period. It's not a period.
Yvonne: His dad, comma.
Jack: Comma.
Annie: Comma.
Annie: His.
Yvonne: And his brother.
Annie: Comma.
Yvonne: Nope. We don't need a last comma.
Annie: (Tries to take marker)
Yvonne: We just need a caret. (Makes it. Hands marker back to A). Now let's read it. Jack, his mom, his dad, and his brother went swimming last summer. They went to the beach. [Yvonne points vaguely at words, but Annie steps in to touch each word with her marker and lead the group during the rereading]. What's the name of the beach?

The individual members' confusions and disparate zones of proximal development became obvious in the context of their suggestions and responses. When peers didn't clarify who 'they' is, Yvonne responded to their developmental levels, as she modeled how to use multiple subjects in a listing format, as well as modeled the use of commas between the items in the list. She pointed out the confusion to the other participants, and modeled the resolution to address the text breakdown. The other participants in the group stepped into her demonstration as they revoiced her modeled words (e.g. repeating after her the word "comma") and they even started to anticipate her next words (e.g. "his" offered by Annie in anticipation of the next listed person, and later, "comma"). This anticipatory set is a critical feature of apprenticeship models insofar as learners exert growing competence through the anticipation and appropriation of the actions, language and practices modeled by the more knowledgeable peer. This type of joint involvement is not as easily obtained by a teacher because of the diffusion of one-on-one learing opportunities in a class of 30 students. Thus, the small group afforded opportunities for students to be integrated into a process with its respective cultural practices, and especially, offered benefits to individuals when it offered them a zone of joint action that was in advance of what the person could manage alone (Wells, 1999).

Yvonne also interrogates the text and the author's ideas (What's the name of the beach?). She points out the questions of the "posited audience" when she underscores the problem of writing for a distant audience to Annie, e.g. "We don't know that . . . . We don't". In this case, "we" represents her alignment with a "hypothesized audience", a group of readers who are remotely removed from the authors' knowledge and experiential context. She and the others in the group created a zone of proximal development, which represented the joint collective knowledge and actions of the group in interaction with each other and the ideas in the text. Through their various moves, Yvonne and the other participants draw attention to the medium of written language itself, focusing on the abstraction of written language that distinguishes it from speech. Their talk flows back and forth between the features of written language and their anticipation of the effect of their various written moves on their intended listeners. Their utterances are filled with dialogic overtones, speaking through and with both local and distant "others" (Wells, 1999).

Nevertheless, the small group does have problems and there are several ways in which it fails to serve the cognitive and social needs in a manner like that exhibited by the teacher. One area in which the small group struggled was in their ability to support the type of metatalk, explanations, and think-alouds, that were provoked by the teacher through her use of step-back moves. The teacher regularly asked students to explain their thinking and think-aloud about the nature of repairs that needed to be made to the text. However, the students in the small group, with the exception of the lowest-performing member, Jordie, seldom positioned themselves or other students to explain what they were doing, and they omitted the teaching or apprenticeship moves that would make visible to others their thoughts and collective actions. The segment below shows the difficulty of the small group in responding to the developmental zones afforded them through the questions of Jordie.

> Yvonne: My brother tried to trip me but I did a back flip. Okay . . . (Inaudible) . . . (Yvonne still writing)
> Jordie: in the air . . . . Put in the air.
> Yvonne: Jordie, he didn't say that.
> Jordie: [looks at Jack]. Don't need that?
> .
> .
> .
> Yvonne: And now, put a period – right here (Points).
> Jordie: Period and another period.
> Yvonne: We don't need another period. That 's the end of our sentence.
> Jordie: Uh-huh. Right there.
> Yvonne: We don't need another period. That's just another . . . (Retrieves marker from his hand).
> Annie: [Makes mark through "my". Then gets up from her seat and comes around to the front of the paper].
> Jordie: No! Aisha, why did you do that? You can't cross that out. That's *not supposed* to be in there [Jordie seems upset].
> Yvonne: No, no, no. Jordan, that's *supposed* to be in there.

The group seldom offered, requested or offered explanations or justifications for their actions or directions. In fact, the students tended to use the language of command and authority in their interactions with others in the construction and revision process (Put a period). It must be realized that this "directive voice" was similar to the voice that was elicited by the teacher in her interactions with the students. She asked them to direct the writing process, and in a similar way, the students commanded each other in the small group activity. However, the apprenticeship discourse enacted by the teacher was obliquely omitted in the talk of students, with the exception of Jordie, who appropriated the teacher's learning stance when he asked the question, "Why?". This novice-like move, a request for an explanation by the more expert members of the group, was a type of move demonstrated by the teacher in the teacher-directed lesson when she requested that the participants explain and justify their actions. Nevertheless, although the group accepted the teacher's apprenticeship moves in the whole-class lesson, Jordie's peers did not respect the inquisitive moves and the resulting zones of proximal development afforded them by Jordie. They did not recognize the intuitive "teacher-like" character of his questions, and they did not take action to responsively address his calls for teaching explanations. Lacking the discursive and pedagogical skills of the teacher and the ability to independently participate in metatalk, they tended to take an authoritative stance and tone with respect to the primacy of their knowledge when they were challenged by Jordie ("No, no, no. Jordie that's *supposed* to be in there"). This authority-based form of discourse leads to insufficiently-developed discussions where students tend to assert ideas but fail to provide full explanations (Linn & Burbules, 1993)

At one point, Yvonne turns to Jordie in frustration, and says: "Would you, please? Jordie, you aren't understanding this. We have to edit. This is a morning message (personal news)." In this manner, small groups may tend to pressure individuals to move along rather than consider alternatives or develop deeper conversations that lead to new knowledge (Linn & Burbules, 1993). The effect on Jordie was marginalizing, and Jordie even stated at one point, "Let's don't do this."

Yet the remarkable aspect of the small group activity was the fact that Jordie persevered in his endeavors to participate in the activity, perhaps fueled by his intense interest to take up the tools and practices that were modeled and deployed by his peers. Rueda et al. (2000) suggest that "fun" and "play" are a necessary element to the continued participation of students. The personal news activity provided occasions that were dense with authentic problem solving and communication of the process and products of problem solving (Rueda et al., 2000). Becoming expert and developing expertise in the personal news activity was how students determined their membership status in the group, and they were compelled in the small group to reach out and seize the tools much like children at a sandbox who are onlookers wait anxiously for their turn to reach out and seize the shovel. In a segment shortly after, Jordie reaches out to seize and appropriate the tools and practices that he had observed in the hands of his peers.

Jordie: [Jordie's hand is raised. His thumb points down.]
Annie: I'm crossing out the 'my' and put in 'his'.
Jordie: Yvonne, you see my thumb like this. That means you're supposed to . . . .
Jordie: Yvonne, you are supposed to take me.
Annie: Jordie . . .
Yvonne: Jordie, I picked you.
Jordie: Too many Jack . . . . There is one right here and one right there.
Yvonne: So what do you want us to do with that?
Jordie: Cross that one out and put . . . Jack . . . Jack went . . . . Wait.
Yvonne: You just said cross it out and that is the same thing.
Jordie: Cross it out and put . . . Ummmm . . . . Cross Jack out and um, put . . . Ummm . . . Me and my mom and Jack went to . . .
Yvonne: Wait. Was it you?
Jordie: No.
Yvonne: Okay, we aren't sure who . . . (Inaudible)

Jordie: (inaudible) That means we have to cross it out.
Yvonne: What should we put here beside Jack.
Jordie: His mom and his dad . . .
Yvonne: It doesn't say his mom and his dad.
Jordie: No. His mom and his.
Yvonne: It says Jack (re-reads) . . .
Jordie: Cross out . . . . Cross out . . . . Cross out that Jack and put a *new sentence* . . . (inaudable).
Yvonne: We aren't supposed to put a sentence right there. How would we cross out Jack and put a new sentence . . . .
Annie: Jack (reads) and.
Jordie: Jack and his mom and his brother went swimming. Not. . . Went swimming.
Yvonne: No, no, no. Look. That's up there. That's up here. Look. Jordie, Jordie, Jordie (Re-reads it.) We're down here. It says Jack went in his mom's new red car.
Jordie: Cross out Jack and put a topic sentence . . . (Looks around).
Annie: It ain't no topic sentence.
Yvonne: We aren't supposed to put the topic sentence right here.
Yvonne: Why don't we just leave it? Leave it.
Jordie: What do that say? (Looking toward plan. Touching)
Yvonne: This is our plan (makes a mark through idea, turns it upside down)
Jordie: Cross out Jack and put a period.
Yvonne: (Shakes head). Let's just leave it like it is. Let's just leave it like it is.

In this episode, Jordie tries to enact several tools and cultural practices that had been introduced and employed by others. Demonstrating his own personal stake in the knowledge being constructed, he appropriates the discourse previously demonstrated by members of the group, including text problems related to textual redundancies ("Too many Jacks"), editing and directing the writing process ("Cross that one out and put . . ."), language substitutions ("His mom and his dad . . ."), sentence construction ("Cross out that Jack and put a new sentence"), and topic sentences ("put a topic sentence."). At one point, Jordie turns to the plan and tries to remind the group about using the plan. Obviously, Jordie had become aware of the notational systems of the culture (Olson, 1995), and his awareness of these systems was beginning to alter the entire flow and structure of his mental functions, creating instrumental acts that needed to become fully aligned with functions in the activity (Wertsch, 1995). Through participatory appropriation, his behavior and words were becoming extensions of previous events (Rogoff, 1995), as he borrowed the language and psychological tools used by others to apply towards goals that were not yet accomplished or fully understood by Jordie. In this way, writers learn to play language games as any social practice by participating in them with others, and through mutual observation and emulation, to learn about their function and meaning by testing their assumptions against those who have the capacity to instruct (Wolff, 1998). Jordie was attempting to take his part in the language game by enacting and testing his hypotheses about the writing tools and language in the situated context of writing. He showed that he was taking an active role in his own development, putting himself in a position to observe what was going on, involving himself in the ongoing activity, influencing the activity in which they were all participating, and demanding some type of involvement with his peers (Stone, 1998). What remained to be accomplished was the provision of supportive feedback by his peers. The type of titrated and scaffolded assistance provided by his teacher, however, seemed beyond his peers' means.

This segment shows the enormous intellectual effort that Jordie was putting forth to try to understand and utilize the tools he has observed in their operational context. "Sustained engagement in an instructional episode requires the maintenance of attention across multiple conversation turns" (Stone, in press, p. 14). Students with learning disabilities may find this difficult, as approximately 30% of the LD population may have co-occurring attention deficit disorder. Taking into account the fact that Jordie was a first grader, this episode showed the powerful attempts that Jordie was exerting to understand and contribute to the writing task. Jordie remained highly engaged throughout the more than 30-minute activity. The power of the collaborative task was that it provided an occasion for a motivational shift in the role of the learner as a subordinate or follower of others' actions, to a more dominant role as a leader or instigator of task-directive speech and actions (Biemiller & Meichenbaum, 1998).

Yet his peers don't fully understand Jordie, and they responded to the instructional dilemmas that he presented with a rebuke to pay attention ("This is not fun and games. We are trying to work here and you are not concentrating."). Rather than respond to the challenge to bridge the gap between his entry-level and the group's, they treat his attempts to participate as misbehavior.

Moreover, the small group was challenged by other demands required for a successful collaborative dialogue that might be fundamental to a successful apprenticeship. Effective participation in a dialogue is no small undertaking for young students because it involves the following social and communicative skills (Gergen, 1995, p. 34): (a) coordination of one's actions and words to what has preceded; (b) generation of words and actions that assign to another speaker authoritative status and coherence; (c) extension of the preceding language and actions in ways that are useful to the exchange; (d) allowing space in the interaction for another's participation, (e) furnishing backchannel information that helps retain the trajectory of the interchange; and (f) avoiding moves that terminate the discussion (e.g. personal threats and insults). Given these social and linguistic constraints, it seems apparent that the development of cohesion and cognition in small groups might overwhelm students at times. Jordie's actions were legitimated only when the teacher entered the group. The following segment reveals the important role of the teacher in scaffolding Jordie's performance and in responding to his zones of proximal development in the small group activity.

T: Where are you, guys?
Annie: Right here.
Jack: My mom . . . it was hot outside.
Annie: I'm going to cross this out.
Jordie: Annie, no. That's how Jack wanted to put it. Jack wanted to put it like that.
Yvonne: No, no, no. Jordie, she is editing.
Jordie: I know. That is how Jack wanted it.
Yvonne No, that is how he said it.
T: Let's go back and reread it and see *what makes sense*. (Annie starts the group from the top) Just re-read this last sentence that you are working on.
Annie: They went because we were hot.
T: Oh! I know what you are talking about. Instead of changing that 'we', did you hear another 'we'.
Jordie: (nods)
T: Where did you hear the other one, Jordan.
Jordie: (looks around)
T: Down here in this last sentence.
Jordie: Right there.
T: There you go. So is that the one you wanted changed, too?
Jordie: And put that one back in, then?
T: Well, did we do it?
Annie: No.
T: So we'll leave that one as 'they'.
Jordie: Cross that one out.
T: That's the one you were talking about?
Yvonne: They went because they were hot.
Jordie: And another one.
T: Yeah, well, that's kind of – not kind of – that's in another word. See, how there are more letters with it?

Jordie presented a wide zone of proximal development that challenged and perplexed his peers. Jordie was an emergent reader with learning disabilities, and his knowledge of the writing practices and language system defied his peers' abilities to instruct and assist him. The teacher, thus, saw what the peers had not: that Jordie was confused about the substitution of "they" for "we", and that he was lacking the word consciousness that might help him distinguish words like "we" and "went". The teacher was able to evaluate his knowledge and then respond by starting at the point where he was and then by challenging, supporting, and teaching within the context of his own actions and partial understandings. For this teacher, small group problem-solving did not mean that it was devoid of her influence and presence. In fact, the small groups provided unique instructional possibilities in terms of the opportunities for the teacher to: (1) conduct online diagnosis that provided direct data on students' thought processes in order to evaluate, develop and further students' literacy understandings; (2) sustain students' participation and motivation to engage in the participatory appropriation mechanisms that underlie current and future development; (3) bridge the gap between independent and successful performance through scaffolding and mediation; and (4) support students in taking up discursive positions that were associated with being an authority over one's knowledge (Gergen, 1995).

What was remarkable was that Jordie continued to persist in his efforts to appropriate knowledge. The acknowledgement of his ideas by the teacher in an instrumental way that altered the group's text served to motivate Jordie further. Although he was only an emergent writer developing his consciousness of words, there were other social practices that he was perfectly capable of grasping in the context of the apprenticeship process afforded him in the lessons. In the last segment of the small group activity, the third graders, Jack and Annie, struggle to compose a concluding sentence. They hesitate and stumble, showing the challenging nature of the task. Though he is only a first grader, Jordie not only models an appropriate concluding sentence, but reminds the group of the social practices concerning the selection of a concluding sentence. Thus, the less skilled writer of the group remains an important player in the language game, and the expertise he enacts in the group shows the distributed nature of learning in collaborative groups.

Yvonne: [Now we need a] Closing sentence.
T: Closing sentence. Okay, how can you close it up?
Jordie: (inaudible)
T: You've got some hands up . . . [T walks away to observe another group]
Annie: What a hot day!
Yvonne: No. [Starts to write, then stops and looks up.] That's more of a title.
Annie: Okay. What a day.
Yvonne: That's more like a title, too.
Jordie: Jordie's hand is raised.
Annie: Jack had a day . . . What a day.
Yvonne: That's too short to be a closing.
Jack: Happy day.
Yvonne: That's too short . . . [Jack directs Yvonne to Jordie]
Jordie: Jack had a . . . Jack . . .
Yvonne: Not . . . a title.

Jordie: Uh, What a happy day.
Annie: What a . . .
Yvonne: That's too short. (It's) a title.
Jordie: I know!
Jordie: (inaudible)
Yvonne: And I thought you said you knew . . . [accusingly].
Jordie: Jack had a great time swimming.
Yvonne: [Registers a doubletake, then starts to write Jordie's sentence].
Jordie: Jack . . . Jack had a great time . . . swimming [dictating text].
Jack: Masterpiece!!!

The small group collaborative space did offer possibilities that extended the learning opportunities for students. The small and intimate situation promoted the students' efforts to engage with the writing tools and dialogue that had been made accessible in the whole class lessons. Many students writing alone would not have had the same opportunities to step into the higher-level practices associated with monitoring, questioning, and constructing text because they needed the distributed expertise of their peers to perform the aspects of the writing process that exceeded their current levels of competence. Yet the small group afforded a unique place for students to take up and dabble with practices that they might not have the opportunities to put into operation in whole-class contexts or independent writing arrangements. Jordie's membership in the small group seemed to propel him to continue to participate and to transform his participation in the larger cultural practices of the community.

Analysis of the interaction patterns and practices of this group highlight the ways in which participation in collaborative spaces might offer students access to roles and responsibilities that are remote or unavailable when engaged in whole class instructional spaces. Both from the perspective of conventional literacy assessment as well as analysis of facility in performing the Personal News cultural practice, Jordie was clearly a novice and the least "abled" member. Yet, he both participated significantly in the cognitive activity of the group as well as in the construction of the actual form and content of the collective text. Further, the small group space provided him with an opportunity to assume cognitive roles, pursue clarification, experience sociocognitive conflict, and engage in the dialectic of negotiating the meaning and navigating the construction of a literate text, whereas his voice and contributions were rarely heard in the whole-class lesson. Thus, the analysis presented in this section suggests that participation spaces differentially support the use and acquisition of mental tools and practices. The small group setting provided students with access to and the opportunity to participate in the cognitive routines of the sociocultural practices of the writing community. Instructional contexts (teacher, small group, individual) are thus consequential to the nature and function of apprenticeship, resulting in different but a balanced set of cognitive affordances.

In summary, the collaborative group seemed to uniquely function to achieve the following benefits (see Stone, in press):

* Recruitment of students' interest and participation
* Transfer of responsibility
* Joint goal-directed activity that allowed risk-taking and hypothesis-testing
* Increased opportunity for participation
* Student participation/choice
* Collaborative and challenging tasks
* Dialogue embedded in activity

DISCUSSION

Cognitive apprenticeship within a social constructivist approach to teaching is not a discovery learning approach, which leaves students to the detection of knowledge (Larochelle & Bednarz, 1998). Quite the contrary, it assumes a strong mediating role on the part of teachers. The challenge for teachers is to develop an instructional discourse that is dynamic in character, and allows for an evolving form of talk tied to the emergent knowledge of students and their active contributions (Larochelle & Bednarz, 1998). In the lessons of the expert teacher, for example, we see her ability to provide students a role in establishing the contours and direction of the dialogue (Gergen, 1995). Yet the teacher is clearly mediating the development of students' literacy knowledge as she creates discursive positions for students associated with the articulation and realization of their authoritative knowledge over the subject matter content.

A second challenge in a social constructivist approach is the demand for a high degree of teacher skill in making useful online assessments about what is occurring in the minds of students (van Glasersfeld, 1998). The focus teacher in this research used the students' discourse to assess knowledge and to take into account the student's conceptual route within the text construction process. "This ability separates individuals who are gifted for teaching from those to whom it is merely a rule-governed job like so many others" (von Glasersfeld, 1998, p. 27). Teachers need a methodology for examining and listening to student thinking (Confrey, 1998). By asking students the equivalent of, "How did you go about getting the answer?", not only does the teacher acquire knowledge about a student, but students themselves discover that they can

decide whether something makes sense – a starting point in the development
of self-regulation (von Glasersfeld, 1998, p. 28). This is especially important
for students with disabilities, given their known difficulties with metacognition
and their failure to employ cognitive strategies (Wong, 1979, 1980). At
the same time, teachers must responsively respond to the developmental states
of knowledge revealed in the assessment by extending knowledge beyond what
the student presently can do without assistance, but not beyond what the student
is capable of knowing. Learning involves the coordination of participation
and the legitimacy of partial, increasing, changing participation within a
community (Lave & Wenger, 1996). Legitimation of partial efforts is critical
for students with disabilities to develop a fuller mastery of the complete task.
The teacher's attention to and responsiveness to individual and collective states
of knowledge is essential for successful instruction in both small group and
whole group activities.

Third, teachers must have models for playing out and making visible the
tools and processes that underlie the construction of authoritative texts. The
challenge for teachers is how to lay open the craft of writing for inspection,
while creating laboratory talk among students that provides another transparent
window into the writing process for other students. Students must see the writing
symbols and the practice-related principles in action, including the false
starts, waverings impasses, as well as to receive assurance, reassurance and
corrections on a need-to-know-basis (Roth & McRobbie, 1999). Teachers
accomplish this through the provision of think-alouds, explanations, and talk
about writing techniques. The creation of an instructional environment where
students feel comfortable engaging in exploratory thought and uncertainty, can
yield multiple benefits, e.g. provoking further insights into the writing process,
as well as increasing the motivation of other students to accept risks in taking
up and making sense of the writing tools and practices.

Fourth, teachers must develop their skill in employing teaching methods that
transfer control to students for engaging in the enterprise of writing. In
the focus classroom, the teacher effectively used step-back moves to provide
opportunities for students co-participate in the writing practice. She also used
collaborative groups so that students might increase their interactions with
others, promoting the opportunity for them to detect text breakdowns, share
their thoughts, explain their ideas, try out writing tools and practices, develop
their literacy knowledge, and construct a discourse for writing phenomena in
small-group and whole-class sessions (Roth & McRobbie, 1999). This ability
to teach by creating collaborative structures that allow the coparticipation of
students in writing practices is rarely demonstrated in most classrooms. Often
teachers teach writing by giving directions or lecturing about writing, yet such

methods deny students access to the full apprenticeship experience that brings them into direct contact with expertise embedded in the context of their own writing actions, thoughts, and problems (Biemiller & Michenbaum, 1998). Instead, reversible roles need to be created that allow students to develop mastery of the writing tools and discourse in the context of their own agency, with opportunities for feedback and social mediation. Over time, it is reasonable that students will come to treat oral and written texts as thinking devices, promoting their active engagement and ownership of the talk and artifacts in a community of practice where participation in processes is assigned social status (Wertsch & Toma, 1995).

Fifth, collaborative groups did seem to have an instructional place in the writing community. The small group that was the focus of this chapter was neither representative nor unrepresentative of the other small groups in the classroom. In fact, each small group developed its own social identity, shaped by the discourses and practices of the participants. However, a theme that ran across our analysis of all groups' interactions was how often we were struck by the engagement of a large number of students in the collaborative discourse. Like Jordie, students were invested in authoring the text, and taking up the social practices of the community because it involved them in social relationships with one other. It was also true that many students availed themselves of the social mediation of their peers by stepping into cultural practices well in advance of their own independent performance (Englert, Berry & Dunsmore, 2000). Importantly, collaborative groups prompted students to think aloud, to use task-directed speech and executive self-monitoring routines, and to engage in discourse-related conversations to a greater extent than that what was feasible in the teacher-led lessons.

Sixth, a critical aspect of learning was the transformation of one's participation in the writing activity. For the students, a critical task of the teacher was to further their participation in the social practices and to reify their ideas through the construction or revision of text. Participation in one social practice tended to open the door to the enactment of other social practices. Conversely, the denial of the legitimization of students' participation in one area resulted in a diminishment of their involvement and ownership of the process. For the teacher, too, learning was a process of transforming her participation from a teacher-directed discourse to a student-directed discourse. These changes took time for students and teachers to understand and master. Such changes, however, reside at the core of the apprenticeship model. How the teacher positioned herself and her students accounted for large differences in the deployment of the writing strategies, discourses, and conventions used by students.

A sociocultural approach to the study of learning and development involves attention to the relationship between collective and individual cognitive activity. Such theories argue that the tools and practices of a particular discourse community come to define the mental activity of the individual as he/she is apprenticed into the ways of knowing and doing which characterize the life, or culture, of the community itself. In the context, then, of an inclusion classroom, the ways in which discourse communities are constructed is consequential for the nature of students participation in the cognitive roles within the collective activity. All talk provides affordances for the appropriation and use of particular ways of knowing and doing. However, the literature on students with disabilities is replete with examples of how didactic instruction or even collaborative groups marginalizes further those students who already struggle with the literate practices of school. We argue, then, that it is essential that teachers become strategic in their use and analysis of the function of talk in supporting the appropriation of the mental, physical, and symbolic tools associated with literate practices.

The first analysis presented in this chapter indicates that the way in which the teacher's facility with whole class discussion had implications for students to gain access to and to participate in the literate practices represented in the Personal News Activity. This analysis revealed some of the central teaching methods associated with social constructivism in writing instruction, including: (a) explicit instruction, modeling, and guided apprenticeships (the discourse, tools, actions, and problem-solving processes of writers) in the situated activity of composing and revising text; (b) the use of discourse moves that transfers control to students so that they can co-participate in the execution and explanation of the specific task-specific actions, decision-making processes, and practices of writers; (c) online diagnosis on a moment-to-moment basis using students' talk and actions as a basis for making informed judgments about their developmental states of knowledge; and (d) individualized assistance and calibrated instruction that scaffolds and supports individuals by furthering their knowledge, participation, and successful performance. Especially important in a successful apprenticeship process are the use of teaching methods that increase the learners' responsibility for taking increasing control of the decisions and processes associated with the accomplishment of the writing goals (Biemiller & Meichenbaum, 1998), while simultaneously allowing the teacher to scrutinize the students' mastery of the problem-solving process in order to supply the needed knowledge and skills at the outer edges of students' competence. Taken together, these methods enabled the focus teacher to adjust her instructional methods in a fluid way to match the instructional opportunities afforded her by individual students' states of knowledge revealed in the text construction activities. Although writing is often viewed as a private or solitary activity, the teacher's instructional methods revealed how writing can be taught as a public and social activity that offered children simultaneous and reciprocal roles as readers and writers, as well as learners and teachers.

In the second analysis, the small group interactions, and Jordie's role in particular, suggested that small group instructional spaces provided students with opportunities to co-participate in cognitive roles that are less readily accessible in a whole group setting. In collaborative activity, there were greater opportunities for students to develop their motivation to shift their role from being a passive follower to being a more active leader and producer of text. Different kinds of learning settings produce different opportunities for knowledge acquisition and application. According to many researchers (Biemiller & Meichenbaum, 1998; Stone, 1998), it is especially important that learners with disabilities be placed in situations where they are asked to assume increasing responsibility to apply what they learn and to direct the learning process. While more competent learners routinely experience the full range of the learning continuum from being a novice to becoming an expert, it is likely that less competent students are provided fewer opportunities to exercise the self-regulatory and metacognitive skills associated with the development of expertise (Biemiller & Meichenbum, 1998). The focus teacher's thoughtful employment of a range of activity settings (both teacher-led and small group) showed how educators might construct learning situations that promote and require students to exercise the cognitive and social dispositions associated with independent and self-directive use of academic talk and skills.

Too often, social constructivism is conflated with other practices and meanings that have confusing interpretations. Some people mistakenly assume that social constructivism is "whole language", entailing little explicit instruction or teacher guidance. This is a mistaken interpretation of both approaches. Others assume that constructivism means peer collaboration and small group activity. The radical application of this view leads educators to simply follow students' leads, offering little of their own expertise to enrich the academic conversation. Our interpretation of social constructivism requires a more complex set of interlocking assumptions about the mutual and codependent roles of teachers and students. Only when instruction is based upon student knowledge can the teaching practices associated with this approach be used optimally; and simultaneously, the ascertainment of student knowledge must be supported and guided through explicit instruction and intervention on the part of the teacher. Our rationale for using these methods is based upon our knowledge of how individuals learn in apprenticeship contexts in real world settings. More importantly, we also see this approach being of vital importance to the instruction of students with learning disabilities, given their known difficulties in the area of metacognition, and the critical role of scaffolding in mediating their acquisition of higher-order thinking (Biemiller & Meichenbaum, 1998; Stone, 1998; in press). We see the instructional techniques associated with this model as being foundational in achieving successful learning outcomes by students with disabilities in writing, but we recognize their relevance to the teaching of other literacy domains, such as reading comprehension (both expository and narrative texts) and literature response.

In addressing the question of when these methods are counterproductive or irrelevant, we have two responses. First, the methods may be attenuated when rote recall is required. If the task involves, for example, memorizing high-frequency sight words, then teaching arrangements that entail stimulus-response-feedback formats might be more advantageous and efficient. In this case, the teacher would: *I*nitiate the interaction by presenting the word, wait for the *r*esponse, and *e*valuate the response, also known as the I-R-E sequence. Nevertheless, we still see how the instructional elements of social constructivism might usefully inform the interaction, such as the provision of teacher scaffolding following incorrect responses, the role of collaboration and peer tutoring in supporting learning, and teacher think-alouds that focus students' attention on the features and sounds of the word. As Duffy and Roehler (1987a, b) have maintained, the mastery of even basic facts and skills requires informed explanations of "what students are learning, how it is done, when it can be used, and why it is important."

Second, inappropriate and excessive applications of any elements of the model can be counterproductive, as is true of any set of teaching practices. Teachers may come to over rely upon certain aspects of the model to the detriment of students' learning. For example, teachers may fail to remove scaffolds and supports, creating a cognitive dependence that prevents students from progressing to independent levels of performance. Similarly, teachers may overemphasize the role of student talk without a similar emphasis on the provision of contingent and responsive instruction that builds deepening levels of knowledge and competence. The absence of teacher explanations and information is counterproductive to the development of expertise. Conversely, teachers may emphasize teacher modeling and explicit explanation without creating activity settings that foster the transfer of control for the talk, tools, and practices from teachers to students. Social constructivist approaches entail an orchestrated and mutual set of teacher and student actions that are designed to accomplish a task, and ultimately, that foster ever deepening levels of student knowledge. This requires a great deal of teacher skill in conducting dynamic assessments of cognitive, social, and motivational states of learners that are aligned to the curriculum through appropriate and contingent teacher actions.

In conclusion, these analyses provide insight into the consequential nature of classroom discourse in mediating individual development. In this chapter, we suggest that pedagogical practices which are informed by sociocultural theories of learning must attend to the situated affordances of speech-in-action and intentional and informed selection by the teacher of roles and routines which best support the development of all students within the context of collective activity. We believe they have much to offer teachers in assisting the literacy learning of many students, but they are particularly well-suited for students with special needs.

ACKNOWLEDGMENTS

This research was part of a larger project, "The Development and Evaluation of an Early Intervention Program for Nonreaders and Nonwriters", funded by a grant from the office of Special Education Programs (No. H023C50089) of the U.S. Department of Education. This research was also partly supported by the Center for the inprovement of Early Reading Achievement, funded by the office of Educational Research and Improvement. The opinions expressed in this article do not necessarily reflect the position, policy, or endorsement of the U.S. Departmnet of Education.

We wish to thank the teachers of Lansing School District who participated on the literacy project that led to to this work, including Karen Hicks, Traci Shepard, Kris Bobo, Charr Hagerman, Megin Turner. We wish to express our appreciation to Troy Mariage for his comments and feedback on an earlier draft of this chapter.

REFERENCES

Artiles, A., Trent, S. C., Hoffman-Kipp, P., & Lopez-Torres, L. (2000). From individual acquisition to cultural-historical practices in multicultural teacher education. *Remedial and Special Education, 21*(2), 79–89, 120.

Bellamy, R. K. E. (1996). Designing educational technology: Computer-mediated change. In: B. A. Nardi (Ed.), *Context and Consciousness: Activity Theory and Human-Computer Interaction* (pp. 134–146). Cambridge, MA: MIT Press.

Biemiller, A., & Meichenbaum, D. (1998). The consequences of negative scaffolding for students who learn slowly – A commentary on C. Addison Stone's "The metaphor of scaffolding: Its utility for the field of learning disabilities." *Journal of Learning Disabilities, 31*(4), 365–369.

Bryan, T. (1998). Social competence of students with learning disabilities. In: B. Y. L. Wong (Ed.), *Learning about Learning Disabilities* (2nd ed., pp. 237–275). San Diego: Academic Press.

Cazden, C. B. (1996). Selective traditions: Readings of Vygotsky in writing pedagogy. In: D. Hicks (Ed.), *Discourse, Learning, and Schooling* (pp. 165–188). NY: Cambridge University Press.
Christie, F. (1993). Curriculum genres: Planning for effective teaching. In: B. Cope & M. Kalantzis, (Eds), *The Powers of Literacy: A Genre Approach to Teaching Writing* (pp. 154–178). Pittsburgh, PA: University of Pittsburgh Press.
Confrey, J. (1998). Voice and perspective: hearing epistemological innovation in students' words. In: M. Larochelle, N. Bednarz & J. Garrison (Eds), *Constructism and Education* (pp. 104–120). NY: Cambridge University Press.
Cope, B., & Kalantzis, M. (1993). The power of literacy and the literacy of power. In: B. Cope & M. Kalantzis (Eds), *The Powers of Literacy: A Genre Approach to Teaching Writing* (pp. 63–89). Pittsburgh, PA: University of Pittsburgh Press.
Donahue, M. L. (1984). Learning disabled children's conversational competence: An attempt to activate the inactive learner. *Applied Psycholinguistics, 5*, 21–35.
Duffy, G. G., & Roehler, L. R. (1987a). Teaching Reading Skills as Strategies. *Reading Teacher, 40*, 414–418.
Duffy, G. G., & Roehler, L. R. (1987b). Improving Reading Instruction through the Use of Responsive Elaboration. *Reading Teacher, 40*, 514–519.
Engestrom, Y., Miettinen, R., & Punamaki, R. (Eds) (1999). *Perspectives on activity theory.* NY: Cambridge University Press.
Englert, C. S., Berry, R. A., & Dunsmore, K. L. (2001). A Case Study of the Apprenticeship Process: Another Perspective on the Apprentice and the Scaffolding Metaphor. *Journal of Learning Disabilities, 34*(2), 152–171.
Englert, C. S., & Mariage, T. V. (1996). A sociocultural perspective: Teaching ways-of-thinking and ways-of-talking in a literacy community. *Learning Disabilities Research and Practice, 11*(3), 157–167.
Englert, C. S., Raphael, T. E., & Mariage, T. V. (1998). A Multi-Year Literacy Intervention: Transformation and Teacher Change in the Community of the Early Literacy Project. *Teacher Education and Special Education, 21*(4), 255–277.
Forman, E. A., & Cazden, C. B. (1985). Exploring Vygotskian perspectives in education. In: J. V. Wertsch (Ed.), *Culture, communication and cognition: Vygotskian perspectives.*
Gee, J. P. (Ed.) (1992). *The social mind: Language, ideology and social practice.* NY: Bergin & Garvey.
Gergen, K. J. (1995). Social construction and the educational process. In: L. P. Steffe & J. Gale (Eds), *Constructivism in Education* (pp. 17–40). Hillsdale, NJ: Lawrence Erlbaum.
Holzman, L. H. (1996). pragmatism and dialectical materialism in language development. In: H. Daniels (Ed.), *An Introduction to Vygotsky* (pp. 75–98). NY: Routledge.
Hutchins, E. (1997). Mediation and automatization. In: M. Cole, Y. Engestrom & O. Vasquez (Eds), *Mind, Culture and Activity: Seminal Papers from the Laboratory of Comparative Human Cognition* (pp. 338–353). NY: Cambridge University Press.
Jakubowski, E. (1993). Constructing potential learning opportunities in middle grades matehmatics. In: K. Tobin (Ed.), *The Practice of Constructivism in Science Education* (pp. 135–144). Hillsdale, NJ: Lawrence Erlbaum.
Kress, G. (1993). Genre as social process. In: B. Cope & M. Kalantzis (Eds), *The Powers of Literacy: A Genre Approach to Teaching Writing* (pp. 22–37). Pittsburgh, PA: University of Pittsburgh Press.
Larochelle, M., & Bednarz, N. (1998). Constructivism and education: Beyond epistemological correctness. In: M. Larochelle, N. Bednarz & J. Garrison (Eds), *Constructism and Education* (pp. 4–20). NY: Cambridge University Press.

A HIGHLY INTERACTIVE
DISCOURSE STRUCTURE

Alan H. Schoenfeld

INTRODUCTION

This somewhat speculative chapter is grounded in observations made during
the detailed analysis of two very different mathematics lessons. The first is a
high school mathematics/physics lesson conducted by Jim Minstrell toward the
beginning of the school year. In broadest terms, the question explored by
Minstrell's class is how to determine the "best value" for some quantity
when a number of measurements have been taken. The day before the lesson
examined here, Minstrell had posed the question in terms of five different
measurements of someone's blood alcohol content. Eight students had also
measured the width of a table, obtaining a range of different values. On this
fourth day of the school year the students discuss whether some or all of the
numbers should be taken into account, and how best to combine them. During
the lesson, Minstrell's questioning style invites contributions from the students.
These contributions provide a significant proportion of the content of the lesson.

The second lesson to be examined occurs in Deborah Ball's third grade
mathematics classroom, in the middle of the school year. Ball's students have
been discussing the properties of even and odd numbers. The previous day they
had met with a class of fourth graders to discuss some of the issues they had
been grappling with – for example, is the number zero even, odd, or "special"?
Ball begins this day's lesson with the request that the students reflect on
their thinking and learning, using the previous day's meeting as a catalyst for

Social Constructivist Teaching, Volume 9, pages 131–169.
Copyright © 2002 by Elsevier Science Ltd.
All rights of reproduction in any form reserved.
ISBN: 0-7623-0873-7

reflection. The ensuing discussion takes on a life of its own, with an intermingling of discussions of content and reflections on student learning.

In some ways the two lessons discussed in this chapter are worlds apart. To begin with the obvious, students in elementary and high school are very different in terms of social and cognitive development. In Ball's class the subject matter content is elementary mathematics, and the agenda is to have students reflect on their understandings. In Minstrell's class the subject matter is more advanced, and the agenda is to have the students sort out how best to make sense of it. Thus the agendas are radically different. Moreover, the two classroom communities are at very different points in their evolution. At the beginning of the year, Minstrell's class has not yet been shaped as a functioning discourse community (that is, the norms of interaction have not been established and internalized). By mid-year, Ball's class has well established sociomathematical norms.

In other ways, these two lessons are very similar. Both Minstrell and Ball work very hard to have their classrooms function as communities of disciplined inquiry. A major instructional goal is for students to experience mathematics/physics as a sense-making activity – as a disciplined way of understanding complex phenomena. A long-term goal of both teachers is for their students to internalize this form of sense-making. They believe it is important for their students to see themselves as people who are capable of making sense of mathematical and real-world phenomena, by reasoning carefully about them. Part of the way that Ball and Minstrell work toward these goals is to have their classrooms function as particular kinds of discourse communities, in which inquiry and reflection are encouraged and supported. Over the course of the year, sociomathematical norms in support of such practices are established. Classroom discourse practices support students' engagement with the content and their reflection on both the content and their understandings of it. One such discourse practice, captured as a pedagogical routine, is the focus of this paper.

This chapter unfolds as follows. I begin with a brief description of the analytic enterprise that gave rise to the discussion in this chapter, the work of the Teacher Model Group at Berkeley. This discussion explains how we came to examine lessons by Minstrell and Ball, and some of what we saw – including the classroom routine that I claim is common to both teachers. I also point to some of the literature on classroom discourse practices, to establish the contrast between traditional discourse patterns and the highly interactive routine used by Ball and Minstrell. With this as context, I move to a description of the routine itself. Following the general description, I work through sections of lessons by Minstrell and Ball, showing in detail how this routine plays out in practice. In a concluding discussion, I elaborate on a conjecture that this routine serves as a mechanism that teachers can use to help their classrooms evolve into highly interactive communities of inquiry.

BACKGROUND AND CONTEXT

The work described here is part of an ongoing body of work conducted by the Teacher Model Group (TMG) at Berkeley. In broadest terms, the goal of the TMG is to provide a rigorous theoretical characterization of the teaching process, employing an analytical framework that explains how and why teachers make the choices they do, in the midst of classroom interactions. Roughly speaking, the idea is that teachers' decision-making is a function of their goals, beliefs, and knowledge. That is, a teacher enters a specific classroom with certain (content-related and social) goals in mind for that day, as well as overarching goals for the school year. That teacher has certain understandings or beliefs about the nature of mathematics, about appropriate teaching practices, and about his or her students. He or she has various kinds of knowledge as well – knowledge of the mathematics, of pedagogy in general, of the students in the class, about the ways that class has unfolded in recent days and where the teacher wants it to go, etc. During the lesson, various things come up. For example, a student may make a mistake, and the teacher may suspect that other students need help with the same concept. Or, a student who has been quiet may risk a suggestion. Any of a million things may happen. How will the teacher respond, and why?

According to the theory, what the teacher does depends on the teacher's knowledge, goals, and beliefs. Take the case of a student saying something incorrect. How serious does the teacher consider this mistake to be? Does the teacher believe mistakes should be dealt with immediately? Does he or she believe in "correcting" mistakes, or in seeking the underlying cause for them? How much time does the teacher have to deal with the issue? What pedagogical methods or classroom routines does the teacher have available for dealing with this situation? On the basis of all of these, the teacher will choose whether or not to address the issue. How the issue is pursued will depend on what options the teacher perceives are available, what the costs and benefits of each option might be, and what the constraints of the situation might allow.

This brief description merely suggests a research agenda, which has unfolded over more than a decade (see, e.g. Schoenfeld, 1998, 1999, for details). That agenda has theoretical components (what do we mean by knowledge, goals, and beliefs? How do they interact?) and a corresponding body of empirical work, in which the theory is used to build models of specific teachers teaching specific lessons. The models serve to test the adequacy and scope of the theory.

Part of the specification of the model of a teacher teaching a particular lesson is the delineation of the cognitive and interactional resources that are available to the teacher and relevant to the lesson being modeled. Here I will not describe the architecture of knowledge used in the model, save to say that TMG's assumptions regarding the organization of memory are consistent with the standard cognitive model. Rather, I will focus on one particular kind of interaction, the classroom routine. As Leinhardt notes,

> Routines are vital. They reduce the cognitive processing load for both the student and the teacher; they are easy to teach because, by second grade, students have a schema of "learn the routine for X" – they expect them. Routines are considered efficient when they elicit an action with a minimum of time and confusion. Effective teachers have management, support, and exchange routines in place by the end of the second day in a school year. They retain 90% of these routines at midyear (Leinhardt, Weidman & Hammond, 1987). But routines are also subtle and set the tone of the class (Leinhardt, 1993, p. 15).

One classic teaching routine, a nearly ubiquitous discourse structure in classrooms in the U.S., is the "IRE sequence" – a sequence in which a teacher initiates an interaction, the student responds, and the teacher evaluates the response (see, e.g. Cazden, 1986; Mehan, 1979; Sinclair & Coulthard, 1975). This structure can be implemented with a fair amount of latitude, in that the student response and the teacher's evaluation of it can range from a word or a phrase to lengthy expositions. However, the stereotype – grounded in reality – is that in traditional didactic mathematics lessons, short IRE sequences are ideal vehicles for fostering student mastery of procedural skills. Typically, at some point in a lesson a teacher will ask students to provide their answers to a set of assigned problems. Students will be called upon to give their answers to the problems in sequence, and the teacher will assess the responses, possibly elaborating on points of importance.

Here, as an example, is part of the dialogue from a U.S. lesson on complementary and supplementary angles (U.S. Department of Education, 1997). The lesson comes from the videotape collection of the Third International Mathematics and Science Study (TIMSS). The tapes that were publicly released were chosen because of their representativeness.

The teacher begins the lesson by going over a homework assignment. After reminding students that measures of complementary angles add up to ninety degrees, he calls on a series of students to give their answers to the problems. The teacher works through the first problem with a student who had not done the assignment, and then continues:

I1. Teacher: What's the complement of an angle of seven degrees? Ho.
R1. Student: Eighty-three degrees.
E1. Teacher: Eighty-three.
I2. Teacher: The complement of an angle of eighty-four, Lindsay?
R2. Student: Sixteen.
E2/I3. Teacher: You sure about your arithmetic on that one?
R3. Student: Oh. Six.
E3. Teacher: Six. Six degrees.
I4. Teacher: Albert, number four.
R4. Student: Seventy-nine degrees?
E4. Teacher: [acknowledges correctness by continuing].
I5. Teacher: Number five, Joey.
R5. Student: Thirty-three.
E5/I6. Teacher: Sure about that? Claudia?
R6. Student: Twenty-three.
E6. Teacher: Twenty-three. You've got to be careful about your arithmetic . . .

Later in the lesson the teacher introduces the students to supplementary and vertical angles. The relevant information for working on the problems he assigns is that vertical angles are equal, and that supplementary angles add up to one hundred eighty degrees. After handing out a work sheet, the teacher continues:

Teacher: Look at the examples on the top. Similar to your warm-up. Look at the figure [below]. . . . Find the measure of each angle.

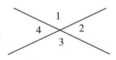

I7. Teacher: If angle three is one hundred twenty degrees . . . and angle three and angle one are vertical, what must angle one be equal to?
R7. Student: One twenty.
E7. Teacher: One hundred twenty degrees.
I8. Teacher: What can you tell me about angles two and three?
R8. Student: That they are vertical.
E8. Teacher: Two and three are not vertical. One and three are vertical. Two and four are vertical. Two and three are supplementary.
I9. Teacher: So, if three is a hundred and twenty, what must two be equal to?
R9. Student: Sixty.
E9. Teacher: Sixty. Two is sixty.
I10. Teacher: What must four be equal to?
R10. Student: Sixty.
E10: Teacher: Okay.

Little needs be said here by way of analysis. In terms of discourse, the I, R, and E labels say it all. The teacher posed a series of "short answer" questions.

When students responded correctly he confirmed the correctness of their answers. When they responded incorrectly he had them re-calculate (in E2/I3 and E5/I6) or, in the case of a factual mistake (E8), he informed them of the correct answer. In terms of sociomathematical norms, an earlier observation made by Lampert hits the nail on the head:

> Commonly, mathematics is associated with certainty; knowing it, with being able to get the right answer, quickly . . ... These cultural assumptions are shaped by school experience, in which *doing* mathematics means following the rules laid down by the teacher; *knowing* mathematics means remembering and applying the correct rule when the teacher asks a question; and mathematical *truth is determined* when the answer is ratified by the teacher. Beliefs about how to do mathematics and what it means to know it in school are acquired through years of watching, listening, and practicing (Lampert, 1990, p. 32).

As noted in the introduction, both Minstrell and Ball have very different goals for their students than the outcomes of traditional instruction described above by Lampert. Rather serendipitously, the TMG wound up analyzing lessons by both Minstrell and Ball. The Minstrell study came about early in TMG work. The first lesson we analyzed (see Zimmerlin & Nelson, 1999) was of a student teacher teaching a rather traditional lesson. While we were engaged in that analysis Emily van Zee, who had worked with Minstrell, joined the group. At that time van Zee was working on the analysis of a lesson taught by Minstrell. The van Zee and Minstrell (1997) analysis focused on a questioning strategy employed by Minstrell, "reflective tosses." TMG believed it would be useful to do a complementary analysis, focusing on Minstrell's knowledge, goals, and beliefs. In addition, Minstrell's lesson was very different from the lesson we had been analyzing. Minstrell was an experienced teacher, while Nelson was a beginner. Minstrell's lesson was non-traditional and of his own design, while Nelson's was traditional. And, while unexpected events in Nelson's lesson had caused him to run into some difficulties, unexpected events in Minstrell's lesson were dealt with smoothly. Studying Minstrell's lesson would be good for theory building: examining radically different cases is an important way to test the scope of an emerging theory, as well as its robustness.

Over a period of about two years, TMG refined its understanding of the Minstrell lesson and constructed a model of Minstrell's teaching (of that lesson). One component of the model was an interactive routine used by Minstrell to solicit ideas and information from his students. This routine, which used Minstrell's "reflective tosses," was a powerful tool for enfranchising the students. It made use of their ideas, rather than information provided by the teacher, to deal with the issues at hand.

Success in modeling the Minstrell lesson led to some confidence about the robustness of the TMG's theoretical constructs. Then, as the model of the lesson was being refined (see Schoenfeld, Minstrell & van Zee, 1999, for a description of the model), members of the research group saw a videotape of Deborah Ball's "Shea numbers" class. This lesson offered new challenges. Although Minstrell's and Nelson's lessons are very different, they share some very important properties. They deal with high school mathematics (and thus with high school students). And, both lessons are driven by the teacher's agenda. In Ball's class the students are third graders, so there are significant differences in terms of the students' knowledge bases, and their cognitive and social development. Equally important, the lesson in question had taken unexpected twists and turns. The agenda appeared to be co-constructed by the students and teacher, in response to ongoing events. The question was, could TMG's theoretical notions suffice to model this lesson – or was a detailed model of this lesson beyond the scope of the theory?

For quite some time the issue was in doubt; in Schoenfeld, Minstrell, and van Zee (1999) the authors noted that they had, thus far, been unsuccessful in modeling Ball's decision-making during the lesson in question. Ultimately, however, a model of the first part of the lesson, with all its unexpected twists and turns, was developed. When the structure of the lesson came to be understood, Ball's decision-making was represented in flow-chart form. At that point, TMG made a surprising discovery. The decision procedure represented by the flow chart was remarkably similar to the decision procedure that we had attributed to Minstrell!

The classroom routine represented by that decision-making structure is the focus of this chapter. I conjecture that this routine occurs with some frequency in "inquiry-oriented" classrooms, and that it helps such teachers to establish classroom communities in which disciplined inquiry is a major feature. The following section of this chapter provides a description of the routine.

A COMPLEX ROUTINE FOR SOLICITING AND WORKING WITH STUDENT IDEAS.

Unlike the IRE sequences described in the previous section, the teaching routine described in this section has as its function the elicitation and elaboration of student ideas. The full routine is outlined as a flow chart in Fig. 1. The discussion that follows provides a brief "tour" of the flow chart.

Each of the rectangles in Fig. 1, labeled [A1] through [A7], represents a possible action by the teacher. Each of the diamonds, labeled [D1] through [D5], represents a point at which the teacher makes a decision.

In broadest outline, the routine operates as follows. In [A1], the teacher introduces a topic to the class. In [A2], the teacher invites comment and calls

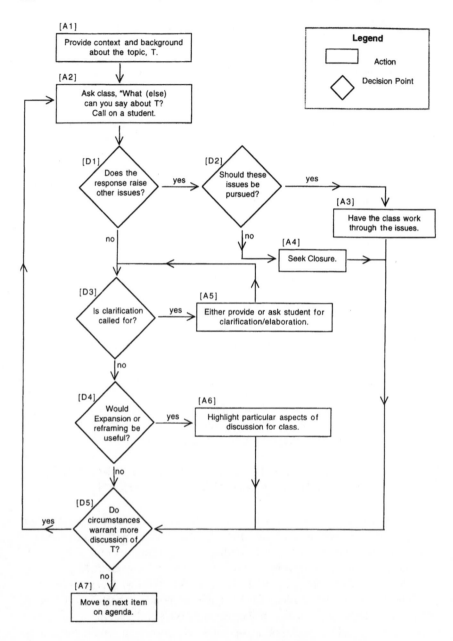

Fig. 1. A Highly Interactive Routine for Discussing a Topic.

on a student. There is always the possibility that the student's response will raise issues beyond those intended by the teacher. If it does ([D1] = "yes"), the teacher must decide whether or not to deal with those issues. That decision is represented by the right-hand branch leading from [D1]. If the student's comment is directly responsive to the teacher's prompt ([D1] = "no"), then the teacher uses that response as grist for the classroom conversation. First, the teacher decides (at [D3]) whether the class would profit from the clarification of the students' comment. If so, the teacher may prompt the student to say more, or the teacher may elaborate on what the student has said. Ultimately the student's comment is clarified to the degree deemed appropriate by the teacher. The next issue faced by the teacher (at [D4]) is whether it would be useful to expand on the student's comment, bringing particular aspects of the discussion to the class's attention. Having made that decision and acted accordingly, the teacher then decides (at [D5]) whether circumstances warrant a continuation of the discussion. If so, the teacher invites further comment. If not, the teacher makes a transition to the next item on his or her agenda.

It should be stressed that all of the teacher's decisions are highly context-dependent. Whether or not the teacher decides to ask a student to elaborate on a given point may, for example, depend on: the time left in that day's lesson; the teacher's perception of the student's readiness and willingness to pursue the idea; whether the class seems engaged; or many other factors.

In the following two sections of this chapter, I show how extended segments of dialogue in Minstrell and Ball's classrooms correspond to the routine described in Fig. 1. Two preliminary comments are necessary. First, I make no claim that Ball or Minstrell either consciously or unconsciously employed the decision procedure outlined in Fig. 1. Rather, the claim is that the routine "captures" the discourse patterns employed by the teachers – and that (see the final section of this chapter) this kind of routine may be a useful pedagogical device for teachers who wish to have their classrooms function as specific kinds of discourse communities. Second, the focus and length of this chapter preclude a detailed, line-by-line analysis of how and why these teachers made the choices they did. Detailed analyses of Minstrell's and Ball's lessons may be found respectively in Schoenfeld, Minstrell and van Zee (1999) and in Schoenfeld (1999).

ASPECTS OF JIM MINSTRELL'S "BENCHMARK" LESSON

Appendix A provides an extended excerpt (roughly 20 minutes of class time) of a lesson taught by Jim Minstrell. Here is the relevant context.

The lesson discussed here is part of a series of lessons specially designed by Minstrell as an introduction to his high school physics course. It takes place the fourth day of the course. The first two days of the course are devoted to introductory activities such as an extensive "name game" and a diagnostic test that documents the students' initial knowledge. On the third day Minstrell begins the substantive content of the course with a non-standard problem of his own design, the Blood Alcohol Content (BAC) problem. In essence, the problem is as follows. Suppose someone has been stopped for drunk driving, and five measurements of that person's blood alcohol content have been taken. You have the five numbers. Which of those numbers should be combined, in what way, to give the "best value" for the person's blood alcohol content?

The Blood Alcohol Content problem is a carefully chosen mechanism for introducing the content and social dynamics of the course. Minstrell has a number of high level goals for his students. He wants them to see physics as a sense-making activity – a way of making reasoned judgments about physical phenomena. He wants the students to see themselves as competent reasoners who are capable of sorting through complex issues themselves. He has, thus, chosen a problem that is meaningful to the students, and which they can engage fully. His discourse style will foster students' growth and autonomy: rather than evaluate student comments and questions, he will consistently (by means of an interactive technique he calls "reflective tosses") turn questions back to the students. Minstrell works to foster a classroom environment in which students feel enfranchised – an environment in which they feel it is their right (indeed, their responsibility) to raise issues and think through them carefully. Van Zee and Minstrell describe the context for the fourth lesson as follows.

> The students worked on the Blood Alcohol Content problem in small groups during the 3rd day of class. In addition, a student from each group independently measured the length and width of the same table. The numbers obtained for the width in centimeters were 106.8, 107.0, 107.0, 107.5, 107.0, 107.0, 106.5, and 106.0. Near the close of the 3rd day of class, Minstrell brought the students together for a brief discussion of reasons for using only some or using all of the numbers in the Blood Alcohol Count problem. For homework, the students were find the best value for the blood alcohol count and to decide whether the driver was drunk. They were also to calculate best values and uncertainties for the length and width of the table. Minstrell and students examined these issues on the fourth day of class during the discussion analyzed here. Minstrell described this as an 'elaboration benchmark discussion' in which he planned to work through a series of issues which the students had already opened and considered in small groups in class and on their own at home (van Zee & Minstrell, 1997, p. 240).

The first part of this fourth lesson is devoted to "housekeeping" issues related to course administration. When those issues have been dealt with, Minstrell turns to a discussion of the Blood Alcohol Content problem. Appendix A picks up the transcript of the lesson at this point. The discussion of Appendix A that follows will indicate that the flow of classroom discourse corresponds, with great fidelity, to the routine described in Fig. 1.[1]

First Implementation of the Routine: Lines 1–70

I claim that the classroom dialogue captured in lines 1–70 of the transcript can be represented by three "passes" through the routine, in lines 1–33, 34–45, and 46–70 respectively.

First Pass: Lines 1–33

Minstrell provides context and background for the discussion (step [A1] of the routine) in lines 1–12 of the transcript. He follows this in lines 13–14 by a request for student input (step [A2]). S1's response in line 15 is on target. Hence [D1] = "no," and he moves to [D3]. S1's comment in line 15 does call for elaboration ([D3] = "yes"), and Minstrell pursues the elaboration in lines 16–33. At this point neither abstraction nor re-framing is necessary ([D4] = "no"); the delineation of various contexts in which the highest and lowest values might be eliminated is sufficient. This completes the first pass through the routine. As the discussion has just begun, circumstances clearly warrant a continuation of the discussion ([D50] = "yes"). Hence Minstrell asks the students for additional comments.

This first pass through the routine is represented schematically in Fig. 2.

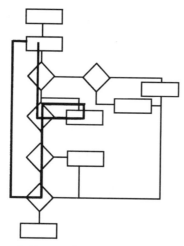

Fig. 2. A Schematic Representation of Lines 1–33 of Appendix A.

Second Pass: Lines 34–45

Minstrell begins the second round of discussion (step [A2]) in line 34. S4's response in line 36, dealing with the elimination of values that are too large or small, is on target ([D1] = "no") and does not need clarification ([D3] = "no"). Following the student's comment, Minstrell chooses to introduce a new vocabulary term ("outliers") and to expand upon the rationale for eliminating outliers ([D4] = "yes"). This completes the second pass through the routine. As there is still much to be said ([D5] = "yes"), Minstrell asks for additional input.

This second pass is represented schematically in Fig. 3.

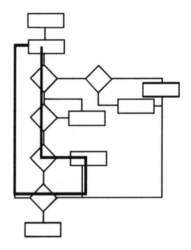

Fig. 3.   A Schematic Representation of Lines 34–45 of Appendix A.

Third Pass: Lines 46–66

Minstrell asks for "another one" (step [A2]) in line 46. S4's response (lines 47–49) is again on target ([D1] = "no") and does not need clarification ([D3] = "no"). As in the previous pass, Minstrell chooses to expand upon the student's answer ([D4] = "yes"); in doing so he completes the pass. In lines 65–66 Minstrell provides the opportunity for a continuation of the discussion. When it appears that the well has run dry, he moves (lines 67–70) to the next item on the agenda (step [A8]), the issue of how best to combine the numbers.

This third pass is represented schematically in Fig. 4.

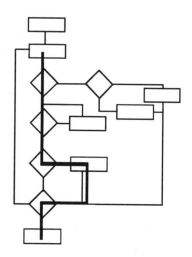

Fig. 4. A Schematic Representation of Lines 46–70 of Appendix A.

Second Implementation of the Routine: Lines 68–251

At this point in the lesson, the issue is how to best combine the given data. There are, of course, three classical measures of central tendency: mean, median, and mode. Rather than lay these out, Minstrell will ask the class "What the heck are we going to do with these numbers?" He has reason to expect, of course, that the students will generate the three measures of central tendency – and if they fail to generate one, he can always "seed" the conversation with reference to it. This situation is ideal for the use of the routine, in that the order in which the students generate ideas doesn't matter. Hence he can solicit suggestions and take them as they come.

I claim that lines 68–220 of the transcript can be represented by four passes through the routine (lines 68–89, 90–109, 110–214, and 214–220). Lines 221–251 represent the adaptive move suggested above, adding an approach to the list when the students fail to generate it themselves.

First Pass: Lines 68–89.
Minstrell begins in lines 68–70 by framing the problem of "best value" for class discussion (step [A1]), and continues in lines 71–72 by asking, "What's one thing we might do with the numbers?" (step [A2]). S5's response in line 73 is on the mark ([D1] = "no") and calls for clarification ([D3] = "yes"), which

Minstrell requests in lines 74–75. S5's definition in lines 76–77 is correct ([D3] = "no"). Minstrell decides ([D4] = "yes") to expand upon the definition in lines 78–89. This is just the beginning of the discussion, so ([D5] = "yes") he will pursue the discussion. This first pass is represented schematically in Fig. 5.

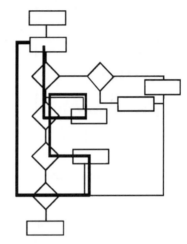

Fig. 5. A Schematic Representation of Lines 68–89 of Appendix A.

Second Pass: Lines 90–109.
Minstrell begins the second pass (lines 90–95, step [A2]) by asking if the students have "any other ideas" for computing the best value. S7's comment in line 96 begs for clarification ([D3] = "yes"), which emerges in dialogue in lines 97–104. Minstrell provides the formal definition of the term they have been discussing ([D4] = "yes") in lines 104–105 and ([D5] = "yes") moves to continue the discussion in lines 105–109.

This second pass is represented schematically in Fig. 6.

Third Pass: Lines 110–213.
Minstrell begins the third pass in line 110, with another request (step [A2]) for "another way of giving a best value." S8's response, which is non-standard, raises a number of very interesting issues ([D1] = "yes") which Minstrell pursues ([D2] = "yes") for quite some time.

A detailed examination of Minstrell's decision to follow up on S8's comments, and the way in which he did so, is fundamental to understanding how Minstrell's teaching reflects his top-level goals for his students (specifically, his goal of

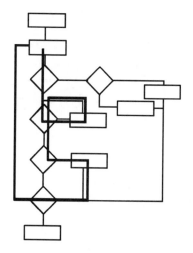

Fig. 6. A Schematic Representation of Lines 90–190 of Appendix A.

creating a discourse community that respects and encourages student initiative). That analysis, which is outside the scope of this chapter, may be found in Schoenfeld, Minstrell, and van Zee (1999). Suffice it to say here that Minstrell takes a substantial amount of time to explore the ramifications of the student's definition. In the process he covers some important subject matter and sends the message that a thoughtful suggestion from a student is important enough to warrant the expenditure of a significant amount of class time.

Minstrell wraps up this discussion in line 213 and ([D5] = "yes") invites the students to make additional suggestions.

This third pass is represented schematically in Fig. 7 (next page).

Fourth (Brief) Pass: Lines 214–220
At this point the mean and the mode have been discussed, but the median has yet to be mentioned. Minstrell begins the fourth pass in line 214, with a request (step [A2]) for another way to approach the problem. S12's response, "you could possibly take the number that appears most often," reintroduces the mode. Minstrell notes this, and then moves to bring closure to the discussion.

Coda: Introducing a Missing Element, Lines 221–251.

Due to the extended unplanned conversation in lines 110–213, it is much later in the class period than it typically would be at this point of the discussion.

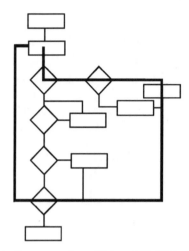

Fig. 7.   A Schematic Representation of Lines 110–213 of Appendix A.

The class has generated two of the three measures of central tendency (mean and mode) but failed to generate the third (median) in response to Minstrell's invitation in line 214. Minstrell introduces it himself in line 221. This adaptive modification of the routine will be considered in the concluding discussion of this chapter.

ASPECTS OF DEBORAH BALL'S "SHEA NUMBERS" LESSON

Appendix B provides an excerpt of the first part (roughly six minutes of class time) of a third-grade lesson taught by Deborah Ball. Here is the relevant context.

This class takes place in January, mid-way through the school year. The discourse community is well established. Ball has worked with her third graders to establish a community that operates according to specific sociomathematical norms, using a vocabulary tailored to those norms. Students make *conjectures*, and they are expected to provide evidence in favor of those conjectures. When a student *disagrees* with another student's conjecture, he or she must provide reason for the dissent: "I disagree because . . ." When a student wants to retract or alter a previously expressed opinion, he or she says "*I revise my thinking.*"

Ball's class has been exploring the properties of even and odd numbers. On the basis of empirical observations they have made some conjectures, for example that the sum of two odd numbers will always be even. They have also dealt with some conundrums, such as the classification of zero. All of the other whole numbers are either even or odd. Is zero even, odd, or perhaps "special"?

Part of Ball's agenda is to have the students reflect on their learning, and on the processes by which they come to understand mathematics. She wants them to understand that it takes a long time to make sense of some things – for example, that last year's third graders, now in the fourth grade, are still grappling with some of the issues that this year's class is working through. Ball had arranged for a meeting between this year's and last year's classes, to discuss even and odd numbers. That meeting took place on the day before the lesson in question. Her agenda as she opens this lesson is to "debrief" the students about their impressions of the previous day's meeting. What issues did it raise for them? She announces "I'd just like to hear some comments about what you thought about the meeting, what you noticed about the meeting, what you learned at the meeting."

As will be seen, the conversation takes some interesting twists and turns; it seems very loosely structured at first. Yet, the flow of dialogue corresponds closely to the routine discussed above: lines 1–8, 9–20C, 20D–24, 25–58, and 59–67 will be seen to correspond to five passes through the flow chart given in Fig. 1. There is much more to the analysis than can be discussed here; see Schoenfeld (1999) for details. The summary given here is derived from that analysis.

First Pass: Lines 1–8.
Ball begins the lesson in line 1 by establishing the context for the discussion (step [A1]) and (step [A2]) calling on Shekira to comment on the previous day's meeting. Shekira's comment in line 2 is on target ([D1] = "no") but needs clarification ([D3] = "yes"). Ball prompts for greater specificity (step [A5]) in line 3 and again in line 5. Given Ball's reflective agenda, Shekira's comment in line 6 does call for reframing ([D4] = "yes"). Ball does so in line 7 and ([D5] = "yes") calls on Shea to continue the discussion.

This first pass through the routine is represented schematically in Fig. 8.

Second Pass: Lines 9–20C
Events move differently in lines 9–20. Ball begins (step [A2]) by asking for more comments about the meeting. Shea's comment is not focused on the prior day's meeting, however. Rather, Shea disagrees with Shekira about an issue of mathematical content ([D1] = "yes"). Ball decides that this issue should be

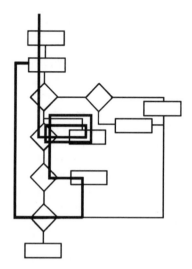

Fig. 8.   A Schematic Representation of Lines 1–8 of Appendix B.

worked through ([D2] = "yes") and she and the class watch (step [A3]) as Shea
and Shekira come to an uneasy accord. In line with her reflective agenda, Ball
comments in lines 20A-C about how difficult some of these issues are. Then
she moves ([D5] = "yes") in lines 20D–F to continue the discussion.

This pass through the routine is represented in Fig. 9.

Third Pass: Lines 20D–24
Ball invites further comment (step [A2]) in lines 20D-F, calling on Lin in line
20G. Lin's comment is on target ([D1] = "no") but invites a follow-up question ([D3] = "yes"), which Ball asks in line 22. Lin's response in line 23 stands
on its own ([D4] = "no"). Still interested in pursuing her agenda ([D5] = "yes"),
Ball asks for more comments. See Fig. 10.

Fourth and Fifth Passes: Lines 25–58 and 59–67
Lines 25–58 are extremely interesting – the question being why Ball, in line
26, embarked on an explicit, announced detour from her reflective agenda.
A great deal can be said about this decision; see Schoenfeld (1999) for detail.
That issue is beyond the scope of the current discussion. Here I restrict my
attention to the routine described in Fig. 1. Ball calls for more comments (step
[A2]) in line 24. From her perspective Benny's response in line 25 raises issues
that she wanted to address ([D2] = "yes"). Ball works through those issues (step

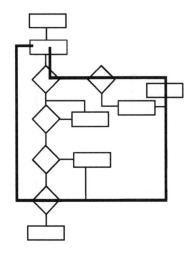

Fig. 9.   A Schematic Representation of Lines 9–20C of Appendix B.

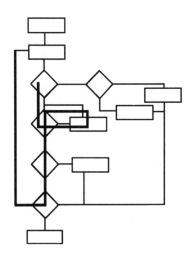

Fig. 10.   A Schematic Representation of Lines 20D–24 of Appendix B.

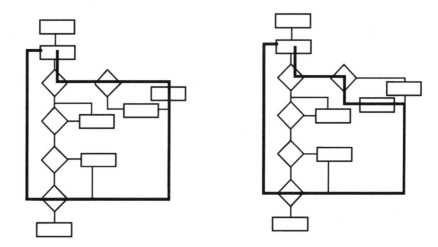

Fig. 11.   Representations of Lines 25–58 and 59–67 of
Appendix B, respectively.

[A3]) in lines 26C through 58. Having done so ([D2] = "yes") she returns to
her reflective agenda.

In line 59, Ball starts the next pass through the routine (step [A2], "I'd really
like to hear from as many people as possible what comments you had or
reactions you had to being in that meeting yesterday"). Shea himself announces
in line 60 that his comment is off topic. Ball misinterprets Shea's comment in
lines 60 and 62 (see Ball, undated); she believes that he is addressing Benny's
conjecture, which had been the focus of lines 25–58. This issue, having been
resolved at some length, does not warrant further discussion ([D2] = "no"),
and Ball moves to obtain closure in line 65. She still wishes to pursue her
reflective agenda ([D5] = "yes"), and in line 67 she asks for more comments.
These two passes through the routine are represented in Fig. 11.

DISCUSSION

If the preceding analyses are right, then the two very dissimilar-looking lesson
segments taught by Jim Minstrell and Deborah Ball share, at one level of
analysis, the same deep structure. Does that matter? I think it does.

This is where the discussion becomes conjectural. What follows is grounded
in my reflections on the way I teach my undergraduate problem solving course

and my understandings of Ball's and Minstrell's intentions and actions. Although the three of us are *very* different people (and teachers), we do have some goals and practices in common. The goals include creating learning environments in which our students experience mathematics or physics as a form of sense-making; in which the students reflect on their learning; and in which they develop certain productive habits of mind. The practices include the routine that has been the focus of this chapter. I suspect that the routine described in Fig. 1 – which is quite flexible, depending on the constraints the teacher imposes on it – can and often does play a significant role in the establishment and maintenance of highly interactive classroom discourse communities.

To establish the context for the discussion that follows, let me describe an apparent paradox. One of the most important goals of my problem solving course is the shaping of the classroom environment in a very particular way – as a community of independent thinkers engaged collaboratively in reasoned discourse. I have written about this goal as follows:

> The activities in our mathematics classrooms can and must reflect and foster the understandings that we want students to develop with and about mathematics. That is: if we believe that doing mathematics is an act of sense-making; if we believe that mathematics is often a hands on, empirical activity; if we believe that mathematical communication is important; if we believe that the mathematical community grapples with serious mathematical problems collaboratively, making tentative explanations of these phenomena, and then cycling back through those explanations (including definitions and postulates); if we believe that learning mathematics is empowering, and that there is a mathematical way of thinking that has value and power, then our classroom practices must reflect these beliefs. Hence we must work to construct learning environments in which student actively engage in the science of mathematical sense-making (Schoenfeld, 1994, pp. 60–61).

If I am true to my word, then my problem solving class should have a pretty free-wheeling atmosphere. Yet, when Arcavi, Kessel, Meira, and Smith (1998) analyzed my problem solving course, they found that this was decidedly not the case as the course got under way. In the first few days of the class, analysis revealed, I exercised a subtle but firm controlling hand. Is this hypocritical, or inconsistent with my avowed goals?

In a word, no. At the beginning of the semester the class had not yet developed the norms of respectful and substantive exchange that are necessary for the successful functioning of a free-wheeling community. One of my major jobs as the semester began was to encourage the students to take risks and express their opinions – but in such a way that they did so on solid mathematical grounds, and without stepping on each other's toes. The more practiced they became at this, the less I needed to provide structure. Ultimately, the community functioned on its own (see Schoenfeld, 1994).

With this as background, let me return to the routine described in Fig. 1. In a sense, the flow chart in Fig. 1 makes things look too straightforward, for there is a great deal of subtlety to the implementation. Teachers have a great deal of flexibility in implementing the routine, because the decision points [D1] through [D5] provide a large degree of latitude. Suppose, for example, that the teacher consistently declines to pursue issues other than those on his or her agenda (that is, [D2] is consistently "no"), and that when clarification is called for, the teacher provides it. The result is that classroom events, although highly interactive, will unfold very much according to the teacher's agenda. On the other hand, the teacher might encourage the students to pursue interesting issues when they arise ([D2] is consistently "yes"), and may consistently turn issues back to the students, pointing out that clarification is needed but leaving it to the students to provide it. When the routine is implemented in this way, the classroom agenda is essentially co-constructed and the classroom community is largely on its way to autonomous functioning. The same routine, then, can be made to function in different ways, depending on the "state of the community." It is reasonable to conjecture that a teacher might use the routine in somewhat constrained ways while the norms of the classroom community are being developed, and then in less constrained ways as the discourse community comes into its own.

I don't want to push the data too far, but this seems to be the case in the two lessons examined in this chapter. Minstrell's lesson is wonderfully enfranchising and interactive (especially compared to traditional presentations). At the same time, his use of the routine in Fig. 1 is also reasonably well constrained. On the one hand, Minstrell employs a large number of techniques that invite student participation in important ways. The simple act of waiting for as long as nine seconds after asking a question (thirteen seconds in other parts of the lesson) makes it clear that his questions are not rhetorical, but are meant to provoke student responses. The frequency of questions is astounding. More than half of Minstrell's dialogic turns involve posing serious questions to the students, and the students' responses provide much of the substance of the discussion. Some of that substance is clearly new – consider for example the exchange in lines 171 to 189. (Minstrell clarifies the suggested procedure and asks the class for its opinion of it. In the ensuing discussion all of the ideas come from the students.) And when a student makes an unexpected comment in lines 111–114, Minstrell devotes a large amount of time to exploring the idea she suggests.

Looked at from the students' perspective, this is a remarkably "open" lesson. Students are actively encouraged to participate and when they do the teacher picks up their ideas and runs with them – even if the discussion leads in unexpected directions. The ideas are worked through carefully. In exploring the properties of S8's proposed "average" (Is this the same as what we usually call average? Does it provide a good summary of the data?), Minstrell models the kind of discourse practices he expects: in this class, new ideas will be honored by being subjected to careful scrutiny! Over time, the students will perceive it to be their obligation to run with each other's ideas in similar ways.

On the other hand, Minstrell remains firmly in charge of the agenda for the class. His questions, while often turning responsibility back to the students, provide clear direction for the conversation; his comments often add substance to what a student has said. His one deviation from his planned agenda, in lines 110–213, has significant "value added." Pursuing S8's question honors student inquiry. It provides the opportunity to explore the properties of the arithmetic average and this proposed variant of it, both of which are plausible extensions of the lesson's content. And it models the process of exploring new ideas. The opportunity is serendipitous and the decision to pursue it spontaneous – but pursuing it is very much in line with the teacher's top-level agenda. Beyond this, it is worth noting that Minstrell's use of the routine to discuss the "best value" has a built-in safety valve. The students may well suggest all three standard measures of central tendency (mean, median, and mode). But if they only mention two, Minstrell can always mention the third himself.

In sum, Minstrell's use of the routine sets the students on the path to autonomy, by providing a structure that will ultimately support free-wheeling classroom discussion – and it is used in a way that is carefully scaffolded. This seems entirely appropriate for one of the first classes of the year.

In contrast, Ball's lesson takes place mid-year, at which point the relevant sociomathematical norms have been well established. (As one indication of this, we have Shea's comment to Shekira in turn 10. The comment is polite; it uses the technical term *disagree*; and his disagreement is backed up with an implicit appeal to the definition of evenness.)

Let us examine the first three passes through the routine. In this part of the lesson Ball plays much more of a facilitative rather than a directive role. In the first pass through the routine, Ball asks questions designed to help Shekira articulate her feelings about the meeting. During the second pass Ball stands aside while Shea and Shekira discuss Shekira's statement that zero "could be even." Her doing so is important, and reflects the state of the community. The conversation between Shea and Shekira is about the mathematics rather than about the meeting – in focusing on the properties of zero, it raises "other issues" than those in Ball's reflective agenda. By standing aside and giving Shea and Shekira room to pursue this conversation, Ball not only honors student initiative but, de facto, gives the students a role in the day's agenda-setting. In the third pass, Ball asks Lin the obvious question – in essence, "how are you going to deal with your current state of confusion?" – and then lets Lin's answer speak for itself.

These actions, I would argue, are entirely in line Ball's goals and with the capacity of the class to function as a productive discourse community. They are consistent with what happens later in the class session, when the agenda is again co-constructed (the class pursues a conjecture by Shea that the number six can be both even and odd) and the students, largely on their own, engage in extended and substantive mathematical discussions.

In sum, the routine outlined in Fig. 1 plays out very differently in the two lessons studied – appropriately so, given the state of each discourse community at the time the routine was implemented. It appears, on the basis of these lessons and my reflection on my own teaching, that this routine – tailored to circumstances – plays a useful role in shaping and then maintaining the productive exchange of ideas. For those of us who believe that classrooms should be homes to communities of reasoned discourse, it can be a useful tool.

CODA

When we were invited to contribute to this volume, Jere Brophy asked the authors to address six specific issues. I have dealt with a number of those issues tacitly in the body of this chapter, but in the spirit of cooperation, let me be explicit in addressing them here. The questions and my responses follow.

What Does Social Constructivist Teaching Mean in the Area(s) of Teaching on Which your Scholarly Work Concentrates?

I hate to start off on an oppositionist note, but I have some serious difficulties with the phrase "social constructivist teaching." For me, social constructivism is a theoretical perspective that can be used to help understand what happens in classrooms – any classrooms. As such, social constructivism doesn't represent or endorse a particular kind of teaching. Be that as it may . . .

I view mathematics as a particularly powerful and empowering lens through which one can make sense of the world. Mathematics coheres – it fits together, and one can make sense of it. I want students to experience mathematics this way, and to come away from their mathematics instruction with a sense of themselves as competent and autonomous reasoners. I may have gone a bit overboard rhetorically in the segment of Schoenfeld (1994) quoted above, but I still believe the bottom line: If we want students to become mathematical sense-makers, we need to construct learning environments in which they actively engage in mathematical sense-making.

Some clarification is necessary here – I want to avoid extremes. On the one hand, a steady diet of straight didactic presentations and imitative exercises deprives students of autonomy and of the sense that they are capable of doing mathematics on their own. On the other hand the equally extreme alternative, a caricature of discovery learning in which students are given interesting problems and set loose with little guidance, is also untenable. The "sink or swim" approach is no more appropriate for learning to think mathematically than it is for learning to swim.

What I think *is* appropriate is a carefully chosen combination of curriculum and pedagogy. What we know in curricular terms is that it is not necessary for students to be taught everything, and then to engage in imitative exercises: it is possible for students to learn (some) things by solving problems, rather than learning things first and then applying what they have learned to so-called "problems." We have also seen – and Ball's and Minstrell's classrooms are prime examples – that students are capable of much more sophisticated reasoning than we tend to give them credit for. However, classrooms that support that kind of reasoning do not tend to occur by spontaneous generation. It is an act of great pedagogical skill to shape a classroom discourse community so that it facilitates productive exchanges among students. It takes vigilance to maintain such a community – although, paradoxically, the "presence" of the teacher may seem diminished as the students become more autonomous and the community seems to function more "on its own." Yet such intellectual communities – classrooms in which students participate in disciplinary sense-making that is structured and scaffolded where necessary and appropriate – are what I hope to see more of.

What is the Rationale for Using These Methods, and What Forms do they Take?

There is a large body of research indicating that students develop their sense of the mathematical enterprise from their experience in mathematics classrooms. The consequences of traditional didactic instruction are all too well known (recall the quote from Lampert, 1990; see also Schoenfeld, 1992; Voigt, 1989). Increasingly, there are "existence proofs" of the kind discussed here, where students learn to engage in disciplined inquiry. Moreover, there is now compelling evidence that some of the new "reform" curricula in mathematics are producing gains on (oh yes!) standardized tests (Schoenfeld, 2002).

The rationale for the "middle ground" approach suggested above is simple. Students are much more likely to develop productive habits of mind when they have the opportunity to practice those habits, and to develop a disposition toward sense-making when they are members of communities that engage (successfully!) in such practices. As suggested above, crafting such communities takes a good deal of work. People are not born knowing how to interact respectfully and productively; they have to be taught to do so. In each classroom, the "didactical contract" needs to be established and negotiated. Students often begin a course with the default assumption that this course, like others, will be run according to the "standard rules;" in courses that operate differently, different expectations need to be made explicit. Moreover, a fair amount of scaffolding is likely to be necessary. In Schoenfeld (1994), for example, I describe the way in which I explicitly violate the normative expectation that my job as teacher is to evaluate the correctness of the arguments they propose.

> The second day of class . . . a student volunteered to present a problem solution at the board. As often happens, the student focused his attention on me rather than on the class when he wrote his argument on the board; when he finished he waited for my approval or critique. Rather than provide it, however, I responded as follows:
>
> > Don't look to me for approval, because I'm not going to provide it. I'm sure the class knows more than enough to say whether what's on the board is right. So (turning to class) what do you folks think?
>
> In this particular case the student had made a claim which another student believed to be false. Rather than adjudicate, I pushed the discussion further: How could we know which student was correct? The discussion continued for some time, until we found a point of agreement for the whole class. The discussion proceeded from there. When the class was done (and satisfied) I summed up.
>
> This problem discussion illustrated a number of important points for the students, points consistently emphasized in the weeks to come. First, I rarely *certified* results, but turned points of controversy back to the class for resolution. Second, the class was to accept little on faith. This is, "we proved it in Math 127" was not considered adequate reason to accept a statement's validity. Instead, the statement must be grounded in mathematics solidly understood by this class. Third, my role in class discussion would often be that of Doubting Thomas. That is, I often asked "Is that true? How do we know. Can you give me an example? A counterexample? A proof?", both when the students' suggestions were correct and when they were incorrect. (A fourth role was to ensure that the discussions are respectful – that it's the mathematics at stake in the conversations, not the students!)
>
> > This pattern was repeated consistently and deliberately, with effect. Late in the second week of class, a student who had just written a problem solution on the board started to turn to me for approval, and then stopped in mid-stream. She looked at me with mock resignation and said "I know, I know." She then turned to the class and said "O.K., do you guys buy it or not?" [After some discussion, they did]" (Schoenfeld, 1994, pp. 62–63. Reprinted with permission).

The net result of this kind of interaction was that by the end of the semester, the class was challenging assertions much more regularly, demanding solid rationales, and often deciding autonomously whether or not an argument that had been presented was indeed correct. I still played the role of Doubting Thomas on occasion, and I had no hesitation in weighing in when I judged that my mathematical input was needed – but in many ways my intervention was needed less than at the beginning of the course.

It is difficult to abstract this kind of interaction into a general rule (and I distrust general rules). Parenthood may not be a bad metaphor, however. The idea is to turn over as much to the students as one thinks they can handle responsibly – and to be nearby with a safety net, just in case.

What are the Strengths/Areas of Applicability of these Teaching Methods, and What are their Weaknesses/areas of Irrelevance or Limited Applicability?

Teaching for deep understanding is hard. It calls for a substantial amount of understanding and flexibility on the part of the teacher – the willingness to explore ideas as they come up, the ability to make judgments about what might be productive directions and what might not, and the ability to provide the "right" level of support for students individually and collectively. Few teachers have had the relevant kinds of experiences as students, much less as teachers. Nor do we, at present, provide opportunities for "on the job training."

As I suggested above, what is needed is a combination of particular kinds of curriculum and pedagogy; assessment plays a critical facilitating or inhibiting role as well. Various "reform-oriented" curricula developed after the issuance of the 1989 NCTM *Standards* support some of the practices discussed here. Evidence is mounting that when teachers are provided professional development consistent with those curricula, and assessments are aligned with them, that students learn a lot more (see Schoenfeld, 2002).

When, Why, and How are Social Constructivist Methods used Optimally?

I'm not sure I can address this question, partly because there's a "chicken and egg" problem. I teach a problem solving course at the college level. In many ways it's "remedial" – I have to teach some things I'd hope my students would have learned long ago. Because of this, I focus more on thinking (problem solving strategies; habits of mind) than I do on specific subject matter content. But, I can imagine a world in which students had learned to think mathematically from kindergarten on . . .

Even so, optimality is going to be elusive for quite some time – until we have much more widespread experience with teaching techniques and curricula as discussed in this chapter. Optimality will also, I think, always be a question of values. Clearly, I value a certain kind of mathematical disposition, and certain habits of mind. But, what do students absolutely have to know? Will I be content if my students can regenerate some things, rather than recalling them, or if they know where to look them up? Your answers may differ from mine. And depending on the answers you give, your pedagogical practices may vary.

When, Why, and How do these Methods Need to be Adjusted from Their Usual Form in Order to Match the Affordances and Limitations of Certain Students, Instructional Situations, etc.?

I think the discussion of the two examples in this chapter suggests an answer, though the answer may be more vague than the reader would like. In some sense, everything is context-dependent. One has certain values and certain goals for one's students; one makes certain (research-based) assumptions about the kinds of environments that will help students attain those goals. The "rest" is scaffolding. But that's easy for me to say . . . .

I'd be tempted to leave it at that, but I do have to address one pernicious misconception regarding such issues. Some will argue that the kinds of practices discussed here are OK for "bright kids," but that "slow kids" need more didactic instruction. To pursue that path is only to exacerbate inequities. Evidence is now becoming available that "reform-oriented" instruction works across the boards. Not only do more students do well when they engage meaningfully with mathematics, but fewer students "bottom out" (Briars, 2001; Briars & Resnick, 2000; Schoenfeld, 2002).

When and Why are these Methods Irrelevant or Counterproductive (and What Methods Need to be Used Instead in these Situations)?

This is a matter of belief, and a matter how extreme one is willing to be (on either the didactic or the "teaching for understanding" side). Take a simple procedure like the one for subtraction. From one perspective, there's one right way to do subtraction (the "standard" algorithm) and the most effective way to teach it is to drill students on it. From another perspective, what counts is understanding the algorithm. If you do, you'll be flexible and have a number of different ways to do subtractions.

Which is "right"? I'm reminded of a story I was told long ago by Fred Reif. Fred needed a blood test. The technician at his HMO said "please give

me the index finger of your left hand." Fred said, "I play the viola and I
have a rehearsal tonight. Please use the right hand instead." The technician
then said, "please give me the index finger of your left hand." Fred repeated
his request. The technician thought long and hard, and then said "I guess
that would be OK."

On the one hand, we can all be horrified at the thought of a technician in an
HMO who doesn't know whether it's OK to take blood from the right hand instead
of the left. On the other hand, Fred pointed out that there are costs involved. Would
you want a doctor to be doing all the blood tests? That could get expensive. The
odds are that less than one patient in a hundred causes the kind of problem Fred
did, so the limited training the technician received was adequate the vast
majority of the time. The optimal solution lies somewhere between those two
extremes – and what you decide is optimal depends on your values.

NOTE

1. I am not claiming that Minstrell, consciously or unconsciously, follows this
routine in an explicit way – any more than one would claim traditional teachers
consciously employ IRE sequences. The claim, rather, is that the routine in Fig. 1
serves as a remarkably accurate post hoc description of the discourse patterns in
Minstrell's classroom.

ACKNOWLEDGMENTS

I would like to thank Deborah Ball and Jim Minstrell for their willingness to
make their lessons available for comment. Thanks to Emily van Zee and Cathy
Kessel for comments on this manuscript, and to all four of the above for their
colleagueship through the years.

REFERENCES

Arcavi, A., Kessel, C., Meira, L., & Smith, J. P. (1998). Teaching mathematical problem solving:
    An analysis of an emergent classroom community. In: A. Schoenfeld, J. Kaput &
    E. Dubinsky (Eds), *Research in Collegiate Mathematics Education, III* (pp. 1–70).
    Washington, D.C.: Conference Board of the Mathematical Sciences.
Ball, D. L. (Undated). Annotated transcript of segments of Deborah Ball's January 19, 1990 class.
    Distributed by Ball at the research pre-session to the 1997 annual NCTM meeting, San
    Diego.
Briars, D., & Resnick, L. (2000). Standards, assessments – and what else? The essential elements
    of standards-based school improvement. Manuscript submitted for publication.
Briars, D. (2001). Mathematics Performance in the Pittsburgh public schools. Presentation at a
    Mathematics Assessment Resource Service conference on tools for systemic improvement,
    San Diego, CA.

Cazden, C. (1986). Classroom discourse. In: M. C. Wittrock (Ed.), *Handbook of Research on Teaching* (3rd ed., pp. 432–463). New York: Macmillan.

Lampert, M. (1990). When the problem is not the question and the solution is not the answer: Mathematical knowing and teaching. *American Educational Research Journal, 27*(1) 29–63.

Leinhardt, G. (1993). On teaching. In: R. Glaser (Ed.), *Advances in Instructional Psychology* (Vol. 4, pp. 1–54). Hillsdale, NJ: Erlbaum.

Leinhardt, G., Weidman, C., & Hammond, K. (1987). Introduction and integration of classroom routines by expert teachers. *Curriculum Inquiry, 17*(2), 135–176.

Mehan, H. (1979). *Learning lessons*. Cambridge: Harvard University Press.

Schoenfeld, A. H. (1992). Learning to think mathematically: Problem solving, metacognition, and sense-making in mathematics. In: D. Grouws (Ed.), *Handbook for Research on Mathematics Teaching and Learning* (pp. 334–370). New York: MacMillan.

Schoenfeld, A. H. (1994). Reflections on doing and teaching mathematics. In: A. Schoenfeld (Ed.), *Mathematical Thinking and Problem Solving* (pp. 53–70). Hillsdale, NJ: Erlbaum.

Schoenfeld, A. H. (1998). Toward a theory of teaching-in-context. *Issues in Education, 4*(1), 1–94.

Schoenfeld, A. H. (1999). *Dilemmas/decisions: Can we model teachers' on-line decision-making?* Paper presented at the Annual Meeting of the American Educational Research Association, Montreal, Quebec, Canada, April 19–23, 1999.

Schoenfeld, A. H. (Ed.) (1999). *Examining the complexity of teaching*. Special issue of the *Journal of Mathematical Behavior, 18*(3).

Schoenfeld, A. H. (2002). Making mathematics work for all children: Issues of standards, testing, and equity. *Educational Researcher, 31*(1), 13–25.

Schoenfeld, A. H., Minstrell, J., & van Zee, E. (1999). The detailed analysis of an established teacher carrying out a non-traditional lesson. *Journal of Mathematical Behavior, 18*(3), 281–325.

Sinclair, J., & Coulthard, R. (1975). *Towards an analysis of discourse: The English used by teachers and pupils*. London: Oxford University Press.

U.S. Department of Education (1997). Attaining excellence: TIMSS as a starting point to examine teaching. Eighth grade mathematics lessons: Unites States, Japan, and Germany. Videotape ORAD 97-1023R. Washington, D.C.: Office of Educational Research and Improvement.

Voigt, J. (1989). Social functions of routines and consequences for subject matter learning. *International Journal of Educational Research, 13*(6), 647–656.

van Zee, E., & Minstrell, J. (1997). Using questioning to guide student thinking. *Journal of the Learning Sciences, 6*(2), 227–269.

Zimmerlin, D., & Nelson, M. (1999). The detailed analysis of a beginning teacher carrying out a traditional lesson. *Journal of Mathematical Behavior, 18*(3), 263–280.

APPENDIX A:
EXTENDED SEGMENT OF JIM MINSTRELL'S CLASS DISCUSSION OF MEASUREMENT

1 T: OK. So we've talked a bit about Blood Alcohol Count, and then we've also got the
2   table measurement to include in this. So those are the contexts in which we can talk
3   about measurement. And let me see if I can remember where we were on Friday in
4   terms of the discussion. And let's see.
5   You can help me out, ah, but I think one of the topics that we had talked a bit about
6   was getting, what I ended up calling, a best value. Getting the best number we can.
7   What is the blood alcohol count number for this person? What is the number for the
8   length of that table? or for the width of that table?
9   And on Friday, some people said, 'let's take all the numbers' and some said, 'let's only
10   take some numbers.' So that was one of the issues that we came up with, whether to
11   take all the numbers that were used in the measurement or whether to only take some
12   of the numbers.
13   And some of the reasons that we listed for taking some numbers were – what was one
14   of them?
15 Sl: Eliminate highest and lowest.
16 T: OK. You might want to eliminate highest and lowest. [writes on board] Is there a
17   context in which, ah, that's done? A measurement context that you can think of where
18   that's done?
19 S2: Math
20 T: In some, in some math situations?
21 S?: [unintelligible]
22 T: Pardon me?
23 S?: [unintelligible]
24 T: You always do that.
25 S?: [unintelligible]
26 T: Teachers always do that, do they? Teachers always eliminate the highest and lowest?
27 Ss: [overlapping unintelligible student comments]
28 T: OK. Sometimes, ah, sometimes in some classes the teacher will, ah, or students will,
29   or teachers will allow students to, or whatever it is, to eliminate the highest and lowest.
30 S3: [partially intelligible]: sometimes scores are eliminated in diving.
31 T: OK. So in diving sometimes you eliminate the highest and lowest? Often in the
32   measurement of diving, you have all those judges eliminate the top and bottom number
33   and take the rest and do something with the rest of them.
34   OK. What's another way at going at taking some of the numbers and not all of them?
35   [S4]?
36 S4: The ones that [unintelligible comment involving eliminating extreme values]

37   T: OK. So we might eliminate – You need to let me know if I'm writing too small or if
38   you don't understand the words that I'm writing down. O.K.?
39   T: That's 'eliminate.' [points to abbreviation on board] All right. Eliminate, ah, what I'll
40   call an outlier. If there are numbers that are just completely out of the ballpark, I mean
41   the rest of these are sort of in a ballpark in there and then there's one that is just way
42   out of there, or two, that are just way out of there, or something like that, then you
43   might just eliminate the outliers, possibly, O.K.?
44   T: And keep all the measures that seem like they're pretty much in the same ballpark.
45   That's another, ah, decision outcome that you might come to.
46   O.K.? What was another one?
47   S4: What about, [it said like in the law that you, um, had like a certified nurse and a doctor
48   I think it was, and you have to eliminate certain people who weren't certified to test the
49   blood or to take the blood].
50   T: O.K. Can you hear her back there [S5]?
51   S5: No.
52   T: No? All right. You want to say that a little louder?
53   S4: You have to eliminate the ones that weren't absolutely certified to take the blood test.
54   T: O.K. In that context or essentially in general then you might want to take those
55   numbers, ah, done by quote the experts, something like that, and then, ah, in there
56   there was a special context like, ah, like for example, ah, some people said, "Oh,
57   goodness, the MD is the one who should do it" and others disagreed with that as
58   being, that person as being the expert; some people said, "Oh what's important is that I
59   take MINE, my measurement, because my measurement I KNOW is right, but
60   anybody else's, I don't know, but MINE I know is right." So there are several ways of
61   getting at 'experts' there; you might even want to question, you know, Who is the
62   expert?" Am I really an expert here?" or "Is the MD really an expert there? so there's
63   some question in there when you start taking it from the experts, you know – who's to
64   decide who the experts are?
65   O.K.? Any other reasons you can think of to only take some of the numbers?
66   [9s pause]
67   O.K. I think that's pretty much the list we had on Friday.
68   All right. Now. We're trying to get a best value and we might take all of the numbers
69   or we might take some of the numbers and then it's, what the heck are we going to do
70   with those numbers? O.K.?
71   So now we've got some numbers there, what are we going to do with those numbers?
72   What's one thing that we might do with the numbers? [S5]
73   S5: Average them.
74   T: O.K. [writes 'average them' on board] We might average them. Now what do you
75   mean by 'average' here. [S5]?
76   S5: Add up all the numbers and then divide by whatever amount of numbers you added
77   up.
78   T: All right. That is a definition for "average".
79   In fact, that's what we'll call an "operational definition". An operational definition is a
80   definition where you, where you give a recipe for how to find what it is that you're
81   talking about. And in this particular case, she's saying, "Add the number of – whether
82   you're talking about some of the numbers or all of the numbers – add those up and
83   divide by however many there are. And that's called the arithmetical average and to get
84   that you add them up and divide by how many there are. O.K.?

85		[talking while writing this on the board] That's an average that you often use in lots of
86		different contexts and it's an average that we'll use in here, but look out! because there
87		are lots of times when that's not the best average to use. On finding the best value,
88		that's a pretty good way to get the arithmetic, or the arithmetic average is a pretty good
89		way of getting a best value. O.K.?
90		Any other suggestions for what we might do? So we can average them – [8s pause]
91		Any other suggestions there for what we might do to get a best value?
92		I'll put up the numbers that we had from the table measurement on Friday in first
93		period, for the length, for the width and the length. As you look at that array of
94		numbers, any other ideas there that come to mind as to how you might go about
95		getting a best value from these numbers you're going to take there? [S7]?
96	S7:	You've got a bunch of numbers that are the same number.
97	T:	O.K. Like what are you talking about there?
98	S7:	107.
99	T:	All right. 107 point zero, 107 point 0, 107 point 0, 107 point 0.
100		Is there any other number in the width column that shows up as much as 107 point
101		zero?
102	S:	No.
103	T:	No. OK? So it's the number that shows up the most often is another way of picking
104		one. That's called the, um, the mode. OK? [writes on board] The number that shows
105		up most frequently. OK. That's another way of getting a best value out of a collection
106		of numbers that you're willing to keep.
107		Does that make sense? Anybody confused here? yet? Haven't confused anybody yet?
108		Then I've got to push a little harder. [4s pause]
109		All right?
110		Anybody think of another way of giving a best value? [S5]?
111	S8:	This is a little complicated but I mean it might work. If you see that 107 shows up 4
112		times, you give it a coefficient of 4, and then 107.5 only shows up one time, you give it
113		a coefficient of one, you add all those up and then you divide by the number of
114		coefficients you have.
115	T:	You lost me.
116	S?:	[unintelligible] [overlapping student comments]
117	S8:	One of those numbers. It's just that the more times it shows up, that makes like makes
118		it a more, um, a more weight.
119	T:	OK. Let me see if I can follow what you're saying then. You're saying one zero seven
120		point zero shows up four times [writing on board] so let me put a multiplier in front of
121		it, {sotto voce: that's what a coefficient is}, of four, and then what, what am I going to
122		do?
123	S8:	Ah, you average that, well then you, just say there are, ah, five numbers, and another
124		one is.
125	T:	Well let's go ahead and use this first column right here.
126	S8:	OK. Then, ah, well, [unintelligible]
127	T:	So everything else only comes up once.
128	S8:	Wait. One, yeah, looks like it. So everything else just gets one.
129	T:	All right. So one and, ah, we've got, ah, one oh six point eight.
130	S8:	Eight.
131	T:	And one?
132	S:	Oh seven point five.

133 S8: Oh seven point five.
134 T: One oh seven point five. And one?
135 S?: Six point five
136 T: One oh six point five.
137 S?: One oh six.
138 T: One, one of six. O.K. Now what do I do?
139 S8: You add all that.
140 T: O.K.
141 S8: And you divide by, [muttering], eight.
142 T: One, two, three, four, and four makes eight?
143 O.K.?
144   [Instructor has written on the board:

145             $$\frac{4\ (107.0) + 1(106.8) + 1(107.5) + 1(106.5) + 1(106.0)}{8}$$

146
147 T: All right. What do you think of that method?
148 Ss: [overlapping student comments including "Forget it." "Too hard."]
149 T: Too hard?
150 Ss: [overlapping unintelligible student comments including "It's the same"]
151 T: All right. So actually it ends up being the same as the arithmetic average?
152 S8: No. Because 107 gets four times the value, so the 107 counts more.
153 T: Ah. O.K. If you were to take the arithmetic average of these numbers, what would
154   you do? What would be the operations that you would go through there?
155   [S5], you were the one who suggested arithmetic average.
156 S5: You'd add all the numbers together and then divide it by 8.
157 T: Now what do you mean by 'adding all the numbers'?
158 S5: You would add each separate number that everybody got; you wouldn't just add one
159   107, you'd add all the 107s.
160 T: O.K. All right. So what [S5] is suggesting is for an arithmetic average is to add this
161   number, then add this number, then add this number, even though it's a repeat of that
162   one, then add this one, this one, and this one?
163 Ss: [overlapping unintelligible student comments]
164 T: Now would that come out the same as this if you did this?
165 Ss: [overlapping Yeah, yes, it would]
166 T: All right. So if you just took the arithmetic average by adding each one of these
167   numbers, all eight numbers, and divide it by eight then, that would end up giving you
168   the same number as this, so this is kind of maybe a quickie way of grabbing some of
169   them, but outside of that, it it gives us the same answer?
170 S8: Yeah. It does. I didn't mean it to when I did it though.
171 T: OK. What about this other method that, ah, that was mentioned, of saying, let's just
172   add up the numbers that are different? like 106.8 and 107.0, 107.5, 106.5 and 106.0,
173   that's all our different numbers, right?
174 S9: Why 107.0?
175 T: Well, because that's a, that's a different.
176 S10: It's different.
177 T: I mean, there's at least one of those, at least one of these, at least these, etcetera, add
178   those up and then take that and divide by 5. How do you like that?
179 S?: No.
180 S?: That doesn't show, doesn't represent it truthfully though, 'cause, I mean, there's a lot

181   more 107s and that's be, that'd change.

182 T: O.K. Wouldn't that give us the same answer as if we just took the arithmetic average?

183 Ss: [overlapping "no"s]

184 T: Can you give me an instance that's a real clear example, that would drive home to me
185   as to why that would give me a different number than if I took all of these and divided
186   by eight? We can do that with the numbers and see that it would come out different.
187   [S11]?

188 S11: If everybody got 107 except for one person who got 99 and then if you took 107 and
189   99 and divided it by 2, it'd be a lot different.

190 T: Does that make sense?

191 Ss: [overlapping agreement]

192 T: So if people go back there and measure the table, 107, 107, 107, 107, 107, 107, 107,
193   107, 107, 107, 107 and somebody else gets 99, so we go over there and we say, Hmm,
194   ah, half way between 107 and 99.

195 Ss: [unintelligible comments]

196 T: Does that make sense?

197 Ss: [overlapping comments, "no"]

198 T: Now I want you to listen to yourselves because a lot of you are saying, "that's a
199   ridiculous situation; of course, it wouldn't be half" – what is half way between 99 and
200   107?

201 S?: 103

202 T: 103?

203 S?: Yeah.

204 T: O.K. Of course it couldn't be 103, right? But you know what? There are going to be
205   some contexts within here in which some of you are going to fall into that very trap
206   right there, if you're not careful. O.K.? So watch out, so watch out for it. Is it clear that
207   one oh, what'd I'd say, 103 would not be a good average for 99 and then all those
208   107s? Is that clear? O.K. All right. Ah. O.K. So this is really not a very good way to
209   do it. Do we agree there? Somehow we need to weight, to weight in there the fact that
210   107 occurs so many times. So we've got this way of doing it, or if we added them all
211   up in there, that would include all those 107s. O.K.? [4s pause]
212   Anybody confused yet? [2s pause] No? [2s pause]
213   O.K. [3s pause] Got to be honest. [4s pause]
214   All right. Anybody else see a different way of approaching?

215 S12: You could possibly take the number that appears most often, like you were saying
216   before, if everyone got 107, and then a couple of people got 99, or like one person got
217   99 and one person got 120, you could pretty much assume that 107 would be nearest
218   to the correct answer and [so that you could just select that].

219 T: O.K. And that's the one that we called the mode there; it shows up the most
220   frequently. O.K. The mode.
221   There's another measure in here that, ah, that, ah, is sometimes used and nobody
222   mentioned it but I'll, I'll go ahead and throw it in here then; it's what's called the
223   'median' measure. Anybody know what the median is?

224 S?: Half way.

225 S?: Half.

226 T: Yeah. If you were to take, if you were to take all of the numbers – this is getting pretty
227   messy there, let me clean that up a bit – if we were to take all of these numbers and
228   rank them, [writing on board] the highest one is 107.5, then it's 107, 107, 107, 107,

229   and then 106.8, 106.5, 106.0, do you see what I did there?
230 S?: Um hum.
231 T: I, what's called ranked them, from the biggest measure that we got to the smallest
232   measure that we got for the width of that table, and then after I rank all of those, I go
233   for the middle number, the middle number. Oh Beep, what do I do here? The middle
234   number right in there.
235 S?: They're the same number so it doesn't matter.
236   Is that zero then? 'Cause it's right in there? [pointing between two numbers]
237 Ss: [overlapping comments: no]
238 T: Nah. 107's above it, 107's below it, right in there, I might even go half way between
239   these two if they differed maybe, but the median number in this case would probably
240   be a nice 107. O.K.? So the median is "the [writing on board] middle number when all
241   are ranked." And ranked, you know, like from the top to the bottom, etc., so then you
242   take the middle number when all the numbers are ranked there. You have to rearrange
243   all the numbers and then take the middle one. And that's called the median. That
244   make sense?
245 S?: Sure.
246 T: OK. All right. Now those are some of the, ah, some of the ways then that we might,
247   we first of all might take all of the numbers to get a best value, or we might take some
248   of those numbers to get a best value, then what we might do with them is that we might
249   average them, or we might go for the number that shows up most frequently, or we
250   might go for the middle number. These are all different techniques for getting a best
251   value.

APPENDIX B:
DEBORAH BALL'S CLASS; FRIDAY JANUARY 19, 1990 THIRD GRADE, SPARTAN VILLAGE SCHOOL, EAST LANSING, MICHIGAN

1 Ball: [A] Okay. A few delays, but I think we're ready to start now.
                [B] I'd like to open, open the discussion today with um – I have a
                few questions about the meeting yesterday that I'd like to ask.
                [C] So, to begin with, I would just like everybody to put pens down, there's
                nothing to take notes about or do right now.
                [D] But I'd like you to be thinking back to yesterday and to the meeting that
                we had on even and odd numbers and zero.
                [E] And I have a few questions. First – my first question is, I'd just like to
                hear some comments about what you thought about the meeting, what you
                noticed about the meeting, what you learned at the meeting, just what kinds of
                comments you have about yesterday's meeting?
                [F] And could you listen to one another's comments, so that we can um,
                benefit from what other people say?
                [G] See what y– what you think about other people's comments? Shekira, do
                you want to start?
2 Shekira: I– I– I liked it because, well, I like talking to other classes and, and when
                you talk to other classes sometimes it helps.

3	Ball:	In what way?
4	Shekira:	It helps you to understand a little bit more.
5	Ball:	Was there an example of something yesterday that you understood a little bit more during the meeting?
6	Shekira:	Well, I didn't think that zero was – zero, um – even or odd until yesterday they said that it could be even because of the ones on each side is odd, so that couldn't be odd. So that helped me understand it.
7	Ball:	Hmm. So y– So you thought about something that came up in the meeting that you hadn't thought about before? Okay.
8	Shekira:	*(nods)*
9	Ball:	Other people's comments? Shea?
10	Shea:	Um, I– I– I just want to say something to Shekira, when sh– what she said about um that, that one, um – zero has to be an odd, an even number bec– I disagree because, um, because what what two things can you put together to make it?
11	Shekira:	Could you repeat what you said, please?
12	Ball:	*(speaks to Bernadette and asks her to listen to this)*
13	Shea:	Okay, um, I disagree with you because, um, if it was an even number, how – what two things could make it?
14	Shekira:	Well, I could show you it. *(Moves toward the chalkboard and points to the number line above the chalkboard.)* Um, I forgot what his name was – but yesterday he said that this one *(points to the 1 on the number line)* and each – this one is odd and this one *(points to the −1 on the number line)* is odd, so this one has to be even.
15	Shea:	But, that doesn't mean it always is even.
16	Shekira:	It *could* be even.
17	Shea:	It *could* be, but . . .
18	Shekira:	I'm not saying that is *has* to be even. I meant that it could be.
19	Shea:	You said it was.
20	Ball:	[A] Before we take this up again, I underst– I– I understand that this is still a problem and that we didn't a – we didn't settle it, we're probably not going to settle it. [B] Um, there's a lot of disagreement about this issue, right? [C] And you saw that the fourth graders who have been thinking about this for a long time also disagree about it, don't they? [D] I'm still kind of interested um, in hearing some more comments about the meeting *itself.* [E] Shekira commented that it was good to have the two classes together because she heard an idea that she hadn't thought about and it made her think about and even revise her own idea when she was in the meeting yesterday. [F] What other comments do other people have about the meeting and what happened yesterday? [G] Lin, do you have a comment?
21	Lin:	Um, I h– I thought that zero was always going to be a even number, but from the meeting I sort of got mixed up because I heard other ideas I agree with and now I don't know which one I should agree with.
22	Ball:	Um– hm. So what are you going to do about that?
23	Lin:	Um, I'm going to listen more to the discussion and find out.

24	Ball:	Other people? Benny?
25	Benny:	Um, first I said that um, zero was even but then I guess I revised so that zero, I think, is special because um, I – um, even numbers, like they they *make* even numbers; like two, um, two makes four, and four is an even number; and four makes eight; eight is an even number; and um, like that. And, and go on like that and like one plus one and go on adding the same numbers with the same numbers. And so I, I think zero's special.
26	Ball:	[A] Can I ask you a question about what you just said?
		[B] And then I'll ask people for more comments about the meeting.
		[C] Were you saying that when you put even numbers together, you get another even number –
27	Benny:	Yeah.
28	Ball:	– or were you saying that all even numbers are made up of even numbers?
29	Benny:	Yes, they are. [This is very hard to make out. There has been significant dispute over whether Benny said "yes they are" or "no, they're not."]
30	Ball:	Bernadette, you said something like that yesterday, too.
31	Bernadette:	What.
32	Ball:	Were you – were you not listening to this just now?
33	Bernadette:	No.
34	Ball:	Benny said a minute ago that when you put even numbers together you get an even number,
35	Bernadette:	Mm-hm.
36	Ball:	But he also said, I think, that all even numbers are made up of other even numbers.
37	Lin:	I disagree.
38	Shekira:	(*says something to Lin*)
39	Ball:	Two even numbers just the same.
40	Benny:	Unh-uh.
41	Ball	The same even number?
42	Benny:	Yeah, like four.
43	Ball:	[A] Like eight is four plus four?
		[B] Are all the even numbers – can you do that with all the even numbers? That they'd be made up of two identical even numbers?
44	Shea:	Not– not– not–
45	Bernadette:	(*looking toward Benny*) You can't. Like six. Six is two, two .... Six you can't get two.
46	Shea:	Six is two *odd* numbers to make an even, to make an even number.
47	Lin:	Three and three –
48	Bernadette:	(*still looking toward Benny*) You need three twos to make six. You can't put a four and a four or a ...
49	Shea:	Three twos???
50	Bernadette:	(*looking toward Benny*) Three's – Three is odd.
51	Shea:	Or, um –
52	Benny:	I know that, but um, um I'm talking about like two plus two is four, and four plus four is eight and I just skipped the six so I just added the ones that, that add. Like the two plus two is four, and four is an even number and I'm just talking about the things that um, like –
53	Shea:	Six can be an odd number.

54	Benny:	What I just said – the um, like two is plus two is four and four plus four is eight and –
55	Bernadette:	So what you're doing is you're going by twos and then what two equals from then you go from – all the way up.
56	Benny:	Yeah, I'm not going by every single number. Like,
57	Bernadette:	Okay.
58	Benny:	Two, four, six, eight.
59	Ball:	[A] More comments about the meeting?
		[B] I'd really like to hear from as many people as possible what comments you had or reactions you had to being in that meeting yesterday.
		[C] Shea?
60	Shea:	Um, I don't have anything about the meeting yesterday, but I was just thinking about six, that it's a ... I'm just thinking. I'm just thinking it can be an odd number, too, 'cause there could be two, four, six, and two, three twos, that'd make six ...
61	Ball:	Uh-huh ...
62	Shea:	And two *threes*, that it could be an odd and an *even* number. Both. *Three* things to make it and there could be *two* things to make it.
63	Ball:	And the two things that you put together to make it were odd, right? Three and three are each *odd*?
64	Shea:	Uh huh, and the other, the twos were even.
65	Ball:	[A] So you're kind of – I think Benny said then that he wasn't talking about *every* even number, right, Benny?
		[B] Were you saying that?
		[C] Some of the even numbers, like six, are made up of two odds, like you just suggested.
66	Benny:	Uh-uh (agreeing with the teacher).
67	Ball:	Other people's comments?

METHODS, GOALS, BELIEFS, COMMITMENTS, AND MANNER IN TEACHING: DIALOGUE AGAINST A CALCULUS BACKDROP

Daniel Chazan and Marty Schnepp

Our language for talking about teaching includes terms like: instructional goals, instructional methods, and teacher beliefs. In a simple-minded way, these terms make sense. Teachers have goals for their students; we teach material and hope and expect that students will learn. Towards these ends, teachers employ methods, means or procedures we hope will help accomplish our goals. And, teachers have beliefs about their students and about how they learn, for example, views that influence our choices of goals and methods to help accomplish those goals. Much teacher education is built on the edifice of these words: goals, methods, and beliefs. For example, in methods courses, teacher candidates are taught to write lesson plans identifying instructional goals and to select instructional methods that will support them.

At another level, these terms are clearly problematic. What counts as an instructional goal? Are goals limited to the content that one is trying to teach? Or do goals include ways in which one wants students to learn to think and act? What is an instructional method? Is wait time a method? Is discussion a method? Whole language? What kind of grain size should one choose when describing methods? And, are beliefs limited to statements with which one might agree or disagree? How about expressions of commitments (like a teacher's commitment to the development of students' critical facilities as a central goal

Social Constructivist Teaching, Volume 9, pages 171–195.
Copyright © 2002 by Elsevier Science Ltd.
All rights of reproduction in any form reserved.
ISBN: 0-7623-0873-7

of instruction), statements where it seems more natural to say that one does or does not share this commitment, or that one has other commitments that supercede this one? Are teachers' commitments beliefs or are they something else?

Beyond these difficulties, and in the face of multiple ways of describing learning and the very nature of human knowledge, it seems important to revisit this simple vocabulary. If learning could be acquiring information, constructing individual connections, reinforcing habits of mind, or reaching intersubjectivity, if knowledge could be socially constructed, descriptive of states of the world, the capacity to participate in activity, or simply a word game, does it still make sense to talk about teachers' choices of instructional methods to meet instructional goals? Or do different views of learning and different views of the nature of human knowledge come with their own goals for instruction and their own instructional methods? For the purposes of describing teaching and teaching future teachers, does it make sense to talk of social-constructivist teaching methods? Or is it better to emphasize commonalities of procedure among teachers who hold different views of learning or of the nature of knowledge and maintain the notion of instructional methods in an unqualified sense?

These are the sorts of questions that we will take up against the background of the teaching of Calculus, discussion of high school AP Calculus classes that one of us, Marty Schnepp, teaches. Schnepp's[1] descriptions of his teaching of AP Calculus make this teaching a useful particular for our investigation of these questions. As he describes below, in this teaching, he is committed to engaging a wide range of students in construction of central ideas of the mathematics of change and accumulation (another way of describing Calculus). And, he is committed to producing accomplished students of Calculus who will be able to go on to further studies in technical fields. He is committed both to helping his students develop substantial understanding of broad issues, like relationships between rates of change and accumulation of totals (as suggested in Thompson, 1994), and detailed, technical facility with specific techniques of differentiation and integration. Schnepp also has strong beliefs about the nature of mathematical knowledge and about how people learn, as well as a commitment to designing teaching that reflects these beliefs. While sometimes the commitments he holds reinforce each other, at other times, they come into conflict and Schnepp experiences tensions. As a result of the tensions between these commitments, at numerous times throughout the year, he faces dilemmas about how to proceed (in the sense of Lampert, 1985). One way to describe these dilemmas is to portray them as a matter of choosing the optimal time to shift instructional method, what we will call his way of working with students.

Exploring how to describe what is changing in the shifts from one way of working to another will allow us to entertain the general questions with which we began.

THREE DIFFERENT WAYS OF WORKING IN A CALCULUS CLASS

To understand the dilemmas Schnepp regularly faces in the spring of each year, we begin with his description and illustration of three ways he works with his Calculus classes. Schnepp then assesses these ways of working, describes how he knits them together, and then articulates a kind of dilemma that he faces regularly in his instruction.

Listening and Assessing; Exploring and Presenting

One kind of teaching I do is based on activities that allow me to assess students' prior understanding. I use these activities to learn about what my students think; to challenge their ideas, when necessary; to help my students develop a disposition to inquire about mathematics and to make sense of it; and to provide a foundation of experiences for a more technical study of the mathematics of change and accumulation (as said earlier, one way of describing Calculus). To these ends, I have assembled a repertoire of simulations of linked changing quantities. These simulations employ various mechanical devices, some of which are linked to a computer (for a description, see Schnepp & Nemirovsky, 2001). These demonstrations (see below for an example) draw attention to the rate at which quantities are changing, and particularly to the notion of variable rate of change. In our explorations, questions regularly arise concerning rate of change in a quantity at an instant and the total accumulation of a changing quantity.

When working in this vein, I pose questions for my students for which they have been taught no previous algorithm for solving. I assign students to groups where they use prior knowledge to construct responses to my questions and solutions to problems that arise in their pursuit of their answers. The products of the students' efforts are discussed and critiqued in a whole group setting; and, as new questions and computational techniques arise, those become the focus of new investigations.

This way of working generates a complex web of mathematical, linguistic, and social interaction. We analyze techniques; review and revise skills; question, clarify and negotiate word meanings; and scrutinize conceptions of scientific models. In the process, students explicitly confront the question of how claims are justified in mathematics. They think about how they would justify a claim for themselves and how to justify the claim to others For many students, this is the first time they have thought about this issue; until now, many have simply worked by assuming that whatever the teacher says is true. In this way of working, I create settings that allow me to hear students articulate their thinking. This allows me to assess their skills and willingness to inquire, understand how their thinking and word use differ from mine and from peers, and to challenge the criteria that they use in deciding to accept something as known in mathematics.

When I work in this way, I do not tell students what they should know or think. I present demonstrations, outline tasks, and facilitate discussions (when they are not orderly). My demeanor is impassive during discussions. I listen in on the small group conversations; typically sitting in a student desk, chin in hand, fingers over my mouth. As I listen intently, I take notes. During presentations, I sit at the back of the classroom with the same posture. I respond to student questions with requests for more information about their thinking or simply ask them what other group members expressed in response to the same question. The explicit message I want to send is that they must do the thinking and that articulate, reasoned arguments are the goal.

When working in this way, I make every reasonable effort to avoid responding directly to the inevitable question, "is this right?" In my view, the danger of responding, "yes what your are doing is correct," or "no what you are doing is wrong because ...," is perpetuating students' reluctance to make sense of and analyze arguments for themselves. If I pass judgment on ideas and methods – to prevent students from pursuing a dead end approach for example – students will learn to look to me to assess validity of arguments and not learn to do such reasoning independently. I am concerned that if I did this they might quickly become hesitant (or too lazy) to move more than a few logical steps beyond the inception of an idea before seeking assurances from me that moving ahead will be fruitful. Well-designed tasks and the phrasing of questions can minimize the incidence of exchanges that end up in an appeal from a student to my authority for an assurance of "correctness" rather than to the student's own logical reasoning to assess validity.

A Sample Activity in this Vein

In this activity, with no introduction other than to take out a sheet of paper and prepare a data table, I mount my bicycle and begin riding on a stationary trainer. As I ride, I read my pedaling rate (recorded in r.p.m. on a cyclo-computer) at 15-second time intervals (for three minutes). I am careful to clearly vary my pedaling rate. The current phrasing of the task (it took me some time to get to this wording) that seems to help students set directly to work without breaking off to ask me questions is:

> Compute an accurate approximation of the number of times Mr. Schnepp's pedals rotated in the 3-minute time interval. And, write at least two questions that arise as you work toward a solution.

Putting the notion of "approximation" on the table seems to allow students the freedom to forge ahead; and, requiring questions as a part of the task allows groups to let their peers in other groups know they see flaws in their method(s). For example, it is common for groups to choose an approach where they assume that the rate from the end of each 15-second sub-interval was maintained for the entire 15-second interval, multiply that rate by 0.25 minute, then total the approximations from each sub-interval to arrive at a final value. These groups typically write questions like, "what do you do with the rate at time 0?" (because it was never used) or "how should we compensate for the fact that the rate was not constant throughout the interval?" Encouraging questions of this sort is a means by which I try to initiate a pattern of self-critique.

When I teach in this way, students are engaged in conversations about solutions, conjectures, and questions that the class has constructed. They learn to critique their own thinking and the ideas of their peers independently, with the idea that they will eventually analyze critically presentations of a textbook or their instructor. Classes are encouraged to reach consensus on acceptable approaches based on the logical strength and weakness of methods they construct, to generalize and develop algorithms for the techniques found to be useful, and to write definitions of terms as a group. As a result, they have a common set of experiences and language to describe rate of change and accumulation.

Suggesting, Introducing, and Calling Attention; Exploring and Presenting

There is another kind of teaching that I do that is similar to the first, indeed it can be seen as a natural outgrowth of the first, but that is different from it. In this way of working, I also teach from student exploration and presentations, but I take a much more active role. I may make suggestions. I may introduce a standard term to name something students have devised. I may enter an exchange and share ideas related to "how mathematicians have come to think about" the issue. Or, in order to bring an idea into play, I may design a new activity to call attention to significant ideas raised by students on prior occasions and tell students I have done so. When working in this way, I also often create exercises that allow students to become proficient with algorithms they have settled upon or assign a task that introduce special cases of functions that I know of that challenge generalizations they have made.

A Sample Activity in this Vein
For example, one year I gave my students a symbolic rule for a function:

$$P(t) = -0.01t^3 + 0.27t^2 + 1.2t + 3, \quad 0 \le t \le 20$$

and suggested that it gave the position of a bicycle as it moves away from a stoplight. I then simulated the bike's motion with computer-driven mini-cars. Two of the questions I asked students were:

(1) What is the bike's average velocity over the 20-second time interval?
(2) At what time(s) do you suppose the number on the speedometer would have been the same as [the average velocity]?

Students in my high school do a great deal of statistical work in Pre-Calculus. They become proficient using the TI-83 graphing calculator's statistical lists for data. In several sections of my Calculus classes in various school years, groups of students used the lists as follows (see chart below): in the first list, they put in times from 0 to 20 in some small sub-interval of times (0.5 sec for example); in the second list, they used the first list and the function rule to list the positions at those times; in the third list, they put in times from 0.5 to 20 seconds, again in 0.5 sec increments; in the fourth list, they used list three and the function rule to find the positions at those times; in the fifth list, they subtracted list two from list four to compute the change in the bike's position; in the sixth list, they finally divided list five by 0.5 sec to find the average velocity over 0.5 second time intervals. They then searched the list for a value close to the value they calculated for the average velocity.

Elapsed time	Position	Elapsed time	Position	Change in position over 0.5 second intervals	Average velocity over 0.5 second intervals
L1	L2	L3	L4	L5 (= L4 – L2)	L6 (= L5/0.5)
0	3	0.5	3.66625	0.66625	1.3325
0.5	3.66625	1.0	4.46	0.79375	1.5875
1.0	4.46	1.5	5.37375	0.91375	1.8275
1.5	5.37375	2.0	6.4	1.02625	2.0525
. . .	. . .	. . .	. . .	. . .	. . .
19.5	54.91875	20	55	0.08125	0.1625
20	55	20.5	54.91625	–0.08375	–0.1675

My intervention, after a group that has done this has presented their results to the class, and peers have had an opportunity to ask questions, is to show students how to use the normal function lists (Y =) and composition on a graphing calculator to do the same thing much more effectively. I ask them to write a rule that will compute the position 0.5 seconds after x, $P(x + 0.5)$, and compare its table of values to $P(x)$. From that point, we construct rules for the change in position, $P(x + 0.5) - P(x)$, and the average rate over a 0.5-second interval starting at $t = x$,

$$\frac{P(x + 0.5) - P(x)}{0.5}.$$

This introduces standard difference quotients. I ask them to algebraically simplify the rules (as a way to make the computations easier), and that usually leads to discussion of changing the 0.5 in the above equation to smaller and smaller values. I have intervened and added to the conversation. But, my contribution builds directly on what students were doing.

My main point here is that in this sort of teaching I play a more active role in the conversation. I initiate and make comments that connect what students are doing with terminology and methods that have been developed by others.

Teaching Skills, Covering the Curriculum; Practicing

There is a third way in which I work with my students. In this way of working, I am focussed on details. As I take to the front of the room, I direct students' attention to the particular details of differentiating and integrating functions with specific characteristics. I standardize methods and cover specific families of functions and skills required by the AP test or a traditional Calculus course. In this way of working, I am typically at the chalkboard presenting a topic for the day, one that students may not have yet encountered. I am introducing new techniques, while taking care to represent them in a manner that links to ideas my students have developed. I then send my students off to do exercises not altogether different from those found in traditional textbooks or straight from a textbook.

A Sample Activity in this Vein

To illustrate how my role is different when I work with students in the third way, here is a description of what I did during one session when we worked in this way. I developed this description from a videotape of the session. Class began with students sitting in groups. I handed out a key for the previous day's homework, a series of separable differential equations to solve. I also handed out a key for a graded assignment that I then returned to students. Groups began checking their homework. While they worked, I handed out a photocopy of the calculator policy from the College Board and topic outline of the AP exam.

I then convened the whole group. I pointed out that I indicated on the topic list the topics we had not covered and discuss the issue a bit. I ask for questions on the first ten problems.

Students ask to look at 8 and 9. I say that I want to look at 9 first. I indicate how I did the problem. As I go through my solution method, I ask fill-in-the-blank type questions. "So what would I have to do in order to . . . ?" As students respond, I write down what they say and work with it towards my solution.

After completing the main step in my solution, I ask if there are questions. No one asks. I finish off the problem by asking students what needs to be done and they fill in the details. In this part of the process, a student makes a mistake, but no other student catches it. I point out the error and ask students how to fix the error. A student indicates how to fix the error and I elaborate on the comment by warning of similar mistakes in general. I review the solution method we have used and give an example of how it would be applied to another problem and discuss difficulties that regularly come up with problems of this type.

We move on and begin exercise 8 in a similar manner. At a certain point in the process, I have them work for a period of time and circulate among the groups. I reconvene the group and discuss the most common solution I saw by directing short questions to one student who solved the problem in that manner. A student questions this student about his solution method. He responds directly to her. When their exchange is finished, I point out an approach that I saw students trying, an approach that was incorrect, and make a tangential remark.

Another student raises her hand and suggests an alternative solution method. As she talks, I write on the board. When she has completed her method, I suggest a third method. Students ask questions about details in the three methods and I answer them directly. I discuss the pros and cons of the different methods and give them a new task to work on. Time runs out.

The Three Ways of Working and their Unfolding

As a teacher, I have many goals for my students. I want my students to be able to understand the Fundamental Theorem of Calculus (see Thompson, 1994 for an argument that many good college students do not develop such an understanding in their Calculus courses) and to appreciate that Calculus is about something. I want them to be able to write their own arguments and come up with their own conjectures. I also want them to know standard terms and to have the skills and knowledge needed to convince others that they have learned Calculus, to enable them to be successful in collegiate mathematics, and to be successful on the AP Calculus test. I am committed to all of these goals; I am not willing to let go of any of these goals.

The three ways of working I described earlier all have their pluses and minuses in terms of the goals that I care about. They help contribute to some of the goals that I have for students (I'm speaking about goals broadly here, not in the narrow sense of content goals that could be reached in one class period), but undermine others. When I am mainly listening and assessing, the process is extremely time consuming and students may not be learning the mathematical facts and methods that I am supposed to cover. But, students *are* being challenged to be intellectually independent and to think about why they believe something should be considered true in mathematics (syntactic considerations rather than substantive considerations, to use Schwab's 1978 terms). When I am more active in discussions of student exploration, my contributions can bring their ideas closer to standard ideas in the curriculum. But, if I become too active, students will quickly apply pressure for me to just tell them how to do it. This can lead to a state of intellectual dependence and does not develop their ability to determine the validity of ideas for themselves. If I teach skills and introduce content, I am much more efficiently ensuring students have seen the required topics and skills of the curriculum. However, this way of working is not necessarily effective at imparting understanding or an ability to independently apply the skills I am teaching.

Since I have this range of goals and each way of working has its limitations, my "solution" to reaching these different goals is to work differently with the students at different points of the year. I don't think I could meet these goals if I chose to work in just one way. Working solely in way 3, I believe would leave students with facts and skills that are not necessarily related or applicable. I don't think that such instruction would lead to robust knowledge and the sort of relational understanding that Skemp (1976) calls for. Similarly, I can imagine that working in way 1 solely would leave students unable to assimilate back into the larger culture easily. If students and teacher launched into a year-long construction of their own mathematics out of their explorations of variation and accumulation, it is unlikely that what they devise would allow students to step into a second calculus course (or applied field) and function effectively. Finally, I cannot understand how one could work in the second way without having students explore.

In my Calculus class, the three ways of working with my students that I have described above follow a particular progression. But, in order to explain this progression, it is useful to give some background on my students. In my high school, students take two routes to my class. One route is through the honors track. Students in this track have studied together in honors classes since junior high school. Other students come to my class from the standard track. In order to arrive in my class, in many cases, these students have taken two mathematics courses at some point during their high school career. In recent years, some students from the standard track come in to my class having some experience with what I have called ways 1 and 2; this is less common with students from the honors track.

I begin very strongly with the first way of working during September. During September, even when my students seem to be struggling and in need of help, I do not step in and provide guidance; I maintain my posture of listening and assessing. I have found that students, especially students from the honors track, will go to extreme lengths in their efforts to goad me into telling them how a problem "should" be solved. Many would prefer I adopt a traditional drill and practice approach to the tasks I assign. Students perceive this to be an easier path to a high grade. Abstract thought, articulating ideas, and critiquing logical reasoning are unfamiliar activities for many of my honors track students and require a considerable amount of effort. But, I believe there is a fundamental difference between what the mind does in trying to locate a sensible place for a new fact in its schema of other known facts, and what is does when it must analyze an idea for validity. In the context of problems for which no previous algorithms or definitions have been presented, asking students to construct a body of mathematical theory through a process of social interaction with peers feels to me like an effective vehicle for getting students to think hard and reflect on what they know. The feedback from peers, who are at a similar level of expertise, is helpful because it represents another perspective; but it is usually open to question because the peer is known to not be an expert either. So, that feedback must also be scrutinized and students learn to continue the analysis until they find something(s) in their repertoire of known things that either verifies or refutes the original idea. They begin to have the ability to assert logical independence, at least as a group.

As a result of our work in September, there is a lot of exploration that students have done and there is much to digest. Starting in mid-October the second way of working comes in. As we meet new topics, I might revert to way 1, but for large chunks of time until the end of January, I work in this second way.

In early February, I return to a large chunk of time in the first mode. We have examined algebraic functions of different kinds. I want my students to have experience with a wider range of functions than we have examined so far. I am interested in having them think about integrating and differentiating functions that are not smooth or continuous, piecewise functions of different kinds, as well as functions with other sorts of discontinuities. The opportunity to do this exploration will stand them in good stead when we formalize continuity and differentiability statements and theorems and investigating the behavior of functions at critical points. Towards the end of the month, I move into the third mode of work. I stay in this mode pretty much through the end of the year, though there is some more exploratory work sometimes during the last few weeks after the AP exam.

As my description indicates, for the majority of the school year, I do not mix and match the third way of working with other two ways of working. I contend that a way of working is not simply a tool in a teacher's repertoire that can be unsheathed and resheathed in a short period of time. I cannot lecture on Monday and Tuesday, ask students to construct ideas on Wednesday and Thursday, then give a lecture on Friday to help with a problem students could not resolve Thursday. I find that if students have so much as an inkling that I will bail them out or that eventually I will "show them how" to do something they are asked to explore in a socially constructive process, they will simply wait for "the answer." My students have years of schooling behind them. I have to sustain my listening and assessing posture for a significant period of time in order to establish a culture of inquiry, rigorous analysis, and productive dialogue.

After a time of impassive facilitating, as students begin to assert their intellectual independence, logical rigor, and begin to confront essential ideas that underlie formal Calculus, I can begin to take part in their conversations, but doing so often feels like walking a tight rope. Too much freedom will make standardizing content later on in the year difficult; too much intervention and guidance can curb students' willingness to think critically.

Once this tight rope walk has established a classroom culture in which I am confident students will continue to work with me acting as a knowledgeable participant and not as the sole expert, I can begin to move into the third way of working. I believe the experience of having constructed their own mathematics gives students a view of the landscape of the mathematics of change. As I shift the focus of activity in the course, moving into the third way of working, my students have in their minds a set of experiences with the questions and quandaries that led to the canonical body of knowledge we call Calculus. It seems to me that the depth of meaning and the richness of the relational understanding (in the sense of Skemp, 1976) my students will construct for the barrage of formal definitions, theorems, computational methods, and applications I am going to throw at them will be greater because of this foundation. They seem much better prepared for what I will introduce than students who have not done this exploration and have to rely solely on algebra and whatever random experiences with changing quantities they might have had prior to entering my course.

But, the shift to the third way of working is a big transition in my class. Here is what that transition was like in the spring of 2000.

I had asked my students to experiment with the function, F(x), that one gets from integrating the function f(t)=1/t from 1 until a variable endpoint x. This problem was once debated by mathematicians developing calculus (see Boyer, 1949). In class (as in history), we had developed techniques for answering this sort of question for polynomial functions. The task I posed was a challenge; 1/t doesn't look all that different than a polynomial, it can be written as t^{-1}. But, with the techniques we had developed F(x) would turn out to be $(-1)t^0$, a constant function. By this time of the year, I assumed that they understood that the function we were looking for should describe how the area under the curve 1/t accumulates from 1 to a variable endpoint.

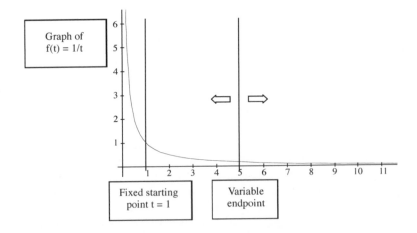

The implication of a constant function as the answer would be that the area under the curve 1/t was unchanging. But, that couldn't possibly be; as x moves the area enclosed by the vertical lines and 1 and x, the x-axis, and the graph of the curve changes. Before we began to discuss their results, I emphasized that we were about to shift the way that we were going to work. Against the background of their exploration, I was going to introduce techniques for integrating functions like 1/t. Here is what I said:

Derivatives and integrals for functions that are not algebraic [like 1/t] are a bit more complicated. But we've got a lot of tools available to us to be able to do that. . . . Anybody have
any questions right now?

Now the way I'm looking at . . . now until the end of the year is we are going to be going
through a lot of stuff, its going to be a lot more traditional in the sense that I'm gonna be
up here talking a lot more. But I'm going to expect you to draw on everything we've done
and if you have questions you've gotta ask them. Alright? So, don't sit back and just hope
that some time . . . at some point later it's going to make sense because you've got to understand things before we start piling stuff up. Because we are going to have a lot of things
that all relates to the stuff we've done before . . . but we're going to move fairly quickly.

Let's talk about values for this function F(x).

Each year, the decision about when to move into the third mode is a very hard
decision. When I do so, I begin the process of standardizing methods for
integrating and differentiating and take up detailed investigations of specific
classes of functions, hopefully without quashing students' disposition toward
inquiry and making sense of the mathematics we are studying. Building on the
foundational understandings of accumulation and change that they have
established, my directed instruction allows the class to cover more material than
does open inquiry, yet hopefully does so in a connected, meaningful manner.
Many of my students take this class so they can receive advanced placement
credit. They will take the national AP Calculus exam in the spring. As a result,
I feel pressure to move into this way of working. I use this way of working to
increase the pace of the course to cover an adequate amount of material to
prepare them for the exam and to send them off to college empowered to step
into new areas of study with the skills that university instructors expect.

While I am happy with the decision to employ these ways of working in
order one after the other, there are dilemmas and tension that never seem to
get resolved in my teaching, as I balance my commitments and outside pressure I feel by changing how I interact with my students throughout the school
year. Each year I face difficult questions. These questions come up in particular about when to make the transition to making presentations about particular
techniques. Questions that come up include:

- Since university instructors expect standard methods, terminology, and a long
  list of specific, automatic skills, how much of the year can I afford to use
  on allowing students to construct understandings of the big ideas at play in
  Calculus?
- How can I continually insist on students building a deep, thorough understanding of material when I have students who do not value or are not
  interested in such understandings and want me to get on to the details that
  will be important for them in technical careers?

- Yet, how can I in good conscience move towards a more traditional instructional paradigm when I know that when I do that more and more students will be left behind in a sea of formulas, definitions, and theorems, many of which feel like technical details of little larger importance?
- And, how can I in good conscience rapidly cover material when those who are able to keep pace will be implicitly encouraged to retain only a list of formulas, definitions, and theorems, without a broad, integrated picture of the subject and its uses?

EXPLORING THE UNFOLDING OF THESE WAYS OF WORKING: A DIALOGUE

Dan: Marty, every time I hear you talk about this class I am impressed anew with the thought that has gone in to creating this experience for your students. When we talk, I am also aware of the incredible tensions that arise for you as you carry out the teaching, in particular, the tension about when to shift into the third way of working. In order to appreciate this tension though, I think I need a better sense of what underlies the choices that you make. You have articulated reasons that it is important for you to work in different ways with your students. But, I think someone might ask why you feel it is necessary to stay with a particular way of working for long stretches of time. Couldn't you meet your goals by mixing up the ways you work with students in shorter timeframes?

Marty: I can see why someone might say that, but I would not agree. I feel strongly that a sustained period of time working in way 1 is necessary to get my students functioning mathematically the way I want them to, before I myself participate in their discussions. I have belabored the point of students wanting me to tell them what to do. But, there is more to it. What I believe happens during my period of impassivity is not only my assessment of what kids know about the previous math they have studied as they try to apply it, but their own assessment of their knowledge. When working in way 1, students confront ways in which they have incorrectly memorized some of what they have been taught and ways in which they misapply previously studied skills. This is not fun for them. It is uncomfortable, particularly for my "honors" students. But I find great benefits from this, beyond correcting particular content problems. Thoughtful students come to realize that simply trying to absorb content from lectures, reading textbooks, and practicing skills without being active learners has left their knowledge base deficient in some respects. This is my trump card over the tendency of students to wait for the teacher when I move into working in way 2. If sufficient numbers of students have come to realize that passive learning will not create strong enough skills, and that active learning, exploration and discussion in particular, is a means by which to create stronger learning, a learning culture focused on inquiry can be established in my room. Some students actually find the intellectual challenges of mathematical inquiry and constructive, critical discourse interesting. The more students who do so, the more momentum the endeavor gains. I don't think this momentum could gather if I didn't stick with way 1 for quite some time.

Dan: What I'm wondering is the degree to which this is a function of your students' prior experience and your setting or whether it might be something more general. Your argument in part seems to be that students can't see you in different roles within a short period of time. It reminds me of the biography of Jaime Escalante and his teaching in LA (Matthews, 1988). Based on experiences early in his career, when he came to the U.S., Escalante looked for an assessment mechanism that would get him out of the role of evaluating his students. His intuition was that in order to ask his students to work hard for him, they would need to feel that he and they were working together on a common goal, on convincing some outsiders that they were good enough.

Marty: I don't think the idea that "students can't see [a teacher] in different roles simultaneously" describes how I think about my decisions in organizing instruction. For example, I can mix and match the first and the second ways of working. Once I feel students are taking to the difficult work of vigilant critique of their own and others' arguments, and I start taking a more active role, I do at times revert to an impassive posture (time permitting). When we take up the derivative of a new function, for example, I will ask them to investigate the new derivative with all the tools they have studied and step back to let them know they must link previous ideas to the new task. I am not going to say a thing until they pursue some line(s) of inquiry (qualitatively sketching its graph using the function's graph, setting up a difference quotient and trying to manipulate it, or comparing it to its inverse and what they know about its derivative, as examples). More generally, I think students learn rather quickly that I say little or simply respond with questions when we begin a new unit, or first take up a new question.

The issue is more how students are going to view my expertise. I'm not sure whether that is a general issue or particular to my context and my students. As I begin to take an active role – as a participant in the discussions, I keep stating how careful I must be to not enter as the expert whose input represents definitive approval or rejection of an idea. One of this things I find myself doing (there are many) to make this possible is to talk in ways that allows me to ally with students in relation to a third party. Not exactly like Escalante, but similar. I make statements that begin with, "what mathematicians do . . ." or "turn to page 320 and read what the textbook says about what Kim just said." A generalized "they" emerges as an entity in my questions and comments. The third party "they" is mathematicians, textbook authors, and my students' future professors of mathematics. It takes some time and evolution in my students' thinking before they are ready for me to move into the third way of working *while* continuing to think. If I want my students to critique textbook proofs and to come up with alternative ideas (as described in Schnepp, 2000), I can't rush this process.

Dan: I think that there is some generality to this issue. Your comment reminds me of when I team taught a senior-level, undergraduate course in the math department with a mathematician. What I realized in that teaching was that the very label mathematician made it very difficult for my colleague to ask students to explore any mathematics. Our students assumed that no matter what they did, my colleague would know exactly what was right or wrong. They were flabbergasted when they asked him a question that came out of their exploration and he said that he would have to think about it and get back to them next time. Of course, they assumed that when he got back to them, he would have it all figured out. It almost seemed that in order for our students to explore a problem, he had to leave the room; he couldn't get away from their perception of his knowing it all.

Marty: But, that isn't the only reason that I have to stick with these ways of working for longer timeframes. Our conversation makes me think of "discovery" learning and difficulties I have with that idea. My parody of discovery learning is when a teacher asks students to explore something in an activity then immediately after students present their solutions, the teacher presents a standard method for solving the problem. I don't see how people can make such swift shifts in their ways of working. It only takes a short time for students to learn that the teacher will show them "the real way" or "the mathematical way" of solving the problem. Students will be reluctant to think very deeply about the next investigation when they know the teacher will simply show them how eventually. And then, I wonder what is the difference between that end result and simply lecturing, other than it takes a lot of time. This seems like an uncomfortable and artificial way of structuring a class.

I am much more comfortable with taking a stance as a listener and working in way 1 for an extended time. I want to hear what my students think, in some detail, and then figure out how to connect what they think to what others have developed.

I also wonder about the teacher guidance that leads to the "discovery" of particular results. I don't find that my students can "discover" ideas like the derivative, for example. They can learn a great deal that will eventually help them understand the careful definition for the derivative that has survived historically by trying to figure out when a bike rider, who is accelerating, achieves a certain speed, given a position function. They gain a great deal of insight from trying to talk about, and calculate, how fast an object is traveling at a specific time before someone show them how mathematicians have settled on defining the derivative. But, their explorations won't necessarily lead them to the particular definition that is in a textbook.

Dan: I also have concerns about discovery learning (see Chazan, 1995), but can't connect those concerns directly to the issue of how long to stick with particular ways of working. So, let's say I accept now that there have to be a range of ways of working and that one needs to stick with them, at least with way 1, for long chunks of time. But, how about issues of order? Do you think that the order has to go 1, 2, 3 as described above, or could it go 3, 1, 2, or some other way?

Marty: I am sure people do work in a mode like what we describe as way 3, then ask students to do various activities to illustrate links or expound upon meanings. But, I have two concerns about that. First, I find it very hard to engage students in the first way of working.

If I had already begun to work with them in the third way, I suspect that transition would be even more difficult. Second, I am concerned about what this teaches students about mathematics and about their own capacity to think for themselves. If the idea is to introduce key ideas to students and then have them work with those key ideas, where do students think the key ideas have come from? I want to emphasize mathematics as socially constructed. An order like 3, 1, 2 wouldn't help with that.

Finally, in my experience, for many students, formal math seems to become less intimidating if they can come to think of mathematics as something other than absolute truth. I think they take more readily to a doing math as exploring a situation and attempting to identify and clearly communicate to others the relationships and methods they find noteworthy in the situation and consistent with the other mathematical things they know. I want students to view axiomatic systems as the well-scrutinized, historically useful efforts of other people to do the same. When students identify a significant idea, try to name it, concisely define what they are talking about with vocabulary from their prior experience(s), and reach consensus on how the term will be used within their peer group, noting the likelihood of revisiting and refining their usage as new circumstances arise, they garner insight into the complexities of historical definitions, theorems, etc. After having done so for themselves as a group, I find students read more critically the definitions they are presented later in the year. They pay greater attention to the detail of phrases and word choices that may have been overlooked reading textbook definitions in the past.

Dan: Because of who you teach, you can't start out playing a more active role and then move to the background. But, I'm wondering in terms of order whether it is possible to move out of the third way of working. Once you start working in this way, is it harder to "revert" to other ways of working, or are you able to do so?

Marty: Realistically, I don't have a lot of experience with this. I almost never have time to switch back. Or rather I should say that I can't switch back until after the AP exam. But then the year is almost over.

Dan: So, you have to stick with way one for an extended time, and the order must be 1, 2, 3, at least at first. Against this background, the central dilemma for you is when to shift into the third way of working. Ultimately, how do you decide when it is time to do this? Your class is an AP class. What role does this play in the timing? Do you think things would be different if this were not an AP class? Or if there were separate AP and non-AP sections of Calculus and students signed up for different classes?

Marty: In terms of the AP designation, several of my colleagues have suggested that eliminating the Advanced Placement test as a goal, or offering AP and non-AP Calculus, would be a way to eliminate my dilemma. But, I have resisted. I do not believe it is that simple. First of all, there are as well motivational issues teaching high school seniors. Finding ways to elicit serious, focused academic work from these students as they prepare to leave high school is not easy, and using the AP test as a goal (in a way similar to Escalante) helps motivate many students. And, the exam is one indicator of whether our discussions of mathematics lead to productive, tangible learning. So, I argue to keep it as a part of the curriculum.

I think it is safe at this point to characterize the dilemmas that I experience as resulting from a larger dynamic in teaching. Teachers are supposed to teach for student understanding, and they are supposed to cover the content of the courses that they teach. Yet, these responsibilities often come into conflict. Sometimes people capture this dynamic as a tension between breadth vs. depth (e.g. Duckworth, 1987). But, in my case, the descriptors seem switched; covering the content is going into depth with particular techniques and teaching for understanding is the breadth and the big ideas of Calculus. At this point in my analysis of my teaching, this ongoing dynamic has many faces. The most prominent can be seen in the question, "how do I cover enough material for the AP exam, yet spend the time working towards goals associated with intellectual independence and mathematical power?" The AP exam can represent an assesment of how well my goal for preparing students to move into fields of technical study at the college level. I move to the third way of working with students primarily for this reason: content is "covered" faster. But, moving at that pace means losing students who may require a different pace to assimilate the material; and, not requiring discussion, writing, and starting to follow standard textbook applications sends a message to just memorize. I haven't found any general way to manage this dilemma. Each year, I agonize over this question once again.

SHOULD WE LABEL "METHODS" AS SOCIAL CONSTRUCTIVIST?

Stepping back from the immediacy of the dilemmas that Schnepp faces early each spring in his Calculus class, we now turn more directly to the question of describing types of teaching.

We begin with some observations about Schnepp's descriptions of his teaching. In describing his teaching, Schnepp articulates beliefs about the nature of mathematical knowledge and about how people learn mathematics, indicates his commitment to creating instruction that represents these beliefs, and describes how he enacts this commitment. In his discussion of mathematics, he raises issues discussed by Philip Kitcher (1983) and Imre Lakatos (e.g. 1976). Though he doesn't articulate an elaborate description of the nature of mathematical objects, in his teaching, there is an important connection between phenomena of our sensory experience of the world and mathematics. Students are expected to learn mathematics from contemplating experiments with mechanical devices; mathematics is not just a word game played on symbols for which sensory experience is irrelevant. At the same time, mathematics is not just simply a matter of description of experience with mathematical objects from some Platonic sphere (perhaps viewed through the window of diagrams and pictures as in Brown, 1999), or a chronicling of the results of experimental measurements.

There are important social elements to the design of his instruction. Students are expected to develop shared understandings with classmates and to coordinate these understandings with those of distant others whose voices are present in textbooks. For Schnepp, this is a representation of mathematics. He is concerned with representing to students how fundamental ideas in the discipline develop. As a result, developing a shared vocabulary is an important component of activity in his Calculus class. In a similar vein, Schnepp indicates that he believes learning to be a fundamentally social process. The very process of having students work in groups is meant to create opportunities for students to clarify their own arguments and to hear arguments of others.

The net result is a consistency across Schnepp's different ways of working, a kind of teaching that Schnepp calls Social Constructivist (Schnepp, in prep.); such a label captures ways in which his instruction and views of his instruction are based in particular views of mathematical knowledge and learning. Schnepp expects his students to engage in a particular way of being in his classroom. Students in his classroom are encouraged to value their own ideas,[2] as well as those of others. They are expected to learn from their own and their classmates fledgling attempts to make sense of phenomena of change and accumulation. And, they are expected to use their nascent understandings to come to grips with the views of others that have withstood critical debate in important social settings and have established their validity. But, Schnepp expects his students to exercise their critical faculties in evaluating views of others, and not simply accept or reject views by virtue of the authority that has been vested in the proponents of a particular view.

In describing how he teaches over the course of the year, it is clear that Schnepp continually makes choices with respect to his actions in class. He has described his rationales for working with students in different ways, as well as rationales for the duration of these ways of working and for the ordering of them in time. In making these choices, is it useful to connect Schnepp's beliefs about learning and knowledge to his methods, to the ways he works with students, in addition to describing the teaching that he does as an enactment of social constructivist views of mathematical knowledge and of learning?

We believe that it is quite important to recognize teachers' beliefs and commitments. But, for us, it does not make sense to attach this recognition to method. Teachers use a variety of methods for a variety of reasons. And, different researchers use the notion of method in different ways. If methods are used to mean broad brush, recurrent instructional processes (as in Berliner & Gage, 1976), teachers with different beliefs can use similar methods with radically different intents. A teacher who believes in discovery learning might ask students to explore and present (as in Schnepp's first way of working). But the rationale for this way of working might be quite different. Such a teacher might be working in this way because he or she believes that students will better remember what they have discovered themselves. Similarly, another teacher might seem to present in order to cover skills in the curriculum (as in Schnepp's third way of working), but without the foundation that Schnepp has laid for his students with the other two ways of working, the nature of this teaching would be quite different than Schnepp's. And, some teachers, like Schnepp, might view a range of ways of working, that others might want to see as to some degree incompatible, as all contributing to teaching that is consistent in its beliefs and commitments. Thus, for us, labeling methods to reflect a teacher's beliefs and commitments is not a sensible way to proceed.

Instead, we are drawn to ways of describing teaching which provide us with more options of aspects of teaching that might be qualified with the adjective social constructivist. For example, Fenstermacher (1999) supplements method with manner and style:

> ... method applies to acts of a teacher undertaken with the intention of bringing about a change in a learner or group of learners. Style pertains to the conduct of the teacher that reflects his or her own personality, without obligation upon any other teacher to act in the

same way. Manner encompasses those traits and dispositions of the teacher that reveal his
or her character as a moral or intellectual being. In slightly different terminology, method
refers to what the teacher does to bring about some sort of result in the learner, style refers
to personality characteristics displayed in the act of teaching, and manner refers to the moral
and intellectual character of the teacher (p. 2).

While we are not sure to what degree manner would encompass the commitment to represent in teaching one's beliefs about the nature of knowledge and
learning, we would be more inclined to link this commitment to intellectual
character in teaching than to teaching method.

CONCLUSION

In the U.S., nominally, educational policies are local affairs. There is no national
curriculum; local school boards decide for themselves. Similarly, teachers are
supposed to develop their own approaches to teaching; preservice teacher
education programs often devote substantial attention to helping preservice
candidates envision the type of teacher that they would like to be. Indeed, there
are even texts (like Fenstermacher & Soltis, 1998) designed for this purpose.

In tension with such individualistic views of teaching, there are more
technical approaches to teaching. The process/outcome tradition of research on
teaching (e.g. Dunkin & Biddle, 1974) treats the choice of methods as amenable
to determination by research. This tradition suggests that teachers should choose
their methods by examining research on the student outcomes that result, not by
their own commitments (see especially p. 51). Research will indicate methods
that produce better outcomes, and those are the ones teachers should use.

For us, tensions between these two ways of thinking about teaching frame a
context for the question of labeling teaching methods according to a teacher's
beliefs about knowledge and learning. If certain methods are labeled social
constructivist teaching methods, would research then determine the jobs for
which, and the circumstances under which, such methods are and are not useful?
It seems like labeling of teaching methods might push in this sort of pragmatic
and comparative direction. How would such a push sit with notions of teachers'
personal approaches and the choices available to them in carrying out district-
mandated curricula?

Here, again, the example of Schnepp's descriptions of his teaching provides
an example with which to reason. It seems like there ought to be ways to
describe teaching that are both attentive to student learning outcomes and to
teachers' commitments and beliefs. In teaching Calculus, Schnepp chooses to
continue to offer the class as an AP class. His students' scores on this exam
are part of what he can use to justify his way of teaching Calculus to his

students, their parents, and their future university instructors. But, those scores, by themselves, do not determine his instruction.

A hypothetical (but plausible) example will help clarify. Suppose that someone were able to do a study that could convincingly suggest to Schnepp that his students' average score on the AP exam would rise if he moved into his third way of working sooner in the year.[3] Though Schnepp cares deeply about student learning, such evidence would not in and of itself convince Schnepp to change his teaching. There are at least three dimensions that might keep him from changing his practice. First, the exam does not assess everything that he would like his students to learn. In particular, it does not assess the depth of their understanding of the Fundamental Theorem of Calculus, nor does it investigate their capacity to explore novel problems for which they do not know an algorithmic solution. Second, if the average AP score rose, Schnepp would still be concerned about the distribution of the scores that would result. Would the increase in the average score be a result of increases in the number of 5s on the exam, but come with an increase in the number of 0s, 1s and 2s as well? An improvement in aggregate learning outcomes may not be desirable. Such an increase might indicate that a small number of students are benefiting at the expense of others. His experience is that the move to the third way of working leaves some students behind. The choice to move into the third way of working in part is a value-laden decision that involves managing tensions between what different students will learn as a result (see Lampert, 2001 for in-depth examination of situations where one must manage tensions between the teaching of some students and others). Finally, Schnepp might also be concerned about the representation of what it means to do mathematics that would result from an earlier move to the third way of working. As a result of the commitments that he holds, there are other goals of importance to him, besides ones valued by what Fenstermacher and Soltis (1998) call the executive approach.

However language for describing teaching evolves, we hope that we have convincingly demonstrated that a teacher's beliefs about knowledge and learning, as well as the degree to which they are committed to representing these beliefs in their practice, are important to describe. Descriptions of teaching which neglect these factors are missing an important component of teachers' decisions about the methods to employ in their interactions with their students.

NOTES

1. Though it is sometimes awkward, when we jointly author text about this teaching, we will refer to the teacher in the third person as Schnepp, rather than in the first person. Text authored solely by Schnepp will use the first person to refer to his teaching.

194   DANIEL CHAZAN AND MARTY SCHNEPP

2. In drawing attention to the emphasis that Schnepp puts on having his students value their own ideas, we do not mean to say that others who are more sophisticated mathematically would necessarily reject the views proposed by Schnepp's students. But, Schnepp's ways of thinking about mathematics and about human learning lead him to put more emphasis on students' individual and shared ways of thinking, even when clearly partial and limited, than teachers with other beliefs might.
3. This of course neglects the difficulties of designing and carrying out such a study.

REFERENCES

Berliner, D., & N. Gage (1976). The psychology of teaching methods. In: N. Gage (Ed.), *The Psychology of Teaching Methods: The Seventy-Fifth Yearbook of the National Society for the Study of Education, Part 1*. Chicago: University of Chicago.

Boyer, C. (1949). *The history of the calculus and its conceptual development*. New York, Dover.

Brown, J. R. (1999). *Philosophy of mathematics: An introduction to the world of proofs and pictures*. London, Routledge.

Chazan, D. (1995). *Where do student conjectures come from? Empirical exploration in Mathematics classes*. East Lansing, MI., National Center for Research on Teacher Learning, Michigan State University.

Duckworth, E. (1987). *"The Having of Wonderful Ideas" and Other Essays on Teaching and Learning*. New York, Teachers College.

Dunkin, M., & B. Biddle. (1974). *The study of teaching*. New York, Holt, Reinhardt, & Winston.

Fenstermacher, G. (1999, April). Method, Style, and Manner in Classroom Teaching. Paper presented at the Annual Meeting of the American Educational Research Association, Session 53.53, Montreal, Canada.

Fenstermacher, G., & J. Soltis. (1998) *Approaches to teaching* (3rd ed.). New York: Teachers College.

Kitcher, P. (1983). *The Nature of Mathematical Knowledge*. Oxford, Oxford University.

Lakatos, I. (1976). *Proof and Refutations: The Logic of Mathematical Discovery*, J. Worrall & E. Zahar (Eds). Cambridge, Cambridge University.

Lampert, M. (1985). How do teachers manage to teach? Perspectives on problems in practice. *Harvard Educational Review, 55*, 178–194.

Lampert, M. (2001). *Teaching problems and the problems of teaching*. New Haven, Yale.

Matthews, J. (1988). *Escalante: The best teacher in America*. New York, Holt.

Schnepp, M. (2000). Proof Positive: An Instance of Mathematical Discovery in the Classroom. *Mathematics in Michigan, 38*(2), 17–19.

Schnepp, M. (In prep.) Theory is practice! In: D. Chazan, M. Lehman & S. Bethell (Eds), Embracing Reason: Egalitarian Ideals and High School Mathematics Teaching. Unpublished manuscript, Michigan State University.

Schnepp, M., & R. Nemirovsky (2001). Constructing a foundation for the Fundamental Theorem of Calculus. In: A. Cuoco (Ed.), *The Role of Representation in School Mathematics*. Reston, VA, NCTM: 90–102.

Schwab, J. (1978). Education and the structure of the disciplines. In: I. Westbury & N. Wilkof, *Science, Curriculum, and Liberal Education: Selected Essays* (pp. 229–274). Chicago, University of Chicago.

Skemp, R. (1987). *The psychology of learning mathematics: Expanded American edition*. Hillsdale, NJ, Lawrence Erlbaum.

Skemp, R. R. (1976). Relational understanding and instrumental understanding. *Arithmetic Teacher*, 26(8), 9–15.

Thompson, P. W. (1994). The development of the concept of speed and its relationship to concepts of rate. In: G. Harel & J. Confrey, *The Development of Multiplicative Reasoning in the Learning of Mathematics* (pp. 179–234). Albany, NY, SUNY Press.

TALKING TO UNDERSTAND SCIENCE

Kathleen J. Roth

PRELUDE: ABOUT THE AUTHOR

As a teacher-researcher who conducts research in the context of my own teaching practice, I see myself as a theoretical pragmatist. I am deeply interested in understanding research and theory related to science teaching and learning. But my interest in this theory is driven by pragmatic concerns: I want to know how to improve teaching practice (first my own practice and then the practice of others). How might research and theory inform my teaching practice (and the practice of others)? How might it help me (and other teachers) enable students to develop better understandings of science and their relationship to science?

OVERVIEW

This chapter examines the issues of talk and understanding in science classrooms. What kinds of talk enable students to develop meaningful understandings of science and scientists' ways of talking and doing science? Recent research in science education has examined classroom discourse from a number of different perspectives. In my work as a teacher/researcher I have been drawing from this research to shape my teaching practice and to study student understanding. In particular, my teaching has been influenced by research in the conceptual change and social constructivist paradigms. Over a decade, I have modified the kinds of talk I foster in my classrooms in response to what I learn

Social Constructivist Teaching, Volume 9, pages 197–262.
© 2002 Published by Elsevier Science Ltd.
ISBN: 0-7623-0873-7

about my students' understandings and confusions and in response to what I learn from the research literature.

As a result of my studies of student understanding and of the research literature, I propose four assertions about the kinds of talk that support the development of students' understanding of science. In describing these assertions, I present examples from my teaching and highlight ways in which conceptual change and social constructivist research influenced the talk in my classrooms. I conclude with comments relevant to the central questions of this book regarding the strengths and limitations of teaching approaches that are based on social constructivist viewpoints. These comments include cautions about classroom talk that have implications for the social constructivist research agenda. Thus, the central question of this chapter is:

Drawing from conceptual change and social constructivist research and from studies of my students' learning, what have I learned about the kinds of talk that help students "really" understand science?

THE PROBLEM OF TALK AND UNDERSTANDING IN SCIENCE CLASSROOMS

Observations of Talk in Textbook-Focused and Inquiry-Oriented Classrooms

In the 1980s, my first experience as a researcher had a profound effect on my thinking about science teaching practice. In particular, I became aware of a problem with the kinds of talk going on in science classrooms. In textbook-focused classrooms, the talk was dominated by teacher telling with teacher-student dialogue limited to the traditional, didactic pattern: teacher initiation ("What kinds of rocks are formed as the result of volcanic activity?"), followed by student response ("igneous"), followed by teacher evaluation ("right"). In hands-on, inquiry-oriented classrooms student talk was much more prominent. Students were actively engaged in talking about their ideas, their observations, and their personal explanations of natural phenomena they observed. The teacher asked more open-ended questions and encouraged students to generate their own hypotheses and theories. In both types of classrooms, however, only a small minority of students developed meaningful understandings of science concepts or about the nature of science (Roth, Anderson & Smith, 1987; Roth, Smith & Anderson, 1984; Roth, 1989–1990).

I was not surprised that the majority of students were not learning in the traditional classrooms where they were primarily listening and only occasionally responding to factual questions with one- or two-word responses. But I was very surprised that students who were actively engaged in "doing" science (making observations and predictions, organizing data, developing explanations for their observations, etc.) and who were constantly talking about their observations and ideas were also failing to understand the central science concepts.

More surprising (and disturbing), was that students in both types of classrooms were developing distorted images of the nature of science and scientific inquiry. In the textbook-focused classrooms, students successfully memorized terms and scientific explanations (e.g. light travels in straight lines, light bounces, light travels through transparent objects, light travels to our eyes to enable us to see). But when asked a "real world" question in an interview situation, such as, "How come you can see the tree out the window, but you can't see through the wooden door?," students at the end of a unit of instruction about how light helps us see gave the exact same explanations as they had given on an identical pretest item. Their explanations had nothing to do with the science terms and explanations they had memorized for science class. To these students, the world of science was in a textbook and had nothing to do with their own everyday experiences.

In the inquiry-oriented classrooms, students like Rachel got tired of doing so many measurements of plants: "I don't know why we kept measuring those plants. I mean it was fun for awhile, but I already know that plants need light, and now I know it again." Rachel learned that science involves a lot of activity that does not help you understand things any better. Because she did not develop better conceptual understandings about plants, the processes of science seemed meaningless and not worth the effort. Driver (1983) critiqued this doing of science in the absence of meaningful conceptual development, suggesting that the "I do and I understand" slogan might more appropriately be, "I do and I am even more confused."

This research and that of others provides compelling evidence that traditional didactic styles of science classroom talk are not adequate to help most students to integrate knowledge with experience, to see relationships between bits of information and phenomena in the real world. In short, students do not *really* understand the science that they are taught in science classrooms. Equally compelling is the observation that open-ended, exploratory talk is not sufficient to help most students make sense of their first-hand experiences in science lessons (Driver, 1994; Millar & Driver, 1987). Clearly, these two types of classroom talk are not helping students develop the kinds of understandings of science concepts and the nature of scientific inquiry that are outlined in the current reform documents (American Association for the Advancement of Science, 1993; National Academy of Sciences, 1996).

What Kinds of Scientific Understandings do we Want Students to Develop?

Like all science teachers, I want to create talk in my classroom that helps my students understand science. But what does it mean to "understand" science, and what do I count as understanding in my students? The national standards documents as well as research on "teaching for understanding" (Wiggins & McTighe, 1998) are calling for something that I refer to as *really* understanding. I take this phrase from an experience I had as a freshman at Duke University. My best friend received the highest grades in advanced calculus courses, while the rest of us struggled in the general calculus classes. I assumed Elizabeth would major in math and was surprised that she had ruled that out as a possible major. "I can't major in math, because I don't understand calculus," she told me. "What do you mean you don't understand calculus?," I replied. I could not understand how she could have been the star student in the advanced calculus class without understanding calculus. But she assured me, "I mean I don't *really* understand calculus."

Drawing from analyses of both philosophy of science and of children's experiences in science classrooms, my colleague, Charles Anderson, and I identified several aspects of scientific knowledge that seem to be more or less universal characteristics of what it means to *really* understand science (Anderson & Roth, 1989; Roth, 1990). Understanding science, for both the scientist and the school science student has the following characteristics:

(a) *It is connected, well-structured.* When I say that scientific knowledge is "connected" or "well structured," I do not mean to imply that it has the sort of static structure that we associate with buildings, or the organization of books in a library. Instead, I use the word, "structure," in the way that biologists use that term. The structures of scientific knowledge, like biological structures, are richly interconnected but also dynamic and constantly changing. Systems of scientific knowledge are also like biological systems in that multiple structures or patterns exist within any given topic or discipline. Thus it is difficult to discuss "the" structure of scientific knowledge, or "the" right answer, not because science lacks structure but because it is highly structured in so many different ways.

Toulmin (1972) uses the metaphor of an "intellectual ecology" to explain the structure of a scientific discipline. Any concept, like an individual organism in an ecosystem, is associated with many other concepts (like an organism is connected to many other organisms in its environment) in a variety of ways and depends for its "life" or meaning on those associations. Adult scientists have developed large systems of richly interconnected ideas and depend on them to do their work.

(b) It is useful in describing, predicting, explaining, designing, and appreciating real-world phenomena. Adult scientists use their knowledge for a variety of purposes that are both socially important and personally rewarding:

- *Describing.* Scientists often use their knowledge for purposes that are essentially descriptive in nature: Providing names for things, measuring them, classifying them, describing their many characteristics. One reason that scientific knowledge is valued so widely is that it gives us the ability to provide precise and accurate names, descriptions, or measurements of natural systems or phenomena.
- *Explaining.* Explanation is a primary goal of science. We acquire scientific knowledge and develop theories to explain how the natural world works. Einstein once called scientists people "with a passion to explain."
- *Predicting.* The ability to generate accurate predictions is a key test of the validity of a scientific theory as well as an important use of scientific knowledge. Scientifically literate adults often use their scientific knowledge to generate predictions about future observations or events.
- *Designing.* Scientific knowledge is also valued because it can be used to design technologies that give us partial control over natural systems and events. Technological applications of scientific knowledge often have great social, political, and economic importance and power.
- *Appreciating.* Finally, scientists are often attracted to their fields as much for personal, aesthetic reasons as for utilitarian reasons. Their scientific knowledge gives them a richness and depth of understanding that helps them to appreciate the wonders, beauties, complexities, and puzzles of the world around them. The more I learn about biology, geology, chemistry, astronomy, and physics, for instance, the more fascinated and awed I am when I am out hiking in the wilderness.

(c) It is constantly changing, building, deepening over time, and raises questions for further exploration. No matter how useful the knowledge it has produced, a scientific field that is no longer changing and developing is characterized as "stagnant" and declines in power and importance. Like living organisms, scientific fields are inherently dynamic; the only alternative to growth is decay.

The same can be said of the knowledge of individual scientists. An important part of what scientists know is how to learn more, how to ask and pursue new questions that have the potential to produce significant new insights. Scientists have a disposition to inquire, to try to make sense of what they do not yet understand, and to demand more satisfying and complete explanations of the world. One consequence of this disposition is that scientists must become accustomed to living in a more or less constant state of uncertainty. Rather than avoiding situations that are confusing or puzzling, rather than avoiding ideas that are different than their own, scientists seek out the puzzles, the contradictions, the different perspectives and try to fit the pieces together.

(d) *It is developed within and shared by a community that cooperatively constructs new knowledge and understanding.* Finally, scientific understanding is a social rather than an individual endeavor. Each individual scientist is a member of a professional community that is engaged in a collective attempt to understand the natural world. Scientists contribute to the development of knowledge in their fields through participation in their professional communities. New knowledge is considered valid only after it has been reviewed and accepted by the community, and scientists are expected to participate in discussions and debates within the community. No individual scientist knows all that there is to know about a topic; the growing body of scientific knowledge is the product, and the possession, of the community.

The Problem of Talking to Understand Science

Thus, understanding science involves much more than memorizing terms and definitions for a multiple choice test on the one hand, or carrying out experiments and talking about observations and personal theories on the other. Discourse in science classrooms, however, tends to emphasize one or both of these kinds of science talk. As a result, the talk in classrooms does not support most students in developing meaningful understandings of science. So what kinds of talk *will* help students develop the kinds of understandings of science concepts and scientific inquiry described above?

IDEAS FROM RESEARCH ABOUT TALKING TO UNDERSTAND SCIENCE

In the years since my first research experience uncovered these problems of talk in other teachers' classrooms, I have drawn from the growing bodies of research literature about classroom discourse and about science teaching and learning to stimulate different kinds of talk in my own science teaching in elementary and middle school science classrooms. Three bodies of research have been especially influential on my thinking about new kinds of talk that might better support students' understanding of science. These three perspectives are: (a) a conceptual change view of learning and teaching, (b) a social constructivist view of teaching and learning, and (c) my own in-depth studies of my students' learning and understanding over the last decade.

Conceptual Change Research

Research in the conceptual change tradition suggested to me that classroom talk should focus more on students' ideas. This line of research has generated compelling evidence about the powerful role that students' own prior knowledge and experiences play in the science learning process (Hewson, Beeth & Thorley, 1998; Minstrell, 1989, 1992; Posner, Strike, Hewson & Gertzog, 1982; Roth, 1984, 1986, 1989–1990; West & Pines, 1985). Students draw from their personal theories and experiences to make sense of ideas presented to them in science classrooms. Unfortunately, the ideas presented in science class are often in conflict with students' personally constructed ideas. If students are not given the opportunity and support to reconcile these differences, they often tenaciously hold onto their personal understandings. They make sense of the teacher's scientific explanations by either distorting the scientific ideas to make them fit their own worldview, or by isolating science explanations into a special "box" called school knowledge (which is memorized for tests, but has nothing to do with students' real-world experiences and beliefs).

This research convinced me that talk about students' ideas should be at the heart of science teaching. But this research also gave me ideas about why students in the inquiry-focused classrooms were not developing meaningful understandings of science concepts. Clearly, getting students simply to talk more in science classrooms was not enough. Conceptual change theory suggested that several conditions must exist before students can change their personal theories and *really* understand scientific explanations of real-world phenomena (Posner, Strike, Hewson & Gertzog, 1982). First, learners must perceive a need to change their ideas – they must find occasions when their own view no longer provides a personally satisfying explanation. Next, they must encounter other ideas that make sense to them as alternative explanations, and they must be introduced to these new ideas in ways that help them see the new ideas as related to their own ideas – that is, as alternatives to their own ideas. Finally, students must find the new ideas useful in explaining a variety of personal experiences and phenomena. The new ideas do not immediately replace students' prior knowledge; instead, students need time and opportunities to try talking about and using the new ideas to explain and make sense of a variety of situations.

To meet these conditions for learning, teacher talk cannot be limited to eliciting and encouraging students' ideas and thinking. Teacher talk also needs to challenge and scaffold students' thinking, so that students receive feedback to help them reconsider and change their personal understandings in light of other evidence and explanations. Conceptual change theory also suggests the need for a balance between open-ended verbal interactions that bring out various student ideas and directed, structured discussions that help students assess why some explanations are more powerful and convincing than others (Roth, Anderson & Smith, 1987).

Social Constructivist Research

Social constructivist research has pointed out the limitations of the conceptual change viewpoint (Anderson, Holland & Palincsar, 1997; Bereiter, 1994; Duit & Treagust, 1998; Tobin, 1998). This perspective has helped me think about a broader range of topics and types of talk that would help students develop a richer understanding of the nature of science as well as knowledge about themselves in relationship to science. In comparison with a conceptual change viewpoint, a social constructivist theory places much more emphasis on the social nature of learning. In this view, it is impossible to think of the individual learner in isolation (Lemke, 1990, 2001). The learning process always includes interactions with others, and these personal interactions influence what is learned. In contrast to an individualistic view of learning, Driver (1994) described the social construction of knowledge:

> Making meaning is . . . a dialogic process involving persons-in-conversation, and learning is seen as the process by which individuals are introduced to a culture by more skilled members . . . . The challenge lies in helping learners to appropriate these [western scientific] models for themselves, to appreciate their domains of applicability and, within such domains, to be able to use them . . . . The challenge is one of how to achieve such a process of enculturation successfully in the round of normal classroom life (p. 7).

In the tradition of Vygotsky (1978, 1986), social constructivists see social interaction to be "central and necessary to learning and not merely ancillary." (Lemke, 2001, p. 296). In both classroom and scientific communities, knowledge construction is "inseparable from the social organization of scientists' [or classroom] activities" (Lemke, 2001, p. 296). Thus, social constructivist theory is critical of the conceptual change assumption that understanding is something that occurs primarily inside the head of the individual learner.

A social constructivist perspective, by highlighting the social construction of scientific knowledge, challenges the view of knowledge as absolute truth. As a result, this view criticizes conceptual change research as too focused on the canon of Western science – too focused on the learning of particular concepts. Instead, they argue that students should be learning as much, if not more, about the nature of science and about scientific ways of knowing and being. In particular, students should learn to see science as a very human and social endeavor, with its own cultural ways of knowing and talking that differ markedly from the cultural backgrounds of many of the students who are studying science in schools. Learning science is thus a process of being enculturated into a special community with its own forms of reasoning and discourse (Rosebery, Warren & Conant, 1992; Michaels & O'Connor, 1990).

Many social constructivists emphasize the role of "enculturation" of students into scientific discourse. In this view, the teacher provides a cognitive apprenticeship for students, modeling and coaching students in how to think like scientists, just as a master tailor models and coaches apprentices under his authority (Collins, Brown & Newmann, 1989; Brown, 1989). Thus, the teacher is a cognitive model, mentor, and coach.

There are others, however, who are critical of this emphasis on enculturation into Western science traditions. They operate from a broader sociocultural perspective. Because science is socially constructed, they argue, it is just one subculture, one way of viewing the world. The textbook image of science as an objective reporting of the "truth" that is observed in nature is not an accurate portrayal of science. Instead, science is just one subculture, one view of the world, and it is a subculture with a lot of power. It often excludes or at least devalues other ways of seeing and understanding the world. Aikenhead (1996, 2000) asserts that enculturation into the Western science subculture supports only those students whose cultural identities harmonize with the culture of western science. Brickhouse (1994, 1998) argues that schools define the community of scientists too narrowly and thus miss the opportunity to connect with communities more in line with students' efforts to forge their personal identities. These theorists argue for a broader vision of science that is more inclusive, and they also advocate teaching students to be critical of the Western scientific community and to compare it to other ways of knowing.

Thus, understanding science from a social constructivist perspective is a process of learning a new way of talking, thinking, and acting, and this is a challenging and social process. Just as a toddler needs to be immersed in rich language environments in order to learn how to talk and behave in her social and cultural community, so learners of science need to be immersed in rich science language environments in order to learn. But science learners are more like toddlers who are born into multicultural, multilingual communities. They must learn how and when to use the knowledge and language of science, and how that language does or does not fit into their own personal and cultural ways of knowing.

Studies of My Students' Understanding of Science

Over the last decade, I have conducted a series of studies as a teacher-researcher, drawing from conceptual change and social constructivist research and theory, to inform my practice and to study the impact of my practice on students' understandings of science concepts and the nature of science. The conceptual change research initially played a central role in changing the kinds of talk that occur in my classroom. But social constructivist critiques of the talk in conceptual change classrooms challenged me over the years to change and modify the kinds of talk in my classroom. In particular, social constructivist research made me question whether my talk was too directive and controlling – driving students to the "one right answer," which of course is the Western science answer. The social constructivist perspective challenged me to broaden the view of science that is enacted in the classroom, to focus on my students' cultural and personal identities as well as non-Western viewpoints on science, and to give students more voice in planning and carrying out their inquiries.

As a teacher/researcher over the last decade, I have conducted studies of students' developing understandings and used the results of these analyses to refine and shape my teaching practice (Roth, 1989–1990; Roth & Hazelwood, 1992; Roth, Peasley & Hazelwood, 1992; Roth, 1993, 1995, 1996, 2001). Although I have taught and studied students' learning on various science topics, I have repeatedly studied and revised a unit about how plants get their food. Since this was the unit that I initially observed being taught by other teachers in the inquiry-focused classrooms, I can compare student learning about this topic across teachers as well as across different iterations of my own teaching. Each iteration had some new focus, some new idea about the kinds of talk that would best support student learning.

To assess my students' progress in developing the kinds of scientific understandings that are connected, useful, changing, and collaboratively developed, I conducted in-depth studies of all of my students' learning (using pre-post unit tests, interviews, lesson videotapes, and regular journal writing to track students' thinking and learning). Assessment of student learning focused on students' abilities to develop connected understandings of canonical knowledge (e.g. photosynthesis, blood circulation, respiration, cells, etc.) that they could use to describe, explain, and design a variety of real-world situations (why seeds will start to grow in a cave but later die, how an aspirin might work to help a headache, how to design an experiment that would clarify the role of the cotyledon, etc.). In addition, students' understandings of the nature of science were explored, primarily through interview tasks and questions.

In my initial studies in other teachers' classrooms, conducted in the 1980s, only 7% of the fifth-grade students ended an inquiry-oriented unit understanding the main ideas that plants (and only plants) get their food by taking in raw materials from the environment (sunlight, carbon dioxide, water) and turning these into energy-containing food, the plant's only source of food. In classrooms where I used a conceptual change teaching model to teach the same content, however, there was a consistent pattern of 80% or more of the students being able to apply their knowledge of plants and photosynthesis to explain a variety of novel, real-world situations (as evidenced on pre-posttest comparisons). In interview situations, an equally high percentage of students constructed coherent and reasonable concept maps about how plants get their food, and many were also able to explain how photosynthesis related to other topics studied during the school year, showing accurate and well-structured links among these ideas. Continuing to build their understandings over time, some students had more coherent concept maps at the end of the year than they did at the end of the unit of study in the fall.

Less formal evidence of student learning is also compelling. For example, there were many instances when students spontaneously raised questions (often outside of science class) that demonstrated they were continuing to think about the implications of the ideas that we had studied. Long after the plants unit had ended, for example, John stayed inside from recess to water the plants. As he was doing this chore, he said to me: "You know, Ms. Roth, I used to think plants just kind of sit there. But they're really busy little things aren't they?" At a parent conference, a parent of one of the seemingly least engaged girls in the classroom said to me: "We were outside raking leaves in the yard and Tina started talking about this huge tree and that it was doing photosynthesis and explaining it all to us. She was wondering about how *much* water it needed to do photosynthesis."

Thus, there is evidence that the teaching strategies and the talk in these classrooms supported many students in developing understandings of central science concepts (see Roth, 1993, 1996; Roth, Peasley & Hazelwood, 1992 for fuller reports). However, in the early years of this work, the evidence of students' learning about the nature of science was disappointing. Students did not understand that the reason I pushed for evidence and encouraged debate about ideas had to do with the nature of science. Instead, they attributed the qualities of our learning community to my personality. As Darla said to me in class one day towards the end of the school year, "Ms. Roth, do you like to argue or something?"

These initially disappointing results regarding students' understandings of the nature of science led me to include in later iterations of my teaching an emphasis on explicit talk about the nature of science and the ways in which our class-room was like (and not like) a scientific community. This teaching approach is consistent with the social constructivist idea of the teacher as a cognitive coach, making explicit and visible for students some of the ways of knowing in science – the language of science. Comparisons of student interview data at the beginning and end of the school year provided strong evidence that this explicit talk was supporting students in changing and enriching their understanding of how science works. The following interview excerpts illustrate how these fifth graders understood the role of evidence and argument in science as well as the socially constructed nature of scientific knowledge:

Interviewer: What else can you tell me about what scientists do?

Ethan: They have to research stuff.

I: OK, tell me how they research stuff?

E: They have to look at different scientists' perspectives and see what they think, and then they try and see if they thought it was any different. And then they maybe could try and find that other scientist and talk about it, and see if he thought it was a good idea.

I: Tell about this, "they look at different scientists' perspectives"?

E: Well, if they were in a book and stuff they might read it, and get some ideas and they might say, "Well, I don't think this is right" and try and change their idea.

I: Do you think it would be easy or hard for scientists to study about humans who lived a million years ago?

Nan: It would be hard because they got to find a lot of evidence, and they got to find a lot of things . . . because there is no proof. Like to find out if early humans got married in churches . . . .. They'd have to go all around the world and try and find like if they find a church or something, they are not going to say that that is a church where early humans go to get married. They ain't going to know.

I: Have your ideas about scientists changed?

Helen: Yes! When I first started science, I used all the stereotypes and now I've learned that they can do anything they want. They can ride a moped, wear grubby clothes. Some work in labs but most of 'em are studying things, finding out things, trying to figure out things.

I: Were there times in science class when you felt like a scientist?

H: When we did the bean experiments. *We* were finding the things out, *we* were the ones that were making the experiments. Some people would like stay in for recess and make up their own experiments.

I: What kinds of talking do scientists do?

H: They have arguments sometimes, they sometimes talk to each other at meetings about what they found out and how they got that information.

I: Can you say more about arguments?

H: Well, some people might believe in one thing and some might believe in the other, like if I said the seeds could grow in the dark, other people might say they can't grow in the dark cause they don't have any sunlight and that's part of food, so you'd do an experiment and find out. They can argue about which one they think is right and then they can try or find out which one is right.

I: Is it a good thing or a bad thing to have arguments in science?

H: I think it's a good thing cause then you learn more about what the other people think and if you're wrong you learn from yourself and sometimes you learn from the other people.

FOUR ASSERTIONS ABOUT TALK THAT SUPPORTS STUDENT UNDERSTANDING OF SCIENCE

So what kinds of talk occurred in these classrooms that might have contributed to the students' successful conceptual learning and their growing understandings of the nature of science? How have the conceptual change and social constructivist research literatures influenced the kinds of talk that supported student learning in these science classrooms?

In the remainder of this chapter, I describe how I have drawn from research in both the conceptual change and social constructivist traditions as well as from research on my own students' learning to shape the talk in my science classroom. These descriptions are organized around four assertions that I make based on my experiences using and studying the impact of different kinds of talk in science teaching and learning.

The assertions are:

(1) *Different kinds of talk are needed for different purposes at different points during the learning process. Overemphasis on one or two kinds of talk in the science classroom limits students' learning opportunities.* To be most effective in helping a broad range of students "really" understand some core ideas in and about science, the science teacher must be aware of a broad range of different types and purposes of science talk. Each particular type of talk is a tool in the teacher's kit. How does the teacher know which type of talk to use at a given moment? Understanding how students learn and the conditions needed to help them change and deepen their ideas (ideas from conceptual change research) helps the teacher search for the right kind of

talk for a particular phase of the learning process. Ideas from social constructivist analyses and apprenticeship views of learning emphasize the changing roles that teacher talk plays during the learning process – from modeling scientific talk to scaffolding students' efforts to "talk science" to gradual fading of such teacher scaffolding.

(2) *Teacher talk is just as important as student talk.* It is not enough to tell teachers to talk less and to let students do more of the talking, though this is an important message. Teacher talk is critical. It must be sensitive to students' emerging ideas and readiness to learn. It is not an easy task to figure out when is the appropriate moment to tell, to coach, to keep quiet.

(3) *Talk about the science content (concepts, facts, observations) is not enough.* My own research and the social constructivist research both point to the importance of including talk that goes beyond the bounds of traditional classroom science talk. There must also be explicit talk about the nature of science and scientific inquiry, about ways of talking and acting in science, about students' personal identities and self-knowledge, and about critiques of science.

(4) *Talk about <u>shared</u> experiences is a critical part of learning to talk and to understand science.* This is important for two reasons. From a learning standpoint, it enables the teacher to scaffold students' thinking. From a nature of science viewpoint, it better reflects how science is done.

THE FOUR ASSERTIONS IN ACTION: EXAMPLES OF TALK IN THE SCIENCE CLASSROOM

Overview

What does this kind of talk look like in science classrooms? The first two assertions will be illustrated together, showing examples of what they look like in action in the classroom. For these two assertions, I draw from a unit about how plants get their food, a unit I have taught and studied with many different groups of fifth grade students. These two assertions will be described in relationship to an instructional model that guides my teaching practice. In each of the five phases of the model, there are distinct (often multiple) purposes for the teacher and student talk. Therefore, the examples are preceded by a brief description of the instructional model. The third and fourth asssertions will each be discussed separately, drawing examples from a variety of contexts across the school year.

The Instructional Model

Figures 1 and 2 describe the "teaching for understanding" instructional model which guides my science teaching practice. Figure 1 describes the phases of instruction, starting with the establishment of a problem that the entire class will study together and the eliciting of students' initial ideas about that problem. The model seems to suggest that these phases of instruction occur in a clear sequence: eliciting students' ideas, challenging students' initial ideas, presenting new ideas, applying new ideas, and reflecting/connecting. In practice, however, these phases occur and re-occur frequently, sometimes within the same lesson. For example, eliciting students' ideas happens in every lesson, whether for the purpose of establishing the problem to be studied, telling the students about scientific explanations, or creating opportunities for students to practice using the new ideas. Figure 2 suggests that the social organization of the classroom is an essential part of science teaching. For students to be willing to share their ideas and make public their confusions and questions, there must be a classroom environment of mutual trust and respect.

Assertions 1 and 2 in Action in the Classroom

Assertion 1. *Different kinds of talk are needed for different purposes at different points during the learning process.*

Assertion 2. *Teacher talk is just as important as student talk.*

Table 1 summarizes the kinds of teacher and student talk that characterize each of the phases of instruction illustrated in the teaching model described in Figures 1 and 2. In contrast with my early studies of classrooms where the talk consisted primarily of either teacher telling or open-ended, student exploratory talk, the talk in this model includes a much wider variety of purposes for both teacher and student talk.

Excerpts of classroom discourse will be used to illustrate these different kinds and purposes of teacher and student talk. The excerpts below are organized into five sections, with each section highlighting the key features of classroom talk during a particular phase of the instruction. While it is difficult to divide the teaching neatly into these five phases, the division will help clarify the changing and multiple purposes of teacher and student talk across a unit of study (in this case, a unit about how plants get their food).

1. **Establish a problem** and **elicit** students' ideas.

Introduce the central question in a way that will engage students' interest and elicit their many different ideas about the question. Students should see that other students have different ways of explaining the same phenomenon.

2. **Explore** phenomena and **challenge** students' initial ideas.

Engage students in experience with phenomena and (direct, hands-on experience whenever possible) that allow them a chance to think through their ideas, to gather new evidence relevant to the central question, and to consider whether their initial ideas still make sense in light of the evidence. Activities are designed to challenge students' preconceptions – to get them finding their initial ideas incomplete or unsatisfying in some way.

3. **Present** new ideas and **contrast** them with students' initial ideas.

New ideas and concepts are not explained to students until their explorations have convinced them of a need for a new explanation. New concepts need to introduced in ways that are likely to make sense from the students' perspectives. Use a variety of representations to explain new ideas (models, role playing, charts, diagrams, etc.). Compare and contrast students' ideas with scientific explanations. Encourage students to critique the new explanation: Does it make sense in light of the evidence we have gathered?

4. **Apply** new ideas and reconcile them with students' ideas – Teacher **Modeling**

Students need opportunities to *practice using new concepts* to explain real world situations. The teacher at first plays an important role as director in this process, at first providing lots of modeling of scientific ways of thinking. For example, after students have attempted an explanation of a problem situation, the teacher might point out aspects of their attempts that are scientifically strong and say, "these are the ways scientists would use this concept to think about this situation."

Apply new ideas and reconcile them with students' ideas – Teacher **Coaching**

Students need numerous opportunities to practice using new concepts to explain real world situations. Teacher modeling in one context is not enough. A variety of activities and questions that engage students in using scientific concepts and in refining their understanding of these concepts will help students see the wide usefulness of the concepts. During these activities, the teacher should actively coach students, providing them with feedback about ways in which their thinking is strong and ways in which they need to be more scientific in their thinking.

Apply new ideas and reconcile them with students' ideas – **Teacher Fading**

Understanding is not occurring until students are able to use new ideas to explain novel situations independently. So it is essential that the teacher coaching fade out as students become more comfortable working with the ideas.

5. **Reflect** on changes in students' ideas and **Connect** with new ideas.

Students need to reflect often on the ways in which their ideas are changing and why. Frequently, the teacher asks: "How did today's activities give you any new ideas about our question? Did you change any of your ideas today? What evidence convinced you to do so? What is confusing to you today? What do we still need to know to help us answer our question?" As students become more comfortable using new concepts without teacher coaching, it is especially important to take time to have students look back at the progress of their thinking and learning. Their awareness of their own conceptual change plays an important role in their valuing of the scientific process.

Fig. 1. A Teaching Science for Understanding Instructional Model.

INSIDE CIRCLE: Instructional Model
OUTSIDE CIRCLE: Characteristics of the Learning Community

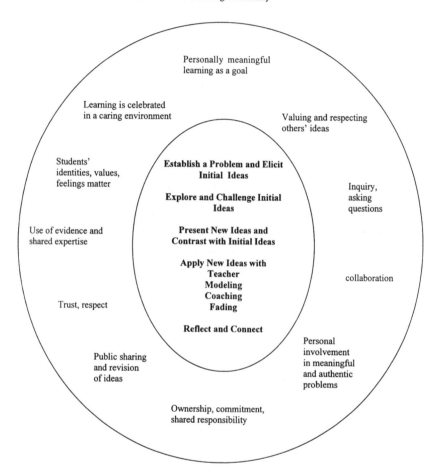

Fig. 2. Teaching Science for Understanding Within a Learning Community.

Instructional Phase I: Establish a Problem and Elicit Initial Ideas. In a unit about plants and photosynthesis, I selected two central questions for the class to explore over 4–6 weeks: How do plants get their food? What is food for plants? The unit began with a discussion in which I elicited students' ideas about how plants get their food. I focused particularly on how plants get the energy they need to live. During this discussion my role was to elicit students'

Table 1.   Phases of a Teaching for Understanding Model of Science Teaching.

Instructional Phase	Intended Student Understanding	Purposes of Teacher Talk	Features of Student Talk
Establish a Problem and Elicit Initial Ideas	*I have ideas about how the world works. Other people have different ideas that are worth my consideration.*	• Elicit students' ideas • Encourage use of evidence and building of arguments • Encourage and make visible multiple viewpoints • Encourage listening to others' personal ideas • Encourage questioning and reconsideration of personal ideas • Ask for elaboration and clarification of personal ideas • Frame and set purpose	• Use personal ideas to build arguments • Make hypotheses • Challenge ideas using personal experience • Support ideas using personal experience • Reconsider personal ideas in response to other arguments • Question
Explore and Challenge Initial Ideas	*My observations and experiences are making me question my ideas and reconsider other peoples' ideas.*	• Challenge students' ideas • Encourage use of evidence, personal ideas to build arguments • Encourage questioning and reconsideration of personal ideas • Encourage listening to and challenging others' ideas • Ask for elaboration and clarification of observations and personal ideas • Frame and set purpose	• Use evidence and personal ideas to build arguments • Reconsider personal ideas • Challenge ideas using evidence and personal experience • Support ideas using evidence • Question
Compare Scientific Explanations with Initial Ideas	*Scientific explanations help me rethink my own ideas and observations. Scientific explanations make sense, because they can be justified by data and my own observations – they don't just appear in textbooks.*	• Tell scientific ideas • Encourage use of evidence, scientific explanations, personal explanations, reasons to build arguments • Scaffold links among canonical knowledge and evidence and students' ideas	• Use evidence, scientific explanations, personal explanations, reasons to build arguments • Reconcile/link canonical explanations and personal ideas • Reconsider personal ideas

Table 1. Continued.

Instructional Phase	Intended Student Understanding	Purposes of Teacher Talk	Features of Student Talk
		• Model scientific thinking • Invite reconsideration and questioning • Ask for elaboration and clarification of scientific ideas in relationship to personal ideas • Frame and set purpose	• Challenge ideas using evidence, scientific explanations, personal experience, reasoning • Support ideas using evidence, scientific explanations, reasoning • Question
Apply New Ideas with Teacher Modeling and Coaching	*Scientific explanations make sense to me, because I can use them to explain or to predict many different things.*	• Coach students' in their use of canonical scientific ideas and ways of thinking • Scaffold links among canonical knowledge and evidence and students' ideas • Encourage use of evidence, scientific explanations, personal experience, reasoning to build arguments • Gradually fade coaching support	• Use evidence, scientific explanations, canonical knowledge, personal experience, reasoning to build arguments • Reconcile/link canonical knowledge and ways of thinking with personal ideas • Challenge ideas using evidence, scientific explanations, personal experience, reasoning • Support ideas using evidence, scientific explanations, personal experience, reasoning • Question
Reflect and Connect	*Scientific ideas change as a result of new evidence, debate, or questions that lead us to design new inquiries.*	• Elicit students' ideas about how and why their ideas have changed, warrants for knowledge, how we know	• Reflect (personal and group process) on learning, how and why ideas have changed, how we know

Table 1.   Continued.

Instructional Phase	Intended Student Understanding	Purposes of Teacher Talk	Features of Student Talk
	My ideas have changed as a result of this process.	• Support students reflections and connections – both as individuals and as a group	• Challenge • Support • Question

ideas, to encourage them to give reasons and evidence to support their ideas (usually drawn from personal experiences), to challenge them to listen to and to consider each other's ideas, and to moderate the discussion. I also wrote a list of each of the suggested ideas on a large, bulletin-board chart, which became a focal point throughout the unit of instruction.

Below is an excerpt from one such discussion designed to elicit students' ideas at the beginning of a unit of study. In the two right-hand columns, I comment on the purposes and features of teacher and student talk. Though the overarching purpose of teacher talk in this lesson was to elicit students' ideas, teacher talk involved a variety of purposes other than simply evoking the students' ideas. For example, teacher talk played a critical role in framing the discussion (highlighting and organizing key ideas); getting students to elaborate on and to clarify their ideas; making different viewpoints visible to everyone; encouraging students to reason, to use evidence, and to reconsider their ideas in light of the conversation.

Speaker	Talk	Purposes of Teacher Talk	Features of Student Talk
Roth	. . . And what I'd like to do is have you guys tell me, what do you think about how plants get their food? I'm going to keep a list up on the board of our ideas. Um, what I would like each of you doing is listening to each other, to see what you think of other people's ideas. Are they similar to yours, or different? Do they have some good evidence for their ideas? Or do you have some different evidence for something else? Okay? So today we're getting up our ideas about food for plants – our hypotheses. Okay. Who wants to – you going to start us off, Dean?	• Elicits ideas • Encourages reasons and evidence • Encourages listening to others' viewpoints	

Speaker	Talk	Purposes of Teacher Talk	Features of Student Talk
Dean	Okay. Fertilizer?		Uses personal ideas
Roth	Okay. Now tell us a little bit about why you think fertilizer would be food for plants.	Encourages reasons and evidence	
Dean	People put it on their plants to help them grow, so –		Uses personal ideas
Roth	Okay. People put it on their plants to help it grow. Okay. Sarah?		
Sarah	Well, I think fertilizer is food for plants in a way, but I don't think it's like one of the natural foods for plants. I think it's more like the Sun and the dirt and stuff is more of a natural food. Fertilizer is like stuff you could put on it to help it grow.		• Supports an idea • Makes a hypothesis
Roth	Okay, so maybe fertilizer is kinda like – you're saying like sun, and dirt? –	Asks for elaboration	
Sarah	– are more natural ways.		Elaborates
Student	And the soil.		
Roth	Okay, soil. Is soil different from dirt, or the same?	Asks for clarification	
Students	[Calling out all at once] Yes/No/The same.		Uses personal ideas
Roth	Somebody tell me about those two words. What are you thinking about when you say "soil"? Is that the same as "dirt"? Tiffany, you say, "yes, it's the same thing"? Who thinks that they're different things? Carey?	Elicits students' ideas about terms	
Carey	Me. I think the dirt is, um, more, um, dirty or something, because they clean the soil.		Uses personal ideas
Roth	Okay. I know what you're saying: that some soil – like if I went out in the playground right now and I dug up some dirt – is that soil or is that dirt?	Asks for clarification	
Students	That's dirt.		Uses personal ideas
Roth	That's dirt. Where would I find soil, Carey?	Asks for clarification	
Carey	In the supermarket.		Uses personal ideas

Speaker	Talk	Purposes of Teacher Talk	Features of Student Talk
Roth	In those bags – in the, in the store? Okay.		
Adam	They talk about, like, treated –		Uses personal ideas
Roth	For right now I'm going to leave these two words separate: dirt and soil. But some people think they're the same thing, and some people think maybe they're different. Right now let's leave them separate, because we're just getting down our ideas right now; we may change our minds later. Um, so what Sarah was saying was that maybe sun and dirt are more like natural foods for the plant, and fertilizer is more like an artificial kind of food? Okay. Good. So we'll put it up on the list. Maria-Yolanda, what were you going to say?	• Frames the question • Encourages students to reconsider ideas • Makes different viewpoints visible	

In the dialogue above, students primarily shared their personal experiences and ideas, and some began forging hypotheses. Since this was their first experience with this kind of talk in science classrooms, these students did not often challenge each other or pose questions. However, as the discussion continued, notice below how teacher talk laid the groundwork for moving students towards more interaction and debate, by making differing viewpoints visible and encouraging students to reconsider their ideas.

Speaker	Talk	Purposes of Teacher Talk	Features of Student Talk
Roth	Tell me what you're thinking about air, Dean.	Elicits students' ideas	
Dean	Well, I was thinking, since, um, it's an organism, that, like, animals and we need air, so I thought they might need air too.		Makes a hypothesis
Roth	Since animals need air, that maybe plants need air? Okay. Would you consider, Dean, air a food for us?	Asks for clarification	
Dean	Kind of.		Clarifies

Speaker	Talk	Purposes of Teacher Talk	Features of Student Talk
Roth	How many people would consider air to be a food? What's our definition of food that we're using?	• Makes different viewpoints visible • Encourages use of canonical knowledge	
Sarah	Well, I don't know, I don't know that; but I just wanted to say that people that are, like, poor and dying and stuff, cuz they don't have food and stuff, well they have air. If air was food, why would they be dying?		• Uses personal ideas • Makes hypothesis
Maria	[Quietly to Sarah] That's a good argument, Sarah.		Supports an argument
Roth	Okay, that's a good argument – right, Maria. That was very nice; Maria complimented Sarah on a good argument. Um, that's a good – that is a good argument. People who are starving, they still have air, but they're still dying. Dean?	• Encourages building of argument • Reflects on group process	
Dean	I just remembered the, um – we use the air, and the trees use the dirty stuff in the air.		Uses personal ideas
Roth	They use the what?	Asks for clarification	
Dean	The like, the dirty stuff in the air.		Clarifies
Roth	Something else in the air?		
Dean	Like the pollution.		Clarifies
Roth	Okay. When you say they use it, do you think it could be a food for them?	Asks for more clarification	
Dean	Yeah.		Clarifies
Roth	Could it be providing them with some energy?	• Asks for more clarification • Scaffolds linking of canonical knowledge with personal ideas	
Dean	Probably.		Clarifies

Speaker	Talk	Purposes of Teacher Talk	Features of Student Talk
Roth	Okay. Um, how many people now are, um – let's think about this air thing, whether air could be food for people? How many people are thinking now that air is a kind of food, that it does provide energy?	Encourages reconsidering ideas	
Students	[A few hands up]		
Roth	Maybe a couple people. How many people are thinking that air would not be food for people?	Makes different viewpoints visible	
Students	[Many hands up]		
Roth	What convinced you, Becky?	• Encourages reconsidering of initial ideas • Encourages use of evidence and reasoning	

Students continued to hypothesize about food for plants, for an entire science lesson. Almost every student contributed some idea about how plants get their food. Throughout this talk students primarily drew from their personal experiences and prior knowledge (Dean's knowledge that people put fertilizer on plants, Carey's description of the "dirt" you can buy at the supermarket, etc.). In some cases the students used their personal ideas to build hypotheses that explained their observations.

The students' personal talk generated a list of 22[1] different ideas about how plants get their food. Each idea was added to the class list of hypotheses about how plants get their food. I then asked the students to look at the list and to see if there were any responses they believed did *not* provide food energy for plants.

During these interactions teacher talk involved more than simply asking for students' ideas and accepting their responses. Teacher talk stimulated students to think about reasons and evidence, encouraged them to listen to each other's ideas and to debate about their hypotheses. I guided the students to consider each other's ideas, and, even at this early stage in the unit, I suggested they might want to change their ideas later on.

Speaker	Talk	Purposes of Teacher Talk	Features of Student Talk
Roth	Anything else on the list that you think maybe does *not* supply energy for plants? Um, Sarah?	• Encourages use of evidence • Encourages reconsidering of ideas • Makes different viewpoints visible	
Sarah	We've been saying this does, for a long time, but just so I – I just thought of it. Well, we said that water doesn't have energy, so why would it be food for plants, if it doesn't have any energy? It may use it to grow, like we use water because we're, we're mostly water in our body, we need water; but, we, I mean – but, doesn't mean that it has energy in it so –		• Reconsiders an idea • Uses reasoning and evidence
Roth	Okay, so we're going to put a question mark – [puts a question mark next to "water" on the blackboard]	Encourages reconsideration of ideas	
Sarah	– I don't know if it's food, it might be food for plants, but it might just be a food that doesn't have energy in it.	Reconsiders an idea	
Roth	What do other people think about the water thing? Cuz she's kind of said – she's using a similar argument that you did, Ethan, about the, um – what was yours? About the air? She's saying that the water – maybe if it's not energy for humans, then maybe it's not, maybe it's not for plants. What do you think, Chuck?	• Elicits ideas • Makes different viewpoints visible	
Chuck	They grow – they grow when you give 'em water and stuff, so it's got to be food.		• Uses personal ideas • Uses evidence and reasoning
Ethan	Some people say that, um, water's food for humans, because it's two-thirds of the body.		Uses personal ideas

Instructional Phase II: Explore and Challenge Initial Ideas. A later lesson in the food for plants unit was designed to challenge an idea held by many of the students: soil is food for plants. At the beginning of the lesson, I wrote the following on the blackboard:

Is soil food for plants?

Evidence

Yes   *No*

As we discussed the question and students suggested evidence for their answers, I wrote their responses on the board. Preceding this lesson, students performed several experiments with bean seeds and grass plants. Therefore, during the discussion on this day, students drew upon observational data, in addition to their prior knowledge and experiences. Armed with direct experiential knowledge from these experiments, the students' talk now involved much more challenging and supporting of each others' ideas. From my perspective as the teacher, the overall goal here was to get students to reconsider evidence for their initial ideas about soil and to raise questions/doubts about their initial ideas. Several different kinds of teacher talk were used to achieve this goal.

Speaker	Talk	Purposes of Teacher Talk	Features of Student Talk
Roth	What do you think about this question: "Is soil food for plants?"	Elicits ideas	
Liz	No. It's just for the roots to hold onto.		Uses personal idea
Maria	I agree that it's "no", because of our beans on the paper towel.	• Supports an idea using evidence • Uses evidence	
Roth	Does everyone know what Maria is talking about?	Encourages listening to others' ideas	
Jill	Yeah, she's saying that the beans grew on the paper towel, and they didn't have soil.		Supports an idea
Tom	I didn't think that would happen. I thought they had to have soil.		Supports an idea

Speaker	Talk	Purposes of Teacher Talk	Features of Student Talk
Jerry	I think soil is food for plants. Well, it's some kind of food, I think, but it just helps a little.		Challenges an idea
Joe	This is about what Jill said. Some of the beans didn't grow on the paper towel. I think they'd grow better in soil.		Challenges an idea using evidence
Roth	If you are confused by what someone is saying, remember that you can ask a question. What would you say in a scientific discussion, like the one we're having now, if you didn't agree or didn't understand? You could say, "Please clarify that," or, "I don't see the point." Adam?	• Reflects on group process • Highlights nature of science • Makes visible differing viewpoints	
Adam	No, soil isn't food for plants. Because it isn't food for humans.		Uses reasons
Jonathon	I disagree – I think the white foamy things in the soil have energy.		Challenges an idea
Roth	Why do you think that, Jonathon?	Asks for clarification	
Jonathon	Well, you could prove it. You could try to grow plants in soil that did not have any white foamy things in it.		• Uses evidence • Proposes experiment
Roth	Hmm, interesting idea. Or, we could buy a bag of the white foamy things and see if we could grow plants in them.	Elaborates on proposed experiment	
Rachel	Well, we could just use the soil we have and pick the white foamy things out of it.		Supports and elaborates on proposed experiment
Roth	That would take a lot of patience. We've talked about the fact that scientists often need a lot of patience to do their work. I'm going to think about this. Rachel, could you write that one in the Question Book? [Rachel gets the book and enters the question.]	• Highlights nature of science • Encourages questioning	
Alonso	But soil does make the plant grow higher.		Challenges using evidence

Speaker	Talk	Purposes of Teacher Talk	Features of Student Talk
Roth	What is your evidence for that, Alonso?	Asks for evidence	
Alonso	Soil and water *together* make it grow high, because the roots grow longer.		Makes hypothesis using evidence
Adam	I'm changing to "yes", because soil is food for worms.		Reconsiders giving reason
Eliza	Maybe the white foamy things are sugar.		Makes hypothesis
Brenda	Maybe soil has sugar in it.		Makes hypothesis
Roth	Great idea! Now try to come up with some evidence to support that. Does anyone have a hypothesis about that?	Encourages use of evidence and hypothesis-making	
Keith	I heard somewhere that worms do not actually eat dirt, that they eat little animals in the dirt.		Uses personal idea
Roth	Keith, let's get that question and your idea in the Question Book. [Keith enters the question and his idea in the Question Book.]	• Makes students' questions visible • Encourages questioning	
Sally	I think they *do* eat the dirt, because what else could they be eating?		Gives hypothesis with reasons
Roth	The worms?	Asks for clarification	
Sally	Yeah – [Pause]		Clarifies
Roger	[Calling out emphatically] – They eat the white foamy things!		Makes a hypothesis
Sally	But how do you know? What is your evidence?		Challenges asking for evidence
Eliza	We could do an experiment, and get a certain amount of soil and worms, and then weigh it. Then wait awhile and weigh it again. If it weighs less, that means the worms ate the soil.		Proposes experiment to gather evidence
Brittany	Yeah, let's do that!		Supports
Maria	But the worms might die – [Pause]		Challenges

Speaker	Talk	Purposes of Teacher Talk	Features of Student Talk
Roth	Okay, we're getting some good ideas about how we might gather some evidence. Take out your book, and open to page 8. [Pause] Tomorrow, we're going to read about an experiment that was done by a botanist way back in the 1600s – before there even was a country called the United States of America. Let's see if his experiment gives us any evidence about our question, "Is soil food for plants"?	• Encourages use of evidence • Frames	

Subsequent activities in the unit were designed to give students more evidence that might convince them that soil is not food for plants. First, students examined the classic experiment performed by the Dutch scientist, von Helmont, in the 1600s. Von Helmont carefully weighed a small tree and a bucket of soil. He planted the tree in the soil and watered it for five years. The tree grew much bigger, but the soil lost only a negligible amount of weight.

Next, I gave the students a highly structured activity in which to work through their emerging ideas about whether or not soil is food for plants. The activity's design provided both the opportunity for students to speak about the evidence from von Helmont's experiment, and for me to diagnose how successfully the von Helmont experiment had challenged students' initial hypotheses that soil provides food for plants. During the activity, an array of magnetic "word cards" were placed randomly on the blackboard. I specifically chose words that would focus the students' attention on our central questions (e.g. 'plants', 'food', 'energy', 'soil', 'evidence', 'von Helmont'). Students took turns coming to the board, selecting a few words, and arranging them in a sentence that made sense. Meanwhile, other students listened and asked clarification questions.

In the subsequent discussion, students again drew from their personal knowledge; however, this time, as a result of the series of activities designed to challenge their entering hypotheses, students added new ideas that emerged from their experiences in the unit. The dialogue below illustrates how several students used evidence from von Helmont's experiment to arrive at the conclusion that soil is not food for plants. Student talk focused more on drawing evidence from the von Helmont experiment and from earlier experiments they conducted with bean seeds and grass plants than on their initial ideas and theories. The task itself challenged student talk to become more structured and more focused on the use of evidence to build an argument.

The dialogue also illustrates that students are still confused. Although I encouraged students to critique each other's statements in the following interaction, I chose not to correct misconceptions at this point (such as the idea that water provides energy for plants). Instead I used the discussion to assess the degree to which students were convinced that soil is not food for plants. Accordingly, the teacher talk here focuses on challenging students' ideas, encouraging students to reason from evidence and to reconsider their ideas, and framing the discussion.

Speaker	Talk	Purposes of Teacher Talk	Features of Student Talk
Roth	Raise your hand if you don't have a sentence ready yet. Ok, let's wait. [Wait time] Is there anybody who is not ready? Who would like to start us off? Let's start with Ellis.	Encourages everyone to think before talk begins	
Ellis	Mr. von Helmont gave us evidence that plants don't eat the soil.		Uses von Helmont evidence
Roth	Okay, let's listen, wait, before we go on o the next one; let's listen to that one and say, "Is that accurate? Does he have a good sentence?" So, Ellis, would you say it again?	Encourages students to consider others' ideas	
Ellis	Mr. von Helmont gave us evidence that plants don't eat the soil.		Uses von Helmont evidence
Roth	Anybody disagree with that? Anything wrong with Ellis'? [Wait time] Great, that's a wonderful sentence. Great start. Okay, we'll go to Billy next and then Theo.	Encourages different viewpoints	
Billy	Water is food for plants, and my evidence is it gives energy.		Makes personal claim (no reason)
Roth	Okay, "water is food for plants", "my evidence is it gives energy"? Okay, any questions for Billy? Travis?	• Encourages students to consider others' ideas • Encourages challenging of ideas	

Speaker	Talk	Purposes of Teacher Talk	Features of Student Talk
Travis	When we were doing the experiments earlier, it said that, um, water does not have energy, so how could it give energy?		• Challenges • Uses evidence from earlier experiments
Roth	What do you think, Billy?	• Elicits ideas • Invites reconsideration	
Billy	[Silence]		
Roth	Do you remember what he's talking about, Billy?	• Elicits ideas • Invites reconsideration	
Billy	Yeah.		
Roth	What do you think? What evidence were you thinking about? [Silence; wait time] Okay, that's a good point, Travis, to think about. Let's remember that we said we didn't think that water has energy in it, and a lot of people, a lot of people in here are wondering about whether water is food for plants or not. If it doesn't have energy, can it be giving plants food? But we know – [Pause] Billy, I thought the evidence you were going to talk about was your experiment that you gave them water and they grew. So if they had water and they grew, wasn't the water their food? That's what we've gotta think about. I want to hear a few other sentences before we go on. Let's see, Kathryn?	• Encourages use of evidence • Invites reconsideration • Scaffolds link between canonical knowledge and student ideas • Frames	
Kathryn	I'm going to go up to the board.		
Roth	Okay.		
Kathryn	Okay, von Helmont put 200 pounds of soil in a bucket, and he proved that soil was not food and energy for plants.		Uses von Helmont evidence
Roth	Okay, good job, Kathryn. Okay, Mitch.	Supports	
Mitch	[Goes to board] Water is food for plants, but it doesn't give them energy.		Makes hypothesis

Speaker	Talk	Purposes of Teacher Talk	Features of Student Talk
Roth	Okay. Any questions for Mitch? "Water is food for plants but it doesn't give them energy." I think it's interesting how you're kind of trying to address Billy's issue and what Travis is saying. So we have a big question here about water. If it doesn't give them energy, is it still food? That's something to keep thinking about. Let's hear from two more people. Uhhh, Michelle –	• Frames • Invites reconsideration • Scaffolds link between canonical knowledge and student ideas	
Michelle	John von Helmont gave evidence that soil is not food for – well, soil – the plants do not eat the soil.		Uses von Helmont evidence
Roth	And Alex.		
Alex	Soil is not food for plants; but some minerals in the soil: that's the food for plants.		Uses von Helmont experiment to generate a new hypothesis

As shown in the above transcript, the word cards structured the class' inter-action, challenged students to articulate their ideas, and made the thinking of a number of different students visible to me and to the other students. From an assessment perspective, I learned that while students were convinced by von Helmont's experiment that plants do not get food from the soil, they were still confused about water (Billy, Mitch) and minerals in the soil (Alex). The next activity was designed explicitly to address these two issues.

While setting up for the next activity, I told students about the activity and how to carry it out. I explained to them that food energy is measured in calo-ries and that we can tell if substances contain food energy by reading nutritional labels. They were to look at various nutrition labels to determine if each substance contained food energy or not. I specifically picked bottles of water, vitamins, and minerals to challenge students to think about the lack of calories (and lack of energy) in these substances. More importantly, both before and after giving directions for the activity, I emphasized the purpose for this activity. During this example of purpose-setting talk, or framing talk, I referenced students' ideas in multiple ways. For example, I indicated the class hypothesis chart and recalled particular students' hypotheses about seeds, water, and minerals being food for plants. In addition, I modified the framing talk to include and to focus on particular ideas raised by Billy and Travis at the beginning of the lesson, during the word card activity.

Speaker	Talk	Purposes of Teacher Talk	Features of Student Talk
Roth	[Stands next to the class list of hypotheses] If we look at our list of hypotheses, about how plants get their food – [Points to "seeds" on the class list] – we've been exploring in our experiments, we've been exploring about seeds – do seeds give food for the plants? What are some ideas we have about seeds? Um, Vicki.	• Frames • Encourages use of evidence • Makes visible multiple viewpoints	
Vicki	The embryo eats the cotyledon and the cotyledon – [Pause]		• Uses observations and canonical terms • Builds argument (no reason)
Roth	So we got some ideas about the embryo eating the food stored in the cotyledon. So, we've got some ideas about seeds. Our grass plant experiment gave us some ideas about light. What I want us to look at today are these two – [Points to class' list of hypotheses] – five and six – because this is one that I think a lot of us are wondering about. Minerals or nutrients in the soil: Are they food by the scientific definition? And then this thing: "People give them food"; and then I think that the people who were suggesting that meant the plant food that you buy at the store? Right? So we're going to explore those two: Do you think minerals or nutrients in the soil are food for plants? And, Do you think, um, the plant food you get at the store is food for plants?. . . [Segue into directions for next activity; next dialogue follows directions] . . . So I want you to be sure to look at the ones that we're wondering about. One thing we were wondering about, that came	• Frames • Encourages use of evidence • Uses students' ideas to modify framing	

Speaker	Talk	Purposes of Teacher Talk	Features of Student Talk
	up earlier today, that **Billy and Travis** were having a good discussion about, is WATER. So look at that. One thing we're looking at today is this number five: minerals or nutrients in the soil – [Points to class' list of hypotheses] – that would be like this plant food stuff. And there's different kinds of plant food in different buckets. There's also, like, vitamins, like you take or I sometimes take. And then there's other things. So I want you to collect some information and be thinking about this question: Are minerals or nutrients in the soil food for plants?		

As students worked and examined nutrition labels, I wandered around the room and spoke with each group. My talk focused on probing students' thinking, and, in particular, challenging them to question and reconsider their ideas about water, minerals and vitamins acting as food for plants. Notice how often both teacher and student talk served the purpose of challenging an idea. The students were just as intent on challenging my ideas as I was on challenging theirs. The following excerpt captures the talk within a small group of one boy and two girls, as I came by their group and joined their conversation.

Speaker	Talk	Purposes of Teacher Talk	Features of Student Talk
Alex	[Looking at Diet Coke can] Diet Coke.		
Vicky	Zero.		Gathers data
Alex	Zero? It doesn't have any – sugar? No sugar.		Gathers data
Vicky	No energy.		Interprets data
Hayley	Yes, it does contain energy.		Challenges
Vicky	But . . . [Inaudible].		Challenges
Hayley	I know, but it still contains energy.		Challenges
Roth	[Joins the group] Which contains energy?		
Hayley	This [Points to Diet Coke can].		
Roth	How do you know?	Asks for evidence	

Speaker	Talk	Purposes of Teacher Talk	Features of Student Talk
Hayley	Because when you drink Coke, it –		Uses personal experience.
Vicky	– But this is *Diet* Coke.		Challenges
Hayley	Yeah, I know, but when you drink Coke it gives you energy, and when you drink Diet Coke, it still gives you a little energy – not as much as Coke.		Uses personal experience as evidence
Roth	So it *feels* like it gives you energy?	Asks for clarification	
Hayley	Yeah.		Clarifies
Roth	[Points to worksheet] What did you find out in terms of these questions, though?	• Challenges • Scaffolds linking of canonical knowledge and student idea	
Hayley	[Waves her arms in the air to suggest "I don't know"]		
Roth	The scientists when they measured this, did they find energy in it? When scientists – [Pause] – How do they know if it has energy in it?		Challenges
Alex	I have no idea.		
Roth	Alex, you do too have an idea. Alex, how do they know it has energy in it? What do they use – how do they measure it?		Challenges
Alex	They use it on specimens, I guess?		
Roth	Yes; so when they measure energy in food, they find out how many calories it has. So, how many calories does Diet Coke have?	• Scaffolds linking of canonical knowledge • Builds argument to challenge student idea	
Hayley	None.		
Roth	So? Hmmm.	Challenges	
Alex	But still . . . [Inaudible].		Challenges

Speaker	Talk	Purposes of Teacher Talk	Features of Student Talk
Hayley	Yeah, because when you wake up in the morning, it gives you energy to get around.		• Challenges • Uses personal experience as evidence
Alex	Yeah, sorta like coffee.		• Challenges • Uses personal experience as evidence
Roth	So, do you not believe the scientists' experiment? [Wait time]	Challenges	
Hayley	[Smiles]		
Roth	They said there was no calories in it. Are you saying you don't believe them?	• Challenges • Links student idea to canonical knowledge	
Alex	I say, yes, kind of.		Challenges
Hayley	[Waves her arms in the air to suggest, "I don't know"]		Reconsiders? Challenges?
Roth	That's a good question. Good thinking.	Supports	

The next phase of this lesson required students to work with a partner, while they considered their observations of the nutrition labels and the following question: Did the activity give them any new ideas about whether to support or to challenge the hypotheses that minerals, fertilizers, and water are food for plants? With their partner they were to agree upon a statement that supported or challenged one of the class' hypotheses about minerals, fertilizers, or water, and then post their findings on the class hypothesis chart. The purpose of this exercise was to encourage students to reconsider their initial hypotheses in light of new evidence. In addition, this process allowed students to prepare for presenting their ideas to the class. Below is an example of the kind of talk generated among the students in a class discussion that followed this activity. During the discussion, student talk included questions and challenges to other students, use of evidence and scientific definitions/explanations, as well as personal knowledge and experiences. Notice below how teacher talk focused on framing the discussion, encouraging multiple viewpoints and making them visible.

Speaker	Talk	Purposes of Teacher Talk	Features of Student Talk
Steven	[Points to can of Surge soft drink] This isn't a food, cuz you don't chew it. It gives food energy, but it's not a food, cuz you don't chew it.		• Uses evidence • Uses personal ideas
Roth	Does anyone have a response to Steven's idea?	• Makes multiple viewpoints visible • Encourages questioning	
Karen	Ooh, ooh, yeah. In the beginning of our talks – in the beginning of the year, we talked about the definition of food, and it says it has energy; and you picked up some juice, and from a scientific perspective, it was a food and it's a liquid.		• Challenges • Uses scientific explanation
Roth	Does that make sense to you, Steven? Steven, I think you're thinking about an everyday way that we talk about food as something we can chew. Do you understand Karen's point?	• Encourages reconsideration • Encourages listening to others' ideas	
Steven	Yeah, but I have a question. Even though the plant food doesn't have calories or energy, is it still food for plants? Because it says, "Plant Food" on the box.		• Questions • Uses scientific explanation
Roth	That's a great question. Can we be sure to write that in our Question Notebook? Vitamins do not provide us with any energy. People cannot live on vitamins alone. They help us, but they do not give us energy. What do you think about minerals and fertilizers for the plants? Is it like vitamins is for us?	• Encourages questioning • Frames • Scaffolds link between canonical knowledge and student ideas	
Travis	Well, we don't think it's food for plants, cuz it doesn't have any energy for the plants, and it doesn't have water either, so it would probably shrivel up and die.		• Uses evidence • Uses personal ideas to make prediction
Roth	Does everyone agree? Or does anybody disagree?	• Makes visible multiple viewpoints • Encourages listening to others' ideas	

Speaker	Talk	Purposes of Teacher Talk	Features of Student Talk
Steven	I disagree, because my plant wouldn't grow, and when me and David did another experiment, we put the plant food in it, and then it grew.		• Challenges • Uses evidence
Karen	But we did fertilizer spikes, and it didn't have any, like, sugar or calories; and most of the things that we've been finding out – that the, what people give plants don't have sugar in them, like the food we eat.		• Challenges • Uses evidence
Roth	How many people wrote down evidence to support, that, yes, plant food provides energy to plants? [Wait time; a few hands go up] How many had evidence to challenge that hypothesis? [Many hands go up]	Makes visible multiple viewpoints	

Instructional Phase III: Compare Scientific Explanations with Initial Ideas.
In this phase of instruction, the main role of teacher talk is to tell students about scientific ideas, terms, and explanations. Telling talk is placed in the context of, and carefully linked with, students' initial ideas and hypotheses. In this way, teacher talk encourages students to reconcile their initial ideas with scientific explanations and to use evidence to make sense of the new ideas. Consequently, student talk focuses on making sense of scientific explanations – for example, by raising questions about established findings and reconsidering students' theories in light of the introduced material.

As our class moved into this phase of instruction, notice below how I framed my presentation of the idea of photosynthesis with a dilemma the students had identified: Is water food for plants?

Speaker	Talk	Purposes of Teacher Talk	Features of Student Talk
Roth	So we have a dilemma, and I want to try and explain something to you and see if that can help us figure out – Do you know what a dilemma is? Who knows what that is: a dilemma? What would be another word for "dilemma"?	• Frames • Links to students' ideas	
Alex	Sorta like procrastinating, but it's not, because it's, it's taking up your time, cuz you can't figure it out, and you can't agree to it.		

Speaker	Talk	Purposes of Teacher Talk	Features of Student Talk
Roth	Okay, it's something – you're on the right track – it's something we "can't agree to", that's right. Travis, what do you think?		
Travis	It's like a problem.		
Roth	Okay, a problem or a puzzle. And we can't sort of agree. Some of us are thinking, "Hey, we've got some evidence that water, water is *not* food for plants, because it doesn't have calories". And then we have evidence that water *is* food for plants, because of all these things you just gave us. So I want you to listen really carefully. I'm going to tell you some things, um, about plants, and see if you can figure out, Is water food for plants? Um, and I'm gonna sorta do some of the things that, um, they did in the skits yesterday. I have some things to show you. I'm going to tell you about photosynthesis, and I want you to think about what is happening to the water, okay? [Reaches for baggie filled with air] What plants can do that people cannot do and animals cannot do is they can take water – [Holds up bottle of water] – which has how many calories? Ellis?	• Frames • Links to students' ideas • Encourages use of evidence to build an argument	

At this point in the lesson, I delivered the scientific explanation for photosynthesis. I used props to model the process: a mixing bowl to represent a cell in a leaf, a bottle of water to represent water, a baggie filled with air to represent air, and a flashlight to represent sunlight. I used egg beaters to mix the raw materials together, and the product was represented by sugar cubes. Following the scientific explanation for photosynthesis, teacher talk emphatically encouraged students to make sense of the presented explanation, to challenge it, and to ask questions. As illustrated below, students generated a number of different questions and discussed them with each other. The teacher talk included a significant focus on "telling" about scientific explanations.

Speaker	Talk	Purposes of Teacher Talk	Features of Student Talk
Ellis	If they've got microscopic holes to get air in, how do they keep the water in through 'em – if they got those holes?		Questions and talks about scientific explanation
Students	Yeah!		Supports
Roth	That's a food question, Ellis. Actually, sometimes the water does go out those holes in the leaf. But the plant gets enough water that it gets some that it can use for photosynthesis, and some that actually does go out the holes in the leaf.	Tells scientific explanation	
Ellis	You said that it makes energy from the light energy, the water and the air, but why does it have to make energy, if it absorbs the light energy?		Questions scientific explanation
Roth	Good question! Okay, I wasn't planning on getting into this much detail about it, but that's such a wonderful question, Ellis. His question was about, if it already got light energy, why did it need to change it into sugar? We can't – how can I explain this? Energy can change forms, and light energy – we can't, and plants can't use just that for food. They have to change it into food energy, before they can use it. So, they have to change the light energy, with the water and the air, into food energy. Maybe we can talk about that more later on, and it'll make more sense. But what I really like about Ellis' question is that he's showing me that he's thinking and that he's trying to make sense of this explanation. Does this really make sense: that a plant could be doing this inside of their leaves? It's pretty – you've got to use your scientific imaginations and think about what's it like to be inside the leaf of a plant and see all this activity going on. Okay, couple of questions. Tom?	• Tells scientific explanation • Encourages students to question and to reason	
Tom	When it rains, how does the water get in the leaves? [This question was addressed by six different students, despite my repeated efforts to set this question aside for now – clearly it was a question of much interest to the students, and they had a variety of ideas about how water gets into the plant.]		• Questions scientific explanation • Makes hypothesis

Speaker	Talk	Purposes of Teacher Talk	Features of Student Talk
Shawn	I got a question: how – why, I mean, – do plants need food – like, I mean, water and soil and stuff?		Questions scientific explanation
Roth	Excellent question. Theo?		
Theo	So they can stay alive.		Uses personal ideas
Roth	Each of the cells in a plant needs food to help it stay alive and to help the plant grow. Did you have another question, Shawn?	Tells scientific explanation	
Shawn	Um, I know, I know that's why, but why does it need all the other things like soil and sun and light and air?		Questions scientific explanation
Roth	Who can answer that question? Why do they need – let's leave soil out of it for the moment.	• Frames • Encourages students to build argument	
Shawn	Why do they need water, sunlight, and air?		Questions scientific explanation
Roth	Why do they need water, sunlight, and air? Eric.		
Eric	They turn it into all food, and then it turns it into – what's the word – photosynthesis, and then they just eat it up.		Uses scientific explanation
Roth	This is a really hard idea. You've got to think really hard to make sense of it. They take water, air, and sunlight, Shawn, to make those into food. Shawn, if the plant only had water, and it had no sunlight and no air, would it be able to live?	Coaches use of scientific idea	
Shawn	No, because it can't make its own food.		Uses scientific idea

Instructional Phase IV: Apply New Ideas with Teacher Modeling and Coaching. In this phase of instruction, the goal is for students to do as much of the talking as possible, so that they may use the new scientific ideas and reconcile them with their initial ideas. Teacher talk models scientific thinking, scaffolds student thinking, and coaches students how to use the new ideas. Since the concept that plants actually make food is difficult for students to understand, our unit of instruction included a variety of contexts in which students could practice using and applying the new ideas. Some of the activities involved designing and carrying out experiments. Others involved solving hypothetical problems.

In the dialogue presented below, students have just been given an established explanation for photosynthesis. They are asked to use the explanation to make sense of an experiment they had done earlier, which involved watching bean seeds grow under different conditions (with and without the cotyledon attached, in the light and in the dark). To structure the task, each small group of students had a book that contained full-page photographs of bean plants at different stages of growth. The students' task was to describe how the bean plant gets its food at each stage of growth. While presenting the assignment to the students, I explicitly told them to use the new idea about photosynthesis and the idea that the cotyledon provides food to the growing embryo. My purpose was to challenge them to make sense of the new idea by trying to use it to explain a phenomenon that they had experienced firsthand. In the excerpt below, I was speaking with two students, Daniel and Theo, as they worked on this task. My goal was to listen carefully to their ideas but also to step in and try to shape their thinking by asking questions and making observations. Since this is the very first time the students have tried to use the ideas about photosynthesis, there is a high level of teacher scaffolding in this conversation. Teacher scaffolding talk would gradually diminish as students became increasingly comfortable and competent in using the new ideas. Notice how the students' talk reveals that they were using the new ideas about photosynthesis but still struggling to fit this idea with their beliefs that water and minerals taken in from the soil are food for plants.

Speaker	Talk	Purposes of Teacher Talk	Features of Student Talk
Roth	[Points to a photograph of a seed under the soil] So how is it getting its food?	Coaches use of knowledge	
Daniel	The embryo is eating the cotyledon.		Uses scientific idea
Roth	Okay, and then – [Boys turn the page to the next picture]		
Theo	The embryo.		Uses scientific idea
Daniel	See? There's the embryo. [Points] Now, this is the embryo, and I think it's starting to get its, uh, either water or the minerals out of the soil.		Uses and personal scientific ideas
Roth	Okay. Does it have leaves yet?	Coaches use of knowledge	

Speaker	Talk	Purposes of Teacher Talk	Features of Student Talk
Students	No.		
Roth	Can it make its food yet?	• Coaches use of knowledge • Focuses attention on canonical knowledge	
Students	No.		
Roth	Okay, so it's mostly getting its food from –	Coaches use of knowledge	
Daniel	The cotyledon.		Uses scientific idea
Theo	Cotyledon.		Uses scientific idea
Roth	Okay, next page?		
Daniel	Now, these are the roots; they are going down to get minerals and water.		Uses scientific idea
Roth	Okay, and especially water, right?	Coaches use of knowledge	
Daniel	Yeah.		
Theo	[Nods yes] And, it's getting the minerals and water.		Uses scientific ideas
Roth	Can the leaves get sunlight yet?	Coaches use of knowledge	
Daniel	No, they're not – they're not out of the ground yet.		Uses observations
Roth	So, can they make their own food yet?	• Coaches use of knowledge • Focuses attention on canonical knowledge	
Theo	Nope.		Uses scientific ideas
Daniel	No, they ain't got sunlight.		Uses scientific idea
Roth	So, where are they getting their food from?	Coaches use of knowledge	
Daniel	The cotyledon.		Uses scientific idea

Speaker	Talk	Purposes of Teacher Talk	Features of Student Talk
Theo	The cotyledon, and the minerals, and the water.		Uses scientific ideas and personal ideas
Roth	Okay, turn the page.		
Daniel	Now it // takes the sunlight.		
Theo	//gets sunlight.		
Roth	Can it get air?	Coaches use of knowledge	
Students	Yeah.		
Roth	Can it get water?	Coaches use of knowledge	
Daniel	Yup.		
Roth	So, what can it do to get food now?	Coaches use of knowledge	
Daniel	Now it can make photosynthesis, and it does the process of making its own food.		Uses scientific idea
Roth	And what is the process?	Asks for elaboration	
Daniel	They mix the air, water, and –		Uses scientific idea
Theo	– Sunlight.		Uses scientific idea
Daniel	Sunlight.		Uses scientific idea
Roth	See if you can figure out the next picture. How's it getting its food there?	Coaches use of knowledge	
Theo	Roots.		Uses personal idea
Daniel	More roots – I think it's spreading more roots out to get more food.		Uses personal ideas
Roth	Is it spreading its roots out to get more food, or to get water?	• Coaches use of knowledge • Asks for clarification • Challenges student idea	
Daniel	Water and food.		Uses scientific and personal ideas

Speaker	Talk	Purposes of Teacher Talk	Features of Student Talk
Theo	Water and food.		Uses scientific and personal ideas
Roth	Food in the soil?	• Coaches (asks for clarification) • Challenges	
Students	Unh-hunh.		
Daniel	The minerals.		Uses personal idea
Theo	Probably just the water.		Uses scientific idea
Roth	Does it have leaves?	Coaches use of knowledge	
Daniel	No, they're starting to spread out.		Uses personal observations
Roth	So?	Coaches use of knowledge	
Daniel	I think, um – never mind.		
Roth	Do you think it could be doing photosynthesis here?	• Coaches use of knowledge • Focuses attention on canonical knowledge	
Students	Yeah.		Uses scientific idea
Roth	Why do you think it could be?	Coaches use of knoweldge	
Daniel	Cuz it's growing more.		Uses personal and scientific idea
Theo	It's getting air, and it could be getting light, and people could, like, be giving it water.		Uses scientific ideas

Later in this lesson, the small groups took turns presenting their ideas to the whole class, with the class challenging and supporting the presented ideas. Daniel and Theo stood up in front of the class together, but Daniel did all the talking. They successfully used the new idea of photosynthesis, but still incorporated their personal convictions that water and minerals are food for plants:

Daniel: The plant is big enough to get water, air, and sunlight and uh make photosynthesis to make its own food. And me and Theo think that um these little hairs on the main root suck up water and minerals from the soil.

Instructional Phase V: Reflect and Connect. Throughout instruction, but especially toward the end of instructional the unit, teacher and student talk in my classrooms focused on reflection and connection. That is, students explicitly talked about how their ideas were changing and why, about new questions and connections they were making, and about how our class was doing as a group of scientists. It was routine practice to end each lesson with some talk or writing about individual student's reflections about any new ideas they started thinking about during the lesson or any issues that raised confusion. And at the "end" of a unit, I engaged students in comparing their pre- and posttest responses, in reflecting on how their ideas had changed (and why), and on identifying remaining questions and confusions.

The following lesson example highlights how difficult it was for students to do this kind of reflection. The day before I was going to introduce the idea of photosynthesis, I ended a lesson by asking students to talk about how their ideas about food for plants had changed so far. I received very few comments, and some students claimed that their ideas had not changed at all. I was puzzled by this response and wondered if the students had just forgotten what they had thought before, if they thought it was bad form to admit your ideas had changed, or if they had not really changed their ideas yet. The following day I passed out the students' pretests and had them look at what they had written three weeks earlier about food for plants. Then I challenged them to revisit this question. In my instructions to them I talked explicitly about the value of revising ideas in science:

> Roth: I was sort of expecting people to be real good thoughtful scientists . . . I was expecting to see a more thoughtful answer. Scientists when they get good evidence, they are willing to reconsider their ideas, change them. I gave you your yellow sheets back (the pretest). I want you to write to me just as if you were talking to me after class or at recess time about whether or not your ideas have changed and why.

As students started to work, I noticed Nan. As she read her pretest answers, she laughed, covered her mouth in surprise, and put her head down on her desk, giggling. Tiffany, sitting next to her, looked at Nan with a broad smile as if she, too, were amused by what she had written earlier. Having students do this reading and writing task prior to the whole class discussion made a big difference in the quality of the discussion, which was lively and full of examples of revised ideas. At one point, Matt brought up an idea that no one else had yet mentioned: "I now think that sun is food for a grownup plant and the cotyledon is food for a seed." This led to a realization among the rest of the students that they, too, were convinced that the cotyledon provided food for the growing embryo. The cotyledon was yet not listed on the class hypothesis chart as a possible source of food for plants, so I went over and added it. I also asked for a show of hands: "How many people think the cotyledon is food for the embryo?" Every student raised her/his hand, and one student exclaimed, "We all agree on something!" There was then a chorus of cheers. There appeared to be a tremendous sense of celebration in that outburst of cheers. I sensed a feeling of genuine accomplishment – that we had patiently considered many different hypotheses, explored carefully sources of evidence, and found at least one satisfying answer that made sense to all of us. Without the reflection process, the students' sense of both individual and group progress would have gone unrecognized. In addition, the reflection process helped individuals clarify their positions and identify their continuing confusions.

Summary Comments about Assertions 1 and 2

The examples above illustrate the many different kinds of talk that supported these students in developing meaningful understandings of science concepts. Both the students and the teachers are using talk for a variety of different purposes at different points in time.

The examples also reveal that the teacher plays a critical role in eliciting different types of student talk. Students do not spontaneously start reconsidering their ideas or challenging the ideas of others or questioning scientific explanations. Teacher talk is critical in eliciting and shaping these kinds of student talk.

Table 1 provides a summary that emphasizes in the left-hand column (pedagogical purpose) that there is a logic to the progression of types of talk across time in the learning process. It also highlights, however, that the teacher has the challenging task of selecting from many different types and purposes of talk at any given point in instruction.

These examples are limited in their primary focus on the development of students' *conceptual* understanding. What about students' understandings about the nature of science and scientific inquiry? What about their understandings of themselves in relationship to science? These questions are addressed in the next assertion.

Assertion 3 in Action in the Classroom

Assertion 3. *Talk about science content (concepts, facts, observations) is not enough.*

My views of what needs to be talked *about* in science classrooms have changed dramatically since the first year I took on a teacher/researcher role. At that time, I was focused on students' conceptual learning. Social constructivists are right to criticize my teaching at that time for being too focused on individual student learning and on a narrow view of science learning. I did not want to "waste" time dealing with students' problems in working together in groups, so I did everything I could to make sure that students who could work well together were grouped together. I was fascinated by students' ideas about science questions, but I did not want to "waste" time hearing too many personal stories that seemed to be taking us off track. I wanted students to learn that science was about questioning and using evidence to build arguments, but I assumed that students would pick this up from the way we acted in science class. I did not think I needed to teach it explicitly. I analyzed my students' thinking about science phenomena carefully, but I failed to look carefully at gender, racial, and ethnic issues in the classroom – I assumed if I listened to students' ideas about the science, that was enough.

Next I turn to examples of the broader range of subjects that I now believe need to be talked about in science classrooms. Each of these ideas was influenced by my research on my students' learning and by social constructivist research.

Explicit talk about the nature of science and scientific talk. My study of my own students' learning at the end of my first year as a teacher-researcher was the first stimulus to broaden my definition of what students need a chance to talk about in science classrooms. From that research, it was clear that my students were not understanding that questioning, the use of evidence, and argumentation are core characteristics of the scientific enterprise. Modeling these scientific processes in the classroom was not enough. There must also be explicit talk about the nature of science and scientific inquiry, ways of talking and acting in science, explicit talk about the language, values, and practices of science. Students need the chance to talk about *why* evidence is so important, and about *why* all evidence is not equal, about *why* scientists debate ideas and measure things and graph things, etc. This finding from my own research is also supported by research in the "cognitive apprenticeship", social constructivist literature.

To address this issue, I have incorporated an explicit curriculum strand about the nature of science and scientific inquiry into each unit of study. At the beginning of the year, students draw pictures of scientists at work, and we talk about the images and stereoptypes of scientists and where they come from. We then "meet" scientists throughout the year – scientists in the community, scientists we get to know through books and videos, scientists we write to. These scientists help us create a class list of characteristics of scientists that we can then contrast with our stereotypical images:

Stereotypes
of Scientists

- Wear white lab coats

- Use tools like test tubes,beakers,
  microscopes

- Are always experimenting
- Wear glasses
- Are men
- Have wild hair
- Are mad, crazy

- Like to be alone
- Work in a laboratory
- Work with poisons, explosives,
  chemicals
- Have beards

Important Parts
of Scientists' Work

- Discover and describe our
  natural world
- Explain the why's and how's
  of our world
- Ask and seek answers to questions
- Solve problems, figure things out
- Study
- Observe carefully and keep notes
- Talk to other scientists
- Write about discoveries, findings,
  questions
- Read journals to find out what other
  scientists are learning

We also use these experiences to develop guidelines for our scientific discussions and debates in the classroom. A classroom chart summarizes the kinds

What a scientist does	What a scientist says
Observe	I see ... I noticed ...
Ask why and how questions	How come ... ? Why ... ? How do they know that ... ?
Think of an idea, theory, or hypothesis	My idea is ... I have a theory ... I think that ... Maybe ...
Listen to others' ideas and ask clarification questions	What do you mean when you say that ... Are you saying that ... I don't understand what you're saying ... What is your evidence?
Agree or disagree with others' ideas	I agree with _____ because ... I disagree with _____ because ...
Give a reason or evidence for your idea	Because ... My evidence is ... The reason I think that is ...

of talk that are valued in our scientific community, along with sentence starters to help students as they learn how to engage in this kind of talk:

What a scientist does	What a scientist says
Piggyback on (add onto) someone else's idea	I want to piggyback on April's idea. I want to add something to what Brian said.
Suggest an experiment or activity to get more evidence.	We could try . . . We could get some better evidence if we . . .
Let your ideas change and grow.	I want to change my idea . . . I think my idea might be changing . . . I have something to add to my idea . . .

The following lesson excerpt provides an example of some of this explicit talk about science talk. In this particular classroom, we began assigning one or two persons from the class to observe each of our science discussions. The observers would be directed to watch for some particular features of our talk, and to help us

Speaker	Talk	Purposes of Teacher Talk	Features of Student Talk
Roth	Let's look at what you wrote in your journal about the model, and I would like to hear some, I want you to listen really carefully to other people. . . . I'm going to listen first for some things that people who said yes, this is a good model and if you have something different from that person, I want you to raise your hand and share it. If you have the same thing, let's not repeat it. Let's get, we've got an empty chair here. Let's have at least one observer today. Who has not been an observer before? Cheryl, you have not before?	• Encourages listening to others • Invites critique of models created by students • Invites community participation in observing the talk	
Cheryl	No.		
Roth	Ok, you help us keep track of things. If lots of people are participating.What else could she keep track of?	• Describes norms of the talk: Importance of having many people participating in the talk	
Renata	People calling out.		Describes norms of the talk: Importance of not calling out during the talk

reflect afterwards on how we were doing as a community of scientists. This excerpt shows how such a process was set up at the beginning of a class discussion:

Speaker	Talk	Purposes of Teacher Talk	Features of Student Talk
Roth	People calling out. What else? Cathy.		
Cathy	If people are in their seats.		Describes norms of the talk: Importance of students being in their seats during the talk
Roth	People not staying where they're supposed to be. Anything else you want Cheryl to watch for?		
Dennis	The differences between our answers.		Describes norms of the talk: Importance of listening for the differences in student ideas
Roth	That's good. Yeah. And what about the differences between our ideas. What kinds of things, Dennis?		
Dennis	How we think about things and what evidence we have and how many different ideas people have.		Describes norms of the talk: Importance of talking about evidence and eliciting a variety of ideas
Roth	So how we're thinking? How many different ideas we have? Okay. Anything Else? Can Cheryl keep track of all that?		

This lesson also illustrates how I began to lead more explicit talk about the tools and research strategies that scientists use. In this case, the tool being explored is a model. The students had previously constructed their own models to show what happens when salt dissolves in water. They had then selected one group's model as the best representation. In this discussion, I asked the students to talk first about what makes this a good model and then to consider ways in which this particular model was not a good model of dissolving. Notice how

Speaker	Talk	Purposes of Teacher Talk	Features of Student Talk
Roth	I wanted to ask you about what you wrote in your journal about the model. First let's hear some reasons why you think that "yes, that is a good model", "I like that model!" Douglas.	Asks for strong points of student-constructed models	
Douglas	It's shows how the salt and sugar particles get into the spaces between the marbles.		• Identifies strength of model • Uses science idea
Roth	Did everybody hear him? Say it again.		
Douglas	It's shows how the salt and sugar particles get into the spaces between the marbles.		• Identifies strength of model • Uses science idea
Roth	And what did you think the marbles represented?	Asks for analysis of the model	
Douglas	Water		Analyzes the model
Roth	So if the marbles represent water, he said he thinks it's a good model because it shows how the salt and sugar gets in between the water molecules. Okay, Something different?	Summarizes student response	
Angela	I think the marbles looked like they are packed in tight together and the salt was getting smaller.		• Identifies strength of the model • Uses science idea
Roth	So you're looking at the salt getting smaller? Okay. Megan?		
Megan	I think it looks like they're really packed in.		• Identifies strength of the model • Uses science idea
Roth	And when you say 'they', you mean?	Asks for clarification about the model	
Megan	The water and the		Clarifies
Roth	The water and		
Megan	Salt particles.		Clarifies
Roth	Salt particles . . . look like they're close in. Good.	Summarizes student idea	

Speaker	Talk	Purposes of Teacher Talk	Features of Student Talk
Roth	Okay, Renata.		
Renata	[pauses, then looks at her journal] Ummm. I think it shows how they stick, go together and how the salt gets smaller and smaller and they're all scrunched together. How they stick to, how they go together.		• Identifies strength of the model • Uses science idea
Roth	So like Angela says, it shows the salt is getting smaller and like how it's how it's touching // . . .	Summarizes student idea	
Renata	// together . . . I [couldn't put that in?] dissolves so I just put that it goes together.		
Roth	Tammy.		
Tammy	Water is bigger, I think it's good because water is bigger than salt and so are the marbles.		• Identifies strength of the model • Uses personal idea that water particles are bigger than salt particles
Roth	So water particles are bigger than salt particles, and it shows it really nicely.	Summarizes student idea	
Erica	I said yes because you can see the two different kinds of particles mixing together.		• Identifies strength of model • Uses science idea
Roth	Okay, you can see the two different kinds of particles mixing together. Cheryl?	Summarizes student idea	
Cheryl	I think the particles, my idea was [inaudible]		Uses science idea
Roth	So you think the marbles represent water too, like several other people.	Summarizes student idea	
Douglas	I got a question. When the salt and the water mixes together you know how the salt dissolves, I wonder if any of the *water* dissolves.		Asks question
Roth	Oooh. That's a good one. Let's save that. Could you write that in our question notebook for us? Now what about reasons why this ISN'T a good model? Because models are never perfectly exactly like the real thing. April.	• Emphasizes importance of questions • Asks for critiques of the model	

Speaker	Talk	Purposes of Teacher Talk	Features of Student Talk
April	Not all the water particles are touching each other.		• Critiques the model • Uses science idea
Roth	Oooh. Not all the water particles are touching each other. Remember when we were being water molecules, and we were always touching each other? Ok, good one. Monica?	Summarizes student idea	
Monica	It's not showing them actually dissolving.		Critiques the model.
Roth	It's not showing them actually dissolving. Ok, and Anne.	Summarizes student idea	
Anne	It doesn't look like the real thing.		Critiques the model.
Roth	[Laughs], And those of us who have worn these glasses, we know what it really looks like, right Anne? Where are they? These glasses. [teacher puts on special glasses that the class uses to represent the need to look at the world with new eyes]. Cathy?	Jokes with students	

student talk includes both talk about specific concepts (e.g. particles and their behavior in solids and liquids) and talk that analyzes/critiques the models.

Explicit talk about students' identities and values. Social constructivist perspectives also challenged me to talk with students about their cultural values and identities. I learned through missed opportunities that I needed to start learning more about my students' identities way beyond their ideas about science. I needed also to consider their personal values, their cultural or racial identities, their interests, their self image and self confidence, their frustrations and worries. At first I thought that all of this was beyond my ability and my responsibility as a science teacher. That is, until I learned from Maria Yolanda, and Miles, and Laticia, and other students whose differences I initially worked hard to ignore. I had wanted to be color blind and blind to the stereotypes attached to those students who are labeled "special education" or "at risk." Kids are kids, and I intended to treat them all the same.

But I learned from these students that I risk missing a connection with them in science if I fail to get to know them at a personally meaningful level. Laticia was the only black student in my class one year. Not only was she new to the school, but she arrived in the middle of the school year so she was also new to our classroom scientific community and the ways of being we had been constructing in our science classroom. Maria-Yolanda was one of a handful of Latino students in my classroom. She most often sat silent in science class, never a disruption but rarely a person whose ideas were heard in science class. Miles was a mainstreamed special education student who had spent his first 4 years of elementary school in special education classrooms and who spent a year sitting almost completely silent in my science classroom. I found out in end-of-year interviews with each of these students that there were things I should have learned about them *while* I was teaching them.

I should have learned, for example, that Maria-Yolanda is socially wise way beyond her years. She understands death and discrimination first hand. And she can be a very forceful and outgoing person on behalf of the issues she cares passionately about:

> I would like to say something to the whole school, like people are out there discriminating against people's race because they are different than you. But nobody is different because they all have the same feelings. Just because their pigment is different, there's nothing wrong with them, they're still human.

Once I had heard this young woman speak so confidently about this issue of importance to her, I realized that I had missed an opportunity to bring this powerful voice into our science discussions. Maria-Yolanda had written eagerly to me in her journal at the beginning of the school year. She even took her journal home and wrote extra notes to me. Some of the notes had to do with science ("I'm shy, I don't like answering questions in front of the class"), but other comments had nothing to do with science (or so I thought at the time I read them):

> When it is windy, I like to stay in the house and read with a glass of cocoa under warm covers.
>
> I am going with the biggest nerd in the school. His name is Eduardo.
>
> What I'm being for Halloween – I might not dress up because it is childish.
>
> Boys are mean to me because I am a different color. It makes me feel unwelcomed.
>
> More than anything I wish I could of seen my sister who died in 1989. Because I never got to see. Now she is in heaven.
>
> Yesterday, I wished Brian never got hit by a car and died.

I remember Maria-Yolanda eagerly showing me her journal entries at the beginning of the year, but I only responded to those that I had assigned for science, passing over quickly those she wrote on her own. I have learned a lot from my failures to connect with students like Maria-Yolanda.

I now welcome talk in science that might at first seem unrelated to the science. And I encourage students to talk and write about their feelings and values and worries and concerns. Daily journal writing entries and end-of-lesson reflection talk are just as likely to be about these topics as about the science concepts: "How are you feeling about yourself as a science learner?" "Would you like to be a scientist like Mary Seeley? Why or why not?" "In what ways are you acting like a scientist in our science class? Does that feel comfortable to you?" "What would you like to ask our visiting scientist about what it's really like to be a scientist? What do you want to ask her about herself and her life outside of work?" "What did you do over the weekend?" "Do you ever think about science outside of school?" "What things are really important to you?"

I also try to create a more welcoming view of science in the classroom. For example, I make it acceptable to talk in the class about ways in which science feels uncomfortable or unwelcoming to certain people. Young girls are often especially passionate about animal rights, and I am now very sensitive to that – making sure that they know there are many different ways of doing science and that it does not always involve hurting or killing animals. When some students were clamoring to do a frog dissection, I opened up a series of discussions, including a visit from a scientist, to talk about animal rights and the use of animals in research. Students were encouraged to clarify their values and positions on this issue, and they debated how to resolve the differences in interests among the group. In the end, students decided that they would have the option to do a frog dissection in one classroom or to visit another classroom and do a virtual dissection on the computer.

We have also had very sensitive discussions about gender. In one class the girls and boys did not want to work together in groups. We talked about the reasons and the advantages and disadvantages of mixed gender groups. The class then did an experiment where we worked in same gender groups for awhile and then in mixed gender groups. There was explicit talk about how the talk went in both situations. The girls were very vocal when they perceived the boys to be dominating or taking over the equipment. And as a group, we talked about strategies of working out these differences within the groups.

In another class, some very quiet girls felt free to raise a question for our group observer: How often do shy girls speak up in our discussions? This led to an interesting discussion about shyness in both girls and boys. After that discussion, I noticed that everyone was much more aware when the self-identified shy people were or were not speaking up.

Explicit talk about critiques of science. As part of our study of a broad range of people who do science, we encountered cases where ageism, sexism, and racism appeared to have played in a role in the development of scientific knowledge. We read about scientists' own accounts of discrimination and asked scientist visitors to our classroom about their own experiences with discrimination and unfairness in the scientific community. The students discussed questions like: Whose ideas count in science? They were very struck by a Native American scientist who had to dissect plants in her training, although this was against her cultural and religious viewpoint. Do scientists have to give up who they are to become scientists? These kinds of questions fascinated the students.

These are just a few examples of the ways in which study of my students' learning and the social constructivist literature challenged me to expand the content of the talk in our classroom. Content was no longer limited only to science concepts and terms. Now there was explicit talk on a regular basis (and integrated with the talk about content as much as possible) about the nature of science, about the ways the students are acting like scientists (and not) in our classroom, and about personal values, feelings, and identities.

Assertion 4 Action in the Classroom

Assertion 4. *Talk about shared experiences is a critical part of learning to talk science and to understand science.*

Some interpretations of social constructivist theories suggest that classroom teaching should look more like on-the-job, one-on-one training by a mentor. If school science learning is going to be authentic, the argument goes, learning should be situated in specific contexts that mirror how learning occurs in out-of-school, "real world" contexts. In a science learning context, students, like real-world scientists, should explore questions of interest to them and design their own strategies for pursuing these questions.

While I cannot argue with the potential value of such self-generated learning opportunities, these contexts provide challenging situations for teachers who are trying to scaffold students' understanding of science – its language, its ways of acting, and its knowledge. It is extremely difficult for a teacher working with 25–30 or more students to do a thoughtful job of listening to students' ideas and responding to their ideas with the kind of talk that will challenge each of them to *really* understand. Remember that *really* understanding involves developing connected and useful explanations of phenomena, learning how to talk science, viewing science knowledge as constantly changing and growing, and understanding the collaborative, human process by which science is created. This is huge task, and the problem is compounded, often to the point of creating mental chaos for the teacher, when students are working on different topics and/or different questions, problems, or projects.

In my classrooms, I sometimes have small groups design and pursue their own inquiries – usually as part of the "application" phase of my instructional model. When students have the freedom to choose what question they will explore and what activities they will engage in to pursue their questions, the management load on the teacher escalates. Even when it is only six different small groups working on six different inquiry projects that are all related to the same general topic, the management demands on the teacher are staggering. I know from experience how difficult it is to be teaching students how to think and talk in scientific ways when you are constantly bombarded with questions of a more mundane nature: "Dr. Roth, our group needs some string." "Dr. Roth, can our group go outside now to take the temperature readings?" "Dr. Roth, we're having trouble with this microscope." "Dr. Roth, we need you to approve our plan of action." "Dr. Roth, does our group have enough time to start a new experiment set up today?" Thus, from a classroom management perspective, the teacher has a greater chance to model and coach scientific thinking when the whole class is focused on a shared inquiry.

But the use of shared experiences, shared questions, and shared strategies for pursuing the questions is important not just because of the cognitive limitations the teacher faces. I argue that the sharing of the experience, in fact, mirrors the typical work life of scientists more than the image of one or two or three scientists going off and exploring their own questions. From a social constructivist point of view, science is a social, political, and collaborative endeavor. Students have a better opportunity to participate in this kind of endeavor in school classrooms if they can interact with students of diverse backgrounds, experiences, and perspectives in trying to understand phenomena in their world.

As I have increasingly helped students analyze our classroom community as a scientific community, I have seen a deepening understanding among my students about how science works. And I no longer worry about the criticism that as the teacher, I am doing too much of the selecting and directing of the science that students are studying. Instead, I think of myself as the prinicipal investigator of a research team, the one who initiated and took the lead in getting funding support for the project. Like the principal investigator, I need a team whose members are interested in and value the plan-of-work I have laid out. But I also recognize that my team can contribute to the research process with new ideas, new questions, and new research strategies. And I recognize that one of the important lessons my team members need to learn is how to talk with each other in ways that benefit the science – this includes talk that challenges, talk that supports, and talk that enables the group to consider and resolve different points of view on a given issue.

TALKING TO UNDERSTAND SCIENCE: LESSONS LEARNED FROM A SOCIAL CONSTRUCTIVIST PERSPECTIVE

So what have I learned from social constructivist research that has influenced my science teaching practice and my students' learning? Social constructivists in both the "cognitive apprenticeship" tradition and in the sociocultural critique tradition have made important contributions to my teaching practice.

Social constructivists working in the "cognitive apprenticeship" tradition have challenged me as a teacher to include explicit talk and coaching about ways that scientists think and talk. My students and I now talk about how we know, how we think about data and evidence, how our ideas differ, and how our thinking is similar to and different from communities of practicing scientists. As teacher, my role in these kinds of conversations is as a "cognitive coach," listening to students' ideas and reasoning strategies and then coaching them in modifying and expanding their ideas and ways of thinking. This kind of talk and coaching enables more students to become members of a scientific community, a community with special norms and standards that are otherwise inaccessible to students who live their daily lives in very different kinds of communities. Research on my students' learning shows that when this kind of explicit talk and coaching about "ways of being" in scientific communities is present, students develop richer and more sophisticated understandings of the nature of science.

Early in my teaching career, a parent challenged my claim during a Fall Open House that I was going to "teach students how to think scientifically." At that time, I had no response to his question. Perhaps he was right, I thought. Perhaps you cannot *teach* someone to think scientifically, you can just immerse a person in the experience of thinking about his or her own observations of natural phenomena and see what happens. Does the person have the ability to think scientifically or not? Some can, some cannot, and teaching makes no difference. A social constructivist teaching approach provides a response to this parent: Teachers can help students learn how to think scientifically if they recognize that "scientific thinking" is like a foreign language and culture into which students can be enculturated. Teachers have traditionally enculturated students into the new culture by taking a tour guide approach, imparting lots of facts and bits of knowledge about the new culture to students. But the social constructivist perspective encourages teachers to become more like families who sponsor foreign exchange students in their homes. The role is not just to impart knowledge to the foreign student, but to help the student figure out how to live, speak, and feel part of the new culture. Similarly, science teachers can become less like tour guides imparting knowledge and more like sponsors who help students move from being tourists to becoming members of the community – learning how to behave, speak, and feel part of a scientific community.

Social constructivists who critique the mismatch between Western science and the diverse cultural experiences of students in our classrooms also have influenced my thinking and actions as a science teacher. This body of research suggests that we can make students' cultural backgrounds more visible in science classrooms and that we can help students connect to science by making visible to them the variety of ways in which science is and can be done. This perspective has helped me figure out ways to connect with students for whom Western science traditions may appear not only foreign but frightening or threatening. More students can become part of classroom scientific communities if the neighborhood of science itself is presented as more diverse in its methods and areas of inquiry and more open to critique and challenge.

TALKING TO UNDERSTAND SCIENCE: CAUTIONS ABOUT SOCIAL CONSTRUCTIVIST PERSPECTIVES

But I also have cautions about the translation of social constructivist theory into teaching practice. Are current enactments of social constructivist teaching . . .

Overrelying on Student-Centered Talk?

In my earliest research studies, I saw the dangers of relying only on didactic, "telling" talk. The emphasis on teacher telling was not helping students *really* understand science. But I also saw the dangers of relying primarily on exploratory, open-ended talk. Engaging students in talking about their ideas and observations was not enough to help them develop well-structured and connected, useful understandings of science concepts. It also did not help them value the inquiry processes, because the inquiry process did not help them understand their world in new and more satisfying ways.

When I later began focusing on students' ideas as a new part of my own teaching practice, I faced the danger of overrelying on student talk about their own ideas. I was fascinated as I listened to and tried to understand the students' ideas and ways of thinking. A teacher collaborating with me observed, "Oh, I get it, science teaching is easy, all you have to do is get the students talking about their ideas." Similarly, many of the students in my teacher education classes who study the science education standards documents and current research on science teaching get the impression that they should never tell students anything – that all the ideas and talk in the classroom should come from the students.

Despite the findings from my own research that this kind of talk is not enough, I sense some of this same enthusiasm for student-centered talk, and the accompanying minimization of the importance of teacher talk, among some researchers in the science education community who advocate social constructivist and inquiry-oriented teaching. As I follow the ways in which many science education researchers in the social constructivist tradition are transforming theory into teaching practice, I worry about the danger of recreating the kinds of talk that characterized the inquiry-based classrooms in my studies back in the 1980s – talk that failed to help students to understand science concepts or to understand the nature of science.

Overemphasizing the Group?

Social constructivist research to date has focused on group processes and interactions within the group. Analyses of the impact of this teaching approach focus on describing the qualities of the learning environment and classroom discourse. While these research studies provide rich descriptions of what is happening in (and sometimes outside of) the science classroom, there is much less attention given to careful studies of individual student learning (Druker, 1998; Gallas, 1995; Kelly & Chen, 1999).

My concerns focus ultimately on student understanding. I worry about individual student learning and understanding. What conceptual knowledge, knowledge about the nature of science, and ways of thinking and acting is each student carrying away at the end of the school year as they each go their separate ways into new classrooms, new world experiences?

Classroom-based studies of social constructivist theories in action typically focus on rich descriptions of classrooms where students are actively engaged in generating and pursuing questions, working largely in small groups to find solutions to their problems (Roth & Bowen, 1995; Moje, Collazo, Carillo & Marx, 2001; Kelly & Chen, 1999). Yes, the descriptions of these classrooms are exciting. There are examples of rich discourse about ideas and evidence taking place among students, with students taking the lead in the process. There are descriptions of teachers wandering about the room, modeling and scaffolding student talk in these independently operating groups.

But I was also initially excited about the "rich discourse" that I observed back in the 1980s in the inquiry-oriented classrooms. If I had written only about my observations of the class as a group, without the studies of their impact on individual students' understanding, I would have produced glowing reports of how these classrooms were operating in many ways like "real" scientific communities. It was only when my colleagues and I closely examined individual student learning that I was forced to confront the evidence that students were not developing meaningful understandings of the science concepts and that they were developing disappointing understandings of the nature of science and scientific inquiry.

Thus, a teacher can create a learning community that looks to adult observers as if students should be learning a lot about science and the nature of science. But that does not mean that students are making the same interpretation. And no matter how wonderful it may be for a student to be part of one of these classroom communities, at the end of the year each student leaves and enters new communities (in and out of school). There the student must rely on her own knowledge and experience as she begins to negotiate her way in a new social setting. It is not enough to say that the class as a whole generated wonderful ideas and projects and engaged in rich debates about ideas and evidence to support them. What about the individual learner? What understandings of science did they develop? What understandings of science and themselves as science learners will they carry with them into new communities and experiences?

Overemphasizing Student-Directed Instruction and Minimizing Teacher-Directed Instruction?

I am concerned about those who translate social constructivist theory into a teaching practice that puts priority on students creating their own topics, defining their own questions and methods of study, and pursuing these inquiries in small groups, with the teacher serving primarily as a resource or a facilitator. This overemphasis on students providing the direction for study minimizes the role of the expert "other" in the learning process and puts huge demands on the ability of the teacher to provide students with effective scaffolding and coaching.

Social constructivists also seem wary of any teacher talk that directs students toward canonical explanations and knowledge. Research on student learning has convinced me that many different kinds of teacher talk are needed to support student understanding and that there are times, especially when students are first trying out new scientific ideas, that the teacher's talk should point students' attention to scientific explanations and encourage students to try out these ideas.

Ignoring the Constraints Teachers Face?

A cognitive apprenticeship model of teaching is based on the traditional learning environment of craftsmen, where a master, an expert, closely guided a handful of apprentices, working together all day long, day in and day out. School classrooms are very different environments. The master teacher will have at least 25 and up to 125 "apprentices" to coach, and he will see each of his apprentices for at most a brief 40 minute period each day. Creating opportunities for students to benefit from talking to and being guided by a more expert "other" (the teacher) in this kind of environment presents special challenges. Teachers must make careful choices about the use of their time; if they talk to students only when students are working independently in small groups, each student will receive only modest, and often decontextualized, scaffolding as the teacher wanders into and out of ongoing conversations in the small groups. How can teachers scaffold and coach students successfully (so that they "really" understand) within the constraints of large numbers of students and limited time with students?

IMPLICATIONS AND LIMITATIONS

Researchers and teachers need to work together to clarify the kinds of talk that will help students *really* understand science. We need more studies that look closely at the role that different kinds of talk are playing in developing student understandings of science. The assertions that I have proposed here are based on a program of research conducted in one teacher's classrooms. The teacher/researcher model used in these studies is both a strength and a weakness. I am convinced from the in-depth studies of student learning across a span of 10 years that these assertions have power. I also recognize that my studies are limited to one teacher, one subject matter, one grade level, and only two school settings, hardly a sufficient sample to understand the diverse classrooms of U.S. schools.

My hope is that the assertions about talk that supports the development of student understanding can serve two purposes. First, I hope they will be a useful starting place in challenging conceptual change and social constructivist researchers to become more pragmatic and yes, even eclectic, if necessary, in translating theory into action in classroom. Second, I hope that the various types of talk described in this paper will stimulate more teachers to become researchers in their own classrooms, implementing more diverse kinds of talk in their classrooms and studying more carefully to assess whether their students are *really* understanding.

NOTE

1. Sun, dirt, soil, minerals, other plants, dead plants, stuff in dead birds, water, makes its own, air, pollution in the air, bugs, flies, nectar, stuff carried by bugs (pollen), liquids

(root beer, juice), powdery stuff you buy at the store, white foam balls in the soil, vitamins, something in grass clippings, hair (cut pieces), care.

ACKNOWLEDGMENTS

The author thanks Marcie Gilbert and Jere Brophy for helpful feedback and editing support.

REFERENCES

Aikenhead, G. S. (1996). Science education: Border crossing into the subculture of science. *Studies in Science Education, 27,* 1–52.

Aikenhead, G. S. (2000). Renegotiating the culture of school science. In: R. Millar, J. Leach & J. Osborne (Eds), *Improving Science Education: The Contribution of Research.* Buckingham: Open University Press.

American Association for the Advancement of Science (1993). *Benchmarks for science literacy.* New York: Oxford University Press.

Anderson, C. W., Holland, J. D., & Palincsar, A. S. (1997). Canonical and sociocultrual approaches to research and reform in science education: The story of Juan and his group. *The Elementary School Journal, 97,* 359–383.

Anderson, C. W., & Roth, K. J. (1989). Teaching for meaningful and self-regulated learning of science. In: J. Brophy (Ed.), *Advances in Research on Teaching* (Vol. 1, pp. 265–309). JAI Press, Inc.

Bereiter, C. (1994). Constructivism, socioculturalism, and Popper's World 3. *Educational Researcher, 23*(7), 21–23.

Brickhouse, N. W. (1994). Bringing in the outsiders: Reshaping the sciences of the future. *Journal of Curriculum Studies, 26,* 401–416.

Brickhouse, N. W. (1998). Feminism(s) and science education. In: B. J. Fraser & K. G. Tobin (Eds), *International Handbook of Science Education* (pp. 1067–1081). London: Kluwer Academic Publishers.

Brown, J. S. (1989). Situated cognition and the culture of learning. *Educational Researcher, 18*(1), 32–42.

Collins, A., Brown, J. S., & Newman, S. E. (1989). Cognitive apprenticeship: Teaching the craft of reading, writing, and mathematics. In: L. B. Resnick (Ed.), *Knowing and Learning: Essays in Honor of Robert Glaser* (pp. 453–494). Hillsdale, NJ: Erlbaum.

Driver, R. (1994). Constructing scientific knowledge in the classroom. *Educational Researcher, 23*(7), 5–12.

Druker, S. L. (1998). The role of culturally-based knowledge in children's scientific problem solving and argumentation strategies: Comparing culturally diverse students in Indonesia. Paper presented at the annual meeting of the American Educational Research Association, SanDiego.

Duit, R., & Treagust, D. (1998). Learning in science – From behaviourism towards social constructivisim and beyond. In: B. J. Fraser & K. G. Tobin (Eds), *International Handbook of Science Education* (pp. 3–25). London: Kluwer Academic Publishers.

Gallas, K. (1995). *Talking their way into science: Hearing children's questions and theories, responding with curricula.* New York: Teachers College Press.

Hewson, P. W., Beeth, M. E., & Thorley, N. R. (1998). Teaching for conceptual change. In: B. J. Fraser & K. G. Tobin (Eds), *International Handbook of Science Education* (pp. 199–218). Dordrecht, The Netherlands: Kluwer Academic Publishers.

Kelly, G. J., & Chen, C. (1999). The sound of music: Constructing science as sociocultural practices through oral and written discourse. *Journal of Research in Science Teaching, 36*(8), 883–915.

Lemke, J. L. (1990). *Talking science: Language, learning and values.* Norwood, NF: Ablex.

Lemke, J. L. (2001). Articulating communities: Sociocultural perspectives on science education. *Journal of Research in Science Teaching, 38*(3), 296–316.

Michaels, S., & O'Connor, M. C. (1990). *Literacy as reasoning within multiple discourses: Implications for policy and educational reform.* Paper presented at the Council of Chief State School Officers Summer Institute on Restructuring Learning. Newton, MA: Educational Development Center, Literacies Institute.

Millar, R., & Driver, R. (1987). Beyond processes. *Studies in Science Education, 14*, 33–62.

Minstrell, J. (1982). Teaching science for understanding. In: L. B. Resnick & L. E. Klopfer (Eds), *Toward the Thinking Curriculum: Current Cognitive Research* (pp. 129–149). Alexandria, VA: Association for Supervision and Curriculum Development.

Minstrell, J. (1992). Facets of students' knowledge and relevant instuction. In: R. Duit, F. Goldverg & H. Niedderer (Eds), *Proceedings of the International Workshop on Research in Physics Education: Theoretical Issues and Empirical Studies* (pp. 110–128). Kiel, Germany: Institut fur die Padagogik der Naturwissenshaften.

Moje, E. B., Collazo, T., Carillo, R., & Marx, R. W. (2001). "Maestro, what is 'quality'?": Language, literacy, and discourse in project-based science. *Journal of Research in Science Teaching, 38*(4), 469–498.

National Academy of Sciences (1996). *National science education standards.* Washington, D.C.: National Academy Press.

Posner, G., Strike, K., Hewson, P. & Gertzog, W. (1982). Accommodation of a scientific conception: Toward a theory of conceptual change. *Science Education, 66*(2), 211–227.

Rosebery, A., Warren, B., & Conant, F. (1992). Appropriating scientific discourse: Findings from language minority classrooms. Working paper 1-92. Cambridge, MA: TERC.

Roth, K. J. (1984). Using classroom observations to improve science teaching and curriculum materials. In: C. W. Anderson (Ed.), *Observing Classrooms: Perspectives from Research and Practice.* Columbus, OH: ERIC Center for Science, Mathematics, and Environmental Education.

Roth, K. J. (1986). *Conceptual change learning and student processing of science texts.* (Research Series No. 167). East Lansing, MI: Institute for Research on Teaching, Michigan State University.

Roth, K. J. (1989–1990). Science education: It's not enough to 'do' or 'relate.' *American Educator, 13*(4), 16–22, 46–48.

Roth, K. J. (1990). Developing meaningful conceptual understanding in science. In: B. F. Jones & L. Idol (Eds), *Dimensions of Thinking and Cognitive Instruction* (pp. 139–175). Hillsdale, NJ: Lawrence Erlbaum Associates.

Roth, K. J. (1993). *What does it mean to understand science?: Changing perspectives from a teacher and her students* (Elementary Subjects Center Series No. 96). East Lansing, MI: Michigan State University, Center for the Learning and Teaching of Elementary Subjects.

Roth, K. J. (1995). Stories of alienation and connection: Examining the neighborhood of science from the margins. Paper presented at the annual meeting of the National Association for Research in Science Teaching, New Orleans.

Roth, K. J. (1996). *The role of writing in creating a science learning community* (Research Series 62). East Lansing MI: Michigan State University, Center for the Learning and Teaching of Elementary Subjects.

Roth, K. J. (2001). The photosynthesis of Columbus: Exploring interdisciplinary curriculum ... from the students' perspectives. In: S. Wineburg & P. Grossman (Eds), *Interdisciplinary Curriculum: Challenges to Implementation* (pp. 112–133). New York: Teachers College Press.

Roth, K. J., Anderson, C. W., & Smith, E. L. (1987). Curriculum materials, teacher talk and student learning: Case studies in fifth grade science teaching. *Journal of Curriculum Studies, 19*(6), 527–548.

Roth, K. J., & Hazelwood, C. C. (1992). *Gender and discourse: The unfolding "living text" of a science lesson* (Research Series No. 60). East Lansing, MI: Michigan State University, The Center for the Learning of Teaching of Elementary Subjects.

Roth, K. J., Peasley, K., & Hazelwood, C. C. (1992). *Integration from the student perspective: Constructing meaning in science* (Research Series No. 63). East Lansing, MI: Michigan State University, Center for the Learning and Teaching of Elementary Subjects.

Roth, K. J., Smith, E. L., & Anderson, C. W. (1984). Verbal patterns of teachers: Comprehension instruction in the content areas. In: G. Duffy, L. R. Roehler & J. Mason (Eds), *Comprehension Instruction: Perspectives and Suggestions* (pp. 281–293). New York: Longman.

Roth, W-M. (1995). *Authentic school science: Knowing and learning in open-inquiry science laboratories*. Dordrecht, The Netherlands: Kluwer Academic Publishers.

Roth, W-M., & Bowen, G. M. (1995). Knowing and interacting: A study of culture, practice, and resources in a grade 8 open-inquiry science classroom guided by a cognitive apprenticeship metaphor. *Cognition and Instruction, 13*, 73–128.

Tobin, K. (1998a). Issues and trends in the teaching of science. In: B. J. Fraser & K. G. Tobin (Eds), *International Handbook of Science Education* (pp. 129–151). Dordrecht, The Netherlands: Kluwer Academic Publishers.

Tobin, K. (1998b). Sociocultural perspectives on the teaching and learning of science. In: M. Larochelle, N. Bednarz & J. Garrison (Eds), *Constructivism and Education* (pp. 195–212). London: Cambridge University Press.

Toulmin, S. (1972). *Human understanding*. Princeton, NJ: Princeton University Press.

Vygotsky, L.S.(1978). *Mind in society: The development of higher mental processes*. Cambridge, MA: Harvard University Press.

Vygotsky, L. S. (1986). *Thought and language*. Cambridge, MA: MIT Press.

West, L. H. T., & Pines, A. L. (1985). *Cognitive structure and conceptual change*. New York: Academic Press, Inc.

Wiggins, G., & McTighe, J. (1998). *Understanding by design*. Alexandria, VA: Association for Supervision and Curriculum Development.

CONSTRUCTING IDEAS ABOUT HISTORY IN THE CLASSROOM: THE INFLUENCE OF COMPETING FORCES ON PEDAGOGICAL DECISION MAKING

Bruce A. VanSledright and Jennifer Hauver James

INTRODUCTION

Ambitious teaching of the sort that promotes understanding and the construction of new knowledge should be goal directed, Brophy and Alleman (1996) argue. It is difficult to contest this claim. But we might ask: What should the goals be? This is a question that is frequently absent from discussions of the construction of knowledge in the cognitive science literature. In that literature, no one really maintains anymore that humans are not fundamentally knowledge constructors (Phillips, 1995). However, there are disputes among constructivist psychologists nonetheless. Much of the disagreement pivots not on normative questions about goals and what knowledge to construct, but around a debate about *how* (the actual mental processes) and *where* (in the mind, or in the interaction of the mind and the world, or somewhere else) such learning occurs. Consider the following brief examples drawn from a much wider array of possibilities.

Vygotsky (1981) speaks at length of the social context in which knowledge is constructed. Memory, cognition and attention, he argues, occur simultaneously at two planes, inter- and intra-mental. Arbitrary distinctions between

Social Constructivist Teaching, Volume 9, pages 263–298.
ISBN: 0-7623-0873-7

individual and social cognition are blurred in Vygotsky's understanding, suggesting that knowledge construction occurs on both planes and in between the two in a reciprocal fashion. Despite psychology's frequent insistence on separating the two spheres, Vygotsky argues that it is fruitless to consider cognitive functions solely on the individual level. As he writes in his general genetic law of cultural development, "Social relations or relations among people genetically underlie all higher functions and their relationships" (Vygotsky, 1981, p. 163).

Von Glasersfeld (1984) seems to disagree. He maintains that any description of the world is relative to the observer doing the describing because it is derived from his or her experience with the world. It appears that he locates the construction of knowledge within the mind of the observer, not fundamentally within a social milieu. The construction process is engendered by sense data emerging from the observer's interaction with objects in the world. Although as Phillips (1995) observes in his review of theories of constructivism, von Glasersfeld attempts to incorporate the social, interventionist act of teaching into his discussion of how individuals construct knowledge, and in doing so "he faces severe problems of consistency here" (Phillips, 1995, p. 8). For more detail on the nature of these debates, see Phillips' (1995) descriptions.

Damon (1991) attempts to find a middle point in this disagreement about how and where the construction of knowledge occurs. It is of particular relevance to our purposes here, so we draw on him at length. Damon invokes a developmental perspective that draws teachers and instruction deeply into the discussion of knowledge construction by learners. Suggesting where his allegiances lie, Damon notes that Vygotsky (1962) was quite clear in making distinctions between what he called spontaneous and scientific concepts that individuals construct. Paraphrasing Vygotsky, Damon observes, "Spontaneous concepts arise directly from a child's own experience and are fully imbued with vivid meaning and flavor of that experience" (p. 388). This idea shares affiliation with von Glasersfeld's (1984) claims. However, again citing Vygotsky, Damon adds:

> Scientific [concepts] . . . are learned as part of a systematic package of formal instruction. The full range and complexity of higher-order thinking only becomes available to a child through schooling experiences that impart scientific concepts. Certain learning acts, therefore, are imbued with developmental priority, in the sense that they enable learners to acquire advanced thinking abilities (p. 388).

With regard to schooling and such formalized learning experiences, Damon, drawing from Vygotsky, takes von Glaserfeld's notions of where knowledge is constructed onto a different plane. That plane prioritizes the types of socially-shared cognitions (e.g. during teaching) that advance thinking beyond spontaneous constructions based in interactions and subsequent descriptions of the world.

Damon (1991) presses this line of reasoning by noting that movement onto the instructional plane in the discussion of knowledge construction often results in discomfort for people because it implies a set of values embedded in defining what is meant by "advanced thinking abilities." Such movement suggests that scientific concepts – those derived from academic disciplines, for example – should be more highly valued than spontaneous concepts learners might construct in their personal excursions in the world. Value choices, Damon argues, are nonetheless "unavoidable if we are look critically at intellectual achievement, let alone if we are to participate in any planned interventions" (pp. 388–389). By planned interventions, we take Damon to be referring to those goal-driven, value-laden, and choice-suffused acts of teaching. These acts are the locations in the classroom context where teachers work out with their students some optimal relationship between directing students toward the aims of the intervention and allowing them room to construct their own ideas about the concepts and goals embedded in that intervention (what Wertsch, 1998, might call appropriation).

Now in this discussion, Damon (1991) wishes to make the point that we need not approach the issue of what types of thinking and knowledge construction to value in a willy-nilly manner. He maintains that "functionality" can serve as the appropriate criteria for judging instructional goals. He suggests that we teachers and curriculum designers, for example, should choose to help children construct ideas and knowledge that enable them to "function" more fully in their everyday sociocultural worlds. Complex ideas that derive from academic disciplines (Vygotsky's "scientific concepts") and that enable increases in "functionality" would rise therefore to the top.

Damon (1991) illustrates with an example in which he describes how he teaches his 12-year-old daughter to solve a mathematical enigma they both encountered in a science museum on a trip in Texas. His daughter, Maria, had become frustrated with her unsuccessful and "spontaneous-conceptual" attempts to address the museum puzzle and walked away. Damon's persistence and greater knowledge of mathematics ("scientific concepts" derived from disciplinary knowledge) allowed him to come to a solution which he in turn could teach his daughter. He notes how both the individual (interpersonal and spontaneous) and socially-shared cognitions (including "scientific concepts") present in his interchange with his daughter played crucial roles in her construction of new knowledge. He implies that, in his daughter's case, the latter enabled "functionality" (solving the enigma) not afforded by the former, an important instructional matter. He concludes by suggesting that such idiographic accounts about teaching for conceptual understanding that stress "deep interpenetration of multiple social forces into cognitive functioning," although often less prized in the research literature, serve as "rich data sources that open windows onto such forces" (p. 393).

On the surface, Damon's (1991) "functionality" criterion offers a compelling argument for addressing the question of which learning goals to pursue and arbitrating whose values will guide definitions of higher-order thinking and understanding. However, we wish to show – in keeping with the importance to the research literature of idiographic accounts demonstrating the "interpenetration of multiple social forces" in the classroom – how such forces can entangle teachers (history teachers in this case) and complicate their efforts at optimizing the relationship between direction towards and the social construction of ideas that enable increased functionality, particularly when those forces send contradictory messages. Some of these forces, as we will illustrate, are far less prone to the kinds of consensus about the value of functionality of higher-order thinking and everyday sociocultural activity than Damon thinks educators and policy makers share (see Damon, 1991, p. 389). This is particularly true in history education. As a result, history teachers committed to social construc- tivist pedagogical approaches, for example, are pressed to adjust and readjust their practices in ways that can undermine the ideal teacher-direction/ student-construction relationship they struggle to achieve.

The classroom context can be thought of as a primary crucible in which Damon's (1991) "social forces" interpenetrate and influence teaching practice. For the purposes of our discussion here, we divide these social forces into two clusters: Those immediate and *internal* forces at work in the daily exigencies of classroom activity, and those more *external* forces that remain several steps removed from the immediacy of daily classroom activity. *Internal* forces, for instance, include the teacher and her appropriated ideas about the nature of subject matter, her students, what they can and should learn, under what optimal pedagogical circumstances, and given the variations in the way they learn. The internal forces also include students and all their manifest and latent experien- tial, prior knowledge, and sociocultural and racial/ethnic differences. *External* forces are comprised, for example, of differing parental expectations and demands, written school district curriculum guides, standards documents, and high- and/or low-stakes tests that students take at selected times during the year. They often influence "externally" because for various reasons (e.g. they send conflicting messages, they compete with one another) teachers do not or cannot appropriate them directly into the daily life of the classroom.

This list of forces is hardly exhaustive. And the distinction we make is for discussion and illustration purposes only. As teachers, we are aware of how complex this terrain of interpenetrating social forces is with respect to classroom life and teaching practice. However, the distinction will assist us in making clearer how striking an optimal balance between teacher direction and learner construction in history education is influenced in various productive *and* unproductive ways by the interpenetration of internal and external social forces in the classroom.

TWO ILLUSTRATIONS OF TEACHING FOR HISTORY FOR UNDERSTANDING

The substance of what follows consists of two illustrations drawn from our own recent teaching experiences. By using the illustrations, we attempt to detail how and why we as teachers made goal-directed choices that enabled our students to construct historical knowledge. Our purpose is to demonstrate how those choices ultimately, and sometimes differentially, influenced *what knowledge* the children in our classrooms had opportunities to construct. Many of these choices were based on our understandings of internal forces within the classroom such as our view of historical knowledge and its disciplinary rule structures, our beliefs about our students various learning capacities and how they interacted with each other, and about ways to build an intervention that provided a useful balance between our direction and students' social constructions of the types of functional ideas Damon (1991) refers. However, because our classrooms were crucibles in which other more external social forces also interpenetrated, we show how those forces – curriculum specifications, state and local standards, and tests – pressed us to modify our choices and adjust our teaching practices in ways that affected our efforts to achieve effective balances. In considering this interpenetration of forces in the social construction of historical knowledge in our classrooms, we use these two illustrations to address the contested questions: What historical knowledge do we adults want our children to construct, who says, and how and why does it matter?

To situate the two illustrations, we begin by introducing ourselves as teachers and classroom-based researchers. Here we speak of ourselves in the third person. Then we switch to the first person as we each describe and discuss episodes from our two classrooms in which we sought in different ways to help our students construct new knowledge about history. We conclude with a discussion of the ways in which different social forces influence and entangle, limit and enable our choices and practices as "constructivist teachers."

We as Teachers and Researchers

VanSledright is a former history teacher who has been conducting classroom-based history education research for a decade, particularly at the upper elementary level where children first are exposed to systematic historical study in most schools in the USA. Through this work, he has contributed to the repeated calls for reform in history education beginning in elementary school.

The larger study from which the first illustration comes began in January of 1999 and concluded that May. The study was a design experiment during which VanSledright taught a group of intellectually, ethnically, and racially diverse fifth graders how to investigate the past and think historically. The choices he made about what to teach the students and how were rooted principally in his appropriation of elements of the National History Standards (National Center for History in the School, 1994) that were consistent with recommendations about teaching historical thinking found the research literature. His primary goal was to teach American history by engaging students in the practice of historical investigation (best exemplified by disciplinary practice) as a means of enabling them to think historically, understand the past, and produce historical interpretations themselves. To pursue this goal, he also operated from a research-based theoretical framework about how historical thinking and understanding occurs for learners, one he had also appropriated based on his own and others' research work.

The emerging theory suggests that learners studying history develop deeper levels of historical understanding when they have opportunities to consciously use their prior knowledge and assumptions (regardless of how limited or naive) about the past to investigate it in depth (e.g. Barton, 1997; Brophy & VanSledright, 1997; Holt, 1990; Levstik & Barton, 1996; Seixas, 1994; Shemilt, 1980; Stahl et al., 1996; VanSledright & Kelly, 1998; Wineburg, 1991). As learners explore the past, attention is must be paid not only to the products of historical inquiry, but to the inquiry process itself. Developing historical thinking and understanding requires opportunities for learners to work with various forms of evidence, deal with issues of interpretation, address questions about the relative significance of events and the nature of historical agency, and cultivate and use thoughtful, context-sensitive imagination to fill in gaps in evidence trails when they arise.

Strategic knowledge dispositions necessary for the development of historical understanding include the capacity: (a) to corroborate sources by evaluating them inter-textually, (b) to make sense of a source author's position in a historical account while also taking into account how the investigator herself imposes her own view on what she reads, and (c) to construct contextualized and evidence-based interpretations. In short, the theory points toward employing variations on the investigative tactics historians use in order to build cognitive capacity to understand what happened in the past. In a sense, the larger study was a test of the educational and pedagogical efficacy of the theory

(VanSledright, 2002). The theory and the classroom practices it evokes is arguably best aligned – both cognitively and epistemologically – with the social constructivism described by Vygostsky and his followers.

In the initial lessons of the design experiment and the ones that comprise the first illustration, VanSledright chose to ask the fifth graders to investigate what is often referred to as the "Starving Time" in the Jamestown colony in the winter of 1609–1610. It was so named after the fact by John Smith who was in England for its duration. In choosing this subject matter focus, his purpose was to introduce students to the intellectual, procedural, and sometimes problematic processes by which historical investigators undertake to explore and understand the past, and simultaneously help students construct initial ideas about life in Jamestown colony. The latter purpose, in part, was driven by school district curriculum specifications for social studies at this grade level, a survey treatment of American history from Native Americans to the Civil War.

James is an elementary school teacher currently working on her doctoral degree at the University of Maryland. She has taught classes at the primary level ranging from kindergarten to fifth grade. Her experience as a teacher has been with a diverse student population in a large school district located in Northern Virginia, where the second illustration takes place. Because of the diversity of her classroom and school community, she has had the opportunity to explore the ways in which social constructivist teaching approaches can be tailored to meet the needs of students of varying cultures, languages and backgrounds. She has conducted a number of action research projects on her teaching and on student experiences in her classroom. She presented one such project at the 2001 AERA Annual Meeting (James, 2001). Other projects have included a mathematics benchmark program developed for the purposes of authentically assessing students' strengths across mathematical knowledge strands, and a study of family stories as a means of inviting student experience into the classroom.

Most recently, James' work has focused on teacher education and the preparation of teachers for diverse classrooms. In particular, she has begun to look at how prospective teachers begin to view their own epistemologies around knowledge in general, and historical knowledge more specifically, and how this ultimately shapes their philosophies of teaching and learning. In the spring of 2001, she conducted a study of prospective teachers and their experience in a social studies methods course. This research project stemmed from her proposal for the transformation of the social studies curriculum, which she developed the semester before. The proposal laid out the pedagogical terrain of history and social studies teaching, presenting a strong case for teaching historical knowledge through an inquiry model, using social constructivist methods (e.g.

Nuthall, this volume). As in VanSledright's case, it called upon recent work which suggests that students should learn to think as historians and construct their own knowledge through the processes of weighing of evidence, corroborating sources, and historically contextualizing their understandings.

Traditionally, students have not been expected to puzzle over authors' intentions despite the fact that such thinking skills would prove valuable to an informed citizen when reading a newspaper, listening to a radio broadcast, or evaluating campaign promises. Rather than constructing their own meanings about text, typically students are asked merely to gather information, with texts (and textbooks in particular) as the ostensibly unmediated bearers of that information. This understanding of learning in history and social studies runs contrary to what Bain (2000) describes as an "epistemic activity" that requires a reconstruction of the past through critical inquiry (p. 332). The teaching of history, he reasons, must reflect the doing of history as is practiced by historians themselves. For Bain, historians construct meaning through a consideration of raw material, or primary documents and artifacts. To do so, they must clarify the context in which an event took place, define the problems under study, work with evidence, and build arguments. Traditionally, students are left unaware of this process of meaning construction, and are only "let in" during the final stage when investigators present their interpretations. Barthes (1968) calls this final stage a "referential illusion," or the misrepresentation of history as received knowledge rather than as something socially construction by historical investigators.

A good deal of the social studies research over the last two decades has focused on students' ability to interpret and think critically about texts, evaluate historical evidence, and build arguments based on constructed meanings (Bain, 2000; Barton, 1997; Levstik & Barton, 1996; VanSledright, in press; Seixas, 1994, 1996; Wineburg, 1991, 1999). For many of these researchers, an educated citizenry is defined by its ability to critically read subtexts in written and spoken rhetoric, define problems, understand context and make conclusions based on evidence, capabilities often ignored in the traditional social studies curriculum. The traditional curriculum was built around a view of historical knowledge as received rather than as constructed. Typically teachers taught this knowledge in a highly-directive, rapid-fire fashion, allowing little room for children to express how they constructed their own understandings of the historical ideas (if and when they did).

The second illustration offered below is taken from a study of James' third-grade class, conducted in the spring of 2000. The purpose was to reflect on instructional decisions she made, which allowed for internal forces such as student identity and experience to become the primary focus of learning in the classroom community. In this sense, she attempted more so than VanSledright to draw students spontaneous concepts into the process of socially constructing knowledge in her classroom. In her study, James (2001) systematically and intentionally focused on her pedagogical choices and the impact those choices had on the direction-construction balance and on student learning. However, as her illustration will show, external forces also interpenetrated James' classroom, necessitating adjustments to her teaching practices that occasionally worked at cross purposes to her efforts at maintaining the direction-construction relationship she sought.

TEACHING ILLUSTRATION ONE (VANSLEDRIGHT): CONSTRUCTING HISTORICAL KNOWLEDGE IN A FIFTH-GRADE CLASSROOM

School and Classroom Context

The fifth-grade classroom was located in a K-5 elementary school in an urbanized section of a school district in southern Maryland. The school's population was large (725 students) and very diverse. Approximately 30% of the students in the school were African-American, 30% were white, and 30% were Hispanic. The remaining 10% included mostly Asian-American students but also a handful of first-generation immigrants to the U.S. whose native languages were not English. In my fifth-grade class, of the 23 students, seven were African-American, six were Hispanic, seven were white, and three were Asian-American. There were 12 females and 11 males. The fifth-grade social studies curriculum, like many in the nation, called for a survey treatment of American history from Natives Americans to the Civil War. I commenced teaching American history every school day at the end of January and concluded at the beginning of May, just prior to the point where state-wide standardized assessments were given. I dealt essentially with two large units: the colonization of North America by the British, and the American Revolution, both required by the school district's social studies curriculum.

Interpreting Evidence: Making Sense of the "Starving Time"

One of the keys to learning to think historically is understanding that evidence trails – those traces of the past left for us to study as we unravel what went before us – are often broken and incomplete, and therefore difficult to interpret. Historical inquirers must scour whatever residue the past leaves us and then carefully reconstruct the historical context under study by building evidence-based interpretations. Investigators must imaginatively fill in missing pieces, as necessary. However, investigators are required to remain within the parameters set by the historical context and evidence at hand.

This task is no small feat for several reasons. Reconstructing a sense of the historical context in a period under investigation is fraught with difficulties because it often remains virtually impossible for us "moderns" to get inside the experiences of the "ancients" studied. Second, the remaining evidence frequently is so sparse and accounts so personally perspective laden that building adequate historicized interpretations is problematic at best, raising issues about the limits of interpretation. And third, attempts to construct a history of events operates on a connection between a reality past and interpretations of that reality which, as Scott (1996) notes, is denied. Investigators claim to relate to us the reality of the past, but their interpretations of it based in the present bar them from fully accomplishing this feat for the reasons I just noted.

Inquiring into the mystery of the Jamestown's "Starving Time" offers an interesting opportunity to develop a type of historical thinking and understanding that brings these key issues into sharp relief. The evidence trail is largely indeterminate. There has been considerable debate over what happened and how to understand the available evidence. Exploring what our Jamestown ancestors left behind provides a powerful opportunity both to test the limits of the ability of inquirers to creatively construct interpretations, and simultaneously use but constrain their imaginations to the historical context and remaining evidence. The investigatory approach I was employing also promised to help my students understand history's rule structure and how practitioners apply it (Bruner, 1960).

Elementary students, however, are taught early to seek out without question texts' literal meanings. In the history classroom, students quickly succumb to the illusion that textbook interpretations demonstrate strict correspondence to what "really happened" in the past. Such reading experiences repeatedly reinforce a fundamentalist epistemological stance concerning historical knowledge. Students can seem confused, for example, by the notion that inquirers might re-interpret history from time to time, in light of new evidence or different historical positions assumed by inquirers. I began teaching under the assumption that, to be successful, I would need to start addressing this stance by helping students construct an alternative, more open view.

Mindful of the reform documents and the research literature, I wanted my students to slowly but perhaps surely learn to think like historical investigators: To remain unseduced by a text's illusion of parroting reality back to us, open to questions, undaunted by indeterminate evidence trails, conscious of the need to interpret and reinterpret, knowledgeable about and secure in understanding that exploring history is a fickle endeavor. Perhaps most importantly, I wanted them to construct the view that giving up on a fundamentalist epistemology did not mean that "anything goes." Instead, I wanted them to be able to appeal to rules within the discipline to arbitrate disputes about what the evidence tells us, as sometimes inconclusive as that might be.

Lesson 1: Initial Interpretations

To introduce the topic, I began by orally reading a couple of paragraphs from an account of the Starving Time by Hakim (1993), *Making Thirteen Colonies* (Chapter 6). Hakim casts events as a mystery, still open to various interpretations because of a limited amount of evidence. She draws heavily on the speculation that then-local Powhatan Indians withheld food and supplies from Jamestown, laying siege to the stockade for the winter of 1609–1610. This deprived the colonists of food stored outside the stockade, precipitating starvation. But she does note that historians remain puzzled about what actually occurred.

After reading the excerpt, I explained to the class that we were going to try our hand at interpreting the Starving Time, testing Hakim's (1993) speculations and, if necessary, coming up with our own. We were going to become "detectives of history." I explained a set of procedures for being what I called "good historical detectives," writing them on a large sheet of paper attached to the chalkboard. These procedures, drawn from disciplinary concepts, included:

- Digging up and reading the evidence;
- Checking the nature of the sources;
- Checking the reliability of the sources;
- Judging the importance of each piece of evidence;
- Building an idea of what happened;
- Making an argument about what happened.

Students were excited by the idea of solving the mystery. Using the desk arrangement in the room (five clusters of four to five desks each), I gave each group a set of documents to read. Helping them construct an idea of the nature of the sources, I described each one, who had written it, and when. I also distinguished between primary sources and secondary sources, explaining why they were considered as such, and then pointed out how "modern versions" of several of the primary sources also were printed on the reverse side to assist them in translating the older English the Jamestown settlers had used. Continuing in this highly directive vein, I asked students to study the documents very carefully and follow the procedures I had outlined. They were to conclude this initial foray into the evidence by writing on notebook paper the result of the last step where they were to make their argument about what they thought happened. I told them that shortly I would ask a member of each group to orally explain their argument.

A period of relative silence followed as students read the documents, rotating them among themselves. After about 10 minutes, a noisy exchange began at each table as students discussed the documents and constructed various arguments about events. At approximately the 20-minute mark, I interrupted students and began calling on group reporters. Again assuming a directive approach, I made it clear that, for this part of the class session, once I called on a group speaker, he or she had the floor and I would limit interruptions.

Group 5 began. Students called them Tables, as in Table 5. Chelsea rose to speak for Table 5. "Worms ate the food," she declared. Several students immediately called out, "No way, no way!" I hushed the interrupters. Coral, another Table 5 member, interjected, "We think the food froze or the food had worms." I responded, "One thought for you and then we'll move on. I didn't read anything in the clues [documents] I gave you about worms." Coral replied, "Well, we're just guessing because we don't know."

We moved to Table 4. Anika stood to speak for her Table.

Anika: We think Mr. Percy [then Jamestown governor] ate it because he's the one who wrote all the letters. And because he was greedy. (laughter from some students)

Dr. Van:[1] What clues do you have to support that he ate the food?

Katie: (from Table 4) Because he wrote the letters.

Anika: Because when the people were eating their shoes, they didn't have any food to be eating because Percy had it all.

Dr. Van: You think Captain Percy was greedy and kept the food for himself. He hoarded the food?

Group: Yeah.

Jeffrey: (interjecting from Table 1) Table 1 thinks that we trust this document [holding up John Smith's comments on the Starving Time, and then reading from the document] ". . . we did not plan well, did not work hard, or have good government."

Dr. Van: (in response to Jeffrey) First, I want to say that you need to wait your turn. But now that you've thrown this out there, I want to ask you, so they got lazy and didn't organize themselves and the food was gone and they didn't know what to do to get more food, so they just sat around and starved? (Table 1 students nod) Interesting. Group 3? Ben.

Ben: But it could be that they were lazy or that Percy ate all the food or maybe they had a war with the Indians . . .

Dr. Van: So which do you think it is? Lazy or Percy the glutton or war with the Powhatans?

Ben: Well, one document says that the Indians fought them and starved them out

[Hakim account] and another says that they were lazy [John Smith's account].

Dr. Van: We have conflicting clues. One says the Powhatans were friendly and they brought corn. John Smith said that. He talks about that in one of the documents. Another document said that the Indians warring with the settlers kept them from getting their food. So which was it?

Ben: We're not sure.

Dr. Van: Last one, Table 2? What's your position?

Brittney: The Native Americans could have been thinking [that] they would get 10 times more food if they took what the settlers had, but maybe the settlers were just lazy.

Dr. Van: So what's your argument here – so what do you think happened?

Brittney: (bashfully) Okay, war.

Dr. Van: So they were starved to death by the Powhatans? [students at Table 2 nod] Okay.

At this point we had to break for lunch. The next day we picked up where we left off.

Lesson 2: The Liar Percy

I began with the observation that we had constructed conflicting interpretations of the Starving Time, not an unusual result when practicing history. I then asked them to revisit the documents and carefully follow the procedures laid out for them the lesson before:

> When you try to solve the mysteries of history, you have to start by looking at the evidence, checking the sources: Where does the evidence come from? When was it written? Is it reliable? Did someone make it up? Because, if you use that source for an answer, you might be missing something. You have to check your sources very carefully. What year was it? Was the author there? Did he or she see it go on? If they were there, they might have some idea. If they weren't there, how would they know? After you check your sources, you develop an idea in your head. Then you make an argument. Something like this: We think what happened in the Starving Time was . . . and then you say why and you cite the evidence.

My goal at this point was to get them to look more closely at the evidence, so that they might refer to it specifically as they defended their arguments. I also wanted them to assess the reliability and significance of the evidence in order to judge one account against another. Here, I was teaching them rules for interpretation and argumentation practiced in the discipline itself. Again, I was very direct about what I was looking for, insisting that we reconstruct a set of extant understandings derived from activities used in the community of historians. By my lights, what I was asking fit well with the my reading of much of the research literature and the reform documents, and fell within the parameters of the theoretical framework underpinning my pedagogy. Earlier, this literature and elements of the reform documents had functioned as an external force. Later, I internalized them, and was busy attempting to internalize them here in the classroom. Doing so was tied to my beliefs about what fifth graders were capable of learning.

We reexamined the interpretations advanced the previous lesson. I observed that only Jeffrey had held up and quoted from a piece of evidence to support his argument. We then discussed how to judge the trustworthiness of different accounts. I tried again to make clear distinctions between primary and secondary sources, asking the students to suggest possible advantages and problems associated with each. I wrote comments on paper attached to the chalkboard next to the procedures I had already laid out the lesson before. These comments included:

- Primary Source: A story told or written down (or photographed) by someone who was there.

- Secondary Source: A story by someone who was not there, but who read/heard about it from a primary source(s).

- Some Possible Problems with Primary Sources:

   (1) Author may not remember all the details.
   (2) Author may see/hear/understand things differently (unique point of view).
   (3) Author's ideas may be influenced by someone else who was there.

- Some Possible Problems with Secondary Sources:

   (1) All of the problems with primary sources, plus . . .
   (2) Author may change the primary source's details.
   (3) Author may put the story in his/her own words.
   (4) Author may not understand what's going on.

My goal here was to entice students to argue for the documents and excerpts they thought were most valid and against those they thought were not. I was attempting to expose the interpretive machinery of historical practice. I took this opportunity to observe:

> Some of us have very different ideas. That's what happens. Often those historians who write the books, they disagree too. They're not sure. Think of Table 5 as a group of historians. They have one idea, one interpretation of what happened. You, Table 4 have another, Table 3 has another, and Table 2 another. We have five different ideas of what happened here. These two groups seem to agree, so we really have four different interpretations of what happened.

I then directed the fifth graders back to the evidence and asked them to repeat the process undergone the class before. This time I said that I wanted them to do a more rigorous job of testing the evidence and then presenting what they had validated to substantiate their arguments.

After about 20 minutes of study and active debate at each Table (e.g. Coral shouted out at one point, "I got it! I got it!"), I called them back to hear groups provide their reconstructed arguments. We began again with Table 5 and with Jamie, their new spokesperson.

Jamie:	In document C1 there's a quote that says [that] George Percy said, "Thanks to God our deadly enemies saved us by bringing us great amounts of corn, fish and meat," and then another guy, John Smith, said he called that time the Starving Time and that he gave the people food.
Dr. Van:	So you think what?
Jamie:	George Percy ate all the food and was greedy.
Coral:	He took the food from everybody else.
Alexandra:	(another Table 5 member) He's talking about one thing, and John Smith's talking about [something else].
Dr. Van:	I have a question. Which of those excerpts is written by John Smith?
Jamie:	Excerpt One.
Dr. Van:	Actually, Excerpt One was not written by John Smith because John Smith was gone.
Alexandra:	Oh, so it should be Percy. Overall, the reason we really think is that George Percy was really greedy. Captain Smith called it the Starving Time, but see George Percy said, "Thank God that we got food," but the captain said it was called the Starving Time, so Percy must have kept all the food to himself.
Dr. Van.:	He forced starvation because he wouldn't share?
Alexandra:	He [Smith] said, "What we suffered was too hard to talk about and too hard to believe. But the fault was our own."
Dr. Van:	What does that mean, "The fault was our own"?
Alexandra:	(quoting Document C-2, Excerpt Two) "We starved because we did not plan well or have good government."
Dr. Van:	But it doesn't say that Captain Percy hoarded the food; it says that maybe they were lazy.
Jeffrey:	(motioning wildly with his arms, then interjecting from Table 1) Yes, it said they had enough food to last a year . . . .
Alexandra:	But he says that they got food from the Indians. So he must have kept the food to himself.
Dr. Van:	Could Excerpt One maybe have been written earlier? Maybe right about the

time John Smith left? And Excerpt Two was written later?

Coral: That means they would have more than enough food to last throughout the
            winter.

Dr. Van: Well, let's see what Table 4 thinks.

Katie: We think exactly what they [Table 5] think. It's Percy, because he wrote the
            letter. Right here it says, "Percy's Account of the Voyage to Virginia and the
            Colonies First Days." *So, maybe Percy lied.* Maybe he said that no one's
            getting any food. If someone else would have written it, those people would
            have said, "Everyone's starving except Percy." But Percy wrote the letters,
            so he was just starving everyone. In the document it said that more people
            were coming and he probably didn't want to share with everyone coming.

Dr. Van: There's no evidence in these documents for this. You're speculating, right?

Katie: Yeah.

Dr. Van: You have to say you're speculating like that, okay?

Katie: Okay, but (insistently) he probably didn't want to share with so many people,
            so he was trying to get rid of the people who were already there by starving,
            and then he wouldn't have to share with them.

We then moved on to the other groups. Tables 2 and 3 quickly supported
Table 5's interpretation, that Percy took the food himself, deprived the others,
and was therefore able to remain alive and write accounts describing the
starvation. Apparently because he was ashamed or afraid of being labeled unjust
and accused of manslaughter, he lied about what happened, concocting a picture
of settlement life more pleasant than it was. At their turn, Table 1 students
rancorously disagreed. They noted that there was no evidence Percy hoarded,
that the other groups were confusing Smith's *ex post facto* account of the
Starving Time with Percy's *a priori* description of initial life at Jamestown and
the benevolence of the Powhatans. They argued that it was far more likely that
either lousy leadership in hunting and gathering food over the winter, or a siege
by the Powhatans explained the Starving Time.

However, the clay had already hardened. "The Liar Percy," who hoarded
food for himself, had become the interpretive refrain of all but the four students
at Table 1. Since the evidence was largely inconclusive, we were left with
competing interpretations on full display, an important lesson I wanted students
to learn. However, on this issue of interpretation, I did add that I thought Table
1's reading appeared more rooted in the evidence, and therefore could be thought
of as more defensible. Most of the students seemed undaunted by my claim,
preferring the intrigue of Percy, the rotund, food-hoarding liar. I chose not to
press the point any further at this particular juncture, saving it for future lessons.

Discussing Illustration One

It should be clear that my efforts in these lessons involved asking students to construct knowledge about both the Jamestown Starving Time *and* the ways in which historical investigators go about the task of constructing that knowledge in the first place. This set of lessons was indeed an exercise in "social constructivist teaching," in the currently fashionable educational parlance. However, a closer inspection of my pedagogy shows me engaged in vacillating between letting students have at the knowledge-construction process on their own and structuring and directing how they did so. It was not the social construction of knowledge for its own sake, with any process and result unilaterally acceptable.

Through the social force of my own standards- and research-based goals internalized to the classroom space via my pedagogical goals, I was attempting to domesticate students' voices to a particular understanding of how historical knowledge is constructed. As I have noted, this domestication process was framed by investigation strategies and procedures practiced within the discipline, what Vygotsky (1962) might loosely call "scientific concepts."

My vacillation between being directive and letting students independently practice what I was directing them to do was bounded by my belief (derived from knowledge of disciplinary norms) that some interpretations are better than others. Better interpretations originate from efforts to stay close to the available evidence, to argue from that evidence, to construct the best interpretation the evidence warrants. Imagination often plays a role because frequently the evidence is insufficient to address all question an investigator might ask. The Starving Time was a case in point. However, given general disciplinary norms (although these are sometimes contested), constructing an interpretation brimming over with unbridled imagination is seldom regarded as good scholarship (see, for example, Masur, 2000, on the flap over Edmund Morris' imaginative biography of Ronald Reagan) and implies sloppy investigatory practice. My pedagogical choices and directive classroom efforts to domesticate student voices were driven by this belief. The knowledge I wanted students to construct, I hoped, would be framed around the social force of historical community norms concerning the relationship of evidence use to interpretation. But why solely privilege the social force of disciplinary community norms?

There were other social forces at work guiding the pedagogical decisions I made. In my judgment, these forces took my goals beyond simply privileging disciplinary norms. I was convinced that helping my students construct an understanding of the disciplinary practices and discourses that guide the historical community had additional, perhaps broader value. Constructing knowledge about history and about the practices of historians can help students develop critical reading and reasoning capabilities. These capabilities are transferable to the everyday world and promote the "functionality" to which I believe Damon (1991) refers. For example, learning to read and reason critically helps students begin the process of intelligently sorting through the welter of claims made by various politicians, marketers, and others who effectively have something to sell. In the arena of democratic politics, for instance, politicians seek to persuade voters that their ideas are best for the country or the state or the locality. Voters need critical reading and reason capabilities to "function" effectively in this arena. They must be able to judge claims against each other in order to make reasonably sound decisions.

Learning how to do so by constructing detailed ideas and discourses about how the process works is essential. The history classroom organized around learning about the past by investigating it offers a range of opportunities to construct and practice such ideas. These ideas permit learners greater "functionality" in our democratic, information-dominated culture than they would have without them, at least on my view. In this sense, I concur with Damon (1991). The mix of being directive at some points and more open to letting students, on their own, practice my directives seemed ideal to me in this teaching-learning context. However, there were yet other social forces in play in the classroom that had impact on my efforts to achieve direction/more-open construction balance, at least one with a counterveiling influence.

The investigative approach I had taken with my students, by mid semester, collided with school district curriculum demands, which I read to be largely an external force and something competing against my goals. As my Starving Time lessons portend by their slow movement (two full class sessions) through one small incident in American history, I would fall behind in my "coverage" of topics listed in the curriculum guide. This made the teacher in whose classroom I was teaching rather uncomfortable. Although she was gracious and most accommodating as I experimented with her students, she nevertheless worried that I would be leaving little time to treat the post-1800 history she needed to teach after my departure. I began to worry with her, entangled on the moral dilemma of offering students opportunities to construct knowledge that I believed enhanced their "functionality," while simultaneously eating up time that otherwise could be spent briskly covering the specified history curriculum, but to ends the research tells us accomplish little (Brophy, 1990; Brophy & VanSledright, 1997). This clearly affected the pedagogical decisions and adjustments I made at several junctures, space restrictions preventing me from discussing them here (see VanSledright, 2002, especially Ch. 4). Suffice it to say, the external force of curriculum coverage threatened to undermine the optimal relationship I thought I had obtained between being directive about rule structures and giving students opportunities to practice constructing a repertoire of ideas and actions around them.

Also in play in this context was concern about a second external force: Standardized tests my students would take in May, at about the point I had agreed with the classroom's regular teacher that I would end my direct involvement in the classroom. In Maryland, the State asks fifth graders (among others) to take difficult tests as part of the Maryland State Performance Assessment Program (MSPAP). The high-stakes nature of this test has been gradually mounting since it was introduced in 1992.

One aspect of the fifth-grade performance measures asks students to read, analyze, interpret, and write about short literature passages. In this respect, one can argue that this aspect of the test holds students accountable for constructing ideas that will help them attain the "functionality" implied by reading and reasoning critically about written text. It then might be only a short step to applying this same idea to spoken text uttered by a politician or by marketers via a television commercial. I reasoned that what I was doing by asking the fifth graders to read, analyze, interpret evidentiary source material, and write about historical events after doing so aligned well with what this feature of the test was intended to measure. I could rationalize my slow truck through the history curriculum on the grounds that what I was doing could well raise the students' MSPAP scores. I am still unsure if the classrooms' regular teacher accepted this idea. It seemed like an uneasy truce we attained on the issue. I thought none too little about this, remaining entangled in the dilemma of choosing from among social forces with competing views about what types of ideas were best for children to construct. Fortunately for me, in the case of the MSPAP tests, they were better aligned to the ideas about history I wanted students to construct than other high-stakes test often are. This made it somewhat easier for me to maintain the type of relationship between direction and open practice I began pursuing with students in the Starving-Time lessons.

As we will see in James' illustration to follow, the state high-stakes tests taken by students where she teaches – barely some 10 miles away, but in testing sense, a world apart – were far from commensurate with the ideas she was inviting her students to construct. The external social forces at work in her school in northern Virginia left her entangled on even thornier pedagogical dilemmas.

TEACHING ILLUSTRATION TWO (JAMES):
CONSTRUCTING HISTORICAL AND SOCIAL STUDIES
KNOWLEDGE IN A THIRD-GRADE CLASSROOM

School and Classroom Context

My third grade classroom was located in a large school district in Northern Virginia. Virginia is one of many states that have recently moved toward greater accountability for teachers and students via a standardized testing program administered at grades 3, 5, 8 and 11. Ultimately, student graduation, school accreditation and teacher pay rest on the results of these exams. As of last year, the testing program, based on the blueprint for the state Standards of Learning (SOLs), was in its third year. Due to a lack of administrative, parental and teacher support, the district in which I worked was slow to adopt the new curriculum and design materials to support instruction in the new SOL units. Thus, the district manuals, state guidelines and available materials made for a complicated web of curricula from which teachers at all grade levels chose what to teach, knowing full well we could not cover everything in both. At Amarette's Elementary School we worked together in teams to develop conceptual units, trying to incorporate as much of the curriculum in a coherent framework as possible. Our third grade team consisted of 11 teachers – eight regular education, one English as a second-language (ESL), one special education, and one Spanish Immersion – who came together weekly to plan and reflect.

Amarette's Elementary is a magnet school, meaning that roughly 20% of our students apply and are bused in from surrounding districts to serve as English speaking models for the neighborhood children. In return for their commuting to school, "magnet" students are given the opportunity to take the math/science portion of their day in our Spanish Immersion Program. The remaining 80% of the student population draw from the neighboring community. This neighborhood consists mainly of low-income housing, the residents of which are immigrant families who often share apartments or houses. Amarette's is a Title I school (due to our percentage of free/reduced lunch qualifiers) which entitles it to additional resources such as instructional assistants, resource teachers and learning labs to support instruction. The student body is comprised of over 900 children.

Within my class of 22 in spring 2001, I had seven magnet students, all of whom were in Spanish Immersion. Four of these children were Caucasian, two categorized as multi-racial, and one of Hispanic descent. The remaining fifteen students came from the neighborhood. Nine were Hispanic, one African, one Pakistani, one Cambodian, one African-American, and two Caucasian. Thirteen were considered LEP, students with limited English proficiency.

Constructing Knowledge About Civil Rights in America

The illustration that follows took place during the third quarter of the school year, February and March of 2001. We had recently finished our unit on economics as was required by the state blueprint, and I had decided to turn to Civil Rights as our next focus of study. According to the district curriculum guides, I was responsible for covering a number of famous Americans, many of whom played integral parts in the Civil Rights movement. The state standards (an external force for me), which did not align completely with the district guides (a more internal force) and often included a great deal more topics and details to be covered, also required that I teach a unit on government and the rights/responsibilities of citizens. It seemed to me that I could bring the list of famous Americans together with a study of the history of our rights as Americans. In this way, I could assist students in constructing their own ideas around the contributions the individual Americans made to our nation's civil rights' history. In order to shed some light on the evolution of this struggle over time, however, I was going to have to provide some historical context for their work. While we had discussed the role of Africans in the early colonization of the Americas earlier in the year, the students had little background knowledge around the changing nature of African-American's rights since that time. I decided to introduce the unit with a novel, *Bright Freedom's Song: A Story of the Underground Railroad*, written by Gloria Houston (1988). It is the story of a girl, Bright Freedom, whose family works on the Underground Railroad helping to transport slaves to safety. Bright is the daughter of a former indentured servant who owes his life to his friend, a former slave, Marcus.

My decision to begin with a novel, and to open up some of the meatier issues of slavery and indentured service for discussion was a result of many months of working to achieve a comfortable environment for student risk-taking. Since the beginning of the year we worked as a class toward managing whole group discussions and debates as well as engaging in small group dialogue. It took many months of discussing group dynamics, having students assume various roles in small and whole group conversations and coming to an understanding of how arguments are made and defended. These, more directed lessons preceded the sort of free-flowing discussions and construction episodes shared here. Unlike VanSledright, whose status as a visiting teacher afforded him less time with his students, I had the luxury of establishing a community of inquiry and knowledge construction over the course of the entire school year. Therefore, by March, much of the teacher-direction/student-knowledge-construction balance was tipped in favor of the latter because I had already created many of the structures and rules that supported it.

As our journey into civil rights history begins, the class is gathered on the floor for a read aloud from the novel and is conversing about the characters.

Abdulahid: Why Freedom's father could work to be free and Marcus couldn't?

Molly: Because.

Molly always had a knack for getting right to the point. I looked her way, my eyes suggesting she do a little better.

Molly: Freedom's father was an indentured servant, not a slave like Marcus.

Abdulahid: (wrinkling his nose.) But why?

Lucas: Because Freedom's father was White. He came over as a servant and made a deal with a landowner. Marcus came over as a slave from Africa. He didn't have any deals.

Lucas had obviously made some sense of our brief discussion on the differences between indentured service and slavery. He seemed, nonetheless, to have missed the greater issue I thought Abdulahid was trying to get at now.

Abdulahid was born in Somalia and had spent the better part of his nine years in Cairo, Egypt. Since he had moved to the United States two years ago, he'd made significant progress as a second-language learner. He was reading just below grade level and had good command of the mechanics of writing along with a strong oral vocabulary. His "ESL errors," as I called them – inconsistency with subject/verb agreement and tense – rarely interfered with the communication of his ideas. In this instance, however, I thought a clarification might help direct the conversation further into the issues at hand.

Mrs. James: I think what Abdulahid is asking is why Freedom's father, as a White man, had opportunities that Marcus didn't have.

Mark's hand rose to his shoulder, and then paused as he considered again what he might say.

Mrs. James: Mark? Did you want to suggest something?

Mark: (clearing his throat) Well, it's almost like Black people weren't people. They were like things. I mean, you could sell them and stuff. They didn't have any rights. But Freedom's father, he wasn't much better, but at least he was White.

Mark spoke directly to Abdulahid, giving an occasional sideways glance to Rochelle, the only other child of African descent in our class. Rochelle played with her shoelaces.

Molly: Well, at least it's not like that anymore. That's just the way it was then.

Mark: (exhaling with some relief) Right.

Rochelle looked over at Molly. They had been good friends on the playground and in the lunchroom all year, but as far as I knew had yet to extend their friendship outside of school walls. At this moment, I wondered if they understood one another's experience at all. For a long time, I had thought children did not see race and color. Today I thought perhaps they just didn't have the language they needed to address it.

The book I had chosen, *Bright Freedom's Song*, allowed me the opportunity to raise what I thought were some important questions for my students to consider. Until this moment, I had not much thought about how those questions might be answered. Where did our understandings about issues like slavery come from? How had we weaved them into our historical knowledge? What was it about our collective conscience that allowed us to feel relief and vindication from responsibility for the inequalities that define our changing nation? Was slavery just some neatly tied bow of decontextualized names, dates, and events around a box stamped "history" that we left unopened for eternity? Or was history itself locked up in that box begging to be lived, interpreted, and understood? All of the pain, loss, fear that defined the period we were discussing in class and that in many ways still defined the experience of minority citizens - where had that gone? My drive home that evening afforded me plenty of time to turn these questions over in my mind.

Later that night as I thought about the next day's lesson, I reached over and pulled a fifth-grade history textbook from my bookshelf. Those of us teaching in third grade were left at the mercy of trade books, but the fourth- and fifth-grade teachers had an honest-to-goodness textbook from which to teach and learn. I had borrowed one. I turned to the chapter on the Civil War, then to a section entitled "The Fight for Rights: 1960–1965." Besides a paragraph on the Emancipation Proclamation and three or four pictures of Martin Luther King, Jr., there was little there.

As I sat at my desk, I mulled over the following thoughts about how to direct my students' construction of ideas. We had to find a way to talk about this stuff; I mean really talk about it, not just make ourselves feel better about it being over, while Abdulahid sat frustrated and Rochelle played with her shoelaces. The book I had chosen certainly provided one viewpoint on history – a White family working on the Underground Railroad (still a rather singular perspective). But what about the Black heroes and heroines of the time? What about the position that slavery was a profitable business venture and should be defended as such? What about the hardships met by those that did escape north and the stories of those who didn't? What about all the ways in which inequality and injustice still rear their ugly heads today? My students may not learn to agree with me or with one another, I thought, but they were not going to leave telling me that the issues of slavery and civil rights had no relevance to their lives. I sought to devise a learning context in which we could discuss that relevance.

The next morning, I arrived early at school to copy an article I had found in the newspaper. The state of South Carolina was in the middle of a battle over whether or not to leave the confederate flag flying over the capital building in Columbia. The NAACP, along with various other civil rights organizations, was leading the fight to have it taken down. I was curious to see what the students would do with the reality that a symbol of the confederate south could still spark such controversy nearly 150 years after the Civil War had ended. I wanted to see what they would do with it and how it would influence the ideas they constructed around these issues.

That afternoon we read the article together as we gathered on the floor for our read-aloud time. Two of the students already had discussed the issue at home. I finally asked, "What do you think?" Right away, some of my students expressed strong reactions. Shedaf insisted the flag should come down. When asked why, she said that it was mean to keep it up, reminding people of slavery all the time. Mike, on the other hand, said that it was their flag and their tradition and since slavery was over, it was silly to fight about it. The two students who had talked about the controversy at home had already decided that the flag was a symbol of slavery and it was unfair to let it fly. Our conversation continued on like this for a few minutes, students taking turns sharing their opinions and challenging those of their classmates. A few became agitated by dissenting opinions. In a more directive fashion, I intervened, restating the rules for generating evidence-based arguments:

> I'd like to try to hold off on making a decision on this if we can. At least until we've had a chance to really think about it. It's okay to have an opinion, remember, but it's even better if you have good reasons for your opinion. Let's see if we can't find out some more about this issue and find some good reasons for the way we think. Maybe we can even change each other's minds?

The students seemed rather unconvinced but willing to give it a try. My goal here was to push students to rely more on their growing understanding of disciplinary norms for defending a position and less on simply their personal convictions.

Returning to our consideration of *Bright Freedom's Song,* that afternoon's reading portrayed a rather gruesome account of a young boy named Cuba who is attacked by a wild animal while hiding out in the Camerons' yard waiting for sundown. I had worried about how the students might handle the scene, but wound up pleasantly surprised. Not only did they listen attentively and maturely, but several began to point to the episode as an example of the horrors slaves had to endure for a chance at freedom.

Jose: Why should we let South Carolina hang a flag that reminds us of that, right, Mrs. James?

Mrs. James: You make an interesting point, Jose, but remember this is just one point of view about this time in history, and it's a fictional story. We'll take a look at some other sources soon and see what they have to say.

We had spent some time earlier in the year conducting research on the "Encounter" in America and European colonization. I spent a good amount of time discussing the ways in which historians construct knowledge around past events and sharing my thoughts with my students. I conducted many lessons in which I directed students to review multiple sources and discuss the case building process in small groups. Much like VanSledright's lessons, we would come together and discuss the varying validity of sources, issues of corroboration and contextualization. As a class we had talked about the upcoming presidential election and ways in which we might determine which messages were more trustworthy in order to make better-informed decisions. These discussions about strategic ways to read texts were ongoing throughout the year, but were becoming less teacher-directed over time as a result of students' growing mastery of the process. Yet, while students were well aware of the differences between primary and secondary sources and were quick to corroborate evidence among texts, they still often attributed greater value to those that seemed to fit their preconceived notions. It was taking some doing to get them to be open-minded and pragmatic about their case building. Then again, I thought, these things take time.

The other civil rights sources we explored included a number of articles the students found at home and on the internet addressing the South Carolina flag question, video clips from "Eyes on the Prize" (documentary series on the civil rights movement), a trip to the Smithsonian exhibit (entitled "Field to Factory"), and several books on famous civil rights activists and the Underground Railroad. By this point in the year, students frequently brought in sources of their own, and we began to build a timeline to keep track of the history of the movement as we discovered it. Very often we read competing accounts of the same event in time or found information left out of one account and included in another. These situations led to further lessons and discussions on point-of-view and evidence corroboration. Before long, students were coming to see themselves as historians who were constructing their own understandings about the past with only sporadic guidance from me, the direction-construction relationship that aspired to my ideal. Molly and Mark decided it might be helpful if we made a pro/con chart to help us decide about the flag issue. This we placed on one end of our timeline under the year 2000. Lucas and Will had stumbled across a reference made to the plight of Jews during World War II in a book about human rights. Taking the initiative, they asked if they might conduct a study of the holocaust to see what they could find about human rights during other times in history. Marika began writing poems about the people we studied who played a role in fighting for the rights of African-Americans. By the time we wrapped up our study, she had written 13 and bound them together for our class library.

Certainly my own understanding of valuable learning experiences, those that allow students the freedom to construct their own understandings around historical knowledge, had the greatest influence on my pedagogical decision-making. I wanted my students to guide the course of our inquiry, as I believe that intrinsic motivation is essential to meaningful teaching and learning. I also believe that such learning is only possible when we allow students and teachers the time to explore in depth the issues and questions which interest them. Yet these internal influences, however strong they were, were not the only factors that I had to consider as the course of the year moved on. The curriculum guides and thoughts about the impending SOL tests pushed me to move on and to "cover" more content. Thus, I asked the students to revisit our discussion of the flag in South Carolina. Their final assignment, I told them, would be to write a page explaining their position by building a persuasive case. We would share our papers the following week. I had already allowed too much time to be spent on students' questions and research if we were going to meet the state expectations by May. I would have to tell students that if they wanted to continue their projects at home, they could share their findings with us later. For now, I had two ancient civilizations and a review unit on exploration to complete before the exams. Here, I was moving back into a more directive role in response to these external forces.

At the end of the civil rights unit, when papers were done and student presentations were underway, I found myself impressed with students' ability to draw from evidence to make their cases. A few – Mark and Molly in particular – had come full circle, first standing on one side of the issue, then the other, finally resting somewhere in the middle. "I can see both sides," they each wrote as they weighed the arguments. Both agreed that injustice was still very much a part of our lives today and that this issue was an important one. "Well," I said to myself, "that was something." Rochelle's paper, however, was by far the most thought provoking. The heart of it read as follows:

The flag in South Carolina reminds all people of the terrible things that happened to so many Black people. It's a symbol of a tradition that made people like animals and business more important than human rights. Many people fought for their freedom during the time of the Civil War and still today. That flag reminds all of us that freedom is not a right that's given to us. You have to fight for it. I think we should leave it up so we don't forget.

Rochelle stood as she read her paper and spoke loudly, clearly. She did not play with her shoelaces that afternoon. She had something to say and we all listened very closely. For some of us, we began to question the positions we had worked so hard to defend. For me (the oldest and "most wise"), tears filled my eyes as I learned a valuable lesson. Beauty is certainly in the eye of the beholder. But so is truth, I believe, and so is history if we allow our students the freedom to arrive at their own disciplined understandings.

Discussion of Teaching Illustration Two

My own experience as a student of history and social studies was very traditional. Lists of dates, names and places filled my spiral notebooks as a child as I worked to memorize "facts" for the weekly chapter tests. A few years in the classroom as a teacher, however, and I realized that my students constructed more ideas, and more sound ones, when I could connect the subject matter to their own experience and when their own questions tended to lead our inquiry, an understanding I quickly appropriated. The more I began to let student interests and questions – one of the classroom's key internal "social forces" (Damon, 1991) – drive my pedagogical choices, the more engaged we all became in learning. Although I had prescriptive curriculum guides and learning targets in hand, I have always been convinced that my students should be able to come to their own understandings of the "facts" and concepts included there. And it is directing the process of this knowledge construction, not the products, which have become the focus of my own teaching and learning. For me, directing how my students engaged that process, and then giving them ample practice in constructing ideas on their own using it, was the most ideal relationship.

In the context of a state (and the school district in reluctant response) that is moving towards standardization and high-stakes testing, however, my instructional goals and decisions come into conflict with the goals of those external policy makers. The sheer amount of information to be covered in a 10-month school year is enough to overwhelm the most organized teacher, which I think I am. For a teacher who is less concerned with efficiency than with meaningful knowledge construction, it is even less conceivable that he or she could get to everything, necessitating difficult choices. The choices I made about what to teach and for how long ultimately rested on my own professional knowledge about what was significant, the prior knowledge and interests of my students, my subject-matter knowledge and confidence with the curriculum, as well as the teaching materials I had at my disposal.

Come May, when the SOL exams are administered, a frenzy of test preparation and review would ensue in my school and students would be drilled on obscure "facts" listed in the SOLs. I still remember Alec's question, "Mrs. James, why does this say Christopher Columbus discovered America when we read about so many other people who explored here before him?" I explained that those who wrote the test had their viewpoint and our job was to make sure we knew what that was – a point I little enjoyed having to make. But what is a teacher to do? We would lose the entire month of May to test preparation, review, and test taking. Still, it was inevitable that students would come across questions about events or details we had not dealt with during the year, despite my best intentions. Entangled on a set of teaching dilemmas, I felt a combination of guilt for not having done a better job of preparing my students for this week of multiple-choice exams, and fear that they would fail to demonstrate their progress on an exam designed to test others' historical knowledge constructions rather than those they had constructed, or their capacity to construct them in the first place. The best I could do was to remind myself that I had taught in a way that made learning powerful and engaging, and that my students had grown in many ways in their capacities to think critically, read and write with purpose, and construct new understandings using the resources around them, even though the test measured little of it.

The SOLs were designed to do just what their name implies: Set standards for learning, or if you will, standardize learning. The exams are tied directly to the standards and weighted with rewards and penalties because the Virginia State Board of Education wants to see that each and every student gets the same "standard" education. However, when education itself relies on human decision making at so many different levels, what is the likelihood of truly standardized teaching and learning? What of the multiple social forces to which Damon (1991) refers? What about the significant class, racial and ethnic variation among students in public schools? What if the stakes were so high that teachers were pressed to adjust the direction-construction relationship strictly by the force of the SOLs and the curriculum it implies, maintaining a quick pace of skill and drill, transmission-style instruction – a style that assumes children are all alike, similarly empty vessels waiting for knowledge to be poured in intact? Is this what we want? Here the normative landscape of policymaking becomes rather complex. It can entangle ambitious teachers who, relying more on internal forces grounded in deep subject knowledge and sensitivity to children and their differences, are professionally committed to helping those children construct powerful ideas that enhance their "functionality" in ways that simply "pouring ideas in rapid-fire sequence" cannot.

Who decides what is included in the state standards and what is left out? Should those standards encourage students to consider multiple perspectives on historical knowledge, as is customary in the discipline? Currently, they do not, effectively defying disciplinary norms. What role do schools and districts have in translating that document into instructional units and helping teachers internalize its force via support to build their knowledge and repertoire of teaching strategies? In the end, the curriculum manuals still sit on the desk of a teacher in an isolated classroom in a school far from the state offices. And that teacher remains the final policy maker for his or her students.

If, as a community of educational researchers, we are able to agree that knowledge is a human construction (e.g. Phillips, 1995) and that students – with some procedural and strategic direction – ought to have the opportunity to construct powerful understandings of the world around them, then programs such as those in Virginia pose compelling problems for educators. The goals of the SOLs appear to contradict the aims of teaching designed to enable students to construct, for example, powerful historical ideas, those that include both knowledge about the past and how that knowledge gets constructed. They intend, by definition, to tilt the direction-construction relationship in favor of the former by circumscribing teaching practices and limiting students' roles to recalling lists of historical details, incidents, and people, what historian Tom Holt (1990) calls "other people's facts." In the discussion of teaching that enables students to construct important ideas ("scientific concepts"), it seems as though, in places such as Virginia, we have forgotten to discuss what we mean by those ideas and why we choose some and not others. Damon (1991) suggests that in such discussions, we could reach ready consensus on what we mean and what we want. However, the difference, for instance, between the types of historical ideas Maryland policy makers encourage their state's children to construct and what is in place in Virginia, belies that consensus. Teachers, those who ultimately must manage the direction-construction relationship, are left entangled amid competing forces.

In my case, I was helping my students construct an understanding of human suffering and the struggle for rights in this country. Like VanSledright, I wanted my students to think critically about the world in which they live, and to begin seeing history through the eyes of people whose experience was other than their own. I wanted them to talk, argue, persuade, and act on their understandings. I wanted to foster their education as responsible, active, democratic citizens. And I wanted them to learn that history is a construction, and that they can construct history themselves if the have the tools that enable that form of enhanced functionality. However, the external force of my state's testing program and learning standards, and the messages they send about what it means to be a

Virginia citizen (a passive one in my view), continually pressed me to alter the relationship between teacher-direction and student-knowledge-construction I was working hard to achieve. Given the sanctions the state threatens to apply for not "measuring up," it will remain difficult to resist the alternatives.

IMPLICATIONS

On our view from a pedagogical and educational perspective, the question of goals – or what knowledge is best for students to construct – is logically prior to questions about how they construct knowledge. In other words, talk of children constructing knowledge is incomplete without first a discussion of what knowledge adults appear to want students to construct. As Damon (1991) observes, this can make some uncomfortable, in part at least, because it has to do with the issue turning on normative questions that the current state of classroom research on history and social studies teaching and learning cannot fully help us resolve. Perhaps this is why such conversations seem to occur so seldom in the literature on teaching students to construct knowledge: Empirical researchers infrequently examine the source and rationales behind the types of history and social studies ideas they observe teachers asking students to construct.

Addressing this issue is a complex undertaking, which may also explain why it so infrequently occurs. Much of the complexity hinges on the fact that examining the everyday "functionality" (e.g. critical analysis of politicians' and marketers' assertions, active citizenship) that certain concepts enable relative to others means exploring the varying epistemological perspectives held by those in positions to make curricular decisions and test items that measure them. Many policymakers are often several steps removed from the classroom (an external force), and attempt to drive pedagogical decision making from a distance, and sometimes regardless of teacher intentions, understanding of students, and appropriated knowledge of discipline-specific concepts and research on teaching and learning (internal forces). And often the policy makers and curriculum- and test-developers epistemological perspectives and commitments are left unarticulated.

For instance, the Maryland State Performance Assessment Program (MSPAP) appears to be driven by state-level policy makers who view knowledge as useful in itself, but more useful in relationship to its application in problem-solving venues. Currently, policy makers there are working out a set of performance assessments that, for example, will (in 2002) ask the state's children to demonstrate the process of constructing historical knowledge by asking them to critically read and analyze primary sources in order to build interpretations of the past, much the way historians themselves construct historical knowledge. These assessments will work from a view of historical knowledge that is reasonably consistent with our efforts to get our third and fifth graders to do the same. State policy makers and test developers appear to be convinced – with Damon (1991) – that asking students to perform in ways that reflect the general epistemological commitments of the disciplinary history community, and their attendant practices, improves students' everyday sociocultural "functionality" in ways that merely recalling historical incidents and details do not. In this way, the external force of a state testing program is aligned with what we know about powerful learning opportunities in history that reflect studies within (i.e. internal to) classroom contexts (e.g. Brophy, 1990; Brophy & VanSledright, 1997; Holt, 1990; Levstik & Barton; 1996; Seixas, 1994; Stahl et al., 1996; VanSledright, 2002; VanSledright & Kelly, 1998). The alignment supports a more optimal relationship between teacher direction and student knowledge construction.

As these MSPAP history performance assessments come on line for third, fifth and eighth graders, school-district history curricula will need to be aligned with them and their underlying connections to disciplinary practice and activity (deployment and application of "scientific concepts") if Maryland districts wish their students to score well. Teachers will be pressed similarly align their teaching practices. With regard to VanSledright's illustration, if curriculum policy makers in the school district in which he taught do not fundamentally alter its survey- and coverage-based fifth-grade history curriculum, teachers there with epistemological commitments akin to his will be entangled in the morass of competing views of historical knowledge much the way he was. However, teachers who view historical knowledge as solely the capacity to recall any number of incidents and details from the past will also be ensnared amid a set of unaligned forces with competing views of what historical knowledge is best for children to construct. Under those circumstances, it will be difficult to develop an educative teacher-direction/student-knowledge-construction relationship.

In Virginia – separated from Maryland by only the thin body of the Potomac River but in some ways a world away – epistemological views about the nature of historical knowledge appear to be quite different. The SOL exams that measure the knowledge children have constructed about history are essentially recall based. Students are asked to pick out the "correct answer" from among the typical four choices on a myriad array of multiple-choice questions. As we have noted, the questions center on recalling what some call historical facts. There are no tasks that ask children to perform on their capacity to construct historical knowledge as is done within the discipline. Judging by the nature of the SOL exams and what they probe, policy makers and test developers at the Virginia State Department of Education hold a fundamentally different idea about the nature of historical knowledge, and what it is good for, than their counterparts in Maryland. Their notion of the optimal relationship between direction towards and the social construction of ideas is tellingly different than in Maryland.

As a result, teachers such as James, with commitments to the importance of helping her third graders construct an understanding (often in a slow and time-consuming manner, as she alludes) of multiple perspectives and interpretations of the "facts," becomes pedagogically entangled on Virginia's version of historical knowledge that differs from her own. James' view of the optimal relationship that supports "functionality," and the knowledge of history (for example) that she understands enables it, grates like sand paper against what the SOL exams suggest by "functional" historical knowledge.

What might account for these two States' apparent policy dissensus regarding views about the nature of historical knowledge and what ideas children should construct? This is a difficult question to address. We would speculate that, in part, it may be political. Virginia is a largely conservative state. Views of historical knowledge there could well turn on efforts to communicate and defend a singular, nationalistic, Anglo-centric story of U.S. history, the type often conveyed in typical history textbooks. Maryland, by contrast, tends to be more liberal. State policy makers are more likely to support multiple interpretations of American history that reflect the diverse populations making up the majority of the voting blocks in the state (e.g. Maryland's Prince George's County has the largest African-American middle-class population in the country).

However, we would further speculate that the explanation may also hinge on economics. Performance assessments cannot be readily machine scored in the way that multiple-choice, right-wrong items can be. Therefore, they are more expensive to administer and analyze. Decisions in each state are likely made on this economic basis (see Darling-Hammond, 1991), where Virginia educational policy makers refuse to invest the additional resources into a type of performance testing program to which policy makers in Maryland have committed themselves. Education, educational outcomes, and educational investments are defined differently in each state.

What role might classroom-based research on teaching and learning history play in mediating the differences in epistemological commitments and the curriculum and testing policies found in these two states and interpenetrating their classrooms? Does it tell us anything about what sort of historical knowledge children construct that produces greater "functionality" for them? Two decades of such research in the U.S. and in Great Britain (some of it cited above) suggest that students of history construct more powerful and "functional" knowledge when they have opportunities to learn about others' interpretations of the American past *as well as* read, analyze, and build their own interpretations based on evidentiary sources (see, for example, a recent review of this research by Voss, 1998). The research repeatedly stresses that asking children merely to reconstruct (via memorization) and then repeat others' accounts of history shows little long-term staying power because the historical knowledge children build as a result is generally neither successfully mastered nor appropriated (see Wertsch, 2000). Both of our idiographic illustrations and the research projects from which they derive (James, 2001; VanSledright, 2002) confirm these wider research claims.

The performance assessment program in Maryland would be more closely aligned then to this body of research than would be Virginia's SOL exams. Whether policy makers in either state use this research to rationalize their standards and assessment programs is an open question. By deduction, we might conclude that, in Virginia's case, this body of research has had almost no impact, and it is not clear why. Consensus among policy makers on what historical knowledge children would be best to construct appears elusive; teachers are left to sort out the details as classroom-based policy makers. Such efforts often leave teachers ensnared in dilemmas that have significant moral and personal implications. Until educators, researchers, and policy makers have a sustained, systematic, and thorough conversations about *what* ideas are best for students to construct and *why* (and the research on teaching and learning could be helpful here), teachers will labor under the uncomfortable weight of mis-aligned goals that, in the case of states such as Virginia, cause them to adjust the relationship between teacher direction and student social construction of ideas toward the exclusion of the latter.

CONCLUSION

Given the complex terrain of competing educational policies and social forces interpenetrating classroom life, we conclude by asking: What are teachers with ambitious intentions about optimizing children's constructions of functional ideas rooted in the research and in domain-specific "scientific concepts" to do, especially when their intentions move against the grain of local and state policies? What stances or pedagogical adjustments can help them navigate this landscape? From a long list of possibilities, we offer the following.

First, teachers will need to be prepared to face competing interests among the social forces that influence construction of ideas in the classroom. Second, ambitious teachers will likely become entangled in dilemmas that competing interests create and they will find that there are no easy resolutions. Tensions will be present at many turns and teachers need to be fully aware that they will have to make and are making difficult decisions. Third, to professionally inform these decisions, ambitious will teachers need to be intellectually savvy about the normative and sociopolitical landscape on which policy makers – often external to daily classroom life – frame out the ideas that they believe are best for students to construct. Ambitious teachers also will need to be intellectually savvy about the epistemological commitments underlying the those policy-makers' decisions. What type of knowledge school districts and state-level policy makers choose to test appears to be a reasonably good indicator of such epistemological commitments.

Fourth, research on the relationship between student knowledge construction and direction toward the "functionality" certain "scientific-concept" constructions offer (e.g. learning strategies and concepts for the critical analysis of evidentiary sources, that in turn promote the exercise of active, critical citizenship dispositions) could serve as an important arbiter in making choices about which learning opportunities to provide. In other words, teachers deeply informed by such research could use it as they addressed many of the difficult pedagogical decisions they face in their classrooms. Normative judgments devoid of research underpinnings will not disappear no matter how much research accumulates. However, accumulated research results can serve to attenuate educational decisions arrived at solely on self-serving political or shallow economic grounds because they can promote powerful counter arguments.

Finally, teachers may have to choose to teach in school districts and states where external educational policies, learning goals, and testing practices align with their professional and research-based goals. Surely, this would force mobility on teachers who are not so inclined or enabled. However, the alternative is to endure the frustrations and the difficult and sometimes conflicting moral decisions teachers such as the two of us faced. As we prepared this paper, an article appeared on the front page the *Washington Post* (Seymour, 2001), noting how a crack mathematics teacher was leaving his school in Virginia to take a job in a private school in the District of Columbia. His reason: "It was SOL this, [and] SOL that. It was not about … 'Let's learn something interesting and exciting today' " (p. A1).

NOTE

1. During my introduction to the class, students asked if they could address me by the abbreviation, Dr. Van, rather than by using my full name. I agreed.

ACKNOWLEDGMENT

The research study that underpins the first illustration was supported by a grant from the Spencer Foundation. The views expressed in the illustration do not necessarily represent the position or endorsement of the grant agency.

REFERENCES

Bain, R. (2000). Into the breach: Using research and theory to shape history instruction. In: P. Stearns, P. Seixas & S. Wineburg (Eds), *Teaching and Learning History in a National and International Context* (pp. 331–352). New York: New York University Press.

Barthes, R. (1968). The reality effect. In: T. Todorov (Ed.), *French Literary Theory Today: A Reader* (R. Carter, Trans., pp. 11–17). Cambridge: Cambridge University Press.

Barton, K. (1997). "I just kinda know": Elementary students ideas about historical evidence. *Theory and Research in Social Education, 25,* 407–430.

Brophy, J. (1990). Teaching social studies for understanding and higher-order applications. *The Elementary School Journal, 90,* 351–418.

Brophy, J., & Alleman, J. (1996). *Powerful social studies for elementary students.* Fort Worth, TX: Harcourt Brace College Publishers.

Brophy, J., & VanSledright, B. (1997). *Teaching and learning history in elementary schools.* New York: Teachers College Press.

Bruner, J. S. (1960). *The process of education.* Cambridge, MA: Harvard University Press.

Damon, W. (1991) Problems of direction in socially shared cognition. In: L. Resnick, J. Levine & S. Teasley (Eds), *Perspectives on Socially-Shared Cognition* (pp 384–397). Washington, D.C.: American Psychological Association.

Darling-Hammond, L. (1991). The implications of testing policy for quality and equality. *Phi Delta Kappan, 73,* 218–224.

Hakim, J. (1993). *Making thirteen colonies.* New York: Oxford University Press.

Holt, T. (1990). *Thinking historically: Narrative, imagination, and understanding.* New York: College Entrance Examination Board.

Houston, G. (1998). *Bright Freedom's Song: A story of the underground railroad.* San Diego, CA: Silver Whistle, Harcourt & Brace.

James, J. H. (2001, April). As students make meaning of culturally relevant pedagogy: A classroom teacher's perspective. Paper presented at the American Educational Research Association meeting, Seattle.

Levstik, L., & Barton, K. (1996). They still use some of their past: Historical salience in elementary children's chronological thinking. *Journal of Curriculum Studies, 28,* 531–576.

Masur, K. (1999, December). Edmund Morris's *Dutch:* Reconstructing Reagan or deconstructing history? *Perspectives: American Historical Association Newsletter, 37,* 3–5.

National Center for History in the Schools (1994). *National standards for United States history: Exploring the American experience.* Los Angeles: UCLA.

Phillips, D. C. (1995). The good, the bad, and the ugly: The many faces of constructivism. *Educational Researcher, 24,* 5–12.

Scott, J. W. (1996, February). After history? Paper presented at History and the Limits of Interpretation: A Symposium, Rice University, Houston, Texas (available on line at www.ruf.rice.edu/~culture/papers/Scott.html).

Shemilt, D. (1980). *History 13–16 evaluation study*. Edinburgh: Holmes McDougall.

Seixas, P. (1994). Students' understanding of historical significance. *Theory and Research in Social Education, 22*, 281–304.

Seixas, P. (1996). Conceptualizing the growth of historical understanding. In: D. Olson & N. Torrance (Eds), *The Handbook of Education and Human Development* (pp. 765–783). Oxford, Blackwell.

Seymour, L. (2001, July 17). SOL tests create new dropouts: Frustrated Va. Teachers switching courses, leaving public school. *Washington Post, 224*, A1, A8–A9.

Stahl, S., Hynd, C., Britton, B., McNish, M., & Bosquet, D. (1996). What happens when students read multiple source documents in history? *Reading Research Quarterly, 31*, 430–456.

VanSledright, B. (2002). *In search of America's past: Learning to read history in elementary school*. New York: Teachers College Press.

VanSledright, B. (in press). Confronting history's interpretive paradox while teaching fifth graders to investigate the past. *American Educational Research Journal*.

VanSledright, B., & Kelly, C. (1998). Reading American history: The influence of using multiple sources on six fifth graders. *The Elementary School Journal, 98*, 239–265.

von Glasersfeld, E. (1984). An introduction to radical constructivism. In: P. Watzlawick (Ed.), *The Invented Reality* (pp. 17–40). New York, W. W. Norton.

Voss, J. (1998). Issues in the learning of history. *Issues in Education, 4*, 163–209.

Vygotsky, L. S. (1981). The genesis of higher mental functions. In: J. V. Wertsch (Ed.), *The Concept of Activity in Soviet Psychology* (pp. 144–188). Armonk, NY: Sharpe.

Vygotsky, L. S. (1962). *Thought and language*. Cambridge, MA: MIT Press.

Wertsch, J. V. (2000). Is it possible to teach beliefs, as well as knowledge about history? In: P. Stearns, P. Seixas & S. Wineburg (Eds), *Knowing, Teaching & Learning History* (pp. 38–50). New York University Press.

Wertsch, J. V. (1998). *Mind as action*. New York: Oxford University Press.

Wineburg, S. (1999). Historical thinking and other unnatural acts. *Phi Delta Kappan, 80*, 488–499.

Wineburg, S. (1991). On the reading of historical texts: Notes on the breach between school and academy. *American Educational Research Journal, 28*, 495–519.

WESTWARD EXPANSION AND THE TEN-YEAR-OLD MIND: TEACHING FOR HISTORICAL UNDERSTANDING IN A DIVERSE CLASSROOM

Cynthia M. Okolo, Ralph P. Ferretti and
Charles A. MacArthur

INTRODUCTION

History Instruction in the Context of Educational Reform

History is a fascinating and intellectually challenging subject. Fascinating because much of it is the story of the human actors and events that have shaped the world in which we live. Challenging because, to understand history, we must grapple with times, people, and motivations that may be very different from our own. To do so, we must overcome *presentism* (Ashby & Lee, 1987; Judd, 1915), or the very natural tendency to interpret the past in light of the present and through the lenses of our own personal experiences.

As standards-based reform has swept through American schools, history instruction has enjoyed renewed attention. Professional organizations (e.g. National Council for the Social Studies, 1994; National Commission on Social Studies in the Schools, 1989) have issued standards recommending the historical content and processes that should direct history instruction at the

Social Constructivist Teaching, Volume 9, pages 299–331.
ISBN: 0-7623-0873-7

pre-collegiate level. States and school districts have followed suit, issuing their own sets of standards and descriptions of performance or products that indicate standards are being met. And, in the majority of states, high stakes tests have been developed to determine whether or not students are able to meet the standards.

Students with disabilities have not been neglected in the standards-based reform movement. The Individuals with Disabilities Act (IDEA) is the major piece of Federal legislation that guides the conduct and funding of special education programs. Several components of IDEA make it clear that students with disabilities are not to be excluded from the curricular expectations and assessment practices required of their peers without disabilities. Rather, IDEA requires documentation on a learner's individualized educational program that educators have considered the relevance of the general education curriculum and the means by which she/he can participate in the state's assessment and accountability system (Destafano, Shriner & Lloyd, 2001; Erickson, Ysseldyke, Thurlow & Elliott, 1998; Yell & Shriner, 1997). A host of concerns have been raised about the degree to which schools and classrooms can adapt their practices to accommodate students with disabilities (e.g. Deschenes, Cuban & Tyack, 2001), and issues about the types of instructional arrangements and support systems needed to ensure progress for all students are unresolved (e.g. McDonnell, McLaughlin, & Morison, 1997; OSEP, 2001). Despite these ambiguities, current practices in special education have undergone a profound shift. Rather than being tracked into a separate, specialized educational system with a different set of expectations, unprecedented numbers of students with disabilities are participating in the general education curriculum and are expected to master the same standards as their nondisabled peers (e.g. McDonnell et al., 1997; McLeskey, Henry, & Alexrod, 1999).

The Value of History Instruction for Students with Mild Disabilities

Our research program has focused on ways to improve history instruction for all learners, including those with mild disabilities (Ferretti & Okolo, 1996; Ferretti, MacArthur & Okolo, 2001; MacArthur, Ferretti & Okolo, in press; Okolo & Ferretti, 1996a, b, 2000). Students who are classified as mildly disabled typically have been identified with one or more of the following disabilities: learning disabilities, mild behavioral disorders, mild mental disabilities, and speech and language disabilities. Although over 75% of the five and one-half million school-age children who receive special education services are considered mildly disabled (U.S. Department of Education, 2000), surveys have shown that social studies is not an instructional priority for students with mild disabilities (Patton, Polloway & Cronin, 1987) and, unlike literacy and mathematics, has not received much attention in the research literature (Curtis, 1991). We contend that this oversight is unfortunate (Ferretti & Okolo, 1996). Beyond the fact that federal policies mandate the participation of students with disabilities in the general education curriculum, there are compelling reasons for improving history instruction for students with disabilities. Setting aside the perennial controversies about the appropriate focus and goals of history (or social studies) instruction (e.g. Wineburg, 2001), most educators concur that it helps prepare students to participate in a democratic society by affording them opportunities to construct elaborate, deep, and tightly interconnected knowledge bases about problems whose solutions inform contemporary society (Ferretti & Okolo, 1996). Surely, this goal is as valuable and relevant to students with disabilities as to those without them.

In addition to being important in its own right, history is a rich domain in which to promote thinking, problem solving, and literacy – areas of keen interest and primary importance to special educators. Historical problems such as: How could the government have protected the rights of the Native Americans during 19th century westward expansion? or, what role should the U.S. have played in the Vietnam War? are representative of the kinds of ill-structured problems (Bransford & Stein, 1984; Simon, 1980) that one encounters in daily life. They do not yield to simple solutions and challenge students to define goals, identify and analyze evidence that can be used to evaluate plausible solutions, develop persuasive arguments in support of proposed solutions, and critically evaluate arguments against the proposed solutions of others (Ferretti & Okolo, 1996; Kuhn, 1991, 1999; Newmann, 1990; Toulmin, 1958). Furthermore, as widely acknowledged by contemporary history educators and reform efforts, historical understanding develops from "doing" history – that is, making use of the available historical record to construct an interpretation of history that is accurate, plausible, and representative. In doing so, the study of history becomes an investigative and interpretative process that consists of gathering information (or evidence) about a historical topic, reading and comparing multiple sources of evidence, asking questions of the evidence, formulating interpretations that are accurate and take into account multiple perspectives, and defending interpretations based on evidence. In this process of historical inquiry, opportunities abound to learn not only about history and historical inquiry, but also to teach and put into practice literacy skills that include reading for meaning, vocabulary development, persuasive writing, and reasoning from evidence.

We do not dispute the need to learn the factual basis of history – the names and contributions of historical actors and the purpose, location, and sequence of key historical events – and the acquisition of such declarative knowledge has been an important component of the instructional units we have developed. We realize that the debate about how to teach history, and which interpretation of history to teach, is a longstanding and sometimes rancorous one (cf. Wineburg, 1996). We will not review the contentions and the merits of various positions here. Rather, as described above, our interest has been in improving students' participation in and knowledge of history as preparation for citizenship, and as a rich domain for promoting problem solving and literacy. The units of instruction we have developed promote history as a problem-solving, interpretative process in which learners are apprenticed into the ways of thinking about and doing history that are consistent with history as a discipline. We view our efforts as focused on the development of students' *historical understanding*, and we will use this phrase throughout the paper to describe the instructional goals we have targeted in our research.

Principles of Teaching for Historical Understanding

The study reported in this chapter was conducted under the auspices of the REACH Institute – a federally funded institute to investigate teaching for understanding in literacy, science, social studies, and mathematics[1]. A major premise of the Institute is that students with disabilities can participate and succeed in complex domains when they engage in instruction that reflects research-based principles of teaching for understanding (Morocco, 2001). Like the other instructional research programs in the Institute, four principles have framed our approach to teaching for historical understanding. First, instruction is built around *authentic tasks* that engage students in constructing knowledge through generative activities such as gathering, organizing, interrogating, interpreting, and synthesizing information to answer questions of historical significance. These tasks entail ideas and ways of knowing that are important to the discipline of history, such as interpreting multiple perspectives and analyzing bias in evidence, and, to the extent possible, use sources and tools that would be used by historians. Tasks are chosen for or linked to problems and issues that have relevance in students' lives.

Second, *social mediation* plays a key role in the classroom as students develop and deepen their understanding of historical events and engage in historical inquiry. Instructional activities include multiple opportunities for students to work with one another in intellectual partnerships to read and interpret historical evidence and create joint projects that demonstrate their understanding of a topic they are investigating. Students bring their own historical, social, and personal perspectives to bear on their inquiries and interpretations, and, in small groups and larger classroom discussions mediated by peers and the teacher, strive to come to shared understandings of the topics they are studying (Morocco, 2001).

Social mediation creates ample opportunities for *constructive conversation*, the third REACH principle of teaching for understanding. Conversation is a central feature of students' historical inquires as they participate in both small group and whole class talk that makes their thinking visible to teachers and peers. Conversation plays a key role in interpreting history; providing students with the opportunity to consider multiple perspectives and to compare, contrast, and negotiate understanding (Morocco, 2001). Conversation provides the teacher with a window on the development of students' understanding and enables her to challenge and deepen their thinking and to promote the discourse and ways of thinking used by historians. Furthermore, conversation is the vehicle through which teachers attend to students' own personal beliefs, interests, and histories. As we will demonstrate later, access to these aspects of students' cognitive and emotional lives enables teachers to make instruction responsive and inclusive

Finally, instruction in domain-specific *cognitive strategies* is embedded in the context of learning about history. Cognitive strategies may be designed to provide students with the tools and ways of inquiry used within a discipline, such as the strategy we have employed to help students analyze and understand the lives of others (discussed below). Or, they may be more generic strategies that assist students in obtaining, analyzing, and communicating information. Literacy-oriented strategies are especially applicable in history as students read and interpret text-based documents and write about or present their findings and conclusions. We embed the explicit teaching of strategies in the context of particular historical tasks for which they can be employed, and we design tasks that elicit their use beyond the context in which they are initially learned. Special education research provides clear documentation that students with mild disabilities can successfully learn and use cognitive strategies, to the benefit of their performance and achievement (e.g. Deshler et al., 2001; Englert, Mariage, Tarrant & Oxer, 1994; MacArthur, Schwartz, Graham, Molloy & Harris, 1996; Palincsar & Brown, 1984; Wong, 1997). However, research also shows that students with disabilities are unlikely to acquire strategies without instruction (e.g. Brown, 1980).

The four principles discussed above are aligned with a social constructivist orientation to teaching and learning (e.g. Palincsar, 1998). They are embodied in the instructional units we have developed and they form a basis for the professional development activities that have accompanied our research program. We acknowledge that some constructivist educators might contend that some of our principles and practices are inconsistent with social constructivism; particularly our focus on cognitive strategies (Prawat & Floden, 1994) and the explicitness with which we teach them (Morocco, 2001). Educators have engaged in vigorous debates about the particulars of constructivist pedagogy, including the role of development versus teaching (Harris & Graham, 1994), the primacy of informal versus disciplinary knowledge (Driver, Asoko, Leach, Mortimer & Scott, 1994), and the degree to which learning is a process of active individual construction versus a process of enculturation into a community of discourse practices (Cobb, 1994). We have employed constructivism as a theory of learning to guide the development and enactment of instruction, rather than as a prescription for the specific means through which understanding is constructed (Bransford, Brown & Cocking, 1999).

Purpose of this Paper

Debate among special educators about the value of and practices associated with constructivist teaching has been no less vigorous and perhaps, at times, even more virulent than the debate in the general education community (cf. Harris & Graham, 1994). Instructional practices espoused by constructivists are at least partially at odds with behaviorally-oriented approaches in special education, in which content is carefully prespecified, sequenced, and delivered via explicit teaching. Behaviorally-oriented models of instruction have been criticized for their mechanistic views of learning, their reliance on decontextualized instruction, and their lack of attention to students' personal interests and cultural backgrounds (Heshusius, 1989, 1991; Poplin, 1985, 1988). However, there is compelling evidence that many students with disabilities benefit from instruction that incorporates pedagogy with the behavioral legacy of explicitness, structure, and sequence (Swanson, Hoskyn & Lee, 1999; Vaughn, Gersten & Chard, 2000). Furthermore, the enterprise of special education is premised on the value of instruction that is tailored to the individual learning and social-emotional needs of students with disabilities. Special educators question the inherent inconsistency in teaching based solely on constructivist practices, a "one size fits all" approach to the education of students with disabilities (Gerber, 1994).

In any case, even the most principled and thoroughly specified program of instruction, regardless of its philosophical underpinnings or educational goals, will be shaped by the local conditions under which it is implemented. Although a literature is emerging to inform our understanding of how constructivist-oriented approaches are enacted in classrooms that serve students with mild disabilities (e.g. Englert, this volume; Ferretti et al., 2001; Morocco, Hindin, Mata-Aguilar & Clark-Chiarelli, 2001; Palincsar, Magnusson, Collins & Cutter, 2001), few of these studies have examined teaching for historical understanding.

The purpose of this chapter is to present a case that illustrates some of the dilemmas that teachers might encounter when teaching for historical understanding through practices consistent with social constructivism. Along with the dilemmas, we highlight the opportunities that all students, including those with disabilities, experienced to extend their understanding and to successfully participate in the classroom community. The teacher in this case, Mrs. L, was an experienced and, by all accounts, effective teacher who ascribed to social constructivist practices. Her experiences, and those of her students, highlight the practical constraints and the cognitive challenges inherent in teaching history as a problem-solving, collaborative, and interpretive process. The manner in which Mrs. L met these challenges, including the teaching practices she adopted, the compromises she made between idealized and actual lesson implementation, and the accommodations she made for individuals and the class, informs us about ways in which teaching for understanding plays out in a diverse urban classroom for students with and without disabilities.

Context of the Study

Mrs. L and Her Classroom

Like the majority of studies we have conducted in our research program, this one occurred in a middle-grade classroom in an urban Northern Delaware school district with a longstanding commitment to the education of students with disabilities in inclusive settings. The district employs a model called Team Approach to Mastery (TAM; Bear & Proctor, 1990) in which students with mild disabilities and those without disabilities are educated in classes taught by both a general and special educator, with part-time assistance from a paraeducator. The recommended ratio of students with and without disabilities in these classrooms is one to three.

The district has mandated specific instructional approaches in literacy, mathematics, and science. Students with disabilities are required, by district policy, to participate in a literacy program that employs a very explicit and sequenced approach to instruction. Other than this mandate, which separates students with and without disabilities for literacy instruction, the ways in which students are grouped and the manner in which teachers' instructional responsibilities are divided are negotiated within each class. In the majority of our project classrooms, science and social studies share a time slot in the daily schedule and are alternated on some systematic basis (e.g. every other marking period). Typically, social studies instruction is planned and implemented almost solely by the teacher who has assumed responsibility for it, and the same is true for science instruction.

The case discussed below is drawn from a study conducted in four 5th grade TAM classes during the 2000–2001 school year. Mrs. L was the general educator, with responsibility for social studies instruction, in the classroom we are about to describe. We met her about five years earlier as she and her teaching partner worked with methods students from the University of Delaware. The teaching practices and behavior management skills we observed in her classroom supported the positive impressions she made on our students. At the outset of the REACH project, Mrs. L and her teaching partner accepted our invitation to become participants, and this study occurred during the third year of their participation.

Ms. L was a veteran teacher, with about 30 years of teaching experience, the bulk of it at the 5th and 6th grade levels. She and her special education co-teacher had been partners in a TAM classroom for over 10 years. Continuing engagement in professional development and leadership activities marked her teaching career. For example, through participation in professional development offerings and systematic reflection on her own mathematics teaching, she had become her school's expert about two inquiry-based mathematics curricula used within the district. She and her co-teacher led a professional development work-shop showing others how to adapt these curricula to meet the needs of students with mild disabilities. Mrs. L. was selected as her school's Teacher of the Year and her students had a higher than average pass rate on statewide tests. As a school leader, she was active on a number of school and district reform commit-tees. Mrs. L viewed her involvement in professional development as an essential part of teaching and reported frustration with colleagues who viewed their responsibilities as limited to interacting with children during mandated school hours.

Other than the differentiated literacy instruction discussed above, students with and without disabilities in Mrs. L's classroom participated together in the same instructional program. Mrs. L taught mathematics and social studies. During these lessons her co-teacher assisted by making accommodations for students with disabilities. Her co-teacher assumed responsibility for inquiry-based science instruction, during which Mrs. L assisted with student discipline, attention to task, and correct use of manipulatives. Social studies occurred every other marking period.

Educating 4th through 6th graders, Mrs. L's school was in an urban neigh-borhood in Delaware's largest city. Students came from neighborhoods surrounding the school and from nearby suburbs. The school housed the district's bilingual program, and thus educated a higher percentage of Hispanic students than other schools in the district. District records showed that 39% of the students were African-American, 41% Caucasian, and 17% Hispanic.

Forty-six percent of the students were eligible for meal subsidies and 7% qualified for special education. During the year in which this study was conducted, slightly over half (53%) of the school's 5th graders met or exceeded state standards in reading, compared to a statewide pass rate of 69%.

Thirty-two students in Mrs. L's class participated in this study. Four of the 32 were identified with a learning disability. All were male, and two were Caucasian. A fifth student had been referred and, by the fourth marking period, had been evaluated and determined eligible for the receipt of special education services. Two other students had been terminated from special education prior to the start of the 2000–2001 school year. Thus, 22% of the students in this class had received special education services over a year's time. Additionally, 5 students received Title I services and 3 attended a program for gifted and talented students. This was a rather low ratio of disabled to nondisabled students for Mrs. L; two years earlier her classroom was composed of 39 students, 19 of whom had disabilities. By the year's end, three additional students with disabilities had joined Mrs. L's classroom.

Other class demographics were as follows. Half the class (50%) was Caucasian and 40% were African-American, with the remaining 10% classified as Hispanic or Asian. Nine students (28%) qualified for free or reduced lunch. Average age was 10 years, 3 months and 47% of the class was male.

Instructional Unit

The instructional unit developed for this study addressed 19th century United States westward expansion, a topic consistent with district and state standards for 5th grade history instruction. The unit focused on the development of students' knowledge about and understanding of the events, people and their motivations, and outcomes associated with westward expansion. We designed the unit to take into account the types of difficulties students with disabilities were likely to experience, including problems reading and interpreting text, difficulties demonstrating knowledge through traditional paper-and-pencil measures, and low motivation.

Substantively, the unit was organized around two themes, or "big ideas," that were taught as analytic strategies to be used in making sense of specific historical events. The first was a *ways of life* strategy, in which students learned to analyze different groups of people by examining their political, economic, religious, and other belief systems. Second, students learned a *migration and conflict* strategy for interpreting events associated with instances of migration, such as that occurring during westward expansion. Building on the ways of life strategy, students learned that aspects of people's ways of life motivate migration and bring them into contact with other groups of people, who often have different ways of life. Conflicts arise, and various outcomes occur as a result of these conflicts.

Students also learned a third strategy, *compare-contrast*, to guide their understanding of similarities and differences between different periods of time, ways of life, and groups of people. Students had opportunities to apply strategies during inquiry projects and in the analysis of video-based information about different groups involved in westward expansion. Mrs. L conducted periodic mini-lessons in which contemporary examples of migration were analyzed using these strategies.

A major goal of the unit was to develop students' understanding of history as a process of interpretation based on the examination of multiple sources of historical evidence. Hence, one set of lessons introduced students to the concept of historical evidence. Students read, viewed, and discussed different examples of primary and secondary sources and considered the advantages and limitations of various categories of evidence. Subsequent lessons addressed the issue of bias in evidence and confronted students with varying video and written interpretations of events occurring during westward expansion. Through extended classroom discussions, students were challenged to examine possible sources of bias and the consequences of basing historical interpretations on biased evidence. In their inquiries, students were continually prompted to provide an accurate interpretation of their topic that took into account various points of view.

Instructional practices were consistent with the REACH principles of teaching for understanding discussed earlier. Students worked in heterogeneous, cooperative groups as they read, viewed, and interpreted historical evidence and completed group inquiry projects. Expertise was distributed within groups and, when reading text, strong readers were partnered with struggling readers in paired reading activities. Groups engaged in two extended inquiry projects during the unit. In the first, students explored life in the 1840s, as a background for understanding how people lived in the U.S. at the start of westward expansion. In the second, each student group investigated either an emigrant or a Native American group that had been affected by westward expansion. With information gained from the two inquiry projects, and from videos presented and discussed in class, students contrasted emigrant and Native American ways of life in order to develop an understanding of sources and outcomes of the conflicts arising during westward expansion. The inquiry projects placed each group in the role of classroom expert about key historical topics and, assuming the role of teacher, each group shared its findings with the class. These collaborative activities were designed to stimulate constructive conversation in which students' questions and interpretations could be addressed and their thinking extended in discussion with other students.

The unit was composed of eight lessons, and was designed to be completed over an eight-week marking period when instruction occurred for about 45 minutes per day on a daily basis. For various reasons discussed below, Mrs. L devoted about 10 weeks to the unit.

Data Collection and Analysis

We collected a variety of measures to evaluate the impact of the unit on students' knowledge, understanding, and attitudes, including multiple-choice knowledge tests, writing samples, individual interviews, attitude scales, and samples of classroom discourse. Two additional data sets informed the construction of the case study presented here. First, we observed and videotaped Mrs. L's class 25 times during the implementation of the unit. Two of the students with disabilities were designated as target students and each observation focused on a target student and his instructional group. Research assistants or the first author recorded notes, during these regularly scheduled observations, that described the nature and duration of each instructional activity, the ways in which the target student and members of his group participated in it, any challenges or difficulties encountered during the activity, and general impressions of students' affective states and of the general classroom climate. Field notes served as a guide to the videotapes. Rather than transcribing and analyzing each videotape, we used the field notes as an index to segments of the video archive that were of particular interest or relevance to the key findings that emerged during our analysis of the field notes.

The second data set consisted of 18 45-minute conversations between Mrs. L and the first author occurring between February and August 2001. The major purpose of these discussions was to gain Mrs. L's perspectives on and insights about teaching for historical understanding in general, and the extent to which the unit had achieved its goals in particular. Segments of videotapes were often used to stimulate recall and to illustrate key activities of interest to Mrs. L and the authors. During these conversations, we also discussed issues related to the development of students' understanding, strengths and limitations of the instructional unit, and the challenges and opportunities that we had observed. Each conversation was audiotaped and transcribed. The field notes and conversation transcripts were analyzed for challenges that arose during the implementation of the unit and evidence of the manner in which Mrs. L addressed these. Emergent findings were discussed with Mrs. L during weekly conversations. Our interpretations of the case study findings were adjusted accordingly and any inaccuracies or misunderstandings were corrected. Mrs. L also reviewed and commented upon a final version of this chapter.

Challenges in Teaching for Historical Understanding in Mrs. L's Class

Our analysis of field notes and the conversations we held with Mrs. L led us to conclude that she confronted two major challenges in implementing the westward expansion unit, in particular, and in teaching for historical understanding, in general. One set of challenges centered on the very practical constraint of the time available to implement the unit and to ensure students' acquisition of instructional goals. The second set of challenges arose from the interaction between students' cognitive and developmental characteristics and the sophisticated demands inherent in development of historical understanding.

Before examining each of these challenges in more detail, it is important to consider further Mrs. L's beliefs about students and teaching. The impact of teachers' beliefs about their students' potential, and teachers' roles in developing that potential, have well-documented effects on instructional practices (Datnow & Castellano, 2000; Stodolsky & Grossman, 2000). Undoubtedly, Mrs. L's beliefs directly affected the manner in which this unit of instruction unfolded in her classroom and the ways in which she responded to its challenges.

Mrs. L's Beliefs about Students and Teaching

As we discussed above, reports of others, our own observations, and external indicators all converged upon Mrs. L's skill and success as a teacher. She held high expectations for herself and for her students and strongly believed that all children can master challenging content. During one interview, she wondered, with a sigh of dismay, why "teachers give up on kids." Noting that many of her children were eligible for free or reduced lunch, she reported that lack of income restricted the educational and enrichment resources available to many families. "So that's the teacher's job, to give them the experiences in a classroom setting that they don't have elsewhere," she concluded.

Mrs. L's philosophies about teaching were aligned with social constructivism and thus the principles and teaching practices in the westward expansion unit were consistent with her own beliefs about teaching. In particular, Mrs. L had a firm belief in the value of inquiry-based activities, in which students worked with physical materials (in mathematics) or historical evidence (in social studies) to construct an understanding of a concept, principle, or event. She did not think social studies textbooks were appropriate for her students, "I don't use a textbook. For a child to look at this book, especially for a child that recognizes he has reading problems, it's intimidating."

As discussed above, she had developed extensive expertise in two inquiry-based mathematics programs used in her district. She attributed her students' successes in meeting state mathematics standards at least in part to what she labeled the "investigative" approach used in her curricula.

> When students do investigative approaches in math or the inquiry lessons in this [westward expansion] unit, for most students, they learn better ... For the most part, in my experience, especially with math, the students learn more and definitely can conceptualize ideas better when they investigate themselves.

When challenged to defend whether or not inquiry-based approaches were appropriate for all students, Mrs. L reported, "There are some who are so completely disorganized in their thinking about everything in general that they need someone else to structure their learning for them, to a degree." She did not see disorganization as a cognitive limitation, or as specific to children with disabilities, but rather as rooted in children's prior experience and developmental maturity. She speculated that some children were used to more structured and explicit approaches, ones in which an adult "does it for them." The challenges these children encountered did not signal the need to provide them with a different instructional approach, but rather the need to better structure and scaffold their participation.

> I would say most of my students who are so disorganized are not mature children and I think it is part of my job to move students beyond that. You have to start somewhere. They need someone to sit down with them and walk them through that process and they can learn from it.

Mrs. L shared the project's beliefs in the value of social mediation and constructive conversation. Students' desks were grouped into clusters of four or five, and groups worked together throughout the day.

> Leaning is social; kids are social. Kids like to play with other kids. They like to talk and laugh. I think I've learned that, if I let them do that in the classroom, then they learn more because they're allowed to be kids, to do what comes naturally ... It makes for a noisy class sometimes, but I think it helps learning.

Mrs. L had clear ideas about the ways in which constructive conversation promoted improved learning in her classroom. She reported that discussions enhanced her own understanding of her students and the way they viewed the world.

> I have found, in class discussions, I have been enlightened by a student's viewpoint; something that I never thought of in that manner, it took a child to help me see a different angle. Listening to kids in the classroom has helped me become a better teacher because I have

learned how to think like children think, so I can anticipate parts of lessons where I think
I need to work more because I don't think the student will understand it.

Similarly, she found that discussions stimulated students' learning by provoking them to examine and defend their opinions and by exposing them to different perspectives:

In my classroom, you're allowed to challenge. You're not allowed to say "you're wrong," but you're allowed to disagree and you're allowed to challenge. Those are words you're allowed to use in my classroom – "I'd like to challenge that." And while you're listening to me challenge what you said, maybe you'll change your perspective; you'll think of something you haven't thought of before.

Social mediation also served important purposes for Mrs. L and her students. She believed that some students, especially those with disabilities, were comfortable working with peers. She noted that sometimes a child could "get through" to another child in ways that she, as an adult, could not. On several occasions, she expressed a firm belief that the distributed expertise and social support inherent in cooperative learning were especially beneficial to students with disabilities.

I think when a child works in a group, the pressure is taken off the child to come up with a product by himself, so when you have four heads working on something and everyone shares the pressure of having to get it done, everyone takes turns. I think you end with a better product and more learning takes place. Because there are those students who do not work well alone, especially children with learning problems. The task can seem too massive to do by one's self and if you have someone to share that with then, yes, you still have to get it done, but it makes the road a little easier to travel . . . . As kids work, they learn that each has something to offer in their own way. You're good at this, and you're good at that . . . .

It was clear, however, that collaboration and tolerance of one another's viewpoints were not left to chance. Mrs. L repeatedly reminded students of her expectations for their participation in shared intellectual endeavors. She told students that all were expected to contribute and did not permit students to opt out of the discussion. On numerous occasions, we heard her bring children into the conversation with comments such as this one, "Jasmine, we haven't heard from you in a while. What do you think?" She expected students to listen and respond positively to each other, often offering encouragement prior to a discussion of challenging or puzzling content, such as the following: "Now remember, no one is going to laugh at anyone's observations. You don't have to agree with someone's observation, but you do not laugh." She described her classroom as a learning community and explained:

My classroom is a place where we all work together, and we know that it's safe to work together. We know that you can be wrong and no one's going to make fun of you because the guidelines have been laid down that we're all different, we all think in different ways. It's OK to be off the beaten track, so to speak. You're able to think more freely, I believe, and not within the constraints of the accepted line of thinking because no one is going to make fun of you .... I liken the learning community to the workplace and I discuss that with the students – this is your workplace for the day. And, while you're not getting paid in money, you're getting paid in education. When you're in the workplace, you need to cooperate with everyone that's there. You don't have to like everybody. I have to say that again and again because kids get very wrapped up in liking and disliking each other and that can interfere with what happens in the classroom. So, you don't have to like me, but you have to work with me.

Mrs. L also put a great deal of thought into the composition of groups. She described how a child's distractibility influenced group selection. She discussed the need to assemble some groups so that one child's tendency to dominate would be offset by peers' assertiveness. For students with disabilities, she found it especially important to assemble a group of tolerant and supportive students.

In summary, Mrs. L had high expectations for her students and positive beliefs about the potential of all, including those students with disabilities. She established and enforced clear norms supporting positive collaboration and constructive conversation. She was well versed in inquiry-based approaches to mathematics and, through her experience and the success of her students, believed that they benefited all learners. However, she also was aware of the range of individual differences in her classroom and was sensitive to needs for scaffolding and encouragement. She did not attribute the need for a more structured experience to disabilities, per se, but rather to developmental and experiential factors that were amenable to instruction. Hence, Mrs. L approached this unit with a positive and optimistic view of teaching and learning. She was no stranger to the principles and practices embodied in the unit, and was disposed to teach in ways that were consistent with social constructivism and with the development of students' historical understanding.

The Challenge of Time

Time is a precious commodity in the classroom. Teachers often lament how much must be accomplished in limited time, and Mrs. L was no exception. The extended discussions and inquiry projects designed to promote the development of students' historical understanding were time-consuming activities. When we asked Mrs. L to comment on the accuracy of time we had allocated to each lesson, she informed us, "I don't like pacing guides. I ignore them. When you're teaching for understanding, I know you have to listen to your kids." Given the difficulties that students encountered in completing lesson activities and understanding major concepts in the unit, which we address next, Mrs. L extended the time allocated to the unit by approximately two weeks and also devoted time during literacy instruction to completing it.

Not only did lessons take longer than expected, but scheduled and unanticipated events cut into the time allocated for social studies instruction. Social studies class regularly began 5 to 10 minutes late due to the time it took students to return from a preceding activity occurring in another part of the building. Rather than usurping time reserved for language arts and mathematics, school assemblies and special programs were disproportionately scheduled during the time allocated to social studies and science.

The attendance records of students with disabilities exacerbated the time pressures experienced by Mrs. L and her students. Both of the target students were frequently absent from school; one missed 40 days over the course of the year for a variety of unverified medical problems. Mrs. L expressed dismay at the instructional time missed by students who needed it most. "Each day we moved forward and when he was out for days at a time, it was difficult to catch up." Group activities and discussion couldn't be replicated for absent students, and, given the limited time available for social studies instruction, Mrs. L found it impossible to help these children make up all they had missed.

Challenges Arising from Students' Developmental Characteristics

Throughout the discussions we held with Mrs. L, she reminded us that she was teaching "10-year-old minds." Her students' cognitive, metacognitive, and social-emotional characteristics were key considerations in her instructional and behavior management practices.

> For a long time I didn't think like a kid. But once I started thinking like a kid, discipline became easier. Because something that would not upset me, but upset a kid, I would react to it as an adult would. But here I've got an upset student and I'm not letting the student know that I feel the student's pain. I, as an adult, am blowing it off because it wouldn't upset me. But a child calls a child stupid – once I start thinking about that as a kid – that really hurts.

Even making the best of their 10-year-old minds, students encountered challenges based on both their level of cognitive development and their relative lack of experience. The concept of time itself posed significant challenges in their understanding of history:

> The fact that they're studying the 1840s, and the idea of what the world would have been like over 150 years ago, is very difficult for them to grasp. The past is the past – it's undifferentiated.

Students' knowledge of distance and geography also limited their understanding of what it might be like to travel 2,000 miles on the Oregon Trail, or to be forced to walk 1,000 miles on the Trail of Tears. As Mrs. L noted, many of her students didn't understand the difference between a city, state, and country. Many had traveled minimally in their short lifetimes, and had little sense of distances or locations. When Mrs. L asked students, during one lesson, to name the river that emigrants followed on the Oregon Trail, they confidently called out "the Mississippi River." Mrs. L took advantage of this response to draw attention to the class map and demonstrate the route one would have to take to reach the west by going south.

To understand issues central to westward expansion, including manifest destiny and the repeated construction and abrogation of treaties with Native American groups, students had to sort through multiple perspectives on and interpretations of an issue or event. As we observed in the classroom, and as noted by Mrs. L, taking the perspective of others was very challenging for 10-year old children. For example, students rejected the idea that members of the starving Donner Party could possibly be desperate enough to resort to cannibalism. And once they knew the disastrous experiences of the Donner Party, they had trouble envisioning how a seductive description of an alternate route to Oregon (Hastings Cutoff), claiming to cut miles and weeks off journey, could have induced the Donner Party to deviate from the main trail. Mrs. L engaged in extensive questioning and prompting to encourage students to consider how the Donner Party members, other emigrants, and Native Americans might have felt about or reacted to events of westward expansion. She often used a physical prompt to attempt to focus the students' attention on a particular perspective. In the middle of a discussion she would gesture placing a hat on her head while telling the students, "OK, now put on your emigrant [or Native American] hat." She later told us, "It may seem juvenile, but it seems to work."

Understanding the perspective of people who are very different than one's self requires more than empathy, however. Students need a rich store of background knowledge about the people, events, and times before they can be expected to see the world through someone else's eyes. One of the primary goals of the unit was to provide students with this knowledge about westward expansion. But even with the rich and detailed information provided in the unit (which, judging by posttest scores, students learned well) it was difficult to overcome the *presentism* that limited students' understanding of the past.

In particular, we observed significant difficulties in the first inquiry activity in which students were asked to investigate different aspects of the way people lived at the start of westward expansion, such as the means by which people traveled and communicated. Students struggled to envision how different daily life must have been. Even when they knew, as judged by statements made during a discussion, that many features of today's world were not available in the mid 1800s, they had difficulty applying this knowledge to build an understanding of how people lived. For example, we observed a classroom discussion in which students showed that they knew the electric light was not invented until around 1880. However, when asked about life in the cities in the 1840s, students described homes with electric light and heat.

Similarly, knowing the date or time period of an invention or event did not ensure students would understand how that invention or event had evolved into its contemporary instantiation. Mrs. L reported that understanding the evolution of transportation systems, such as the railroad, posed significant challenges.

> It's difficult for them to appreciate the fact that building the railroad system started with laying the track, the enormous amount of work and labor involved in this, the dangers of the job. Kids tend to think of the world back then as it is today – you just go out to the station and get on the train. I spent a lot of time with this group and, even then, it was tough to get the kids to see that there were only a few railroad lines, that they were restricted to major cities, that people anywhere in the country couldn't travel on trains wherever they wanted to go.

It is instructive to contrast students' experiences with the two inquiry projects. The first required students to investigate rather abstract categories of information related to aspects of daily life. We provided students with a number of different sources of information to read about these topics; some drawn from books written for children and others from websites. Most of the information was in the form of expository text. We provided a range of materials – from simple to more challenging – to accommodate the different skills of readers in the class.

Although this lesson took about three times longer than we had allotted for it in the unit plan, when the class presented the results of their investigations, it was apparent that some groups had learned practically nothing about their topic. Not one to accept students' lack of understanding, Mrs. L provided them with additional materials about their topics that distilled relevant information into one-or two-page handouts and worksheets addressing a few key concepts.

In contrast, the second inquiry project, in which students investigated one of six groups of emigrant or Native American people, was much more successful. We were able to locate a number of children's books about the groups, some in narrative and some in expository form. Mrs. L reported that the materials were appropriate to students' skills and interests, and students' class presentations demonstrated that they had developed an accurate and comprehensive knowledge base about the group they investigated. It may be the case that students became better at analyzing and interpreting evidence through the practice and instruction occurring between the first and second inquiries. Or, perhaps it was inherently easier for students to understand and organize information about groups of people than about more abstract categories related to ways of life. We will return to the teacher's choice of narrative, as a vehicle for promoting students' understanding, in the next section of this chapter.

In a related observation, students exhibited a strong tendency to personalize their study of westward expansion. They expressed greater interest in those topics that were relevant to their personal interests and chronological ages. For example, when generating questions they'd like to explore about the 1840s, many asked about the daily lives and routines of children. "Students are interested in what life was like for kids in the 1840s, not in generic categories of information such as technology or communication," Mrs. L warned us. Yet, we sometimes observed a curious lack of connection between students' personal lives and their interpretations of historical events. For example, in several discussions of reasons for migration, students from minority religions did not bring up issues of religious freedom, nor did students of color raise issues of discrimination. However, students' personal knowledge and prior experiences did play a role in their willingness to delve into historical information. Several students foreclosed the possibility of learning more about a topic because they had one previous encounter with it. For example, several students had viewed a television version of *Little House on the Prairie*, and thus insisted that they knew enough about life on the farm in the mid-1800s. Or, students who had seen a museum exhibit about a topic believed they were now fully informed and needed to read no more about it.

In summary, the time available for social studies was limited, given that other events often were scheduled during this time and social studies and science were offered only every other marking period. Mrs. L extended unit activities when it was clear that her students did not understand key points or as activities required additional time for completion. She devoted addition time on the unit during language arts. Students were engaged in literacy activities as they developed their knowledge and understanding of westward expansion, and thus Mrs. L believed these arrangements were appropriate. However, students with disabilities participated in differential literacy instruction, and thus missed out on some of the additional time allocated to unit activities. In addition, the frequent absences of some frustrated attempts to ensure their mastery and participation.

The cognitive tools and experiential backgrounds that students had available to them, as 10-year-old learners, also posed challenges to their participation in unit activities and, ultimately, to the development of their historical understanding. Their concepts of time and distance were limited, as was their knowledge of geography. Historical empathy (Ashby & Lee, 1987), or taking the perspective of others who lived in very different circumstances and times, was constrained by students' own cognitive characteristics and by the knowledge they could bring to bear upon the lives of others. Students were most interested in historical issues and events that made some personal connection to their own lives, yet showed some difficulty drawing on their own experiences to enhance historical empathy. Abstract categories of information were more challenging for students to investigate and understand than were narratives about people and their experiences. In the next section, we will examine the ways in which Mrs. L responded to these challenges as she implemented the unit.

Mrs. L's Responds to the Challenges of Teaching Historical Understanding

Mrs. L was acutely aware of the challenges she and her students confronted in the implementation of this unit. She used a variety of teaching practices aimed at capitalizing on students' strengths and interests while supporting and deepening their understanding of westward expansion and of the process of historical inquiry.

Orchestrating Constructive Conversations

As we have reported elsewhere, constructive conversation, designed to build students' understanding, has been a key element of successful history instruction in the diverse classrooms we have studied (Ferretti et al., 2001). Whole-class discussions were frequent occurrences in Mrs. L's class, and they included many elements associated with effective teaching practices. For example, Mrs. L typically opened a discussion with a review of information from previous lessons. She defined key terms and vocabulary and provided a clear goal for the discussion. Earlier, we described the fact that she enforced clear expectations that all would participate and be respectful of one another's opinions. She invited the participation of those who remained on the periphery. Discussions provided Mrs. L with the occasion to monitor student understanding and to immediately clarify misunderstandings. She frequently revoiced students' comments and contributions and then expanded upon them or asked other students to extend the ideas they contained. We observed her to adapt the pace of the discussion, its explicitness, and the examples she used to suit the responses and mood of her class.

As discussed earlier, students seemed to have difficulty applying their personal and school-based knowledge to a concept or issue under consideration. Classroom discussion offered an opportunity for Mrs. L to weave together students' personal interests and experiences and their knowledge of related topics with their developing understanding of a topic under discussion. As we discuss below, her personalization of history heightened students' interest and provided vivid examples of how experiences in their own lives could help them understand history. Through pointed questioning and prompting, she helped students draw on what they knew to synthesize points in a lesson, or topics across the lessons, that otherwise might have remained as inert and isolated knowledge.

Mrs. L rarely asked convergent questions of her students during classroom or individual discussion.

> If you ask them "what life was like – was it hard," they'll say, "yes," and leave it at that. Or they'll say life is hard because you led them to say that. So, I use questions that ask them to describe or compare – terms that ask them what they think.

However, she adapted the type of questions she asked in order to encourage the participation of some of the students with disabilities. She noted that eliciting a response to an open-ended question from some students with attention deficit disorders was "like pulling teeth." To these students, she directed more pointed questions that could be answered in a single word if necessary. She also took great care to make all students feel valued for their contributions, even when they were tangential and did little to advance the discussion.

> I knew some [of the questions students generated] were insignificant, but I wrote them down. I didn't want any student to feel their contribution was unsuccessful. In other situations, I may acknowledge that the student made a contribution by telling them, "I'm, glad you said that, it shows you're thinking."

In order to complete lessons within the time constraints she faced, Mrs. L continually weighed the needs and emerging understanding of her students against the expectations embedded in each lesson and made a series of compromises. The press of time was especially noticeable during whole-class discussions. Each of the two inquiry projects was designed to begin with a class brainstorming session, in which students were to generate questions they'd like to explore about a topic, and then make predictions about what they would find. The question-generation sessions in the 1840s inquiry project extended over four class sessions. Students generated a number of interesting questions, such as "how did people know where they were" and "how did kids get to school." But they also generated less relevant and tangential questions, to which Mrs. L felt compelled to give equal time. Mrs. L attributed the variability in the quality of questions to students' lack of background knowledge. While supporting the practice of student-generated questions, she concluded that the value of this activity did not offset its time-consuming nature. As a consequence, Mrs. L abandoned the question-generation activity in the second inquiry so that more time could be devoted to reading, interpreting, and discussing the topics addressed in that lesson.

Externalizing Supports for Historical Understanding
The cognitive strategies that we built into the unit, such as the ways of life and the compare-contrast strategies, were designed to provide explicit support for the development of students' understanding. In lesson plans accompanying the unit, we provided charts, timelines, and other visual representations of information and strategy components. We intended these materials to provide external and public reminders of the cognitive processes in which students would engage when analyzing and interpreting history.

Mrs. L made frequent use of these external supports. She recorded question-generation and discussion sessions on large paper or on the chalkboard. Charts, maps, lists, and timelines from the unit were posted throughout the room. When students investigated multiple perspectives on an issue or event, Mrs. L found that charts or tables, in which students laid out perspectives, side by side, were valuable. She explained:

> Kids with learning problems have trouble processing, so if you have something to look at, that draws focus to what you're talking about, they can learn better.

About two weeks into the unit, Mrs. L's co-teacher informed us that some of the students with disabilities were having difficulty understanding "how it all fits together." She asked us to create written outlines of each lesson's main ideas, which we subsequently distributed with the lesson materials. Mrs. L recommended that we incorporate more visual representations of information into the unit and had many excellent suggestions for ways to color code and organize these materials to draw students' attention to key ideas and relationships among them in order to "help students think and stay focused."

Personalizing History
As described above, Mrs. L recognized the power of students' interest in exploring history from a personal perspective. Throughout the unit, we found ample evidence of the ways in which she attempted to relate history to students' personal experiences and interests. She often introduced topics by inviting students to share what they knew about a topic or by describing personal experiences related to it. For example, when introducing the concept of viewpoint, she explained to students that they were going to explore this topic by investigating viewpoints about homework. After a collective class groan, she asked students to indicate, with a show of hands, whether they thought teachers should give more or less homework. She then chose a representative from each side of the issue to explain their point of view. These attempts to personalize history seem highly successful and students were eager to contribute to these discussions.

But personalizing history could also be time-consuming and sometimes led to revelations of personal issues that Mrs. L could not afford the time to address. For example, in the first lesson of the unit she invited students to reflect upon the importance of history by asking: "What has happened to you in the past and how does that affect your life today?" This led to a lively discussion, with students eager to contribute stories from their own lives. About 10 minutes into the discussion, Mrs. L called on a student who described a very personal story about the breakup of her family. With other hands raised and stories waiting to be told, Mrs. L felt compelled to move the discussion along to the next topic in the lesson. "I could have spent the whole class on that one question," she later mused.

Privileging Narrative

Throughout the unit, Mrs. L capitalized on students' interest in stories, particularly those describing the experiences of children. "They love stories," Mrs. L reported, and recommended that we replace the compare-contrast writing assignments in the unit with narrative writing, such as creating a diary of what their life might be like in the 1840s. "If you want to see what they've learned about the 1840s, you'll learn much more if you ask them to write narrative," she cautioned us. Although we made frequent use of narrative in the unit activities by incorporating a number of stories and videos to introduce key concepts and as sources for inquiry projects, Mrs. L and her teaching partner extended our efforts. Each teacher incorporated a book about the time and events of westward expansion into their literacy instruction, with accompanying writing assignments related to the story. Mrs. L also brought in a number of different children's books about westward expansion and created a center in the classroom for students to use during free time.

Easing Cognitive Complexity

Making frequent use of narrative appeared to be one way in which Mrs. L reduced the cognitive complexity inherent in understanding key groups and issues associated with westward expansion. We observed a number of other instances in which Mrs. L adapted explanations, vocabulary, questions, and materials to suit the developmental level of her students, or to better accommodate her understanding of the 10-year-old mind.

Although instruction for students with disabilities has been widely criticized for "watered-down" curricula and decontextualized activities (Heshusius, 1989, 1991; Poplin, 1985, 1988), Mrs. L found that, rather than being stimulated and motivated, students could be discouraged and overwhelmed by complex problems.

It's [not just history], it's really across the board. I'm thinking about teaching problem solving in math and lots of times when a student is presented with a problem, and the child perceives it as being a very difficult problem, if I change the numbers in a problem to simple numbers, they know the answer without even using pencil and paper. When I tell them, "that's the same problem, I just took out the difficult numbers, or eliminated a step," then the process becomes clearer to them. The idea of people leaving their homeland and coming to the U.S., and the conflict that resulted, or to try and justify their reasons for coming here, that is abstract for them [the students] because of the difficulty that children of this level have with identifying with these issues. It's the same thing as with math that I was just describing. You give them a situation they can identify with, make it simple; a close-to-home problem, like you're being bullied in your neighborhood so your family decides to move. Then it starts to click with them.

On several occasions, Mrs. L commented on abstractness of the language we used in the ways of life strategy. Although we incorporated terms consistent with middle-grade social studies curricula and standards, such as politics and economy, Mrs. L always paired these terms with more "kid-friendly" language when discussing them in class. "I'd say "economy, or money and jobs, adding more student-friendly terms when I talked about these concepts." It's important to note, however, that Mrs. L did promote discourse associated with history and historical inquiry throughout the unit. For example, we observed her reminding students that they were not talking about "stuff," but about evidence and prompting students to give the proper label to a piece of evidence (e.g. diary, primary source).

Mrs. L made adjustments in a lesson designed to help students understand differences between primary and secondary sources, a key concept in the Delaware 5th grade social studies standards. The unit offered a definition that differentiated primary sources by the time of their creation (during or after the fact) and the relationship of the author to the event (having first-hand or second-hand knowledge). We attempted to illustrate that both primary and secondary sources could be biased. However, Mrs. L found that our treatment of primary and secondary sources was too complex.

What I found with some of my lower achieving students and some special education students, too, is that this needs to be put into simpler terms. So, I said, "the person was there for a primary source and, for the secondary source, the person was not there at the event being discussed." We used some common childhood experience [to introduce the source], a birthday party, I think, and they identified with that. I presented a situation in which you wanted to write your grandmother who lived far away and couldn't come, to tell her what the birthday party was like. I asked them, "who would know better – you or somebody down the street who didn't come but heard about it?" They all said, "well, I could tell my grandmother about it because I was there and I know what happened."

We pointed out to Mrs. L that this explanation might lead students to the inadvertent conclusion that primary sources are more accurate than secondary sources, thus ignoring the fact that primary sources also are subject to bias. She agreed with this observation, adding:

> But I thought it was better that the kids understand this [the relationship of the author to the event being described]. I'm hoping that 7th and 8th grade teachers revisit this and you can get into the subtle points of bias and primary sources. I think, the first time hearing it, you almost have to make it black and white for the kids to understand it.

CONCLUSIONS

In this chapter, we have featured the experience of one teacher as she led a classroom of learners with and without disabilities toward the development of historical understanding. The unit she implements, which was developed by the authors, embodies practices that are consistent with social constructivism, in general, and that are designed to promote history as an interpretative and analytic process of inquiry. Mrs. L's professional dispositions and beliefs, and her previous experiences and teaching practices, seem highly consistent with the goals and teaching practices embedded in this unit. Thus, she seems to provide us with an informative example of how teaching for understanding unfolds in a diverse, 5th grade classroom, and how instruction is shaped by institutional constraints and students' characteristics and responses.

It is important to reiterate that Mrs. L seemed to be a highly successful teacher. In addition to her qualifications, experiences, and honors, discussed earlier in this chapter, her students made statistically significant gains on the knowledge and understanding measures used to assess outcomes in this study. Her classroom included a higher percentage of students with disabilities than the school at large, but, otherwise, the demographic profile of her classroom was comparable to the school as a whole. Yet, pass rates on the 5th grade state test, administered in the spring of 2001, were substantially higher in Mrs. L's class than in other 5th grade classrooms in this school. The percentage of 5th graders passing or exceeding state standards at Mrs. L's school were 53% in reading, 51% in mathematics, and 41% in writing. Pass rates in Mrs. L's class were 66% in reading, 86% in mathematics, and 75% in writing. Thus, at least as measured by statewide tests, her students were fortunate to be in her classroom.

The challenges encountered by Mrs. L's students as they engaged in historical inquiry and grappled with key concepts of westward expansion have been documented by other researchers and educational reformers. The limitations of students' (and adults') knowledge of geography and history have been the subject of criticism and derision from a variety of camps, ranging from E. D. Hirsh (1987) to the Tonight Show's Jay Leno. Developmental psychologists (e.g. Flavell, 1985; Piaget, 1969, 1970), cognitive scientists (e.g. Anderson, 1981; Bransford, 1979; Brown, Bransford, Ferrara & Campione, 1983; Wineburg & Fournier, 1997), and history educators (e.g. Barton & Levstik, 1996; Brophy, 1990; Lee & Ashby, 2000; Wineburg, 1991) have studied the developmental nature of children's concepts of time and location, their abilities to take the perspective of others, and their skill in applying personal and school-based knowledge to novel situations and problems. Mrs. L's observations about students' needs and characteristics, their approach to learning history, and the challenges they encountered were quite consonant with the findings of these literatures.

What is most significant about Mrs. L's case is not that the development of historical understanding is a tough task, or that student characteristics shaped what and how they learned, but the ways in which Mrs. L adapted the task of teaching for understanding to accommodate her students' 10-year-old minds. Mrs. L did not view students' cognitive, metacognitive, and social-emotional development as placing upper limits on students' historical understanding and inquiry, but rather adjusted the unit we developed, and her teaching practices, to make the most of students' interests and capabilities.

Discussion, or what we have defined as constructive conversation, was a central feature in shaping students' understanding throughout the unit. Mrs. L's efforts to personalize history drew students into the conversation, maintained their interest, and enabled them to draw upon their own knowledge and experiences. Clearly established and consistently enforced expectations for class discussions and other collaborative intellectual ventures offered a safe environment in which all students, including those with disabilities, felt welcome to participate. Questioning, prompting, and physical gestures to elicit perspective-taking scaffolded students' efforts to make sense of multiple perspectives and to coordinate various sources of knowledge and information.

Mrs. L's experience had taught her that effective cognitive apprenticeship requires teachers to make thinking explicit (Bain, 2000). Mrs. L valued and made effective use of the ways of life, migration and conflict, and compare-contrast strategies. Together, she and her students created and employed visual and graphic representations to record, organize, and externalize historical thinking processes, such as question generation and comparisons of different point of view.

On several occasions, Mrs. L felt compelled to reduce the complexity of goals and activities that we had envisioned for the unit. The adaptations she made were in response to her students' difficulties in dealing with abstract vocabulary and categories of information and in making sense of expository text. Social constructivist educators might have been alarmed by the revelation that, in one activity, Mrs. L brought in worksheets and one-page handouts to help her students better understand the features of mid-19th century transportation and communication systems. We have a different view on the eclecticism we observed in Mrs. L's teaching, however. There is no "pure" version of social constructivist teaching, or of teaching for understanding. Rather, as an educator committed to teaching for understanding, Mrs. L incrementally increased the structure and explicitness of teaching practices and instructional materials to bridge the gaps between her students' knowledge and cognitive abilities and the cognitive demands of the curriculum. Mrs. L's flexibility seems an essential element in the student-centered and pedagogically responsive teaching that characterizes social constructivism.

One highly practical but important observation from Mrs. L's classroom is that engaging in historical inquiry and developing rich historical understanding of a topic takes time. The social studies were not an instructional priority in Mrs. L's district. The shared time slot for science and social studies was a common occurrence in other classrooms that had participated in our project, and thus was not unique to Mrs. L's school. It's worth noting that, in the year this study was conducted, the district was administering its first round of statewide assessments in social studies. Although scores were to be reported publicly, there were no contingencies attached to the performance of students, classrooms, and schools, as was the case with reading and mathematics.

The challenge of time is significant to consider as Mrs. L's district, and others, seek to attach consequences to the mastery of complex historical knowledge and understanding. Some educators have branded standards-based instruction as overly ambitious and elitist; as a reform movement likely to benefit only the advantaged and talented (e.g. Hofmeister, 1993). As an educator in a diverse urban school, Mrs. L clearly disagreed with such a perspective. Her beliefs, and the performance of her students, provide a compelling demonstration of the opportunities inherent in teaching for understanding and the potential of all students to attain high standards. However, as Mrs. L noted, in the westward expansion unit students were often making a first pass at some sophisticated vocabulary, concepts, and processes. Unless educators make a serious commitment to allocating the time needed to develop students' historical understanding, and provide multiple opportunities over time for engaging in the analytic and interpretative processes of historical inquiry, we will be hard pressed to achieve these goals.

In conclusion, we revisit the six questions about social constructivist teaching that frame this volume. The first two questions, *what does social constructivist teaching mean in teaching for historical understanding* and *what is the rationale for using these methods, and what forms do they take,* relate to features of our units of instruction and the rationale for their inclusion. We have attempted to design units that accomplish two goals: (a) they promote history as an inquiry-based, analytic, and interpretive process, and (b) they are accessible to students with a variety of learning and behavioral characteristics. Key instructional features of these units are student engagement in basic forms of inquiry used by historians (authentic tasks), social interaction among students in the construction of historical knowledge and understanding (social mediation), constructive conversation among peers and between teachers and students, and instruction in domain-specific and more general cognitive strategies. Our rationale for these methods is rooted in our beliefs about the appropriate focus of history instruction and builds upon extant research about instructional approaches that have been effective in teaching and learning for understanding with diverse learners.The third question asks us to consider the *strengths and applicability of the teaching methods and their weaknesses and areas of irrelevance or limited applicability.* Our data support the contention that the approaches we have used help diverse groups of learners (including those with disabilities) acquire historical knowledge, develop historical understanding, and improve their attitudes and self-efficacy (cf. Ferretti et al., 2001; MacArthur et al., in press; Okolo & Ferretti, 2000). As we discussed earlier, specific features of these units may offer unique benefits to students with disabilities. As Mrs. L reported, group work distributed expertise, provided social and academic support, and took the pressure off individuals with disabilities. Constructive conversations offered opportunities to assess and extend students' developing understanding and address alternative conceptions and inaccuracies on the spot. Through these conversations, Mrs. L invited and reinforced the participation of reluctant contributors and built a supportive intellectual climate.

The instructional methods employed in these instructional units also introduced significant and sometimes unanticipated challenges, which speak to limitations in the approaches we employed. Logistical challenges included the need to find substantial chunks of time to complete unit activities and the dilemmas of managing classroom discussions, particularly when students were encouraged to contribute individual reflections and personal experiences. Perhaps the greatest challenge encountered by Mrs. L and our other project teachers, however, relates to the difficulty of cultivating historical understanding in ten-year-old minds – minds that are constrained by limited knowledge of and experience with key constructs that support historical understanding.

Mrs. L's responses to these challenges address another framing question for this volume: *when, how, and why these methods need to be adjusted from their usual form.* We discussed a variety of adaptations made by Mrs. L in response to her students' cognitive and social/emotional characteristics, and showed that some of these involved the provision of more structure, the simplification of key vocabulary and concepts, and a reduction in student-centered discussion. On a continuum anchored by social constructivism on one end, many of Mrs. L's adaptations moved instruction toward the opposite, or teacher-directed end of the scale.

Mrs. L's adaptations in favor of more teacher-directed instruction raise issues related to the fourth question addressed in this volume, *when, where, and how are social constructivist methods used optimally?* As we described above, social constructivist approaches probably have a higher chance of success when they are consistent with a teacher's attitudes and beliefs about teaching, learning, and student competence. Despite her professed beliefs about the value of social constructivist teaching, Mrs. L deviated from what many might consider its core principles. However, her judgments about the need to vary approaches were always in response to practical constraints, student needs, and emerging understandings. Thus, we conclude that social constructivist methods are optimal when they're used flexibly and are adjusted to meet characteristics of the classroom and its inhabitants. The imposition of more structure and direction may be needed when content is particularly challenging and when students have little background knowledge. Furthermore, not all students are equally prepared to productively participate in the types of activities at the heart of social constructivist teaching, including peer collaboration and classroom discourse. Some students, including those with disabilities, may need instruction and guidance in order to fully partake of these instructional opportunities. Finally, historical inquiry was not a common occurrence in the lives of the students who participated in this study. Time was limited, and the social studies were addressed during only about half the school year.

With repeated experience in features of instruction such as collaborative inquiry and classroom discourse, students may develop skills that enable the teacher to shift the balance of instruction toward more open-ended and student-directed approaches and to teach in ways that are more consistently aligned with social constructivism. Thus, the nature of instruction, and the compromises made by Mrs. L in this particular study, may represent one point along an evolving continuum of social constructivist teaching in her classroom and with these particular students.

Finally, the sixth question asks us to consider *when and why social constructivist methods are irrelevant or counterproductive.* We're reluctant to make strong claims in response to this question; it is not an issue that we have explored in a systematic manner in this study or others. We can offer the observation that, in some of our studies, students have shown few gains when classroom organization and management are not well developed. Frequent behavioral disruptions, widespread dissent among student groups, and poor use of instructional time have turned inquiry activities and discussions into chaotic and frustrating events (Okolo & Ferretti, 1996b). Teacher content knowledge also can constrain student learning in the more open-ended and student-centered inquiries and discussions that characterize our approach to teaching history. In these situations, teachers' knowledge about and understanding of topics are critical to the provision or resources for inquiry and for the stimulation and support of rich and motivating discussions (Okolo & Ferretti, 2000). We view these issues as ones that must be addressed in the context of staff development and coaching that supports teaching for historical understanding.

NOTE

1. The research reported in this paper was supported by Grant No. H180E30043 and Grant No. H023V70008 from the U.S. Department of Education, Office of Special Education Programs, and by a Dwight D. Eisenhower Professional Development State Grant (No 84.281B).

ACKNOWLEDGMENTS

We gratefully acknowledge Mrs. L's contributions to this paper and to other studies and curriculum development efforts of the REACH project.

REFERENCES

Anderson, J. R. (1981). *Cognitive skills and their development*. Hillsdale, NJ: Erlbaum.
Ashby, M. G., & Lee, P. (1987). Children's concepts of empathy and understanding in history. In: C. Portal (Ed.), *The History Curriculum for Teachers* (pp. 62–88). London: Falmer Press.
Bain, R. B. (2000). Into the breach: Using research and theory to shape history instruction. In: P. N Stearns, P. Seixas & S. Wineburg (Ed.), *Knowing, Teaching, and Learning History* (pp. 331–352). New York: New York University Press.
Barton, K. C., & Levstik, L. S. (1996). "Back when god was around and everything": Elementary children's understanding of historical time. *American Educational Research Journal, 33*(2), 419–454.
Bear, G. G., & Proctor, W. A. (1990). Impact of a full-time integrated program on the achievement of nonhandicapped and mildly handicapped children. *Exceptionality, 1*, 227–238.
Bransford, J. D. (1979). *Human cognition: Learning, understanding, and remembering*. Belmont, CA: Wadworth.
Bransford, J. D., Brown, A. L., & Cocking, R. R. (1999). *How people learn. Brain, mind, experience, and school*. Washington, D.C.: National Academy Press.
Bransford, J. D., & Stein, B. S. (1984). *The IDEAL problem solver*. New York: W. H. Freeman.
Brophy, J. (1990). Teaching social studies for understanding and higher-order applications. *The Elementary School Journal, 90*, 351–417.

Brown, A. L. (1980). Metacognitive development in reading. In: R. Sprio, B. C. Bruce & W. F. Brewer (Eds), *Theoretical Issues in Reading Comprehension. Perspectives from Cognitive Psychology, Linguistics, Artificial Intelligence, and Education* (pp. 453–481). Hillsdale, NJ: Lawrence Erlbaum.

Brown, A. L., Bransford, J. D., Ferrara, R. A., & Campione, J. C. (1983). Learning, remembering, and understanding. In: J. H. Flavell & E. M. Markman (Eds), *Handbook of Child Psychology: Vol. 3, Cognitive Development* (pp. 789–166). New York: Wiley.

Cobb, P. (1994). Constructivism in mathematics and science education. *Educational Researcher, 23*(7), 4.

Curtis, C. K. (1991). Social studies for students at-risk and with disabilities. In: J. P. Shaver (Ed.), *Handbook of Research on Teaching and Learning* (pp. 157–174). New York: Macmillan.

Datnow, A., & Castellano, M. (2000). Teachers' responses to Success for All: How beliefs, experiences, and adaptations shape implementation. *American Educational Research Journal, 37*(3), 775–799.

Deschenes, S., Cuban, L., & Tyack, D. (2001). Mismatch: Historical perspectives on schools and students who don't fit them. *Teachers College Record, 103*(4), 525–547.

Deshler, D., Schumaker, J. B., Lenz, K. B., Bulgren, J. A., Hock, M. F., Knight, J., & Ehren, B. J. (2001). Ensuring content-area learning by secondary students with learning disabilities. *Learning Disabilities Research and Practice, 16*(2), 96–108.

Destafano, L., Shriner, J. G., & Lloyd, C. A. (2001). Teacher decision making in participation of students with disabilities in large-scale assessment. *Exceptional Children, 68*(1), 7–22.

Driver, R., Asoko, H., Leach, J., Mortimer, E., & Scott, P. (1994). Constructing scientific knowledge in the classroom. *Educational Researcher, 23*(7), 5–12.

Englert, C. S., Mariage, T., Tarrant, D, & Oxer, T. (1994). Developing a school-based discourse for literacy learning: A principled search for understanding. *Learning Disability Quarterly, 17* (1), 2–32.

Erickson, R. N., Ysseldyke, J. E., Thurlow, M. L., & Elliott, J. L. (1998). Inclusive assessment and accountability systems: Tools of the trade in educational reform. *Teaching Exceptional Children, 31*(2), 4–9.

Ferretti, R. P., MacArthur, C. A., & Okolo, C. M. (2001). Teaching for historical understanding in inclusive classrooms. *Learning Disability Quarterly, 24*, 59–71.

Ferretti, R. P., & Okolo, C. M. (1996). Authenticity in learning: Multimedia design projects in social studies for students with disabilities. *Journal of Learning Disabilities, 29*, 450–460. (Reprinted in K. Higgins & R. Boone (Eds) (1997). *Technology for Students with Learning Disabilities* (pp. 131–146)). Austin, TX: Pro-Ed.

Flavell, J. H. (1985). *Cognitive development*. Englewood Cliffs, NJ: Prentice Hall.

Gerber, M. M. (1994). Postmodernism in special eduation. *The Journal of Special Education, 28*(3), 368–378.

Harris, K. R., & Graham, S. (1994). Constructivism: Principles, paradigms, and intergration. *The Journal of Special Education, 28*, 233–247.

Heshusius, L. (1989). The Newtonian-mechanistic paradigm, special education, and contours of alternatives: An overview. *Journal of Learning Disabilties, 22*, 403–415.

Heshusius, L. (1991). Curriculum-based assessment and direct instruction: Critical reflections on fundamental assumptions. *Exceptional Children, 57*, 315–329.

Hirsch, E. D. (1987). *Cultural literacy: What every American needs to know*. Boston: Houghton Mifflin.

Hofmeister, A. M. (1993). Elitism and reform in school mathematics. *Remedial and Special Education, 14*(6), 8–13.

330   C. M. OKOLO, R. P. FERRETTI AND C. A. MACARTHUR

Judd, C. H. (1915). *The psychology of high school subjects*. Boston: Ginn.

Kuhn, D. (1991). *The skills of argument*. Cambridge: Cambridge University Press.

Kuhn, D. (1999). A developmental model of critical thinking. *Educational Researcher, 28*(2), 16–25, 46.

Lee, P., & Ashby, R. (2000). Progression in historical understanding among students ages 7–14. In: P. N. Stearns, P. Sexias & S. Wineburg (Eds), *Knowing, Teaching and Learning History. National and International Perspectives* (pp. 199–222). New York: New York University Press.

MacArthur, C. D., Ferretti, R. P., & Okolo, C. M. (in press). On defending controversial viewpoints: Debates of sixth-graders about the desirability of early 20th century American immigration. *Learning Disabilities Research and Practice*.

MacArthur, C. A., Schwartz, S., & Graham, S., Molloy, D., & Harris, K. (1996). Integration of strategy instruction into a whole language classroom: A case study. *Learning Disabilities Research and Practice, 11*, 168–176.

McDonnell, L. M., McLaughlin, M. J., & Morison, P. (1997). *Educating one and all. Students with disabilities and standards-based reform*. Washington, D.C.: National Academy Press.

McLeskey, J., Henry, D., & Axelrod, M. I. (1999). Inclusion of sudents with learning disabilities: An examination of data from reports to Congress. *Exceptional Children, 66*(1), 55–66.

Morocco, C. C. (2001). Teaching for understanding with students with disabilities: New directions for research on access to the general education curriculum. *Learning Disability Quarterly, 24*, 5–13.

Morocco, C. C., Hindin, A., Mata-Aguilar, C., & Clark-Chiarelli, N. (2001). Building a deep understanding of literature with middle-grade students with learning disabilities. *Learning Disability Quarterly, 24*, 47–58.

National Council for the Social Studies (1994). *Curriculum standards for social studies*. Washington, D.C.: Author.

National Commission on Social Studies in the Schools. (1989). *Charting a course: Social studies for the 21st Century*. Washington, D.C.: National Commission on the Social Studies in the Schools.

Newmann, F. M. (1990). Higher order thinking in teaching social studies: A rationale for the assessment of classroom thoughtfulness. *Journal of Curriculum Studies, 22*, 41–56.

Office of Special Education Programs, United States Department of Education (2001). *Record of the expert strategy panel on students with disabilities access to, participation in, and progress in the general education curriculum*. Washington, D.C.: Author.

Okolo, C. M., & Ferretti, R. P. (1996a). Knowledge acquisition and multimedia design in the social studies for children with learning disabilities. *Journal of Special Education Technology, 13*(2), 91–103.

Okolo C. M., & Ferretti, R. P. (1996b). The impact of multimedia design projects on the knowledge, attitudes, and collaboration of students in inclusive classrooms. *Journal of Computing in Childhood Education, 7*, 223–252.

Okolo, C. M., & Ferretti, R. P. (2000). Preparing future citizens: Technology-supported project-based learning in the social studies. In: J. Woodward & L. Cuban (Eds), *Technology, Curriculum, and Professional Development: Adapting Schools to Meet the Needs of Students with Disabilities* (pp. 47–60). Thousand Oaks, CA: Corwin Press.

Palincsar, A. (1998). Social constructivist perspectives on teaching and learning. *Annual Reivew of Psychology, 49*, 345–375.

Palinscar, A. S., & Brown, A. (1984). Reciprocal teaching of comprehension-fostering and comprehension-monitoring activities. *Cognition and Instruction, 1*(2), 117–175.

Palincscar, A. S., Magnusson, S. J., Collins, K. M., & Cutter, J. (2001). Making science accessible to all: Results of a design experiment in inclusive classrooms. *Learning Disability Quarterly, 24*, 15–32.

Patton, J. R., Polloway, E. A., & Cronin, M. E. (1987). Social studies instruction for handicapped students: A review of current practices. *The Social Studies, 78*(3), 131–135.

Piaget, J. (1969). *The child's conception of the world.* Totowa, N. J., Littlefield, Adams & Company.

Piaget, J. (1970). *The child's conception of time.* New York, Basic Books.

Poplin, M. S. (1985). Reduction from the medical model to the classroom: The past, present, and future of learning disabilties. *Research Communications in Psychology, Psychiatry and Behavior, 10*, 37–70.

Poplin, M. S. (1988). The reductionist fallacy in learning disabilities: Replicating the past by reducing the present. *Journal of Learning Disabilties, 21*, 389–400.

Prawat, R. S., & Floden, R. E. (1994). Philosophical perspectives on constructivist views of learning. *Educational Psychologist, 29*(1), 37–48.

Simon, H. A. (1980). Problem solving in education. In: D. T. Tuma & R. Reif (Eds), *Problem Solving and Education: Issues in Teaching and Research* (pp. 81–96). Hillsdale, NJ: Erlbaum.

Stodolsky, S. S., & Grossman, P. L. (2000). Changing students, changing teaching. *Teachers College Record, 102*(1), 125–172.

Swanson, H. L., Hoskyn, M., & Lee, C. (1999). *Interventions for students with learning disabilities. A meta-analysis of treatment outcomes.* New York: The Guilford Press.

Toulmin, S. E. (1958). *The uses of argument.* Cambridge: Cambridge University Press. Toulmin, 1958

United States Department of Education (2000) *Twenty-Second Annual Report to Congress on the Implementation of the Individuals with Disabilities Act.* Washington, D.C.: Author.

Vaughn, S., Gersten, R., & Chard, D. J. (2000). The underlying message in LD intervention research: Findings from research syntheses. *Exceptional Children, 67*(1), 99–114.

Wineburg, S. S. (1991). Historical problem solving: A study of the cognitive processes used in the evaluation of documentary and pictorial evidence. *Journal of Educational Psychology, 83*(1), 73–87.

Wineburg, S. S. (1996). The psychology of learning and teaching history. In: D. C. B. R. Calfee (Ed.), *The Handbook of Educational Psychology* (pp. 423–437). New York: Macmillan.

Wineburg, S. (2001). *Historical thinking and other unnatural acts.* Philadelphia, PA: Temple University Press.

Wineburg, S., & Fournier, J. E. (1997). Picturing the past: Gender differences in the depiction of historical figures. *American Journal of Education, 105*(2), 160–185.

Wong, B. (1997). Research on genre-specific strategies for enhancing writing in adolescents with learning disabilities. *Learning Disability Quarterly, 20*(2), 140–159.

Yell, M. L., & Shriner, J. G. (1997). The IDEA amendments of 1997: Implications for special and general education teachers, administrators, and teacher trainers. *Focus on Exceptional Children, 30*(1), 1–20.

DISCUSSION

Jere Brophy

In this concluding chapter, I attempt to both synthesize and compare and contrast what the contributing authors have had to say in Chapters 1–8. I begin by characterizing the chapters along several dimensions, then turn to some of the issues raised and their potential implications for research and practice, and then consider some of the unique contributions of each chapter.

DIMENSIONS FOR COMPARISON

All of the authors rooted their teaching principles in either sociocultural theory or the notion of a disciplined-based learning community (or both). Several also emphasized the activity of inquiry, either in the general Deweyian sense (Wells), or in the context of the knowledge construction processes featured in the disciplines of mathematics (Schoenfeld; Chazan & Schnepp), science (Roth), or history (VanSledright & James; Okolo, Ferretti & MacArthur). In addition, Nuthall combined sociocultural theory with ideas drawn from research on information processing and memory; Roth combined it with ideas drawn from work on conceptual change teaching; and both Roth and Englert and Dunsmore added emphasis on the concept of cognitive apprenticeship. All of the authors spoke of relatively specific and goal-oriented discourse genres, not merely "discussion" as a generic instructional method.

A broad range of subjects and grade levels was included. Wells presented a general model of inquiry teaching and illustrated it with excerpts drawn from several subjects and grade levels. Nuthall and Schoenfeld also wrote at relatively general levels, the former illustrating with material from middle school science and social studies teaching and the latter with material from

Social Constructivist Teaching, Volume 9, pages 333–358.
Copyright © 2002 by Elsevier Science Ltd.
All rights of reproduction in any form reserved.
ISBN: 0-7623-0873-7

elementary mathematics teaching, high school mathematics/physics teaching, and college mathematics teaching. The remaining chapters were couched more specifically within grade level and subject-matter contexts: early elementary literacy/writing (Englert & Dunsmore), high school mathematics (Chazan & Schnepp), middle school science (Roth), middle school history (VanSledright & James); and elementary school history (Okolo, Ferretti & MacArthur).

All authors discussed both a general instruction model and some of the specific tactics that would be used in implementing it. Wells and Chazan and Schnepp placed relatively more emphasis on the general model whereas Nuthall and Schoenfeld placed relatively more emphasis on the specific tactics.

All of the authors also considered both discourse and activities/tasks. Most placed relatively more emphasis on discourse, although Wells and Okolo, Ferretti, and MacArthur placed at least as much emphasis on activities/tasks.

Four of the chapters placed most of their emphasis on discourse within the whole-class context, but all of them considered small-group contexts along with the whole-class context, and four also considered the activities of individuals working on their own. For Nuthall and for Englert and Dunsmore, social constructivist teaching occurs more in the small-group setting than the whole-class setting.

Other chapter comparisons include the following. Wells, Nuthall, and Englert and Dunsmore most strongly, and Schoenfeld and Chazan and Schnepp least strongly, based their instructional principles on assumptions drawn from explicitly sociocultural theories of learning. The latter chapters were based on more general social constructivist ideas, especially the notion of discipline-based learning communities. All of the chapters spoke to some extent about social-izing students into discipline-based discourse genres, although Wells and Nuthall placed less emphasis on this idea (probably because they described generic rather than discipline-specific instructional models).

All of the authors except for Englert and Dunsmore emphasized the notion of inquiry, with Wells and Okolo, Ferretti, and MacArthur placing special emphasis on it. The absence of emphasis on inquiry in Englert and Dunsmore's chapter may be due to the fact that their chapter focused on the earliest grade levels. Also, the notion of inquiry doesn't fit as well within a language arts/writing context as it does within the other subject-matter contexts represented in the volume, although it could be argued that some of the literature analysis and appreciation activities that occur in the literacy context are parallel to some of the inquiry activities that occur in other subject-matter contexts.

All of the authors emphasized establishing a learning community in the classroom, with Wells, Schoenfeld, Chazan and Schnepp, and Roth giving this idea particular emphasis. Wells, Nuthall, Chazan and Schnepp, and Roth all stressed that it takes considerable time to socialize students to learning community norms. These authors contrasted, however, in the degree to which they expressed confidence that students would acquire these norms and begin to display them consistently, even when working independently. Wells was the most optimistic in this regard, arguing that students would eventually spend much of their time working independently of the teacher (usually in small groups rather than on their own), thus simplifying classroom management demands on teachers and freeing them to circulate and spend most of their time monitoring and scaffolding students' inquiry activities. Nuthall and Roth, in contrast, expressed low confidence in students' potential for working at length independently, and discussed the need for relatively simple tasks, continuous monitoring, and clear accountability mechanisms.

All of the authors talked about teaching within discipline-based subject-matter contexts. Englert and Dunsmore (literacy), Schoenfeld (mathematics), and Chazan and Schnepp (mathematics) were the most clearly focused on disciplinary discourse genres, tools, and activities. Other authors enlarged on their disciplinary bases in varying degrees, with VanSledright and James being notable both for couching history teaching goals within broader social studies goals and for talking about integrating instruction to address not only history goals but language arts and critical thinking goals.

Finally, the authors tended to say more about goals (usually emphasizing dispositional goals over more specific knowledge and skill goals) than about the assessment of students' attainment of corresponding outcomes. However, both Nuthall and Roth not only assessed student outcomes but also adjusted their developing instructional models in the light of these outcome data. Okolo, Ferretti, and MacArthur also collected outcome data, but the remaining authors did not. Englert and Dunsmore did consider process data (e.g. whether or not students who asked questions got the explanations they needed when working in small groups), and more generally, stressed the need to constantly assess what students are thinking. Schoenfeld emphasized that assessment is important and cited studies of reform mathematics programs that included outcome data, but did not include such data in discussing his own work or that of Ball or Minstrell. I find it worth noting that the authors who made the most use of outcome data (Nuthall and Roth) were the least optimistic about the overall feasibility and effectiveness of social constructivist approaches to teaching, especially approaches that call for the students to function independently much of the time.

The chapters by Wells and by Nuthall were placed first in the volume partly because they (along with Schoenfeld's chapter) discussed relatively generic aspects of social constructivist teaching that cut across subjects and grade levels, but also because they set a tone for the volume by illustrating both most of the commonalities and most of the differences along the dimensions just described. Wells's chapter is clearly the most optimistic, and Nuthall's chapter is arguably the most pessimistic, in the beliefs expressed about the feasibility of establishing classroom learning communities in which students carry major responsibilities for establishing and carrying out knowledge construction agendas, working largely independently of the teacher much of the time. Yet their depictions of social constructivist learning settings and activities overlapped considerably, being rooted in the same basic version of sociocultural theory (although Wells included a strong emphasis on inquiry as well). Despite this shared vision, Wells described a glass mostly full (challenging but feasible for successful implementation by teachers with the right philosophy and the knowledge needed to select suitable learning activities and scaffold students' engagement in them effectively), but Nuthall described a glass mostly empty (time consuming and difficult to implement, and even then, feasible mostly only in small groups and with close teacher monitoring and frequent intervention).

The remaining chapters fell in between Wells and Nuthall on the optimism/pessimism dimension. They tended to depict subject-matter learning as acculturation into disciplinary or discipline-based learning communities, in which students acquire the discourse genres and learn to use the tools developed by the communities as they participate in authentic knowledge construction activities. They characterized the discipline or subject matter in ways that featured both content and process goals, couched within broader dispositional goals involving acquiring discourse genres and other knowledge generation tools and applying them in appropriate contexts in and out of school. These goals typically were rooted in discipline-based ideas about epistemology (e.g. mathematics as making meaning and acquiring skills that will be used in real-world applications). Commitments to such goals provided a rationale for emphasizing depth of development of key ideas over breadth of content coverage, as well as for emphasizing overall dispositions over specific content (and sometimes, even specific skills). Establishing learning communities that use the discipline's discourse genres and knowledge generation tools was viewed as the key to helping students attain priority goals.

The more optimistic chapters (the majority) depicted social constructivist teaching as the default mode, with transmission or other forms of teaching used only when needed (e.g. to establish an initial base of common input or to "step in" and scaffold when students encounter difficulties). Less optimistic chapters depicted social constructivist teaching as an option for use at particular times or in particular situations rather than as the default mode for all-day, everyday teaching. Some cited the breadth/depth dilemma in noting that teachers' content coverage responsibilities preclude using social constructivist models all or even most of the time. Others spoke of constraints on when it can be used successfully (e.g. only in small-group settings, only after a common base of knowledge or experience has been established, only when the teacher is available to monitor closely and intervene as needed).

Social constructivist teaching is commonly contrasted with transmission teaching, but the contributions to this volume suggest that it also should be contrasted with superficially similar forms of teaching that engage students in discussion or hands-on learning activities but without orienting them toward clear learning goals, scaffolding their progress, or holding them accountable for goal attainment. Schoenfeld, Chazan and Schnepp, and Roth all explicitly distinguished their teaching models from these unfocused forms of discourse or activity, and Englert and Dunsmore implied the need for such distinctions in discussing the need for teachers to monitor activities closely and "step in" when necessary. I suspect that the remaining authors also would endorse distinctions between the kinds of social constructivist teaching that they envisioned and superficially similar forms of discourse or activity that are not structured or scaffolded with particular learning goals in mind.

ISSUES THAT REQUIRE RESEARCH ATTENTION

The authors tended to agree that socializing students to the point of functioning as a learning community requires starting early and taking time (possibly months). The point of starting early is to socialize students to ask genuine questions and begin to rely on themselves and their peers as resources for constructing answers to those questions, rather than automatically looking to the teacher or the textbook as the authoritative source. There was disagreement on whether learning community discourse genres are feasible in whole-class as well as small-group settings (with Nuthall expressing general pessimism in this regard and several other authors suggesting that the whole-class setting is feasible only when certain conditions are in place, such as a common prior experience that provides a basis for grounding the discussion).

There also was disagreement about whether teachers can move back and forth between learning community modes of discourse and other forms of teaching. Schnepp was the most pessimistic in this regard, arguing that it takes a great deal of time and determination on the teacher's part to get students to accept the idea that they will be expected to work out problems on their own, and that reversion to a transmission mode or even a willingness to give ready answers to students' questions will quickly undo painstakingly constructed learning community norms.

There was a range of opinion (and some silence) on whether it is important for students to have choices, or at least input, in identifying topics for discussion or questions for inquiry. There even was some disagreement on whether students are capable of making good decisions in this regard. Wells was the most optimistic, envisioning classrooms in which much of the time is spent in small-group inquiry on topics that students have proposed themselves (with teacher approval vis-à-vis overall goals) and depicting students themselves as the ultimate judges of the degree to which they have attained learning goals. Most other authors implied, and some explicitly stated, not only that the state, school district, or teacher would establish learning goals for students, but also that the teacher would structure learning activities, scaffold student progress toward these goals, and hold students accountable using various forms of assessment. Authors who emphasized accountability and outcome data were least likely to suggest that students would work independently of the teacher much of the time.

In talking about productive whole-class or small-group discourse, most authors stressed the need for common experiences and vocabulary to establish a base of prior knowledge that can be assumed, referred to, and used in negotiating understandings and debating the merits of proposed solutions to problems. In this regard, prior hands-on experiences were usually depicted as preferable to less immediate forms of prior knowledge, partly because these experiences would be valuable for motivating and guiding subsequent inquiry.

There was a range of views on the relative need for or value of teacher presentation vs. elicitation of students' thinking when initially establishing key ideas. Several authors noted that the potential for relying on elicitation for this purpose depends on the students' capabilities for generating, inferring, or discovering valid ideas on their own. None of the authors specifically addressed the signal-to-noise ratio problem that I raised in the introduction to this volume, but most of them addressed discourse management issues that merit research and analysis of lesson excerpts: How does one decide when "the well of student ideas has run dry," so that it is time to shift from an idea-collection phase to an analysis phase or to transmit to students those ideas that they didn't generate on their own? When and why should teachers revoice or elaborate on students' ideas vs. simply accepting them or adding them to a list under construction? When and how should teachers accommodate student questions or comments that would divert the lesson from the planned agenda, and what should they do when they believe that such accommodation would be inappropriate at the moment? How deep should teachers lead students into issues that are not central to their instructional goals (either for now, or perhaps ever)? When should teachers accept misconceptions without comment and when should they correct them immediately or take other action (e.g. asking other students if they agree) to address the misconception and try to ensure that students do not believe that it is true (even temporarily)? How can teachers monitor the engagement of low participators, and when and how should they take action to involve these students more directly?

Besides talking about strategies for managing discourse once an activity was underway, most authors emphasized the need to select appropriate activities in the first place and structure them with reference to the instructional goals. For example, VanSledright chose the "starving time" at Jamestown as the basis for engaging his students in historical inquiry because it is an interesting and mysterious topic about which historians disagree, so consultation of source material followed by construction and debate of proposed explanations afforded his students opportunities to engage in authentic historical inquiry. This would not have been possible if the students had been asked to develop explanations for a noncontroversial historical event for which there is broad consensus about what happened and why. Similarly, the questions about food for plants that Roth posed to her students, along with the activities in which she engaged them, provided a natural basis for scientific inquiry and discourse (moreso than, for example, "What is photosynthesis, why is it important, and how does it work?").

Most authors viewed learning within the context of acculturation into a specialized community, including appropriation of its discourse genres. However, there was disagreement about whether this can be expected to occur automatically through repeated experiences or whether some things must be explicitly taught by the teacher. Okolo, Ferretti, and MacArthur emphasized the need for explicit teaching of cognitive strategies. Nuthall and Roth spoke of tactics designed to support students' acquisition not only of desired information processing capabilities, but of metacognitive knowledge and self-regulatory capabilities for using these tools thoughtfully and purposefully. VanSledright and James spoke of the difficulties involved in getting students to the point where they not only use disciplinary discourse genres and tools, but use them in the ways that practitioners of the discipline use them. Several authors included post-discourse activities (pair sharing, writing in journals, etc.) to give students opportunities to articulate what they had just learned or negotiated. Most included final reflection/debriefing sessions as well.

Authors differed not only in their relative emphasis on assessment but in what they meant by assessment and how they would conduct it. Some referred to relatively conventional tests of knowledge or skills whereas others emphasized "online" assessment of what students are thinking. The latter authors also tended to emphasize activities that make students' thinking visible (by requiring oral or written discourse). Wells and Englert and Dunsmore were the least conventional in their comments on assessment. Wells suggested that students themselves are the best judges of their progress (some of the other authors would doubt this on the grounds that students often do not know what they do not know or may be laboring under misconceptions). Englert and Dunsmore included group products as potential assessment data, whereas other authors emphasized the need for individual accountability.

Many of the authors referred to the problem of competing standards as complicating goal setting and assessment. Competing standards raise thorny professional issues, especially when teachers see certain standards as counterproductive (not merely as lower in priority than other standards that they wish to emphasize). Positions on these issues are related to the degree to which authors depict teachers as autonomous professionals vs. as public servants responsible for carrying out policies established by their states or districts. The depth vs. breadth issue is basic here as well. Most authors did not take firm positions, instead commenting on the dilemmas involved and noting that one must allocate sufficient time to allow for realistic accomplishment of whatever goals one adopts as top priorities.

REACTIONS TO INDIVIDUAL CHAPTERS

Wells

Wells's chapter describes the CHAT model that combines Dewey's inquiry with basic principles of sociocultural learning. The latter principles are common to most of the other chapters as well, although typically treated within the context of a single discipline or subject matter. Wells's four types of activity in the spiral of knowing (experience, information, knowledge building, and understanding) also appear frequently in other chapters, although usually not labeled as such or treated as phases in a sequence.

Wells presents an appealing vision of committed learners constructing knowledge collaboratively and persistently, with teachers needing only to drop hints here and there once they have successfully engaged students in a productive line of activity. He is unique in his emphasis on inviting students to propose their own inquiry topics (subject to negotiation with the teacher with regard to their suitability given the activity's goals), encouraging students to manage their inquiry (in small groups) largely independently of the teacher, and viewing them as the best judges of their progress. He also is unique in analyzing the construction of knowledge according to both the participant structures and the types of activities involved. His model is the broadest and the most generalizable across subject areas.

Wells claims that inquiry approaches are preferable when depth of understanding is the goal and time permits, and that allowing students to negotiate topics for inquiry (and later presentation) is ideal. An inquiry unit early in the year helps establish a learning community ethos. Open-ended, hands-on inquiry also is preferable when introducing a brand new topic (to provide students with an experience base). However, he notes that information giving (by teachers or texts) is appropriate as part of providing basic input when launching a new topic, when providing assistance to enable individuals or subgroups to complete their activities, when reading aloud to the class to expose students to fictional or nonfictional sources from the wider world beyond the school, and when bridging from students' informal language to the more formal language of disciplinary genres (typically when revoicing or expanding on students' ideas).

I find his vision inspiring but troubling, on at least three counts. First, given typical time constraints and coverage responsibilities, I don't think that many teachers will be able to use inquiry methods to the extent that Wells implies that they should (this reservation applies to most of the other chapters as well). Second, I don't share Wells's optimism about what students can be expected to accomplish by managing their inquiry and assessing their progress, in collaboration with peers but largely independently of the teacher. Finally, I am troubled by Wells's views on assessment. He appears to believe that students' learning can be assessed adequately merely by monitoring their discourse participation and activity products. My experience has been that educators who confine their assessment to these informal methods tend to construct unjustifiably rosy views of their students' accomplishments. In particular, they tend to: (1) read more than they should into students' responses, assuming that valid discourse about one or two components of a network of knowledge is evidence that the student possesses connected knowledge of the entire network, and (2) take valid comments made by one or two students as evidence that the rest of the students also have attained the same understandings. I share Nuthall's pessimism in this regard, so I believe that relatively formal assessment of the learning of each individual student is required to produce a reliable and valid picture of the degree to which the students have attained the instructional goals.

Nuthall

Nuthall describes the nature of social constructivist teaching and the kinds of learning that it is intended to produce, critically appraises the claims made about it, and suggests conditions under which it is most likely to be effective (concluding with a list of seven principles). Like Wells, he considers whole-class, small-group, and individual activity settings. However, he projects a more teacher-structured version of social constructivist teaching, and one that focuses more on discourse than inquiry.

Tactics for managing the discourse include using questions sparingly, listening closely to what students say and responding in ways that connect the discussion so far and position it to move forward, staying with the same topic for several turns and involving more of the students in contributing ideas to it, helping students to clarify their ideas and become more explicit and consistent, making sure that they interact respectfully, and revoicing or reformulating their comments to expand them into more complete statements and emphasize key concepts and causal linkages (bridging). Nuthall considers these tactics with respect to three kinds of learning: (1) acquiring meanings, (2) acquiring and modifying well-thought-out knowledge, and (3) acquiring new ways of thinking and solving problems.

Nuthall's classroom research involves collecting unusually rich data sets, including transcripts of the utterances recorded by microphones attached to individual students. The latter transcripts reflect not only what students say in public discourse situations, but also what they say when speaking to partners or fellow members of small groups and even when speaking aloud to themselves. They often indicate that students' understandings of a term or idea are retained in much the same form as they were encoded originally. These understandings are not necessarily improved if incorrect, transformed to more formal or generalized encodings, or connected to other understandings to form the knowledge network that the teacher wants the students to construct.

Individual students' understandings of the same term or idea may vary considerably; their use of processes and skills may not be accompanied by sufficient metacognitive monitoring and self-regulation to provide a basis for ready access in future application contexts; and much of what is experienced is likely to be forgotten (or transformed and assimilated back to previously held beliefs or strategies) unless it is reinforced through repeated exposures and application opportunities. These findings are disturbing and should give educators pause in considering what outcomes are reasonable to expect from engaging students in particular learning activities (I refer here to all educators, not just those emphasizing sociocultural or social constructivist principles).

His findings have led Nuthall to call for more teacher presentation of concepts and skills and tighter structuring and scaffolding of students' activities than most social constructivists envision. They also have led him to set narrow parameters in identifying the contexts in which he believes that social constructivist teaching is likely to be effective. For acquiring meanings, he emphasizes the need for shared recent experiences that are understood in common ways to provide a basis for discussion. For acquiring and modifying well-thought-out knowledge, he suggests that participants in the discussion must share a substantial body of prior knowledge, experience the discussion in essentially the same ways, share the same interpretations of its purposes, engage in free exchange of beliefs and ideas, and revisit the key ideas being constructed at least three or four times (if these are expected to become part of the established knowledge of all of the students). Concerning acquiring new ways of thinking and solving problems, he finds that it is not difficult to get students to imitate strategies modeled by the teacher or their peers, but much more difficult to develop these strategies to the point that students can use them independently of the contexts in which they were learned.

Taking these and other constraints into account, Nuthall claims that social constructivist teaching works best: (1) in the context of activity-based teaching in which discussion focuses on experiences that students have shared, and (2) in small groups rather than whole classes. He describes these activities as evolving through four stages: (1) instructions, (2) carrying out the activity, (3) preparing a report, and (4) discussing the results (with an accountability system in place and the teacher monitoring carefully to track individual thinking and intervene as needed). He assumes that the activities will be selected and structured by the teacher rather than the students, but indicates that these activities should involve issues that students can identify with and believe are worth resolving. Nuthall's depictions of small-group, activity-based learning settings are parallel in many ways to those described by Wells, but with much more structuring and scaffolding by the teacher and much less independent student activity. Whereas Wells depicts social constructivist teaching as the default mode, Nuthall concedes that it has its place but only under certain rather restrictive conditions.

Beyond its general pessimism, Nuthall's chapter is unique in several other respects, mostly connected to his data collection. More than other authors, he speaks of individual differences in the prior knowledge that students bring to activities, in their levels of participation in the activities, and in the specifics of what they take away from an ostensibly common experience. He also places strong emphasis on the need for accountability systems and for close teacher monitoring of group processes and readiness to intervene at critical moments. Finally, he is unique in his claim (based on his data) that students need not only initial exposure to key ideas but three or four follow-up revisitings to cement these ideas in memory.

Englert and Dunsmore

Although focused on literacy, Englert and Dunsmore's chapter complements and elaborates on Wells's chapter in providing a general summary of basic sociocultural ideas about learning and teaching. Whereas Wells emphasizes both sociocultural and inquiry principles, Englert and Dunsmore stick to sociocultural principles but explore them in more depth, emphasizing in particular genre socialization, cognitive apprenticeship, and establishing contexts for situated tool use that make students' thinking visible. In the context of an interesting analysis of a teacher studied in the first year and again in the sixth year of her affiliation with the authors' project, this chapter elaborates on two key aspects of sociocultural teaching: (1) how teachers facilitate whole-class discussions to provide students with opportunities to participate in literate practices, and (2) how small groups provide students with opportunities to participate in cognitive roles that are less available to them in the whole-class setting.

The authors note that opportunities for students to hear discourse and (voiced) inner speech associated with tool use and to see practice-related principles and tools in action are especially important in writing instruction, because written language requires considerable covert abstraction, metalinguistic awareness, self-monitoring, problem solving, and self-regulation of one's own thought processes. Teachers accomplish this by modeling writing processes and practices, creating instructional dialogues that challenge and support students as they create texts, and providing responsive instruction and graduated assistance to them as they develop expertise.

Englert and Dunsmore's analysis of tactics for managing whole-class discussions focuses on the interplay of step-in moves (modeling, explaining, and prompting) and step-back moves (asking for explanations, for opinions about what to revise, for decisions about text construction, or for direction concerning the specifics of the writing process), juxtaposed in the process of helping students to acquire the discourse, tools, and practices of writers and to assume increasing responsibility for constructing and revising texts. The teacher does much of the intellectual work at first, modeling writing practices and explaining when they are used. However, by engaging in dialogue with students about ongoing text construction, the teacher gradually positions herself more in the role of apprentice and the students more in the role of expert. The assistance provided through step-in moves is graduated to match students' current expertise, beginning with relatively complete modeling or explanation, then shifting to "joint involvement episodes" in which the teacher provides the first half of some interlocking discourse and the student is cued to provide the second part, and eventually moving to open-ended questions that require students to generate most of the needed direction and explanation on their own.

Englert and Dunsmore portray the small group as an important context for sociocultural teaching because it allows students in general, and inhibited or learning disabled students in particular, to engage in much more writing-related talk than is possible in the whole-class context. They illustrate this using data showing startling differences in individual students' active participation in these two contexts. They also note that the small-group context provides teachers with many more opportunities to hear what students are thinking than they get when the students are in the whole-class context or working alone.

Englert and Dunsmore contrast the cognitive apprenticeship model with discovery teaching, noting that the former assumes a strong teacher mediation role and does not leave students to detect knowledge on their own. They close their chapter by identifying six challenges involved in implementing the cognitive apprenticeship model well: (1) developing an instructional discourse that is dynamic and allows for an evolving form of talk tied to the emergent knowledge of students and their active contributions, (2) assessing what is occurring in students' minds as they participate in the text construction process, (3) skill in using explanations, think-alouds, and talk about writing techniques to model text construction processes in ways that make them visible to students, (4) mastery of step-back moves and other methods for transferring control to students as they develop expertise, (5) engaging students in productive small-group collaborative activities and monitoring those activities to assess and respond to students, and (6) learning to transform their own participation in writing activities from a primarily expert role to a primarily apprentice role.

Along with its focus on literacy/writing and its longitudinal comparison of a teacher's management of the "morning personal news" activity, Englert and Dunsmore's chapter is unique in its analysis of the interplay of step-in and step-back moves, its detailed exposition of the cognitive apprenticeship model, its emphasis on monitoring what students are thinking, and its ideas about taking advantage of the range of zones of proximal development represented in a group or class. In addition, along with Okolo, Ferretti, and MacArthur, Englert and Dunsmore are notable for their attention to the participation of learning disabled students in social constructivist learning activities.

Schoenfeld

Schoenfeld's chapter presents a model and way of analyzing social constructivist teaching that potentially is as broadly applicable of those described by Wells or Nuthall, but his personal focus and most of his examples come from mathematics instruction and are construed in terms of apprenticeship into the mathematical community. He emphasizes that specific knowledge and skill goals need to be couched within larger agendas built around major dispositional goals (e.g. inducing students to view mathematics as a form of sensemaking, to reflect on their learning, and to develop productive habits of mind). He describes a mathematical learning community in which members grapple with problems collectively, discuss the relative merits of proposed solution methods, and negotiate understandings.

Schoenfeld's research group has been charting teacher decision making and related tactical moves used in managing lessons and activities, to characterize teaching routines within an analytic frame that is general enough to apply across grades and subjects, yet specific enough to support analyses of relationships between teachers' instructional routines and their knowledge, goals, and beliefs, as well as questions about which kinds of teaching are likely to be associated with particular goals and outcomes.. His chapter focuses on what the group has learned about a routine for soliciting and working with students' ideas. He illustrates the routine as it appears in excerpts taken from elementary mathematics teaching by Deborah Ball and secondary physics/mathematics teaching by Jim Minstrell. These lessons differ in level of students and subject matter, time of year/stage of establishment of mathematics learning community norms, and relative emphasis on initiating new learning vs. consolidating/applying previously learned concepts and principles. Yet, all of the teachers' instructional moves can be accommodated (and represented graphically) within the decision making template that Schoenfeld's group has developed for charting attempts to solicit and work with students' ideas.

In addition, qualitative analysis of lesson excerpts illustrates ways in which the routine plays out somewhat differently according to the teachers' overall dispositional goal priorities and immediate lesson objectives. Minstrell's tactics used in the first week of school when he is focusing on establishing basic mathematics community norms have much in common, for example, with Schnepp's way of working with students early in the year, as well as with the tactics that Schoenfeld himself uses in establishing a mathematics community in his university classroom. Similarly, Ball's tactics used later in the year within an established mathematics learning community have much in common with the tactics that the experienced teacher described by Englert and Dunsmore used when managing whole-class discourse within an established writing community.

I find Schoenfeld's modeling of routines and use of associated graphic templates to be very useful for thinking about teaching tactics questions that are of special interest to me. However, I sometimes found myself wanting more information. For example, the decision points in the routine featured in his chapter take into account whether the answer is relevant and whether it needs clarification/focus or elaboration, but not whether it contains a misconception. I wonder if the model might need additional decision points referring to tactics to be used when the answer is relevant but incorrect (and within that, whether the error involved reflects something of fundamental importance such as a major misconception or something relatively minor such as an error in calculation). I also would like to see more elaboration of the cues or rationales that underlie certain decisions. For example, one of Minstrell's students says (in Line 96), "You've got a bunch of numbers that are the same number." Schoenfeld says that this comment "begs for clarification." I agree, but I would like to see suggested criteria for teachers to consider when deciding whether to simply accept student comments or to ask for clarification.

Schoenfeld's chapter also suggests the need not only to clarify the tactics and decision points involved in using particular instructional routines, but also to address higher order questions about the affordances and constraints associated with these routines (that have implications for when and why the routines should or should not be used). For example, parts of the excerpt from Ball's teaching raised the "signal-to-noise" issue for me, especially Shea's "Six can be an odd number" comment and the extended "Shea numbers" segment that developed from it. When I am reading either Ball's own analysis of this segment or Schoenfeld's analysis presented in this volume, I follow their reasoning and tend to agree (temporarily) with their argument that Shea's comment was appropriately handled using what Schoenfeld describes as the routine for soliciting and working with students' ideas (plus Ball's subsequent follow up). However, upon later reflection, when I think about the signal-to-noise ratio issue and about Nuthall's troubling data indicating that many students remember misconceptions they have heard rather than more accurate target conceptions, I wonder if Shea's comment should have been handled with a different routine entirely – a routine for immediately addressing misconceptions in ways that not only correct them but make it likely that they will be forgotten and the accurate conception will be remembered. This is just a question (all right, a hypothesis!) rather than a claim that I am prepared to support with data at this point, but it illustrates the kind of higher order, "which routine to use when and why" question that I think needs research attention.

Schoenfeld closes his chapter with a coda indicating that extremes of either transmission or social constructivist teaching are less desirable than a judicious blend. He adds that we should be seeing more social constructivist teaching than we are seeing now (because research continues to indicate that very little such teaching goes on in most schools), and that decisions about how much of what kind of teaching to emphasize ultimately depend on the learning outcomes that the teacher values. I agree, but I would add that value-based decisions about instructional goals and methods imply assumptions about process-outcome relationships, and that these assumptions are tenuous given the paucity of research assessing the effectiveness of social constructivist teaching for producing specified student outcomes.

Chazan and Schnepp

This chapter used an interesting format in which mathematics education professor Chazan interviewed high school mathematics teacher Schnepp about his "ways of working" with his advanced placement calculus class. These include: (1) initial establishment of a learning community, during which students explore problems, present their solution ideas, and then critique one another's ideas and negotiate synthesis (with Schnepp mostly listening and assessing); (2) additional student exploration, presentation, and critique/synthesis, but now with Schnepp playing a more active role by making suggestions, introducing mathematical terms for terms that students have discovered or invented themselves, and calling attention to significant ideas by explaining them or engaging students in specially designed activities that will challenge them to become more proficient with algorithms or to reassess generalizations developed to date; and (3) providing more conventional teaching and skills practice in order to cover the content more quickly and prepare students for their advanced placement tests. Schnepp emphasizes that these three ways of working with students have to be introduced in the order given to ensure that students learn to think for themselves and engage in the desired mathematical discourse.

Schnepp emphasizes higher order dispositional goals similar to those emphasized by Schoenfeld. His three ways of working with students involve trade-offs with reference to those goals. The first way challenges students to be intellectually independent and reflect on their mathematical thinking, but it is time consuming and would not allow him to teach all of the mathematics that he is supposed to cover if he used it throughout the year. The second way allows him to bring student contributions closer to the formal mathematical versions emphasized in the curriculum, but requires him to be careful not to become too active and thereby encourage students to begin pressuring him for directiveness and "answers." The third way allows for more efficient coverage of the prescribed curriculum but is not as effective for imparting understanding or teaching students to apply what they are learning independently.

Schnepp contrasts his approach to discovery learning, which he describes as having students spend a short time working on their own and then giving them "the" answers. He also notes that certain formal concepts are extremely unlikely to be discovered by students, let alone to be given the formal definitions used in the discipline.

Unique aspects of Chazan and Schnepp's chapter include: (1) the idea that part of the rationale for pushing students to communicate mathematical ideas to one another is that this will enable them to get feedback from peers who are operating on a similar level of expertise (which will expose them to multiple perspectives, but perspectives that are easier to question because the peer is known not to be an expert either), as well as (2) the motivational principle of aligning with the students to work together on the common goal of convincing outsiders (test makers, future professors) that their mathematical knowledge is "good enough." Schnepp can be viewed as a realist who has developed workable plans for addressing multiple and partially contradictory goals. He distrusts tests, for example, partly because he doesn't think that they get at dispositional goals or address individual differences effectively, yet he admits that the looming advanced placement test serves as a motivator for high school seniors prone to "senioritis."

The two mathematics chapters share an emphasis on couching more specific knowledge and skill goals within larger, yearlong dispositional goals. They also are compatible in most other respects, although Chazan and Schnepp focus on the molar aspects of their model whereas Schoenfeld focuses on moment-to-moment tactics in managing discourse.

Chazan and Schnepp also conclude by suggesting that decisions about curriculum and instruction ultimately depend on value commitments more than on data linking processes to outcomes, and they include a hypothetical example to illustrate. I found the argument and example enlightening, but I would argue for instead broader and better aligned assessment that would provide a solid basis for systematically checking out, rather than simply assuming, the efficacy of adopted methods for accomplishing the intended goals. Just as much as mathematics educators would like to see teachers succeed in empowering students to function as mathematicians, I would like to see teachers and teacher educators (in all subjects) empowered as assessors and researchers of the validity of the process-outcome assumptions built into their goal commitments.

Roth

Roth's chapter describes how she broadened her original conceptual change approach to science teaching in order to incorporate sociocultural ideas about socializing students into a science community (paying as much attention to process as to content), then made additional adaptations based on her experiences with students (especially, getting to know them better as individuals and welcoming their personal contributions). Her search for a satisfactory approach was motivated originally by dissatisfaction with both narrow transmission models and hands-on, inquiry-oriented models that produced a lot of student talk but not enough clarity about the purposes of investigations. Neither approach enabled students to use their knowledge to address problems or questions amenable to solution through scientific reasoning.

Roth has adapted the cognitive apprenticeship model by casting herself as the leader of a scientific research team and her students as the other team members. Within this context, she implements a five-stage conceptual change approach to teaching for science understanding: (1) establish a problem and elicit students' initial ideas; (2) explore phenomena and challenge the elicited ideas; (3) present new ideas and contrast them with the students' initial ideas; (4) use modeling and coaching to help students apply the new ideas and reconcile them with their own ideas (then fade these and other forms of teacher support); and (5) engage the students in reflection on changes in their ideas and connections with new ideas). Both student talk and teacher talk are important components of each of these stages, with the kinds of student and teacher talk emphasized evolving as learning progresses. The conceptual change focus of this model is unique to Roth, but many of its other aspects (inquiry, eliciting and using students' ideas, scaffolding learning through modeling and coaching, etc.) have much in common with principles espoused in other chapters.

Roth's model appears comparable with those of Wells and Schnepp in its macro-level aspects, and with those of Ball and Schoenfeld in its micro-level aspects. However, Roth more clearly sets the agenda and scaffolds the students' activities throughout the unit, being more comparable to Nuthall in that respect. She structures what students talk about in the first place by introducing a problem or activity to frame the discourse, then guides the discourse to keep it on track, focus on big ideas, etc. (although she is willing to take side roads, up to a point, to address student questions or comments that she views as useful).

Roth's lesson examples highlight the dilemma of sticking with the planned agenda versus exploiting teachable moments. For example, her students initially generated 22 different ideas about how plants get their food. Should teachers faced with this situation explore all 22 ideas, or would it be better to quickly dispense with many or even most of them in order to focus on correct ideas and the most widely held misconceptions? An interesting technique that Roth reports using when students raise a question that she does not want to stop to address is to instruct the student to write the question in the class's question notebook to ensure that it will be addressed at some future time.

Roth's examples also point up some of the scaffolding dilemmas that arise in content-rich subjects (primarily science and social studies), especially the issue of how much information about a topic is just the right amount to impart to students "for now." For example, in order to enable students to engage in scientific reasoning about whether water and other substances are or are not food for plants, Roth had to explain that, from a scientific standpoint, a substance is a food for some organism if the organism derives energy from the substance. In the process, she also noted that food energy is measured in calories and that we can tell if substances contain food energy by reading the nutritional information on their labels. Students had to take this information on faith because at this point they had no real understanding of what calories are, and Roth declined to try to develop such understanding at this point in their science education (presumably because doing so would not be cost effective or perhaps even feasible given the students' ages and prior knowledge). Yet, despite this lack of deep understanding, possession of the knowledge that foods must contain energy as reflected in calorie content was sufficient to enable the students to collect information and engage in reasoned argument about whether various substances were food for plants. At this point, very little theory or research exists to inform curriculum developers' and teachers' decisions about which aspects of a topic can or should be included and which can or should be omitted in lessons for students at a given grade level, and within what is included, which aspects should be "front loaded" through initial instruction and which can or should be withheld until students are engaged in subsequent discussion or inquiry activities.

Roth's chapter also points up some of the issues involved in selecting examples or other representations of concepts or principles. Most theory and research developed to date on these issues has been done by mathematics educators, who commonly warn teachers, for example, not to always display geometric figures as situated on horizontal planes, so that students do not develop the idea that a triangle (or rectangle, etc.) is not a triangle unless it is so situated. Representation issues in science and social studies are even more complicated than those in mathematics because many of the concepts involved are multidimensional, so that distinguishing them from related concepts can be complicated. To help her students develop firm scientific concepts of food, Roth needed to engage them in consideration of a variety of examples that were not food (water, fertilizer, etc.), yet incorporated one or more dimensions in common with food. Questions calling for students to compare and contrast examples and non-examples of key concepts or principles are frequently needed in structuring the discourse that occurs in social constructivist teaching, and attention is needed to criteria for determining what examples to introduce and what kinds of questions to ask about them.

Some of the unusual or even unique aspects of Roth's chapter include the impressive quantity, variety, and ultimately successful level of outcome data she has collected; her use of unusual props to demonstrate concepts (Schnepp is noteworthy in this respect as well), her engagement of students in comparing their pre-unit responses with their subsequent ideas to help them recognize the degree to which their thinking has changed; and her assignment of one or two students to act as observers of science discussions who will provide input to a later analysis of the key features of that day's discourse and their implications for how the class is developing as a scientific community. The latter technique is part of Roth's larger emphasis on the need to provide explicit instruction about the nature of science and science inquiry rather than assume that students will develop these understandings automatically through participation in scientific discourse.

Even though Roth has developed methods that are generally very successful in helping her students attain the target understandings, her views are much closer to those of Nuthall than to those of Wells (and most of the other chapter authors) when it comes to assumptions about what students can be expected to accomplish without close teacher structuring and monitoring. Her teaching is social constructivist in many respects, but she emphasizes the need for explicit modeling of key ideas and processes, sustained efforts to attack misconceptions and induce conceptual change, explicit attention to metacognition about scientific discourse, and careful monitoring of small groups to keep them on task and be prepared to intervene if necessary. These concerns have led her to emphasize whole-class settings rather than small-group settings in her instruction.

One conspicuous omission in Roth's chapter is the breadth/depth issue. I raise it because I believe that it is of special relevance to the work of Roth and others (especially conceptual change teaching researchers) who have responded to initially unsatisfactory outcome data by improving their units until they consistently succeed in enabling students to display the target understandings. What typically happens is that the units become significantly longer and more complicated, to the point that they extend across several weeks or even months. The upside of Roth's thorough teaching of photosynthesis is that her students typically display deep and connected knowledge of key concepts (and few if any misconceptions) on post-unit tests and interviews, but the downside is that sticking with this approach across the school year would limit middle-school science classes to only studying photosynthesis and a very short list of other key concepts or processes. Even if this prospect were not rendered unrealistic by the current zeal for content standards and related high-stakes tests that pressure teachers toward broad (but shallow) coverage, I suspect that relatively few educators would be willing to go this far in privileging depth over breadth.

VanSledright and James

The chapter by VanSledright and James focuses in some detail on these external coverage pressures and the depth/breadth dilemmas they create. It also speaks to several major issues and ideas addressed in one or more other chapters: the challenge of planning curriculum and instruction to address multiple goals simultaneously; the need to juxtapose what Englert and Dunsmore called "stepping in" and "stepping back" moves in managing discourse; the need to explain the behaviors expected in whole-class discourse and small-group inquiry activities and to coach students until they become able to fulfill the roles embedded in these activities productively; and the challenges involved in not only teaching students the discourse genres and knowledge generation tools used in a discipline but getting them to use these genres and tools in the ways that practitioners of the discipline use them.

Unique aspects of the chapter include the authors' emphasis on teaching subject matter in ways that help students function more fully in their everyday sociocultural worlds, their comments on state standards and tests, and their examples of strong student emotional responses to content that caused their units to unfold somewhat differently than they had planned. In VanSledright's case, students got so carried away with the notion that "the liar Percy" hoarded the food and then created a cover story later, that most of them ignored better evidence indicating a different explanation for the food problem and therefore failed to engage in the kind of historical reasoning that the activity was designed to support. In James's case, student questions and comments indicating both strong emotional reactions to slavery and curiosity/ignorance about the beliefs and attitudes associated with it led her to supplement her unit plans to add activities relating to the Confederate flag controversy in South Carolina.

In my view, part of the reason for the problems reported by VanSledright and James (and for parallel problems reported by some of the other authors) was the students' very limited prior knowledge. Across the subject areas, guidelines for establishing learning communities and socializing students to norms for discipline-based dialogue and reasoning typically emphasize principles of reflective and critical thinking (students should attend carefully not only to alternative views expressed but also to the arguments and evidence advanced in support of these views, and should be prepared to cite relevant arguments and evidence in support of the views that they put forth themselves). Even if students already understand and accept these guiding principles, they may find them difficult to put into practice when they do not possess enough background about an issue to be able to make informed decisions about the warrants for competing arguments. For example, VanSledright's students might have engaged in a higher level of historical reasoning if they had begun the discussion with more prior historical knowledge about the context for the "starving time" and the people and events involved in it (and perhaps also psychological and other knowledge that might have informed their ideas about the likelihood that various events would have occurred, could have been kept secret by the people involved,

and so on). More such knowledge might have enabled "the liar Percy" enthu-
siasts to realize that other explanations were more likely.

However, too much background information, especially if presented in ways
that seemed to dictate certain conclusions and rule out others, would have
reduced the degree to which the activity afforded opportunities to engage in
authentic historical reasoning. Thus, along with Roth's example of telling
students that energy is measured in calories and calorie content can be read
from food labels as a way to support their arguments about whether different
substances are food for plants, VanSledright's "starving time" example illustrates the need for criteria for deciding what type and amount of background
information is optimal for scaffolding students' inquiry, problem-solving, and
decision- making activities. Failing to provide students with enough background
information may cause them to flounder or resort to power-assertive tactics, but
providing them with too much information or steering them too obviously
toward a foregone conclusion may rob the activity of its potential authenticity.

Okolo, Ferretti, and MacArthur

This chapter compares most directly with that of VanSledright and James, in
that both chapters focus on history taught as preparation for citizenship but with
emphasis on apprenticing learners in ways of thinking about and doing history
that are emphasized by disciplinary historians and both address the challenges
of time constraints and adapting instruction to students' cognitive levels. This
chapter also shares with Englert and Dunsmore's chapter a concern about
students with learning disabilities, an emphasis on cognitive apprenticeship, a
focus on structuring conversations that make students' thinking visible to teacher
and peers, and examples drawn from lessons taught by a teacher involved with
the authors' project. More generally, the chapter shares the emphasis on sociocultural principles and apprenticing learners into discipline-based learning
communities that appear in most of the chapters.

Four basic principles stressed by Okolo, Ferretti, and MacArthur are: (1)
authentic tasks, (2) social mediation (in whole-class discussions and in reading
and communicating about historical evidence or creating joint products in pairs
or small groups), (3) constructive conversations that make thinking visible to
teacher and peers, and (4) domain-specific instruction in cognitive strategies.
Their chapter is unique in its emphasis on explicit teaching of cognitive strategies, especially to learning disabled students.

The chapter is notable for the authors' collection of a rich data set on
processes and outcomes and for its comparison of two extended group inquiry
projects (of which one worked notably better than the other). The teacher's

emphasis on group inquiry projects is similar to that of James, and was similarly motivated (based on their experiences over time, both teachers have concluded that their students learn better and retain more when they engage in group investigations). Like Schnepp, she believes that students (especially those who are learning disabled) often learn as well or better through interactions with peers than with her, partly because working in the group reduces pressures on the individual.

The teacher's comments about setting up group inquiry projects address an issue that was not addressed in other chapters: assigning individual students to groups in ways that support their likely progress toward learning goals. Her principles include providing for a range of abilities in each group, offsetting one student's tendency to dominate by including at least one other student who is assertive, and making sure that learning disabled students have tolerant and supportive group mates. She uniquely notes that reliance on groups creates special problems in helping students who are frequently absent from school or out of class for special education to "keep up." Teachers can transmit to these students whatever they taught to the class as a whole and can provide them with copies of assignment sheets that they missed, but they cannot recreate the discourse that occurred in small-group contexts.

The teacher has many useful ideas about teaching history to "10-year-old minds" that address limitations in students' cognitive capacities or prior knowledge and experience. Responding to these challenges requires her to include a lot of transmission teaching along with social constructivist teaching. Overall, her approach could be characterized as a compromise that employs whole-class presentation of information (either through personal explanation or storytelling or through videos, texts, or other input sources) and small-group inquiry projects.

The contrasts in the effectiveness of the two inquiry projects described in the chapter are instructive. Although firm conclusions are not possible from these two examples because relatively generic increases in the students' knowledge levels and inquiry skills probably contributed to the fact that the second project was more successful than the first, it appears likely that there were important differences in the suitability of the topics/questions used in these respective projects as bases for structuring inquiry. As with Roth's questions about food for plants and VanSledright's selection of the "starving time" for historical investigation, the contrasts between the two inquiry projects described in this chapter point up the importance of structuring students' inquiry around topics or questions that afford authentic inquiry opportunities and yet also are suited to the students' zones of proximal development, access to information sources, and so on.

The authors identify several techniques that this teacher has developed for adapting their units to "the 10-year-old mind." Many of these involve considerable structuring and scaffolding of students' learning, including explicit teaching of strategies and provision of learning supports such as charts, timelines, lists of ideas generated, outlines of main ideas, simplification of definitions, and substitution of "kid-friendly" language for more formal terms used in the unit plans. The authors portray this as realistic and reasoned eclecticism. I tend to agree, for the most part, partly because the authors report that this teacher's students do better than other students at the same school on state tests in reading, writing, and mathematics. However, I expect that some standards-oriented educators would accuse her of "dumbing down" the curriculum, and some social constructivists would complain that her teaching features too much transmission and teacher domination and not enough co-construction of knowledge and reliance on peers.

I found it interesting that this teacher used the authors' recommended question generation activity as the way to introduce the first inquiry project, but abandoned this in favor of using the time for reading and interpreting data in the second inquiry project (maybe this is another reason why the second project was more successful). She had found that, along with some questions useful as vehicles for pursuing the unit's learning goals, this activity yielded many less desired questions. My experience has been that this problem routinely occurs when students with very limited prior knowledge about the topic are asked what they would like to learn, especially when these students are children.

Even much more constrained and focused questions can yield more than the teacher may want to address, such as when Roth's students generated 22 possibilities when asked about food for plants. The same problem can develop when teachers invite students to share what they know about the topic or describe personal experiences related to it (as noted by Okolo, Ferretti, and MacArthur). KWL and related techniques call for introducing topics by asking students to state what they already *k*now (or think they know) about the topic and what they *w*ant to learn about it, then revisiting the students' responses as part of the culminating reflection on what they *l*earned. These are often very productive teaching techniques, but the experiences of the teacher featured in this chapter suggest that they may not be suitable for all lessons or units, and that even when they are suitable, the teacher's description of the topic will need to be constrained so that the exercise elicits primarily productive statements and questions from students.

This teacher found, as have myself and others, that children more readily respond to and use narrative structures rather than analytic structures (cause/effect, compare/contrast, etc.) in learning history. Consequently, she recommended that the authors replace assignments calling for analytic structures with assignments calling for narrative structures, adding that what the students wrote in the latter assignments would more accurately reflect their learning. This is one place in which standards-oriented readers might criticize this teacher for "dumbing down" the curriculum, complaining that her approach would limit the students to historical content and activities amenable to narrative structures and restrict their opportunities to learn historical content and engage in historical knowledge building activities that require analytic structures. Others, probably including the teacher, would reply that the former is appropriate historical teaching for 10-year-olds (and younger students), whereas the latter should be withheld until later grades. This is the kind of argument that should lead to design experiment work, in which different approaches to representing historical content and engaging students in activities couched within analytic structures are assessed for their feasibility and cost effectiveness at different grade levels.

CONCLUSION

In this discussion chapter, I have identified many points of comparison across the chapters and even more questions and issues raised, and neither of these totals approaches those that will accumulate as others begin to make such comparisons. Furthermore, few of these questions or issues have been subjected to sustained analysis and research. Consequently, one way to respond to this volume is to invoke the irritatingly familiar observations that: (1) it raises more questions than it answers, and (2) it concludes that much more research is needed.

Although valid, these observations do not begin to reflect the volume's value. A great many insights and hypotheses can be derived from it, initially through reading the contributions of its individual chapter authors and subsequently through comparing and contrasting their insights and arguments. Thanks to their efforts (and even though some of them don't like the term!), a richer literature is now available on social constructivist teaching, at several levels. First, the various contributions exemplify forms of teaching that social constructivist educators espouse and provide opportunities to see how these forms are adapted to different grade levels, subject areas, and other context factors. Second, the contributions provide a great deal of information about the affordances and constraints of social constructivist approaches, carrying implications about when, why, and how they are optimally implemented and when and why other approaches might be needed in addition or instead. Third, along with general models and principles, the contributions offer unusually detailed elaboration of instructional strategies and tactics, including both routines and special adaptations for special situations. Finally, each chapter offers information about implementation problems and special techniques or adaptations that are not only unique within this volume but rarely if ever addressed elsewhere in the scholarly and professional literature.

For these and many other reasons, I thank the authors for contributions that have significantly broadened and deepened my understanding of social constructivist teaching. I believe that it is safe to say that their contributions will bring similar benefits to other readers, as well.